Alexander George Findlay

Sailing Directory for the Coast of the United States

Between Boston and the Mississippi, including the Gulf of Florida, and the Coast of Cuba to Havana

Alexander George Findlay

Sailing Directory for the Coast of the United States
Between Boston and the Mississippi, including the Gulf of Florida, and the Coast of Cuba to Havana

ISBN/EAN: 9783337188054

Printed in Europe, USA, Canada, Australia, Japan

Cover: Foto ©ninafisch / pixelio.de

More available books at **www.hansebooks.com**

SAILING DIRECTORY

FOR THE COAST OF THE

UNITED STATES,

BETWEEN

BOSTON AND THE MISSISSIPPI,

INCLUDING THE

GULF OF FLORIDA,

AND

THE COAST OF CUBA TO HAVANA

TO ACCOMPANY THE CHART.

BY ALEXANDER GEORGE FINDLAY,
Fellow of the Royal Geographical Society.

LONDON:
PUBLISHED FOR RICHARD HOLMES LAURIE
53, FLEET STREET, E.C.
1875.

PART I.

BOSTON TO CHARLESTON.

CONTENTS.

	PAGE
NOTES ON THE BEARINGS AND VARIATIONS OF THE COMPASS, 1875	1

SECTION I.

BOSTON TO NEW YORK.

BANKS and SHOALS off Cape Cod, &c., 2; St. George's Banks, 2; Cashe's ― ― ― , the Fippenies and Stellwagon's Bank 5

MASSACHUSETT'S BAY, 6—23; Cape Ann and Thatcher's Island Lighthouses, 6; Londoner Rock, 6; Gloucester Harbour, 7; Baker's Island Lighthouses, 8; Manchester and Beverly, 10; Salem, 11; Marblehead, 12; Nahant, 13, 14; Boston, 14—19; Scituate, &c., 19; Plymouth, 20; Barnstable, 21; Wellfleet and Cape Cod Peninsula, 22; Highlands Light, 22; Cape Cod Harbour and Provincetown 23

EASTERN COAST OF CAPE COD PENINSULA, 25; Chatham Harbour, 26; Monomoy Island, 26; Butler's Hole.......,...................................... 27

NANTUCKET AND VINEYARD SOUNDS, 28—42; Nantucket Island, 28; Martha's Vineyard, 29; Sankaty Head Light, 29; Nantucket Shoals, 29—33; Nantucket Harbour, 33; Edgar Town, 35; Hyannis Harbour, 36; Directions for Nantucket Sound 38

Vineyard Sound, 39—42; Gay Head Light, 40; Nobsque Light, 42; Buzzard's Bay, 43; New Bedford, &c., 44; Mattapoiset 45

Rhode Island, 46; Newport or Rhode Island Harbour, 47; Narraganset Bay, 48; Point Judith and Lighthouse, 48; Block Island Lights 49

CONTENTS.

LONG ISLAND AND SOUND, 50—75; Montauk Point and Light, 50; Block Island Sound, 50; Gardiner's Island and Bay, 51-2; Greenport, 53; Plum Island Lighthouse, 53; Gull Islands and Lighthouse, 54; the Race, 54; Fisher's Island and Sound, 56; Stonington, 58; New London, 59; Bartlett's Reef and Lightvessel, 61; Connecticut River and Saybrook, 61; Falkner's Island and Lighthouse, 62; New Haven, 63; Stratford Point Light, 64; Bridgeport, 64; Black Rock Harbour, 65; Penfield's Reef and Light, 65; Norwalk Islands, 65; Sheffield Island and Light, 66; Captain's Islands, 66; Huntington Bay, 67; Hempstead, 68; East River and Hell Gate, 69—72; General Directions for Long Island Sound, 72; Long Island, South Coast, 74; Pondquogue and Fire Island Lights 74-75

NEW YORK HARBOUR, 76—84; Highlands of Navesink and Sandy Hook Lights, 76; Lights and Channels, 77; Tides, 78; Directions, 79; General Directions for approaching New York 80-84

SECTION II.
SANDY HOOK TO CHARLESTON.

Barnegat and Little Egg Harbour, 85; Absecum and Great Egg Harbour, 87; Five Fathom Bank 88

DELAWARE BAY AND RIVER, 88—94; Cape May and Cape Henlopen Lights, 89; Shoals on the North side, 89; Channels and Directions, 90; Cohansey, 92; Blake's Channel, 93; Wilmington, 93; Philadelphia 94

COASTS OF DELAWARE AND MARYLAND, 94—98; Fenwick's Island Lighthouse, 94; Winter Quarter Shoal and Lightvessel, 95; Assateague Island Lighthouse, 95; Chincoteague Shoals, 95; Metompkin Harbour, 96; Smith's Island, 96; Directions, Delaware to the Chesapeake, 96; the Capes of Virginia 98

CHESAPEAKE BAY AND RIVERS, 98—112; Cape Charles and Cape Henry Lighthouses, 99; Lights in the entrance of the Chesapeake, 99, 100; Shoals in the entrance, 100; Lynhaven Roads and Hampton Roads, 101; Directions for entering, 102; Cape Henry, or Lynhaven Bay, to York River, 103; to Mobjack or New Comfort Bay, 104; New Point Comfort to the Rappahannock and Potomac Rivers, 104; Potomac to the River Patuxent, 106; Patuxent to Annapolis and Baltimore, 108—112; to Susquehanna River 112

CAPE HENRY TO CHARLESTON, 113—126; Body Island and Light, 113; Cape Hatteras and Light, 113, 114; Hatteras Shoals and Cove, 114, 115; Hatteras Inlet, 116; Albemarle and Pamplico Sounds, 116; Cape Lookout Lighthouse and Shoals, 117; Beaufort Harbour, 117; Wilmington, 118; New Inlet, 119; Cape Fear and Frying Pan Shoals, 119; Cape Fear River, 120; Winyah Bay and Georgetown, 121; Cape Roman Lighthouse and Shoals, 123; Bull's Bay and Rattlesnake Shoals, 124; Charleston.............................. 125

Remarks on the Winds, &c., on the Coast of South Carolina 126

Alphabetical Index 127

SECTION III.

CHARLESTON TO HAVANA AND THE MISSISSIPPI.

P. GE

CHARLESTON TO CAPE FLORIDA, 127—145; Pilots, 127; North Edisto Inlet, 127; St. Helena Sound, 128; Port Royal, 129; Tybee Inlet and Savannah, 131; Observations on the Winds, &c., of South Carolina, 134; Great Warsaw Sound, 134; Ossabaw Sound, 135; St. Catharine's Sound, 135; Doboy or Darien Inlet, 126; St. Simon's, 137: St. Andrew's, 138; St. Mary's, 139; Fernandina, 139; Nassau, 140; St. John's, 140; St. Augustine, 141; Cape Canaveral, 143; Indian River Inlet, 143; Jupiter, Grenville, Hilsboro', and New River Inlets, 144; Cape Florida, 145; Fowey Rocks Lighthouse... 145

The FLORIDA REEFS AND KAYS, 145; General Description, 145—148; Lighthouses and Beacons on the Florida Reefs, 148—152; Harbours and Anchorages on the Florida Reefs, 152—160; Legaré Anchorage, 152; Bahia Honda, 153; Kay West, 153; Marquesas Kays, 157; the Tortugas 158

DIRECTIONS FOR FLORIDA STRAIT... 160

The GULF STREAM .... 161—163

The BAHAMA BANKS, 164; Little Bahama Bank, 164; Maternillo Reefs, 164; Providence N.W. Channel, 165; Great Bahama Bank, 165; Gun Kay and Lighthouse, 166; Salt Kay or Kay Sal Bank 167

NORTH COAST OF CUBA, 168; Port Sagua La Grande, 168; Bahia de Cadiz Kay, 169; Cardenas Bay, 171; Matanzas, 171; The Harbour of Havana 173—175

The COAST OF FLORIDA, &c., 176; The Tortugas Bank, 176; Chatham Bay, 176; Charlotte Harbour, 177; Tampa Bay, 177; Cedar Kays, 179; St. Mark's, 181; St. George's Sound, 182; Apalachicola, 183; Cape San Blas, 164; St. Joseph's Bay, 184; Sta. Rosa Bay, 185; Pensacola Bay, 186; Mobile, 188; Mississippi Sound, 191; Ship Island, 192; Biloxi Bay, 192; Chandeleur Islands, 193; River Mississippi, 193; Pass a l'Outre, 194; N.E. Pass, 195; S.E. or Balize Pass, 195; South Pass and Jetties, 195; S.W. Pass, 196; Pilots, 196; Directions for Approaching the Mississippi... 196

APPENDIX—Cautionary Weather Signals.. 193

U. S.—Part I.—Insertion.

Digitized by the Internet Archive
in 2007 with funding from
Microsoft Corporation

http://www.archive.org/details/sailingdirectory00findiala

THE EASTERN COASTS OF THE UNITED STATES.

⁎ Throughout this Work, the given Longitude is the Longitude from Greenwich. The Bearings and Courses are those by Compass, unless where otherwise expressed: but those given thus [*W.S.W.*] signify the True; and the given Direction of Wind, Tide, and Current, is always to be considered as the True.

THE VARIATION OF THE COMPASS, 1875.

Off Boston, 11° 20′ W.; Plymouth, 11° 15′ W.; Cape Cod, 11° 45′ W.; Vineyard Sound, 10° 45′ W.; Nantucket South Shoal, 10° 20′ W.; Rhode Island, 9° 45′ W.; East entrance to Long Island Sound, 9° W.; New London, 8° 50′ W.; Sandy Hook, entrance to New York Harbour, 7° W.; Cape May, 5° 10′ W.; Mouth of Delaware Bay, 4° 45′ W.; Entrance to Chesapeake Bay, 2° 45′ W.; Cape Hatteras, 2° 15′ W.; Cape Lookout, 1° 20′ W.; Cape Fear, *no variation;* Charleston Harbour, 1° 40′ *East.*

Savannah River, 2° 30′ E.; Cape Canaveral, 3° 10′ E.; Cape Florida, 3° 20′ E.; Cay West, 4° 10′ E.; New Orleans, 7° 20′ E.

SECTION I.

BOSTON TO NEW YORK.

The descriptions of the Coasts of the United States which succeed, are derived from, and are made to accord with, the fine series of charts drawn up by the officers of the United States Coast Survey. This great work was determined on in 1807, but was not properly commenced till ten years later, under Mr. F. R. Hassler, who continued it for many years. In 1842 a new plan was organized under Professor A. D. Bache, who, as is well known, continued it far towards completion.

The elaborate charts of the coasts and harbours, which were published by the Hydrographic Bureau at Washington, contained generally, besides the topographical and hydrographic details, brief sailing directions applicable to its area. To these attached notes we are largely indebted for the subsequent directions.

The chart and its plans have been faithfully reduced from the same authorities.

(2)

BANKS AND SHOALS OFF CAPE COD, ETC.

The approach to the north-eastern portion of the United States is somewhat embarrassed by dangerous banks, of which the shoal spots on the Great George Bank are the outermost, and which lie at 100 miles eastward of the peninsula of Cape Cod. These and others to the E.N.E. of Boston Bay require much caution, and therefore the following notices are necessary to be attended to.

ST. GEORGE'S BANK.—This bank was very little known until it was regularly surveyed in 1821, by the United States schooner *Science*, and the sloop *Orbit*, under the orders of Captain Isaac Hall. The following description is a copy of his report :—

There are properly *four shoals on St. George's Bank;* the whole of them are included between the lat. of 41° 34' and 41° 53' 30", and long. 67° 18' and 67° 59'. Between them are from 15 to 35 fathoms of water.

The largest, and on which is the greatest danger, is the most southerly and westerly. It is somewhat triangular, with a long and narrow spit, making out from the S.E. angle. The S.E. point is in lat. 41° 34', long. 67° 40' The West point is in lat. 41° 42', long. 67° 59'. The N.E. point is in lat. 41° 48', long. 67° 47' The eastern side of this shoal, although somewhat irregular, runs nearly S.S.E. and N.N.W., having on it from 3 ft. to 9 fathoms at common low water. It is composed of a great number of sand pits, very narrow, so that the width of a narrow vessel will make several fathoms difference in the depth of water. The general range of the spits is from S.E. to N.W. As there are no rocks, they are consequently liable to change, in some measure, their position and ranges. On the eastern edge, even in calm weather, unless it be either high or low water, the tides run with greater rapidity, and form considerable breakers, when setting to the westward, and a large waterfall when setting to the eastward. This is accounted for by a knowledge of the fact, that directly on the edge of this shoal there are from 12 to 16 fathoms water, so that the edge forms a sort of dam, stopping the force of the flood-tide, and over which the ebb falls.

When there was any considerable wind, we observed that the breakers were higher within the edge to the westward than on the edge; and I have no doubt (says Captain Isaac Hall) that the water there was still shoaler, and that we should have seen the sand had it not been for the heavy sea. The breakers were such, unless it was entirely calm, that it was impossible to go among them with boats; nor was it considered safe to attempt it with the vessels. For, besides the danger of striking on the hard sand-spits, the vessels would have been liable to have been filled by the breakers. Even on the eastern edge, and at nearly slack water, the vessels were at times nearly covered with them; and it was therefore not thought necessary to attempt it, as the object of the survey, to ascertain if there was danger on the shoals, and the situation and extent of this danger, could be accomplished without the risk. Had not the sea been very smooth, and at high water, we should not have been able to have got on where we found only 3 ft., reducing it to low water. The prevailing wind was to the eastward; and I have no doubt that this place would have been bare, with any continuance of an off-shore wind.* I think there are no rocks about the shoals. We had one cast on the S.W. side, which indicated rocky

---

* This tends to confirm the assertion made by the Cape Cod fishermen, that part of the shoal has been seen quite dry, with sea gulls sitting upon it.

ST. GEORGE'S BANK.

bottom, in 15 fathoms; but I believe it to have been some sharp stone that the lead struck upon.

The centre of the northern shoal is in lat. 41° 53' 30", and long. 67° 43'. It extends E. and W., about 4 miles; the shoalest part, having 6 fathoms, is very narrow, and composed of hard sand; but there are not more than 12 fathoms of water for 3 miles to the southward of the above latitude. On the North side, at 2 cables' lengths from the shoal, the sloop dropped into 33 fathoms. The breakers on this shoal are very heavy; and when there should be a sufficient sea to endanger a vessel, they might be seen some miles, and heard at a considerable distance; and as the shoalest part is not more than a cable's length idside, and no danger near it, a vessel might avoid it.

To the eastward of the last-mentioned shoal, in lat. 41° 51', long. 67° 26', is another *small shoal*, with 8 fathoms water, having, however, considerable breakers. There are but 17 fathoms for 3 miles to the northward of it; but very near to the eastward are 31 fathoms, and from 20 to 30 fathoms to the S. and W.

The centre of the East shoal is in lat. 41° 47', long. 67° 19'. It is about 2 miles long from E. to W., and has 7 fathoms water. To the southward there are but 17 fathoms for 2 miles; but in other directions there are from 20 to 30 fathoms.

The above shoals, I am confident, are all which are on St. George's Bank; their positions and sizes may be relied on, as well as the soundings which I have laid down; they were ascertained by a vast number of celestial observations, taken with good and well-adjusted instruments, on board the two vessels, and very carefully and faithfully calculated. The rates of the chronometers were found by a transit instrument previously to sailing from Boston, and after our return; and all our observations recalculated for the small variation that appeared.

At anchor, in different places, and on different days, we determined the set and strength of the tides, and, as nearly as possible, their rise and fall. The rise of them is from 1 to 1½ fathom. They set round the compass every tide, setting S.E. every full moon, and running from 1 to 4 knots per hour, at a mile distance from the breakers. The mean rate is, however, materially varied by the winds. They set strongest at W.S.W. and E.N.E., and which is, undoubtedly, the strength of the flood and ebb. From these causes and variety in the tides arises a principal danger in approaching the shoals. When under way about the shoals, in a few hours time we found ourselves drifted far out of our reckonings; and to ascertain our situations, when both vessels were under way, we took continued observations for the longitude by the chronometers, and, at the same time, double altitudes for the latitudes; which latter were calculated by Brosinus's new and certain method. By allowing for the set of tides, as ascertained at anchor, the observations and reckonings agreed very nearly; so that the latitudes and longitudes of every place may be considered as certain. Should, therefore, any vessel fall in with these shoals, a knowledge of the course and strength of the tides will prove of the greatest importance; and they can, by the preceding facts, be calculated for any day and hour.

In proceeding from Cape Cod to the shoals, at 5 leagues from the light, there are 86 fathoms, muddy bottom. The water gradually deepens to 133 fathoms, and then decreases towards the shoals. In lat. 41° 51', long. 68° 11', there are 90 fathoms; in lat. 41° 50', long. 68° 3', there are 49 fathoms, sand and gravel, on the western edge of the bank; the water then shoals fast. To the northward of the shoal, in lat. 41° 59', long. 67° 52', on the South side of the North channel, there are 60 fathoms, soft mud; in lat. 42° 12', long. 67° 51', there are 102 fathoms; in lat. 42° 10', long. 67° 18', there is no ground at 175 fathoms. To the eastward we did not ascertain the extent of the bank. At 2 miles southward of the S.E. point of the shoals there are from 20 to 26 fathoms, which soundings continue 20 miles to the southward and westward.

The bottom, on the bank, so far as we examined it, is of such a narrow character, that it is difficult for a vessel to ascertain her situation by it; we often found a great variety of soundings in a very short distance, such as sand of various colours, and differently mixed, coarse and fine gravel, pebbles of various colours, stone, sponge, and shells. Notwithstanding this variety, some general character of the soundings may be useful. The mariner therefore will find, to the westward of the shoals, and at some distance from them, the bottom to be coarse sand and gravel of all colours; to the N.W. a mixture of white, black, and yellow sand; to the North, black and white sand; to the N.E., chiefly gravel and pebbles; to the East, fine white and yellow sand; and in lat. 41° 57', long. 66° 40' some white moss; to the S.E., fine white and yellow sand; and to the South, generally white sand.

As the shoals are approached, in whatever direction, the soundings become coarse, and are frequently mixed with shells of different kinds. Near the shoal much of the bottom is pebbles; and to the East of the largest and most dangerous shoal there are stones the size of hen's eggs, with moss and sponge on some of them.

Near the S.E. point are from 15 to 20 fathoms; a prevailing character of the soundings is green shells, chiefly of the species called sea-eggs. If a vessel be far enough South to avoid danger, she will have no shells.

The reports that rocks have been discovered on these shoals, are undoubtedly incorrect; at the western part of the bank we saw, in strong tide rips, large quantities of kelp and sea-weeds, which, at a distance, had the appearance of rocks, but on sounding we found good water and a regular and clear bottom.

It will be seen by the bottom that the holding ground is not good; but the vessels employed in the survey, by having a long scope of cable, frequently rode out a considerable gale of wind for 22 hours, on the East side of the main shoal, and also to the windward of it; the sea breaking very high at the time, we being in 10 fathoms water.

It may be worthy of remark, that at one cast of the lead, on examining the arming, I found one-third black sand, one-third white sand, and one-third green shells, in as distinct dimensions as they could be drawn.

Since this survey, in 1821, the shoal has been surveyed by Captain Charles Wilkes and others, in the U.S. brig *Porpoise*, in the year 1837, and from this report the following is taken.

The shoalest water found on any part of the bank was 2½ fathoms, or 15 feet, reduced to low water; and this is only to be found in two small places, viz., in lat. 41° 40' 13", long. 67° 44' 10", and lat. 41° 40' 33", long. 67° 44' 30". The whole of the shoal is composed of hard sand spits; fine sand on the shoalest places, and coarser as the water deepens, until it becomes large pebbles without sand.

The rise and fall of tide is 7 feet, extremely regular, the first part of the flood setting N.N.W., the latter part N. by E.; and ebb S.S.E. and S. by W. The flood runs 4½ hours, the ebb 5½ hours; the greatest velocity, 2 6-10ths of a mile; and half an hour to two hours in changing, going round with the sun North by way of East. The wind has but little effect on the velocity. High water, full and change, at 10^h 30^m.

Clark's and *Little George's Banks* are proved by later examinations not to be accurately defined, and are but parts of the shoal ground of George's Bank.

CASHE'S LEDGE.—This is a dangerous reef, about half a mile in extent each way. Its soundings are very irregular, having from 10 to 4 fathoms in the length of a boat. There are 17 fathoms within a cable's length of it, deepening a short distance

THE FIPPENIES—STELLWAGEN'S BANK.

to 90 fathoms, on the western side. On approaching the shoal you may find 60 to 35 fathoms, brown sand, with black stones and broken shells; then 30 fathoms, where it becomes rocky. The currents on the ledge are exceedingly rapid and devious. On the shoalest part there are said to be only 12 ft. at low water. By observations made, on four successive days, by the master of H.M. sloop *Beaver*, the latitude is 43° 1′ 0″. The longitude has been deduced from that of Cape Anne as from 69° 6′ to 69° 12′.

Such is the statement, exactly as it has appeared in our North Atlantic Memoir, since the year 1815, respecting this dangerous rock. Yet by a later examination by the United States' Coast Survey, by Passed Midshipman Ammen, it was recommended to be called *Ammen's Rock*. As we see not the slightest reason for such change, notwithstanding the difficulty and perseverance shown in its exploration, the original name certainly must remain..

The latitude of the rock, deduced from the two days' observations, June 5th and 6th, 1849, is 42° 56′; the longitude 68° 51¼′ W. The least water on this rock is 26 feet; a less depth has been reported by the fishermen, but they sound with their fishing lines, perhaps not accurately marked, and with a lead insufficient to press down or pass through the thick kelp that covers the rock. The extent, having less than 10 fathoms, is about half a mile in a N.W. by W. and S.E. by E. direction, and very narrow. It is surrounded by deep water at a short distance, particularly on the S.E. side, where the depth increases suddenly to 60 fathoms.

South of the flat rock there is a gully, 90 fathoms water, which runs in upon the bank in a south-westerly direction. Upon the South side of the gully, 3 miles South of the flat rock, there is a shoal of 7 fathoms, whence the soundings run suddenly to 15 and 30 fathoms, on all sides except the East, where it deepens suddenly to 80 fathoms.

N. by W., 9 miles from the flat rock, there is a shoal of 14 fathoms; between them there are from 10 to 35 fathoms, rocky bottom; on the rocky bottom there is kelp of 45 ft. in length, but on the flat rock there is none.

THE FIPPENIES is a bank of some 10 miles in extent within the 50-fathoms line, at 8 or 10 miles S.W. from the same depth, on the western edge of Cashe's Ledge.

The Fippenies are some shoaler soundings than in the gully between them and Cashe's Ledge; they consist of a bottom of 36, 38, and 40 fathoms, to a depth of 55 fathoms, and are situated 18 miles to the W. by S. of the Ammen's Rock of the Cashe's Ledge. The extent of the shoal ground is about 8 miles North and South, and 3 miles across East and West. Thirty-six fathoms is the depth about the middle, which is in lat. 42° 49′, long. 69° 13′. In the gully between the Fippenies and Cashe's Ledge are from 60 to 90 fathoms.

Stellwagen's Shoal Ground.—Commander H. S. Stellwagen, U.S.N., by his soundings has shown the existence of this bank of over 2,000 square miles, extending from George's Shoal to the westward, 25 miles; to the S.W., 50 miles; to the southward, 30 miles. Its eastern limit being not yet defined, having on it as little as 9 fathoms water, in some places rocky bottom, on others its western edge.

STELLWAGEN'S BANK.—This is an extensive bank of 13 to 18 fathoms on the western side of the foregoing shoal, and fronting Massachusetts Bay, situate almost immediately in face of the harbour of Boston. It commences at about 6½ miles N.N.W. from the lighthouse on Race Point, where is situate a small shoal spot of 9½ fathoms, thence it extends in a curved form, the curve being to the eastward, 18 miles in a northerly direction to its North end (13 fathoms), which is situate 16 miles S. by E. ½ E. from Thatcher's Island, Cape Ann. The soundings close to its edge are

30 to 20 fathoms, deepening rapidly eastward and westward, the 100 fathoms line being at little more than 10 miles from its eastern side. Between its northern end and Cape Ann the depth is 40 to 55 fathoms. It forms an extremely valuable guide to vessels making Boston in thick weather, as a single cast of the lead upon it, the soundings eastward of it being so deep, is sufficient to determine a vessel's position with some degree of certainty. It has been buoyed, a *red* buoy having been placed on the 9½ fathoms patch at its South end, a *black* and *white* one in the middle, and a *black* one at its North end.

MASSACHUSETTS BAY.—The space comprehended between Cape Ann and Cape Cod is called Massachusetts Bay, and it lies outside of Boston Harbour, which deeply indents the eastern side of the State of Massachusetts. The opening of the bay is about 40 miles in width, and has the Stellwagen Bank across a considerable portion of this distance.

CAPE ANN is the eastern point of an island of that name, and off it are several islets and rocks, of which *Straitsmouth Island* is the northernmost of the more conspicuous ones, and it has a local light *fixed*, as a guide to Rockport, and the channel inside the *Salvages* which lie farther out.

THATCHER'S ISLAND LIGHTHOUSES.—The island contains about thirty acres of land, surrounded by an ironbound shore, and is about a mile to the East of Cape Ann Island.

Upon Thatcher's Island are two lighthouses, 112½ ft. from the base to centre of lanterns, and 165½ ft. above the sea; each lighthouse is built of gray stone, while the lanterns and railing are painted *black*. They both exhibit *fixed* lights, visible 20 miles off, all round the horizon. The northern tower is in lat. 42° 38' 19", and long. 70° 34' 10", the southern one bearing S. by W. ¾ W., distant 298 yards. A fog whistle is sounded, giving in every minute a blast of 8 seconds, and a blast of 4 seconds with an interval of 4 seconds between the blasts. From the North lighthouse the Londoner Rock bears S.E. by E., half a mile.

Thatcher's Island affords no harbour, nor is there any safe anchorage very near it; there is, indeed, a passage between it and the main, through which small vessels may pass, even at low tide; but the water is shoal, and the bottom is covered by large stones. So soon as the lights are discovered by the mariner, he may be certain of his situation; for, being two separate lights, they cannot be mistaken for the single light of Boston, or of Cape Cod; or for the Plymouth lights, which are double, but within a *very short distance from each other*. The latter can be brought to range in one only in a S. by W. ¾ W and N. by E. ¾ E. direction; while those of Plum Island (Newbury Port), when in a line, bear about W. by S. and E. by N. The Plymouth lights cannot appear so arranged from the North until you are on the shore, and from the South only when nearly in with the land. The lights of Cape Ann are therefore of great utility to all vessels in their passage in or out; as they at once serve to point out the situations of the Salvages and Londoner, and for a point of departure to vessels bound coastwise or to sea.

The Londoner Rock bears from the body of the island S.E. by E. half a mile. After getting the West light to bear N. ¼ W., you are to the westward of the ledge; then haul to the N.W. to bring the lights to bear N.E. by E., and steer S.W. by W. for Eastern Point, which is about 7½ miles distant from Thatcher's Island. Then your course is W. by S., distance 7½ miles to abreast the lights on Baker's Island.

Beacon.—On the *Londoner Ledge* is a wrought iron shaft, 40 ft. high, surmounted by an octagonal lattice, or open work of cast iron, 7 ft. high, and 5 ft. in diameter, painted *black*. The following are the bearings from the beacon :—Dry Salvages, N. ¾ E.; Straitsmouth Island Lighthouse, N.N.W.; Northern Lighthouse, Thatcher's

GLOUCESTER HARBOUR AND LIGHTS.

Island, N.W. ¼ N.; Southern ditto, N.W. by W. ¾ W.; Eastern Point Lighthouse, S.W. by W. ½ W.

When you come from the eastward, and make Cape Ann lights in the night, bring them to bear S.W., and run direct for them, which course will carry you within the Londoner; and when you pass these rocks, bring the two lights in one bearing, N. by E. ⅜ E., and then steer S.S.W. ¼ W.; keeping this course one mile will carry you clear of *Milk Island*, which is very low, and cannot be seen in a dark night. When you judge yourself to the westward of this island, you haul to the westward until you bring the lights to bear E.N.E., when you must steer W.S.W. about 5 miles, which course will bring you to the eastern point of Cape Ann Harbour.

If you want to go inside the Salvages, keep close aboard Halbert Point, which has a tree on the eastern point of it, and steer S.S.E. for Straitsmouth Island, but be careful to avoid Avery's Rock, by keeping the lights on the dry point of Straitsmouth Island, till you get up close aboard; then haul round the point, and S.S.E. will carry you to the lights. To avoid the Londoner, you must keep the lights close aboard the body of the island on which they stand. The Londoner lies half a mile off, breaks at all times of tide, is quite dry at low water, and bears E.S.E. from the middle of Thatcher's Island. A long shoal runs off N.E. half a mile distant from the Londoner. Between the Londoner and Thatcher's Island there are 3 fathoms at low water. From the Salvages to Halbert Point and Sandy Bay, there lies a large spot of flat ground, which at low water will take up a large vessel. Outside the Salvages is very bold. Halbert Point bears from the Salvages W.N.W. 2½ miles distant, and the Salvages bear from the lights N.N.E. 3 miles distant.

Gloucester Harbour is 6 miles south-westward from the lighthouses of Cape Ann. The entrance is 1½ mile broad, between the *Eastern Point* and ledge, on one side, and the high land called *Norman's Woe*, on the other.

Lights.—On the *East Point* of Gloucester Harbour there is a *white* lighthouse 33 feet high, which shows a *fixed* light at 60 feet above the sea, visible 13 miles. A bell is sounded in foggy weather.

On *Ten Pound Island* (an islet within the harbour) there is also a small lighthouse showing a *fixed* light, visible 12 miles off.

A ledge extends out from East Point some distance, upon which (with the exception of the southern prong) is a depth of 7 to 18 ft. at low water. The southern prong, or East Point Ledge, runs out from the lighthouse nearly a quarter of a mile in a S.W. ⅜ S. direction, and has near its extremity a very dangerous rock, named *Webber's Rock*, which is awash, or nearly so, at low water. The depth close to this part of the ledge is 3¾ fathoms, which rapidly increases seaward to 7 and 8 fathoms. The northern prong, or *Dog Bar*, extends from the lighthouse about N.W. by W. rather more than one-third of a mile, and has upon it 5 to 18 ft., gradually increasing towards its extremity, and has a *black* buoy No. 2 on its South edge; outside this prong, and in the same line of direction from the lighthouse, is the Round Rock, situate in the middle of the harbour.

The *Round Rock* has a depth of 13 ft., and lies in line with and midway between East and Mussel Points, and from it East Church appears just open to port of the lighthouse on Ten Pound Island. It is marked by a *black* buoy No. 1.

Norman's Woe is a high rocky islet on the West side of the harbour. It is situate W. by N. from the lighthouse on East Point, and from it a ledge of 7 to 16 ft. extends out south-eastward one-eighth of a mile.

Ten Pound Island Ledge is a small rock of 12 ft. water, lying in the middle of the harbour, at about one-third of a mile S.W. ¾ W. from the lighthouse on Ten Pound Island, with a *black* buoy No. 4. Close to it is a depth of 5¾ fathoms.

Ten Pound Island is surrounded for a short distance by a *ledge ;* and a *rocky ledge* also extends towards it from the eastern shore, leaving between only a very narrow channel of 10 ft. water.

Field Rocks are on the western side of the harbour at a quarter of a mile from the shore, and half a mile westward from Ten Pound Island. They are above the surface at low tide, and are marked by a *black* buoy No. 3.

Babson's Ledge is a rock of 13 ft. water, lying about 200 yards southward from Fort Point, the West point of the inner harbour. It has a *black* buoy No. 5. There is no safe passage between it and the point.

Pinnacle Rock.—This rock is just within the entrance of the inner harbour, at about 80 yards south-westward of the Spindle Rock off the large wharf. It rises to a point, over which are only 9 ft. at an ordinary tide, and there is deep water around it at not more than 10 ft. from its centre.

Directions.—Approaching Gloucester from Cape Ann, beware of the Londoner, a rock 200 yards in extent, half a mile S.E. by E. from Thatcher's Island South light. There is a channel to the westward a quarter of a mile in width, with 5 and 6 fathoms, but strangers should pass to the eastward, not approaching the lights nearer than 1 mile till they bear N.W. With the lights on Thatcher's Island in range, bearing nearly N. by E. ¾ E., distant 1 mile, steer S.W. by W. ¼ W. 5 miles, till East Point light bears almost North, and then haul round the point to the northward and westward, keeping half a mile from it to avoid Webber's Rock and the Dog Bar Ledge.

To anchor in the *South-east Harbour,* the anchorage south-eastward of Ten Pound Island, where is a depth of 5 to 3¼ fathoms on sand, mud, and broken shells, bring the lighthouse on Ten Pound Island to bear N.N.E. ¼ E., and steer thus until within half a mile off, or between it and Black Bess Point, when the course should be altered to E.N.E. ¼ E. If it be desirable to run from this anchorage to the inner harbour, it should be remembered that the passage between Ten Pound Island and the eastern shore is too much obstructed by rocks to be available; but that a vessel of light draught may run between that island and Ten Pound Island Ledge, there being a depth, according to the chart, of not less than 3¾ fathoms at low tide.

If intending to enter the *inner harbour,* bring Ten Pound Island light to bear N.E. and steer N.E. ¼ N., passing between Norman's Woe Rock and the Round Rock Shoal, and also between Field Rock and Ten Pound Island Ledge. When the light bears E.S.E., distant 300 yards, steer N.E. by E. ¾ E. into the harbour.

The northern part of Massachusetts Bay, to the westward of Gloucester Harbour, is indented by many inlets, which form the harbours of Manchester, Beverley, Salem, Marblehead, &c. The approaches to these harbours are between numerous rocks, islets, and shoals, whose relative position can only be understood by referring to the chart. Most of the dangers are marked by buoys or spindles, but as implicit reliance cannot be placed on these, either an intimate acquaintance with the channels, or the aid of a pilot, is indispensable to safety.

The following is a brief enumeration of the dangers and marks :—

Half-way Rock is the outermost from the coast, and one of the most conspicuous. It lies about half-way between the lighthouses of Thatcher's Island and Boston (hence its name), and nearly 2½ miles from the nearest land. It is 180 ft. in diameter, 40 ft. high, and has a depth of 12 fathoms or even more water immediately off it. On it there is a pyramidal beacon, bearing a spindle 15 ft. high, on which is a copper ball. The rock bears from the lighthouses on Baker's Island S. ¼ E., 2 miles.

BAKER'S ISLAND Lighthouses.—The island is about half a mile in extent, and has a shallow flat of 8 to 10 ft., extending from its north-western side about one-third of a mile, close to which is a depth of 3 and 4 fathoms. On the island are two lighthouses, 29 and 52 ft. high, and only 40 ft. apart, bearing from each other N.W. and S.E., which exhibit *fixed* lights at 64 and 87 ft. above the sea, visible about 14 miles; the southernmost of these is the highest. Near the East and South sides of the island are soundings of 5 and 3 fathoms, the latter depth being in the narrow passage separating the island from the Baker's Island Breakers, a channel which must only be attempted by those perfectly acquainted with the navigation. The island is represented as affording no convenient landing place, and its northern and eastern sides are high and rocky.

Baker's Island Breakers consist of an extensive flat which runs off from the South side of Baker's Island, a distance of seven-eighths of a mile in a S.E. by S. direction. On it there are from 2 to 6 ft. water, and several of the rocks are dry, so that it is extremely dangerous, and must be cautiously avoided by all vessels approaching from the southward and eastward. Two of the rocks bear the name of the *North* and *South Gooseberry*, and another the *Pope's Head*. The edges of this flat are steep, there being a depth of 6 and 8 fathoms immediately off them.

Some reefs, called Outer and South-east Breakers, lie one-third to three-quarters of a mile from the outer edge of Baker's Island Breakers, in the direction of S.E. by S. ¼ S. from the lighthouses. They are marked by *black* spar buoys, and have deep water around them. To clear them keep southward of the line of bearing—Half-way Rock, W.S.W. ¼ W.; or do not go south-westward of the lighthouses bearing W.N.W. ¼ W.

Searl's Rock, with 9 ft. water over it at low tide, lies above half a mile S.E. from the lighthouses. It is marked by a *buoy*.

Misery Island is about a mile from Baker's Island, and is joined by a bar to Little Misery, which makes the North side of the channel opposite Baker's Island. *Misery Ledge* has 8 ft. least water, and bears N.W. by W. ¼ W. 1¼ mile from the lighthouses. The South part of Little Misery Island is three-quarters of a mile N.W. ½ N. from the lights.

Hardy's Rocks, distinguished by a beacon, lie W. ¾ N. from Baker's Island lights, distant five-eighths of a mile. The rocks appear at half-tide. On the East end of *Bowditch's Ledge* is a beacon, rebuilt in 1872 as a granite pyramid, surmounted by a mast and cage, painted black. It is altogether 47 ft. high from low-water mark, and bears from Baker's Island lighthouse W.N.W. 1¼ mile distant.

Cat Island is about S.W. by W., 1½ mile from Baker's Island, and a mile from Marblehead Neck, ranging nearly between the two. On its N.W. end is a high beach, directly opposite the point of Marblehead, called Peach's Point. The shore is irregular and rocky. On the southern side of the island are three high rocks, two of which are connected with the island by bars of sand, uncovered at low water. The other stands boldly up between these two, but more southerly. On Cat Island Rock is a spar 40 ft. high, to the top of which is attached a cask, a useful mark from sea.

On the North end of Cat Island there is a large white building used as an hotel, the cupola of which bears S.W. by W. 2 miles from Baker's Island lights.

Archer's Rock.—At about a quarter of a mile westward from the North end of Cat Island there is a small rock of 15 ft. water, named Archer's. It has a depth of 4 and 5 fathoms close to it, and is marked by a buoy, the position of which is W. ¼ S. from the hotel on the island.

At 1½ cable's length from the East side of the North end of Cat Island there is a dangerous patch of 20 ft. water, named Martin's Rock, which is marked by a buoy; and nearly midway between the island and the North Gooseberry Rock, there is a patch of sunken rocks dry at low water, which is also marked by a buoy. These latter rocks, named the *Brimbles*, bear from the lighthouses on Baker's Island S.W. by W. ¼ W., distant 1⅞ miles, and S.S.E. ¾ E. 3 cables' lengths from Eagle Island.

Satan or Black Rock is a black rock nearly level with the water, situate half a mile eastward of Cat Island, in the direction of Halfway Rock. It has a depth of 8 and 10 fathoms close to it, and is marked by a buoy.

Gooseberry Ledge is a small patch 1⅞ mile S.S.W. ½ W. from Baker's Island lights. It has 15 ft. water upon it, and is marked by a buoy.

Marblehead Rock is high out of the water, and will be at once recognised by the *beacon* upon it. It is three-eighths of a mile S.E. by E. from the lighthouse on Marblehead Neck, and may be closely rounded on its eastern side.

Eagle Island.—This is a small island, situated a little more than half a mile northeastward of Cat Island. It has a flat of 3, 6, and 12 ft. extending from it half a mile to the northward, upon which there are several dangerous rocks; its edges are also steep-to, so that it requires care to avoid. The north-western edge of this flat may be avoided by keeping Fort Sewall open northward of Gray's Rock; on this edge of the flat there is a spar buoy.

House Island is nearly two-thirds of a mile eastward from Misery Islands, and on the East side of the entrance to Manchester Harbour. It is connected to the shore by a shallow flat.

MANCHESTER.—This harbour is the north-westernmost of those within the range of islands and shoals. It has a depth of 3 to 6 fathoms, hard sand and rocky bottom. The *Whale's Back*, dry at two-thirds ebb, lies in front of the entrance, about midway between House and Great Misery Island. It is marked by two buoys, and within it is *Saulis Rock*, also marked by a *buoy*, and which is dry, except with high springs. There are other buoys and marks within the harbour, which affords good shelter from most winds, especially from the northward.

To enter Manchester Harbour you must bring the southern light on Baker's Island to bear S. ¼ E., and run North 1 mile, where you may anchor on good bottom.

N.B. Eastern Point bears from Baker's Island lights E. by N. ¼ N. 7½ miles distant. Halfway Rock bears from the lights S. 2° E. 3 miles distant. Hardy's Rocks bear from the lights W. ¾ N. distant three-quarters of a mile, and are marked by a spar buoy.

In thick weather a gun will be fired from the lighthouse, in answer to any signal which may then be made.

BEVERLY is 8 miles westward of Manchester Harbour. To enter the harbour of Beverly, follow the directions for Salem Harbour, hereafter given, till you bring the *Haste* to bear E.S.E., then run W.N.W. about 2 miles, and you reach *Beverly Bar*, which is a spot of sand running out from the southern or Salem side of the entrance, and has a *black* spar buoy upon the head of it, above a quarter of a mile from the shore. The bar has very shoal water on the eastern or outer side, near it, but good anchorage within. There is good water at the head of the bar.. Having passed the bar, there is a sandy point from the Beverly or northern side of the entrance; and beyond this point are the *Lobster Rocks* marked by a square granite *beacon*, which bear from the head of the bar West a little South, and not half a mile distant, and they are above water at half-tide. To avoid this point, after having well cleared the bar, you will steer towards Ram-horn Rock, which has also a *beacon*, and is to be seen at half-tide, bearing S.W. by S. from the head of the bar, one-eighth of a mile distant. There are several fathoms of water within a vessel's length of Ram-horn Rock. Giving this a good berth, you then clear the sandy point, and steer for the Lobster Rock beacon, bearing from Ram-horn beacon N.W. by W., distant about one-quarter of a mile. Giving this a good berth, you are then opposite to the wharves, and may anchor in deep water, and in a very safe and excellent harbour.

SALEM is the oldest and largest seaport but one in old Massachusetts. Its Indian name was Naumkeag. It is nearly surrounded by water, lying between two inlets of the sea, called the North and South Rivers. Its situation is low, but pleasant and healthy. It was the birth-place of Dr. Nathanial Bowditch, the author of the Practical Navigator. The Eastern Railroad passes through Salem, and has a branch thence to Marblehead.

Lights.—To the North of Salem Harbour a fixed bright light is shown on Hospital Point. Seen in range with the main light on Baker's Island, it leads up to the Main ship Channel entrance. As an additional guide between Baker and Misery Islands, the light is shown stronger in that direction.

About 6 cables to the southward of the preceding a *fixed bright light* is shown at Fort Pickering, on the North side of entrance to Salem Harbour. The light is shown from a red iron tower; it is elevated 25 ft. above the sea, and to be kept on the starboard side in entering. A *red light* is shown on Derby Wharf, 1 mile S.W. by W. ½ W. from Fort Pickering light, and these two lights in line clear the Haste Shoal. There is good anchorage S.W. by S. half a mile from Fort Pickering light, with Derby Wharf light bearing W. by S.

If bound into this harbour, or those adjacent to it, and you fall in with Cape Ann, supposing Cape Ann lights to bear N.N.W. about 2 miles distant, your course will be W.S.W. about 3 leagues, then W. by S. ¼ S. 7 or 8 miles, which will bring you up to the lights on Baker's Island.

But, should you fall in to the southward, when proceeding for the lights, you should, so soon as you have made them, bring and keep the northern or lower light open to the eastward of the other, and thus run for them. This will carry you to the eastward, and clear of the South Breaker of Baker's Island, which is very dangerous. Hospital Point light, in line with the Baker's Island lights, clears the outside ledges as above described.

Should the wind be westerly, when beating up, you should not stand to the southward or westward farther than to shut one light in with the other, otherwise you will be in danger of the South Breaker above mentioned; neither stand to the northward farther than to bring the lights W. by S. ¼ S., or you will be in danger of *Gale's Ledge*, a ledge which bears from the lights E.N.E. 1½ mile distant. In this course you must guard against the Whale's Back, which dries at one-quarter ebb. It is marked at each end by a *red* spar buoy, that to the East is No. 6, and to the West No. 8, which bears from the lights N. by E. four-fifths of a mile.

The *Common or Ship Channel into Salem* is between Baker's Island and Misery Isles. It is about a mile wide; and you may, so soon as you are in mid-channel, between Baker's and Misery Islands, steer W.N.W. till you have passed Bowditch's Ledge, or until *Cat Island* comes open to the westward of Eagle Island; then haul up for the Haste, above mentioned.

You may safely anchor in 5 fathoms; but, to proceed farther, pass the Haste at the distance of about half a mile on the port, and steer S.W. by W., which will carry you to the harbour. Observe, however, that a rocky ledge stretches from the N.E. end of Winter Island, and that a rock called *Abbot's Rock*, marked by a stone *beacon*, lies abreast of it, to avoid which keep a quarter of a mile from shore. This rock had 7 ft. over it at low water.

Be cautious, when keeping off shore, in order to avoid Abbot's Rock, that you do not go so far as to get on the *Aqua-vitæ*, sunken rocks, lying E.S.E. nearly half a mile from Fort Pickering, and marked by a beacon.

Should you, when coming from the south-eastward, find yourself near the beacon on *Halfway Rock*, you may bring it S.E., and steer N.W. $\frac{1}{4}$ W. for the Haste, passing near the *Satan or Black Rock*. The latter is above water, steep-to, and bears S.W. by S. 1$\frac{3}{4}$ mile from Baker's Island. It should be left on the port hand, and the black spar *buoy* on the *Brimbles*, and the red buoy marking Mid-channel Rock, 1$\frac{1}{4}$ cable W.S.W. from *Eagle Island*, on the starboard. By continuing this course, you leave the Haste on the port, and enter the Ship Channel, whence proceed as above directed. Common tides here rise about 12 ft.

The other channels into Salem Harbour, although useful to those well acquainted, and generally marked by buoys, &c., should never be attempted without a pilot.

MARBLEHEAD is the southernmost of the group of harbours on this side of Massachusetts Bay, and to which Baker's Island lights form the chief leading mark.

Light.—On the north-western part of the harbour, which trends in about a mile to S.W., is Fort Sewall, and on the N.E. point is a white lighthouse, which shows a bright fixed light, elevated 43 ft., seen 12 miles off. The dangers within the harbour are marked by buoys on the more prominent points, so that when once the entrance is made out there is little risk in entering.

Vessels bound to Marblehead, falling to the southward, and running for the lights on Baker's Island, after making them must keep the North and lower one open to the eastward of the southern light, and run for them, which will carry them to the eastward, and clear of the South Breakers off Baker's Island, which bear from the lights from S.E. $\frac{1}{4}$ S. to S.S.E. $\frac{3}{4}$ E., distant 2$\frac{1}{4}$ miles, and has the buoy on the S.E. part, as before described.

Having made the lights with a westerly wind, and beating, when within 2$\frac{1}{4}$ miles of them, you may not stand to the southward and westward so far as to shut the northern light within the southern one, on account of the South Breakers; nor to the northward farther than to bring the lights to bear W.S.W. $\frac{1}{2}$ W., on account of Gale's Ledge, which bears from the lights N.E. by E. distant 1$\frac{3}{4}$ mile.

Drawing near the lights, take care to avoid the ledge called the Whale's Back, marked at each end by a *red buoy*, which bears from the lights N. by E., distant four-fifths of a mile.

In going into Marblehead, and being up with the lights, give the North point of Baker's Island a berth of one-quarter of a mile, or less. Having the lights in a line, you will be up with the point. When the South light is open with the North light, you have then passed the point (leaving Misery Island on your starboard hand, which bears from the lights N.W. $\frac{1}{2}$ N. four-fifths of a mile). Then steer S.W. by S., or S.S.W., until you bring the South light to bear N.E. by E. $\frac{1}{4}$ E., then steer S.W. by W. $\frac{1}{4}$ W. 3 miles, for *Marblehead Harbour*. You will leave Hardy's Rocks, Eagle Island, and Gray's Rocks, and their buoys, on the starboard hand; Pope's Head, Brimbles, and North point of Cat Island on the port hand. The Brimbles bear from Eagle Island S.S.E. $\frac{1}{4}$ E., distant half a mile; and Gray's Rock, from the North point of Cat Island, N.W. by W. seven-eighths of a mile.

Falling in with the South point of Baker's Island, and it blowing hard from the eastward, if you cannot avoid it, you may pass the point by keeping it well on board, say at the distance of from 20 to 50 fathoms from the shore, where you will have from 4 to 5 fathoms of water. When up with the S.W. point, steer W.S.W., which will carry you between the North Gooseberry and Pope's Head, leaving the former on your port hand, and Pope's Head on your starboard hand, between which you will

MARBLEHEAD.

have from 3½ to 5 fathoms of water. So soon as you have passed Pope's Head, haul to the northward, until the South light bears N.E. by E. ¼ E.; then steer S.W. by W. ½ W. for Marblehead Harbour.

The South entrance of the harbour of Marblehead is bold, and may be approached with safety with the light on the point of the neck at the S.E. side of the harbour, bearing from N.N.W. to W. by N., until you are within half a mile of it; then bring the light to bear W. by S. and run for it until within 2 cables' lengths; then steer N.W. by W., until the lighthouse bears S.S.W.; then steer S.W., and anchor with the light bearing from E. by S. to N.E. by E. from a quarter to half a mile distant, in 6 fathoms, good holding ground, and clear bottom, secure from all but easterly gales.

Vessels coming from the eastward, and running for Halfway Rock, distinguished by its beacon, must not bring the rock to bear to the southward of W.S.W., to avoid the South Breaker, which bears from Halfway Rock N.E. ½ E. distant 1 mile. Being up with Halfway Rock, and bound into Marblehead, bring the rock to bear E.S.E. ¼ E., and steer W.N.W. ½ W. for Fort Head, distant 3 miles, leaving Cat Island on the starboard hand, which bears from Halfway Rock W.N.W., distant 1¾ mile; and Marblehead Rock * on the port hand, which bears from Halfway Rock W. ⅜ N., distant 2 miles. Black Rock bears from Halfway Rock N.W. by W., distant 1½ mile. Cat Island Rock and Point Neck bear East and West of each other, distant about 1 mile.

Vessels, being up in Boston Bay, may, by bringing the Boston light to bear S.S.W., run N.N.E. for Marblehead Rock; they are distant from each other about 12 miles. Halfway Rock and Boston light bear from each other S.W. and N.E., distant 15 miles.

From the light on the N.E. point of Marblehead Harbour to Nahant Head, the South extreme of the rocky peninsula, the distance is 25½ miles, and within this space are numerous rocks and shoals.

The first of these to the South of the light are *Tom Moore's Rocks*, which stretch off the Marblehead Peninsula at three-quarters of a mile from the lighthouse, and have a buoy at their outer edge with 4 fathoms close to.

Tinker's Island is a small rocky islet lying off the South end of Marblehead Neck, to which it is joined by a sandy flat, nearly dry at low water. At about a quarter of a mile south-westward from its South end, and separated from it by soundings of 3¾ to 9 fathoms, is a rock named *Roaring Bull*, which is marked by a buoy.

Pig Rocks, Ram Islands, and *Sammy's Rock* are all situated at various distances from the shore between Marblehead Neck and Phillip's Point, the North point of Nahant Bay. The *Great Pigs*, the outermost of these rocks, are as much as 1½ mile from the land, and there being deep water in their immediate vicinity, great care is requisite when passing along in thick weather.

Nahant Bay, on the North side of Nahant Peninsula, has a depth of 12 to 7 fathoms, the latter being at about 1¼ mile from the shore, and almost close to the edge of a shallow flat of 12 to 7 ft., which thence extends westward to the beach.

---

* Marblehead Rock bears S.W. about three-quarters of a mile from the western part of Cat Island. It is above water, and may be approached to a short distance without danger. On the rock is a monument, or beacon, painted white at the bottom and black at the top; it is about 8 ft. in the base and 15 ft. in height. The course and distance from Halfway Rock to Marblehead Fort is W.N.W. ¼ W. 3 miles, leaving the beacon on Cat Island Rock on the starboard, and the monument on Marblehead Rock on the port side. The monument bears from the beacon W.S.W. ¼ W. seven-eighths of a mile.

The North point of the bay (Phillip's Point) has a rocky ledge jutting out from it some distance. There being no shelter in the bay, vessels should only anchor in it with winds from the land.

Egg Rock Lighthouse.—In front of Nahant Bay there is a small rock, named the *Egg*, upon which is a lighthouse, 25 ft. high, which shows a *fixed red* light at 87 ft. above the sea, visible 8 or 10 miles.

NAHANT PENINSULA.—The Nahant Peninsula, or Rock, as it is sometimes called, is about 2 miles in extent, and connected to the shore at its northern end by a low beach, dry at low water. The Nahant Rock is a remarkable spot; it has an hotel upon its summit, which is a place of great resort for the metropolitan New Englanders; its area is about 2 miles by three-quarters of a mile, and it is distant nearly 2 miles from the main land, to which it is connected at low water. The ground swell, with its majestic heave, is here going on for ever.

The promontory itself is never wholly left by the ebb; but from its western extremity there extends a narrow ridge, scarcely broad enough for a horse-path, impassable for the rocks and seaweed by which it is matted, and extending just at high-water mark from Nahant to the main land. Seaward from this ridge, which is only the connection with the continent, descends an expanse of sand, left bare six hours out of the twelve by the retreating sea, as smooth and hard as marble. For 3 miles it stretches away without shell or stone, a surface of white fine-grained sand, beaten so hard by the eternal operation of the surf that the hoof of a horse scarcely marks it, and the heaviest wheel leaves it as printless as a floor of granite.

Lynn Harbour.—Nahant Peninsula forms, with the coast on its western side, a large shallow bay, the upper part of which takes the name of Lynn Harbour. Lynn is a large and flourishing town situate at the head of the harbour, which is much resorted to by the smaller class of coasting vessels. Shoals, dry at low water, occupy the whole of the harbour, leaving between them narrow channels of generally only a very moderate depth. The depth on the bar is only 2 ft. when the tide is out.

There is good anchorage in front of Lynn Harbour in 5 or 6 fathoms, where vessels may ride in bad weather. The mark is the hotel on Nahant Head, E.N.E.

BOSTON.

From the South end of the Nahant Peninsula to Minot's Ledge lighthouse, on one of the Cohasset Rocks, the distance is about 11 miles, and in this interval are the various entrances to the extensive series of channels and bays which collectively form the harbour of Boston.

This labyrinth of islets, shoals, and rocks cannot be properly understood by any verbal description. The chart, reduced from that issued by the United States Coast Survey Office in 1857, with subsequent emendations, will afford a far better guide than any lengthened directions.

The assistance of a pilot is always necessary, and this cannot be too strongly insisted on, for notwithstanding that the principal dangers are beaconed and buoyed, and the points of approach well lighted, yet it should never be attempted without either an exact knowledge or with the aid of a competent pilot.

BOSTON LIGHTHOUSE.—The principal lighthouse is on *Little Brewster Island*, on the North side of the principal entrance in latitude 42° 19′ 39″ N., and longitude

BOSTON—MINOT LEDGE LIGHTHOUSE.

70° 53' 5" W. It is a white circular tower 80 ft. in total height, showing a brilliant revolving light every half minute, elevated 98 ft., visible at 16 miles off. An air trumpet is sounded in foggy weather, giving blasts of 7 seconds at intervals of 43 seconds.

MINOT LEDGE LIGHTHOUSE is $6\frac{3}{4}$ miles S.E. $\frac{1}{2}$ E. from the Little Brewster Island lighthouse, and stands on the outermost of the Cohasset Rocks. It was originally an iron pile structure, which disappeared during a heavy storm, and was succeeded by the present dark grey granite tower, 100 ft. in total height, and showing a brilliant fixed light at 92 ft. above the sea, visible 15 miles off. A fog bell is sounded when necessary.

The Narrows Light, on the West end of the Brewster Spit or Bar, abreast the Narrows, is a *red fixed* light, exhibited from a screw pile lighthouse, and may be seen 7 miles off. It bears westward $1\frac{1}{4}$ mile from the Boston lighthouse.

Long Island Lighthouse. is a white iron tower 22 ft. high, on the N.E. end of Long Island, on the South side of President Road. The light is fixed, elevated 80 feet, visible 15 miles off.

DANGERS.—The *Graves* are a parcel of dry rocks which appear white, lying to the northward and eastward of Boston light. On the N.E. ledge is an iron *bell-boat*, in 10 fathoms water, Long Island light bearing W.S.W. $\frac{1}{2}$ W., $4\frac{3}{4}$ miles distant, and Boston light S.W. $\frac{1}{2}$ S., $2\frac{3}{4}$ miles distant.

Thieves Ledge, of $4\frac{1}{2}$ fathoms, lies E. $\frac{1}{2}$ S. of Boston light, distant 3 miles.

Harding Ledge is dry at low water, and on the drying part a shaft is raised, having on its summit, which is $31\frac{1}{2}$ ft. above low water, a cast-iron ring, set horizontally, with twelve wooden pendants attached to the rim. This beacon is entirely black, and from it Boston lighthouse bears N.W. $2\frac{1}{4}$ miles ; Martin's Ledge, North, $2\frac{1}{4}$ miles ; and Minot's Ledge lighthouse, S.E. $\frac{1}{4}$ E., $4\frac{1}{4}$ miles. A *black bell-boat* lies off the N.E. side of the ledge.

Martin Ledge lies nearly midway between Thieves Ledge and the Graves, and has on it 13 ft. at low water. Outside the ledge, in 6 fathoms, there is a *red* nun buoy, No. 2, the Graves bell-boat bearing N. $\frac{1}{4}$ E. $1\frac{1}{4}$ mile ; Harding bell-boat S. $\frac{1}{4}$ W., nearly $2\frac{1}{4}$ miles, and Long Island light W. $\frac{1}{4}$ S., $4\frac{1}{2}$ miles distant. Between the Outer Brewster and Martin Ledge, on the last-mentioned range, lies Tewkesbury Rock, with 9 ft. on it at low water.

N.W. nearly from Martin Ledge, between Green Island and the Graves, is a ledge of sunken rocks, called the Roaring Bull, S.W. of which is a shoal spot of 10 ft., and N.E. is a spot of 18 ft. water.

Barrel Rock, which was situated N.W. by W. from the North part of Green Island, has been removed by blasting, and now has a depth over it of 22 ft. at mean low water. Vessels can therefore pass over its site in safety.

Devil's Back.—West of Green Island, half a mile distant, is a ledge of rocks, called the Devil's Back, on the northern part of which is a *black* buoy, No. 1, in 18 feet water, Long Island light bearing W.S.W., $2\frac{1}{2}$ miles distant.

Half-tide Rocks.—E.N.E. one-third of a mile from Devil's Back buoy, lies Maffit's Ledge, on which are 12 ft. water ; and S.S.E. $\frac{1}{4}$ E. of the same buoy are the Half-tide Rocks, in Hypocrite Channel, near which is a *red* spar buoy, No. 2.'

Egg Rocks or *Shag Rocks* lie East of the North point of Little Brewster Island. The ledge is about one-third of a mile long, and runs N.E. and S.W., nearly. N.E. of the ledge, about half a mile distant, is a shoal spot with 18 ft. water, and about midway between the eastern points of Middle and Little Brewster Islands is another spot of the same depth.

Nash Rock, with 2 ft. water upon it, lies on the northern side of the main ship channel, one-third of a mile S.W. of the western part of Little Brewster.

Kelly's Rock, with 15 ft. water on it, lies to the westward of Nash Rock, about midway between it and George's Island, and is also in the main ship channel. Operations for the removal of this danger have been carried on.

Tower Rock lies off the S.W. extremity of Brewster Bar, in mid-channel. It has on it 17 ft. water.

Black Rock is on Brewster Bar, in the north-eastern part of Black Rock Channel.

Ram Head.—A ledge of rocks, called Ram Head, makes off the northern part of Lovel's Island, on the northern part of which is a *black* can buoy, No. 5. Long Island bearing W.S.W. ½ W., 1¼ mile distant.

Nix's Mate lies between Long Island and Lovel's Island, about half a mile from Long Island light. On it there is a square granite *beacon*, with octagonal pyramid on top, painted black.

A *black* nun buoy, No. 9, has been placed on the North end of Nix's Mate, in 15 feet at low water.

Hospital Shoal.—Between Rainsford and George's Island is Hospital Shoal, or *Wilson Rock*, on the northern part of which is placed a *black* nun buoy, No. 1, in 18 ft. at low water. Long Island light bearing N.N.W. nearly 1¼ mile.

The *Toddy Rocks* lie E.S.E. ⅛ E. from the buoy on the Hospital Shoals; near them is placed a *black* nun buoy.

Quarantine and Hangsman Rocks.—South of Rainsford Island are the Quarantine Rocks, and South of the rocks lies *Hangsman's Ledge*, on which is a granite open-work *beacon*, with a small square cage on the top. The rocks are dry at low water.

There is a *rock* with 12 ft. water on it, bearing S. 45° W. from Boston light, distant 700 yards. The new beacon on the spit open to the North, with the hotel on Long Island, leads clear to the South of it.

Another *rock*, with 15 ft. on it, bears S. 75½° W. from Boston light, 770 yards distant, and from the new beacon on the spit South and East, distant 240 yards. The hotel on Long Island shut in entirely with the North part of George's Island, leads clear to the South of it.

Another *rock*, with 17 ft., bears S. 85¾° W. from Boston light, 2,343 yards distant, and from the old beacon on the spit S. and S.W., 117 yards. Nix's Mate, on the northern edge, or at the farthest the centre, of Bunker Hill monument, leads clear to the South of it. If Bunker Hill monument is not visible, keep Deer Island beacon on the North end of Apple Island, while passing the range of the old beacon spot on the little head of the Great Brewster.

Tewkesbury Rock bears E.N.E. from the Outer Brewster, distant a quarter of a mile, with 9 ft. on it.

The *outer ledge* of 17 ft. bears E.N.E. from Boston light, 2 miles distant.

There is a *red* nun buoy, No. 10, on Seventy-four Bar, in 15 ft. water, about 20 fathoms West of the old wreck, which has but 9 ft. on it at low tide. It lies with Nix's Mate beacon, W. ¾ N.; Nix's Mate buoy, N.W. by W. ¾ W.; and Deer Island Point beacon, N.W.

Directions.—Coming from the vicinity of Cape Cod, you should keep to the northward of the direct course, if the wind is N.E.; and to the westward if it is S.W., making allowance for the tide. With a leading wind a direct course may be made good on the flood; but the ebb sets toward Minot's Ledge light.

If from the vicinity of Cape Ann, no particular precautions are necessary.

Should you fall in with the Scituate land, in a depth of 10 or 12 fathoms, without having seen the light on the Cohassets Rocks during the night, or thick weather, run North into 17 or 18 fathoms, and steer W.N.W. for Boston light. From the lighthouse on the Cohassets Rocks, Boston lighthouse bears N.W. ¼ W., distant 7 miles. Davis's Ledge lies E. by S. ¼ S. from Cohassets lighthouse, and has a buoy placed to the N.E. of it to mark the danger.

When near the land and, approaching Minot's Ledge, bring the point of Scituate to bear South, and steer North, which will clear Davis's Ledge, three-quarters of a mile to the eastward, and when you get the lighthouse on the Cohassets Rocks to bear West, steer N.W. by W. for Boston lighthouse, which will lead to the N.E. of the bell-boat on Harding's Ledge; but in thick weather it is more prudent to steer N.W. until up with the bell-boat, bearing West, then W.N.W., allowing for wind and tide. From off Nahant Head, and bound for the main ship channel, bring the light on the Egg Rock to bear N.N.W., and steer S.S.E., to pass the Graves, at half a mile to the eastward of the bell-boat riding on them, and when it bears N.W. by W. ¼ W., steer S.S.W. until up with the bearing for entering the channel. Vessels may pass inside the Graves, keeping 1 cable's length from the S.W. point.

Vessels working to windward in Boston Bay up the harbour, may, in the daytime, stretch safely anywhere between Minot's Ledge and Nahant Head until up with the Graves on one side and Harding's Ledge on the other. Do not come nearer the N.E. part of the Graves than half a mile, but the Harding's may be approached pretty near to the bell-boat. Inside of the line from the Graves to the Hardings you may stand to the southward to within half a mile of the shore, and to the northward to within three-quarters of a mile of the East end of the Outer Brewster, or the East end of the Shag or Egg Rocks.

When up with the Egg Rocks, you must stand no farther to the northward than. to bring Boston and Long Island light in range, and in passing Point Allerton be careful not to go inside the buoy. A vessel, not having a pilot, even if a stranger, may beat up to the anchorage inside the lighthouse, in the daytime, by making short boards, and keeping 2 cables' lengths from Lighthouse Island, but should wait there for a commissioned pilot. If you are working up for Boston Harbour in the night, you will avoid the Cohassets and Harding's Ledge by not standing farther to the southward than to bring Boston light to bear W.N.W. When within 2 miles of the light, go no nearer than to bring it to bear West, and when near Egg Rocks you must not pass to the North of Boston and Long Island lights in range.

Main Ship Channel.—When abreast of the lighthouse, bearing North, and in mid-channel, a W. ½ N. course made good leads to the pile lighthouse on the spit; but if the tide is ebb, or you are on the North side of the channel, steer West or West-southerly, so as to avoid getting on the False Spit. Leave the lighthouse on the starboard hand, and steer N.W. ¼ W. past George's Island. In this course you will have Nix's Mate beacon and the middle of Bunker Hill monument in range until up with the eastern end of Gallop Island. From this point the course through the Narrows is N.W. by N., keeping in mid-channel and steering for the high land on Deer Island until up with Nix's Mate, which leave on the port hand.

When you are passing Nix's Mate you should have Deer Island beacon on the N.E. end of Apple Island for a light ship, and off the South part of Apple Island for a vessel of heavy draught. By observing either of these marks, you will avoid the shoal ground about Nix's Mate. A W. ¼ N. course leads from Nix's Mate through President Roads, until the new beacon on the high part of Long Island is just clear of the N.E. bank of Spectacle Island, when the course is N.W., keeping the marks astern in range until abreast of the beacon on the S.E. part of Bird Island.

U. S.—Part I.   D

In steering this latter range, it will lead safely past the Lower Middle, Castle Island Rocks, Governor's Island Point, the Upper Middle, and in the best water over the shoal ground above the Upper Middle. When up with the beacon on Bird Island, steer N.W. by W. ¼ W. towards the State House, until abreast of the buoy on the Slate Ledge, and then N.W. by N. for the anchorage.

Hypocrite Channel is between the Outer Brewster on the South, and the Sunken Rocks to the northward, thence between the Green and Little Calf Islands to Ram Head, where it joins the Broad Sound Channel. This channel is intricate, and only fit for those acquainted with it, and therefore not to be attempted without a pilot.

Black Rock Channel leads from the main ship channel at the pile lighthouse into the Hypocrite Channel, and is never used by large vessels except in the winter time, to avoid the ice in the Narrows. This channel, too, is narrow and dangerous, and not fit for strangers to attempt.

Broad Sound Channels.—*The South:* Vessels intending to enter by the South Channel may stand in anywhere between Nahant Head and the Graves, and steering to the South of West, until they bring Nix's Mate beacon to bear S.W. by W. ¼ W., may run for it.

The mark for this channel is Nix's Mate, in the middle of the northern and highest of the Blue Hills. This channel is short and straight; its range is perfect, and is safe at half or three-quarters flood for the largest ships; especially for vessels outward bound. Vessels going out this way will leave Ram Head, Aldridge's Ledge, and Devil's Back buoys on the starboard hand, and the Little Faun and Great Faun beacon on the part hand; and in running out of Broad Sound will keep Egg Rock open with Nahant Head.

The *North Channel* passes nearer Deer Island, and is separated from the South Channel by a middle ground. The buoys are passed in the same way as in the latter. The range for this channel is the North head of Long Island (on which the lighthouse stands), in line with the second bluff on the West side. This channel cannot be recommended, and should not be attempted in bad weather, even by small vessels.

There is another channel out, used by vessels in light winds on the ebb, to prevent being set into the Sound at Nix's Mate, or the East end of Lovel's Island. This is to the southward of President Roads, Spectacle Island, and Long Island, and through Nantasket Roads to the main ship channel South of Boston light, and is termed the *Back* or *Western Way.*

NANTASKET ROADS.—To take Nantasket Roads from outside, when Boston light bears North, three-eighths of a mile distant, steer W. ½ S. to the buoys on the Centurion; leave these on the starboard hand close to; and steer W.S.W. until Long Island light opens clear to the S.W. part of George's Island, then haul up for the light, and run in for the anchorage.

Anchorages.—*President Roads*, South of a line from Nix's Mate to Castle Island, in sticky bottom.

Nantasket Road.—Nix's Mate just on with Gallop Island, and Boston light shut well on to George's Island, give the best ship anchorage. Heavy vessels anchor farther South.

There is a convenient refuge for coasters in N.E. winds under Spectacle Island.

Vessels caught in bad weather near Nahant without a pilot may anchor to the West of Nahant, in from 5 to 6 fathoms, by opening Lynn Harbour, and bringing the hotel to bear E.N.E.

Vessels waiting for a pilot may anchor in the main ship channel anywhere between the lighthouse and Nantasket Beach.

Dangers.—The principal dangers in and about Boston Harbour are the rocks and ledges near the shore, under the surface, and surrounded by deep water. Persons ignorant of the ground are cautioned not to approach them without a pilot. The following are particularly to be avoided:—Davis's Ledge, near the Minot's; Martin's Ledge and Tewkesbury Rock, near the Outer Brewster, and Maffit's Ledge, North of the Devil's Back, which are dangerous to vessels beating into Boston Bay and Broad Sound.

To vessels outward bound from Boston lighthouse, who would wish to fall in with Cape Cod, the course is S.E. by E. ¼ E., distant 11 leagues, thence 3 leagues to the lighthouse; and when it bears S.W., 2 leagues distant, you may then steer S.S.E., which will carry you out of the South Channel.

Vessels in Boston Bay, which bear away for Cape Cod Harbour, must endeavour to fall in with Race Point lighthouse, which shows a flashing light, and run for it till within half a mile; when it bears E.N.E. haul up E.S.E., or as near as the wind will permit, and anchor in from 10 to 4 fathoms, in Herring Cove, where there is good shelter with the wind from N.N.E. to S.E. by E. Should the wind shift to the N.W., Provincetown Harbour is under the lee to which we refer; should you first make Cape Cod light, bring it to bear E. by N., and run for it till you have soundings in 14 or 15 fathoms; then steer N.E. until the light bears E. by S.; then run in N.W. for the harbour.

Between Cape Ann and Cape Cod there are from 50 to 17 fathoms: the latter 4½ miles N. by E. from the Race light, with 55 fathoms inside. S.E. by E. ¼ E. from Boston light to the Race light there is a ridge of rocks and sand of 7 to 23 fathoms water, with a small gully of 37 fathoms, 20 miles from Boston light. To the North of this ridge the bottom is generally muddy, and the depth from 40 to 50 fathoms.

It is high water, full and change, off Race Point, at 10^h 45^m. Vessels leaving Cape Cod, bound to Boston, should calculate the tide, as the flood sets strongly to the S.W. off Cape Cod, from the Race to Chatham; flood sets to the South, ebb to the North; southern tide 9 hours, northern tide 3 hours.

BOSTON, the capital of New England, and the second place, in point of commerce, in the United States, consists of three parts—Old, South, and East Boston; and its harbour is one of the best in the United States. The Eastern Railroad commences at East Boston. The Lowell Railway runs on the bridge over Charles River, and the Worcester and Providence Railroads run from the South side of the city. By means of these communications, this city has become the focus of much commerce.

SCITUATE.—At 4½ miles S. by W. from Minot Ledge lighthouse is the entrance to Scituate Harbour. *Cedar Point* makes the North chop of the harbour; the first cliff, so called, making the South chop. There are four of these cliffs extending towards the North, the southernmost of which is the highest. The harbour is small, having only about 12 ft. of water on the bar at high water, middling tides.

From the northerly part of Cedar Point a ledge, called *Long Ledge*, extends N.N.W. nearly 1 mile. Ledges extend from all the four cliffs, but none between; and half a mile from shore will clear all, except for large vessels.

There is a passage within the Cohasset Rocks, used by coasters, which is found by giving the light a berth of half a mile, and running N.W. by N. to the southerly entering rock.

At about 2 miles W. by N. from Cedar Point is a meeting-house, and near the N.W. side of the harbour is a farmhouse, with two large barns at a little to the

North. To enter the harbour, the mouth of which is about one-third of a mile broad, bring the meeting-house or farm-house to bear about W. by N. from the middle of the entrance, and run in, on that direction, for the farm-house, until you have passed the bar, which is a hard bed of stones and gravel that does not shift; and, after passing the bar, and coming on sandy bottom, haul up and anchor near the beach, on the South side of the harbour.

The Coast to the southward of Scituate trends south-eastward for 8 miles to *Brant Point*, and offers nothing remarkable.

Off Brant Point is *Howland's Rock*, a ledge of only 7 ft. water, lying at 1¼ mile due West from the shore, with Gurnet lights bearing S. ¼ E., distant 4¼ miles. Within this ledge, at the distance of three-quarters of a mile, is *Egg Rock*. These dangers are marked by a buoy; close outside is a depth of 4 to 9 fathoms.

To the southward of Egg Rock the coast is formed by a narrow neck of land, called *Salthouse Beach*, enclosing the northern part of Plymouth Harbour, and terminating in Gurnet Point. On this coast, at 3½ miles from Brant Point, and 2 miles northward of Gurnet Point, is a very dangerous reef, called the *High Pine Ledge*, which extends out for a mile, and has 7 ft. water on the reef, and dries in one spot. It is marked by a *black* spar buoy, lying in 15 ft. water, with the Gurnet Rocks bearing S. ¼ W., Captain's Hill W. ⅜ S., and Brant Point N. by W.

Gurnet Point Lighthouses.—The point is a round hummock at the termination of Salthouse Beach. Two white octagonal wooden lighthouses stand on it, 30 ft. apart, N.W. and S.E., and each 33 ft. high, showing bright *fixed* lights, elevated 93 feet each, and visible 15 miles off, and are so situated that they cannot be brought in a line to the northward, unless to those on shore. But to the southward these lights may be brought in one, and lead clear of Brown's Island or Bank. On Salthouse Beach stands (or stood) one of the huts erected for the reception of shipwrecked mariners. There is a breach in the inner beach, which exposes the shipping, even at the wharves at Plymouth during an easterly storm.

PLYMOUTH.—This harbour may be known by a round hummock, lying on its northern side, called the *Gurnet*, upon which the two lights are established; and on its southern side by a double high land, called *Monumet*. The Monumet side is full of shoals and quicksands, which dry in several places; but on the Gurnet or North side there is a fair channel, in which you may ride safely with any wind but an easterly one. But, should an easterly wind happen to blow so hard as to force you from your anchor, you must run farther up the harbour, and anchor within the sandy island called *Brown's Island*.

The harbour of Plymouth is capacious, but shallow, and is formed by a long and narrow neck of land, called Salthouse Beach, extending southerly from *Marshfield*, and terminating at the Gurnet Head; and by a smaller beach within, running in an opposite direction, and connected with the main land near Eel River. Plymouth is interesting as being the oldest European settlement in New England. It was the landing place of some English emigrants on December 22nd, 1620.

In coming from the northward, bound to Plymouth, you must not bring the lights to bear South of S. by W. to clear High Pine Ledge, which lies about 2½ miles North of the Gurnet. Off this ledge there is a spar buoy (red, No. 6). When in the channel, abreast of these lights, run up W. ½ S. for Duxbury Pier light, and leave it on the starboard hand. In running in from South to East, bring 'Gurnet's' lights in range until Duxbury Pier light bears W. ½ S., when you will be midway between the lights and nun buoy on Brown's Island Shoal; then steer W. by S. until Duxbury Pier bears W. by N., when you will be midway between red buoy No. 6 and black buoy No. 5; then steer W. ½ N. Pass between red buoy No. 8 and black buoy No. 7, leaving Duxbury Pier light one-half cable's length on starboard hand; then steer North, and anchor under the lee of Muscle Bank in from 5 to 8 fathoms of water, or continue on same course between red buoy No. 10 and black buoy No. 9, and anchor in " Cowyard " in from 4 to 5 fathoms of water. This is a good harbour for vessels overtaken in easterly storms. Depth of water in channel at low tide, 18 feet.

Duxbury Pier Lighthouse, on the North side of the channel, within Saquish Head, is a red iron lighthouse, constructed in 7 ft. water, from which a fixed white light is shown at an elevation of 40 ft. above the sea, and visible 11 miles off.

If bound into Cow Yard, steer North half a mile, passing to port, or on the West side of Duxbury Pier, and giving it a berth of 100 yards. Anchor in 4½ fathoms, with Duxbury Pier light S.E. ½ E.

When beating into Plymouth Harbour, do not stand into less than 3 fathoms on the northerly tack. On the southerly tack the best guide is the rips marking the edge of Brown's Island or Shoal, which can be distinctly seen.

White Horse Lone Rock,—The South point of Plymouth Bay is named *Elisha's Point*, it should not be closely approached, because a rock, known as the White Horse Lone Rock, lies off it at a short distance, in the immediate vicinity of which is a depth of 6½ fathoms.

Manomet Point.—At 2½ miles south-eastward from Elisha's Point, and 5¾ miles southward from Gurnet Point is Manomet Point, off which are the dangers termed the *Mary Ann Rocks*. These are from half to three-quarters of a mile from the shore, and have a depth of 7½ fathoms close to outside them, and 5½ fathoms in the narrow channel which separates them from the sunken ledge jutting out from the point.

A 6-feet sunken rock, named *Stellwagen's Rock*, has been discovered at about a mile from the shore, from which Manomet Point bears nearly North 2 miles. It has a depth of 5 and 7 fathoms in its immediate vicinity.

From Manomet Point southward, the shore of Cape Cod Bay is lined by a flat of 10 to 16 ft., which extends out in some places more than a mile. In other respects there is deep water over the whole surface of the bay, with the exception of the extensive Billingsgate Shoal, mentioned subsequently.

It is high water on the bar, on the full and change, at 10^h 19^m.

Should you make the Gurnet lights in the night, during hard northerly or north-west winds, and cannot get into the harbour of Plymouth, you may run for that of Cape Cod, the point at the entrance of which bears from the Gurnet lights E. ¾ S. about 10 miles. It is bold-to, and, unless it be very dark, you may see the sandy hills before you can get on shore.

BARNSTAPLE.—The entrance of the port of Banstaple bears S. by W., 19 miles from Race Point light, and S.E. ½ S., 7 leagues from the Plymouth or Gurnet lights. A *fixed* harbour light is established on Sandy Neck. On advancing from the northward, keep into 5 fathoms of water until the lighthouse bears S.W. by S. ¼ S., which will bring you up to the red buoy No. 2 on the bar; haul close round this buoy, leaving it on your starboard side; then steer S.W. by W. ¼ W. for black buoy No. 1, clearing it on the port hand. Be careful to make the above courses good, as the flood sets strongly over Yarmouth Flats, and the ebb strong to the northward over the bar. Continue to run for the light until within a cable's length of the beach, and follow the shore round the point. There is safe anchorage inside, abreast of the light, against all winds, the light bearing from S.W. to N.E., in from 5 to 2¼ fathoms. There are 7 ft. of water on the bar at low water, and the tide flows 10 ft.

Vessels drawing 8 ft. may, at high water, bring the light to bear S.W. ½ W., and run directly for it. High water, full and change, at 11^h.

WELLFLEET.—*Billingsgate Island lighthouse*, at the entrance of Wellfleet Bay, is 5 leagues S.E. by S. from the light on Race Point, and exhibits a *fixed* light at 52 feet above the sea, and is situated so far up Barnstaple Bay that it cannot be mistaken for any other. The island is about 13 ft. above high water, and from the West end extends a long shoal of hard sand, 10 or 11 miles from W. by S. to W. by N. from the lighthouse, and in a N.W. to W.N.W. direction, 5 or 6 miles.

The surface of the bay is almost wholly occupied by shallow flats, even, or nearly so, with the surface at low water, and there are some rocks in the middle of the bay, bearing the names of *Middle*, *Lumpfish*, *Wood's Beach*, *Sand*, and *Channel Islands*, the situations of which can be best seen by a reference to the chart. The most dangerous of these, or those most in the way of vessels, are marked by buoys. Between these rocks, and in a direction nearly parallel to the islets, is a channel averaging in depth 2½ to 5¼ fathoms, access to which is over a bar of 7 ft. Vessels anchor in this channel and obtain shelter from almost all winds.

When running for Wellfleet Bay it is necessary to give a wide berth to the western side of Billingsgate Island, because a shoal of 8 to 15 ft. extends from it nearly 5½ miles W. by S. ½ S. from the lighthouse. This is marked by the buoy at its extreme point, but thence it gradually increases in breadth eastward until its base includes the whole of the islands forming the West side of the bay; consequently it forms a very prominent danger to vessels approaching from the northward. Although so dangerous to vessels bound to the bay, most excellent shelter from northerly gales can be obtained under it. Its ledges are steep-to, especially on its southern side, where the lead will drop from 10 to 14 ft. into 4½ fathoms.

When bound to Wellfleet from Cape Cod, get the lighthouse on Race Point to bear East 1½ mile, and steer S. ½ E., maintaining at the same time a good lookout for the buoy on the extremity of Billingsgate Shoal. When up with it, pass it on the West side, and bring the lighthouse on Billingsgate Island to bear E.N.E., and then steer E. by N. ¾ N., until the lighthouse bears N.E. by E. ½ E., at which time you will be 2 miles from it, and in a depth of 4 or 4½ fathoms, sandy bottom, and should anchor.

When beating up the channel, care must be taken not to approach too near Billingsgate Shoal, as the soundings decrease rapidly. Good anchorage may be obtained farther in the bay in 3 or 4 fathoms water on soft bottom, at four-fifths of a mile S. ¾ E. from the lighthouse, but the approach to it should not be attempted by vessels of burthen without a pilot.

There is a small *fixed* light on Mayo's Beach at the head of Wellfleet Bay, visible about 11 miles off.

CAPE COD PENINSULA.—Cape Cod is the northern part of the peninsula of Barnstaple, anciently called Namset, and now that of Cape Cod or Codd. On the hook of the Cape is *Provincetown*, distinguished by its useful harbour of refuge, which has a depth of water for any ships. This harbour, generally known as Cape Cod Harbour, has a light on Long Point, and another on Wood End to the S.E. On the West extremity of Cape Cod, called Race Point, is a small lighthouse; and there is a larger, called that of the Clay Ponds, or the Highlands, 8½ miles more to the S.E.; and still farther to the South are the three lights on *Nauset Beach*. The inhabitants depend chiefly on the cod-fishery for subsistence.

The Highlands Light, or the *Clay Ponds*, in lat. 42° 2' 21", and long. 70° 3' 38", is erected on land elevated 140 ft.; which, with the elevation of the lantern, makes the whole height 195 ft. above high-water mark. The light is bright and *fixed*.

CAPE COD HARBOUR AND PROVINCETOWN.

There is generally a haze over the Cape, and the light is seldom seen at more than 6 leagues off. A first-class Daboll trumpet is sounded here in thick weather, giving blasts of 8 seconds' duration, at intervals of 30 seconds.

If outward bound from Boston lighthouse, and you would wish to fall in with Cape Cod, the course is E.S.E. 13 leagues; thence 3 leagues to the lighthouse. When up with the lighthouse, and it bears S.W. 2 leagues, you may thence steer to the S.E.

If inward bound, and you want to fall in with the back of Cape Cod, bring the light to bear S.W. 2 leagues distant, then steer W.N.W. for Boston lighthouse.

Race Point Lighthouse is a rubble-stone whitewashed tower, 31 ft. high, built on the point, at 155 ft. distant from high-water mark. The light, elevated 47 ft. above the sea level, is a fixed bright light, varied by a bright flash every 1½ minute. It is visible 12 miles off between S.E. by S. ½ S. by the westward to N.E. ¾ E.

A *steam fog whistle* is sounded at this station in thick weather, two short blasts in quick succession, followed by an interval of 44 seconds.

Race Point is very bold-to, and has a number of fishermen's huts on it. To the southward of Race Point is what is called Herring Cove, where there is good anchoring half a mile from the shore (the wind being from East to N.N.E.), in 4, or even in 3, fathoms.

Good anchorage may be found in a N.E. gale, by running for Race Point Light, giving it one-third of a mile distance as you pass it, as soon as it bears E.N.E., when you will be safe with the wind from N.N.E. to S.E. by E.; haul up E.S.E., and anchor in from 10 to 4 fathoms. This lighthouse was erected to guide vessels into Provincetown or Cape Cod Harbour, and to enable those which are caught in Boston Bay with an easterly gale to find safe anchorage.

CAPE COD HARBOUR and PROVINCETOWN.—Vessels bound for Provincetown or Cape Cod Harbour, may run for the light on Race Point when it bears S.S.W., or anywhere to the eastward of it.

Sailing Directions for entering Provincetown Harbour:—When three-quarters of a mile off shore, with Race Point light bearing East, run S.S.E., until Cape Cod light opens South of Long Point light, or Wood End light, described below, bears S.E. by E. ¾ E.; then run S.E. ½ S. until Cape Cod light opens South of Wood End light, or Wood End light bears E. ½ N.; then run S.E. by E. ¼ E., until Townhouse at Provincetown, opens East of Wood End light, or Wood End light bears N. by E.; then run E. by N. until Townhouse opens East of Long Point light, or Long Point light bears N.N.W. ½ W.; then run North until Wood End light is in range with Long Point light, or Long Point light bears S.W. by W. ½ W.; then W. by N.; and anchor in from 8 to 4 fathoms of water, with Wood End light bearing S.W. by S. ¼ S., and Long Point light S.E. ¾ E.

In running from Race Point to the Wood End, you must not make too free with the land, as there are some shoals which extend above a quarter of a mile off shore. The northern one lies 1¾ mile S.S.W. from Race Point light, called *Shank-painter Bar*, and has 9 ft. on it; and another called the *Wood End Bar*, with 8 ft. at low springs. The shoals consist of hard sand; while outside the bold edge of this shoal water there is sand, mud, and clay, and within a very short distance, 30 fathoms and upwards. Cape Cod light, open South of the Wood End light, carries clear of these.

In beating into Provincetown Harbour, stand to the eastward into 4 or 3½ fathoms, but no farther westward than into 8 fathoms, in order to avoid the spit of Long Point, which is steep to 9 or 10 fathoms.

Lights.—At Wood End a red light, revolving every 15 seconds, is shown from a brown brick tower 41 ft. high. The light is elevated 45 ft. above the sea, and visible

BOSTON TO NEW YORK.

11 miles off. From Wood End lighthouse Race Point bears N.W. by N.; Townhouse, Provincetown, N. by E. ¼ E.; Long Point light, N.E. by E. ¼ E.; Cape Cod light, East; Billingsgate Island light, S. by E. ¾ E.; Sandy Neck light, S.S.W.; Plymouth lights, W. ½ N.; Minot's Ledge light, N.W. ¼ W. Upon Long Point, at the entrance of Cape Cod Harbour, there is a *fixed* harbour light. It is close to the point, and is 28 ft. above the sea.

In running from Race Point to Wood End, after you pass the Blackland or Hummocks, avoiding the shoals previously mentioned, you will come up with a low sandy beach which forms the harbour, extending between 2 and 3 miles to Wood End, marked by its lighthouse; it is very bold, and you will have 25 fathoms within a quarter of a mile of the shore.

Long Point, the extremity of Cape Cod Peninsula, is bold-to, and has 10 fathoms water within 100 yards of the lighthouse; but to the eastward of it, there is a spit, called the *Long Point Bar*, which has only 3 fathoms on it at a quarter of a mile East by compass from the light. From this the village of Provincetown bears about a mile, and extends along the shore nearly 2 miles, and has several wharves and jetties. In the deeper water of Cape Cod Harbour, the depth is 9 and 10 fathoms; the bottom is of soft mud; but in the shoaler water, which gradually extends towards Provincetown, it is of hard sand.

Vessels caught in *Boston Bay*, in an easterly gale, should endeavour to make Race Point light. If you can make the light, run within half a mile of it; so soon as it bears E.N.E. haul up E.S.E., or as near that as the wind will permit, and anchor in from 10 to 4 fathoms of water, where you will find a lee with the wind from N.N.E. to E.S.E. Should it shift to N.W., you have Cape Cod Harbour under your lee. Large ships should not bring the light to bear more westerly than N. by W., and steer S. by E. to pass Wood End Bar in 10 fathoms. So soon as the light on the high land of Cape Cod bears E. by N., run N.E. until you get into 8 fathoms, where you may anchor with the high light bearing East.

Large ships should bring the light on Race Point to bear N. by W., and steer S. by E. until the Long Point light bears N.E. by N., in order to pass Wood End Bar in 10 fathoms; continue this course until Long Point light bears N.E. by N., then steer N.E. until you are in 8 fathoms of water, when you should anchor with the high light on the high lands of Cape Cod, bearing from E. ½ N. to E. ¼ S.

At full and change it is high water off Race Point at 11ʰ 45ᵐ; rise from 12 to 15 feet. On leaving Cape Cod, if bound for Boston, you must calculate the tide, as the flood sets strongly to the S.W.

The lighthouse of Cape Ann and the high light of Cape Cod bear from each other S.S.E. ¼ E. and N.N.W. ¼ W., distant 13½ leagues.

The curvature of the shore, on the West side of Provincetown, and South of Race Point, is called *Herring Cove*, which is 3 miles in length. On Race Point, besides the lighthouse, stand about a dozen fishing-huts. The distance from these huts to Provincetown, which lies on Cape Cod Harbour, is 3 miles. The passage is over a sandy beach. It would be difficut, if not impossible, for a stranger to find his way thither in the dark. Not far from Race Point commences a ridge, which extends to the head of Stout's Creek. With the face to the East, on the left hand of the ridge, is the sandy shore; on the right is a narrow sandy valley; beyond which is naked sand, reaching to the hills and woods of Provincetown.

On this ridge, halfway between Race Point and the head of Stout's Creek, is (or was) a hut. It stands a mile from *Peaked Hill*, a land-mark well known to seamen, and is about 2½ miles to Race Point. At the head of Stout's Creek is (or was) a second hut. Stout's Creek is a small branch of East Harbour, in Truro.

From the head of Stout's Creek to the termination of the salt marsh, which lies on both sides, and at the head of the East Harbour River, the distance is about three miles and a half. A narrow beach separated this river from the ocean. It is not so regular a ridge as that before described, as there are on it one or two hills, which the neighbouring inhabitants call islands.

The shore, which extends from this valley to Race Point, is unquestionably the part of the coast most exposed to shipwrecks. A N.E. storm, the most violent and fatal to seamen, as it is frequently accompanied with snow, blows directly on the land; a strong current sets along the shore; add to which, that ships, during the operation of such a storm, endeavour to work to the northward, that they may get into the bay. Should they be unable to weather Race Point, the wind drives them on the shore, and a shipwreck is inevitable.

From the valley above mentioned the land rises, and less than a mile from it the high land commences; on the first elevated spot (the Clay Ponds) stands the *lighthouse*, previously mentioned. The shore here turns to the South; and the high land extends to the table land of Eastham. This high land approaches the ocean with steep and lofty banks, which it is extremely difficult to climb, especially in a storm. In violent tempests, during very high tides, the sea-breaks against the foot of them, rendering it then unsafe to walk on the strand, which lies between them and the ocean. Should the seaman succeed in his attempt to ascend them, he must forbear to penetrate into the country, as houses are generally so remote that they would escape his research during the night; he must pass on to the valleys, by which the banks are intersected. These valleys, which the inhabitants call Hollows, run at right angles with the shore; and in the middle, or lowest part of them, a road leads from the dwelling-houses to the sea.

From Fresh Brook Hollow, the tenth from the Higlands lighthouse, to the commencement of Nauset Beach, the bank next the ocean, is about 60 ft. high. There are houses scattered over the plain open country; but none of them are nearer than a mile to the shore. In a storm of wind and rain, they might be discerned by daylight; but in a snow-storm, which rages here with excessive fury, it would be almost impossible to discover them, either by night or by day.

Nauset Beach begins in lat. 41° 51', and extends 10 miles to South. It is divided into two parts, by a breach which the ocean has made through it. This breach is the mouth of Nauset or Stage Harbour; and, from the opening, the beach extends North 2½ miles, till it joins the main land. It is about a furlong wide, and forms *Nauset Harbour*, which is of little value, its entrance being obstructed by a bar. This northern part of the beach may be distinguished from the southern part by its being of a less regular form. Storms have made frequent irruptions through the ridge on which beach-grass grows.

Lighthouses.—On an elevated part of the beach, about 4½ miles North of the mouth of Nauset Harbour, are *three* lighthouses, circular buildings 18 feet high, painted white, and 50 yards apart North and South. They each show a bright fixed light at 93 ft. above the sea level, and visible 10 miles off; abreast of these lights the tides divide and run in opposite directions.

The southern part of Nauset Beach, most commonly called Chatham Beach, and sometimes Potanumaquant Beach, begins at the mouth of Nauset Harbour, and extends 8 or 9 miles South to the mouth of Chatham Harbour. A regular, well-formed ridge, which in the most elevated part of it is 40 ft. high, runs the whole length of it, and, with the exception of a few spots, is covered with beach-grass. This beach forms the barrier of Chatham Harbour, which, from Strong Island, North, receives the name of *Pleasant Bay*. A mile South of the entrance of Nauset Harbour it joins the main land of Orleans, except in very high tides, when the sea flows from the north-eastern arm of Pleasant Bay into the harbour of Nauset, completely insulating the beach.

The beach of Cape Malabar, or the sandy point of Chatham, stretches from Chatham, 10 miles into the sea, towards Nautucket, and is from a quarter to three-quarters of a mile in breadth. It is continually gaining South. On the East side of the beach is a curve in the shore, called Stewart's Bend, where vessels may anchor with safety in 3 or 4 fathoms of water, when the wind blows from North to S.W. North of the Bend there are several bars and shoals. A little below the middle of the beach, on the West side, is Wreck Cove, which is navigable for boats only.

The whole of the coast, from Cape Cod to Cape Malabar, the S. end of Monomoy Island, is sandy, and free from rocks. Along the shore, at the distance of half a mile, is a bar, which is called the outer bar, because there are smaller bars within it, perpetually varying. This outer bar is separated into many parts by guzzles, or small channels. It extends to Chatham; and, as it proceeds southward, gradually approaches the shore, and grows more shallow. Its general depth at high water is 2 fathoms, and 3 fathoms over the guzzles; and its least distance from the shore is about a furlong. Off the mouth of Chatham Harbour there are bars which reach three-quarters of a mile; and off the entrance of Nauset Harbour the bars extend half a mile. Large heavy ships strike on the outer bar, even at high water, and their fragments only reach the shore. But smaller vessels pass over it at full sea; and when they touch at low water, they beat over it, as the tide rises, and soon come to the land. If a vessel is cast away at low water, it ought to be left with as much expedition as possible; because the fury of the waves is then checked, in some measure, by the bar; and because the vessel is generally broken to pieces with the rising flood. But seamen, shipwrecked at full sea, ought to remain on board till near low water; for the vessel does not then break to pieces; and, by attempting to reach the land before the tide ebbs away, they are in great danger of being drowed. On this subject there is one opinion only among judicious mariners. It may be necessary, however, to remind them of a truth, of which they have full conviction, but which, amidst the agitation and terror of a storm, they too frequently forget.

CHATHAM HARBOUR, on the south-eastern part of the peninsula of Cape Cod,, sheltered by the narrow spit of Nauset Beach, is a convenient station for the fishery. It has but 11 ft. of water at low tide, and the bar is frequently shifting. The vicinity has been remarkable for shipwrecks, as already shown. The access, however, was much improved by two lighthouses, 40 ft. high, on the point called *James's Head*, the lanterns of which are 70 ft. above the sea, and show *fixed* lights, which may be seen 5 or 6 leagues off, and are very useful to vessels bound to Nantucket, &c. But since their erection the beach has extended 2 or 3 miles, so that they are now only serviceable in running over the shoals. A pilot is therefore indispensable.

MONOMOY ISLAND, a narrow sandy ridge about 4 miles in length, is apparently a prolongation of Nauset Beach, which was parallel to the low shore of the Cape Cod Peninsula, leaving the shallow opening into Chatham Harbour at 3 miles southward of the lighthouses. To the south-eastward af its southern part is an extensive cluster of shoals, the northern abutment of the Nantucket Shoals.

The Lighthouse on *Cape Malabar*, the S.E. end of Monomoy Island, is a red iron tower, 30 ft. high, which shows a bright fixed light, elevated 41 ft., and seen 12 miles off. A *lifeboat* is maintained near the lighthouse.

BUTLER'S HOLE.

The S.W. point of Monomoy curves to the northward, and shelters an anchorage called the *Powder Hole*.

The Pollock Rip is one of the shoals eastward of the South end of Monomoy Island. It consists of two parts, the outermost 4 miles from the island, and each has patches of not more than 9 or 10 ft. water.

The Pollock Rip Lightvessel, moored in 6 fathoms, 3¼ miles S.E. by E. ¼ E. from Monomoy lighthouse, on the southern side of the shoal, 1½ mile S.E. from its shoalest (7 ft.) spot, is coloured *red*, and exhibits a *fixed* light at 45 ft. from the water, visible 12 miles in clear weather; and in the daytime a *red* hoop-iron day mark is hoisted at the mast-head. During foggy weather a bell is rung, and a horn sounded every alternate 5 minutes. A S.S.W. course up to, or a N.N.E. course for 2 miles from this lightvessel, will, if made good, take a vessel through the slue or swashway, over the shoal, in not less than 3 fathoms; the *black buoy*, distant half a mile North from the lightvessel, must be passed close to on its eastern side. Another first-class nun buoy No. 2, is placed N.N.E. from this vessel, on the broken part of Pollock Rip, which should be kept close on the port hand in going to sea through northern slue.

An E. by S. ¼ S. course from this lightvessel, or by keeping this lightvessel in line with the Shovelfull lightvessel, until Chatham lights bear N. by W. ¼ W., leads clear to the East of the broken part of the Pollock Rip.

The Shovelfull Shoal extends for three-quarters of a mile southward of Monomoy Island, and is nearly awash in many parts. To the West of it is an irregularly formed shoal, nearly 4 miles in extent, North and South, called the *Handkerchief*, which has extensive patches of from 6 to 12 ft. of water. There is a channel between its eastern edge and the Shovelfull Shoal, nearly half a mile wide, with from 4 to 7 fathoms on it. This shoal, like the Shovelfull, is marked by a lightvessel.

BUTLER'S HOLE is the channel to the southward of the shoals last named, and is bounded to the south-eastward by the *Stone Horse* or *Broken Rips*, being 1¼ mile in width, with from 7 to 10 fathoms throughout. The prominent points and edges of the banks on this channel are marked by *black* buoys to northward, and *red* buoys to southward; but too much dependance should not be placed upon these. Besides the Pollock Rip lightvessel, previously mentioned, it is well marked by the two following:—

The Shovelfull Lightvessel is moored in the southern part of the channel between that shoal and the Handkerchief Bank, W. by N. ¼ N. from the Pollock Rip lightvessel, and to the southward and westward of the Monomoy lighthouse. It is painted *green*, and shows a *fixed* light 40 ft. high, visible 11 miles off. A *red* hoop-iron work at the mast-head serves as a day-mark, and in foggy weather a bell is rung and a horn sounded every alternate 5 minutes. By preserving a W. by N. ¼ N. course from Pollock Rip lightvessel, you will not have less than 4 fathoms up to the Shovelfull; and by passing a *red* buoy, and leaving the latter lightship close on your port hand, and the opposite *black* buoy on the South edge of that shoal on the starboard, you may steer N. ¼ W. towards Powder Hole on the northern shore of the sound.

The Handkerchief Shoal Lightvessel is schooner-rigged, with a *black* oval grating day-mark at each mast-head, and her hull is painted *straw* colour, with "Handkerchief" in large black letters on each side. It lies in 5½ fathoms, 1½ mile southward of the South part of the shore, with Monomoy lighthouse N.E. ¼ N., and Great Point lighthouse S. ¼ W., and shows a *fixed* light 40 ft. above the level of the sea, visible 11 miles off.

This and the Pollock Rip and Shovelfull lightvessels serve as excellent guides to vessels entering Nantucket Sound through Butler's Hole, for, by steering West for nearly 3 miles from Pollock Rip lightvessel, or till Monomoy lighthouse bears North, and then shaping a S.W. by W. course towards the Handkerchief lightvessel, which may be passed on either side, they will go clear of the Pollock Rip, Shovelfull, and Handkerchief on the starboard, and of the Broken Rips or Stone Horse Shoal on the port hand, in not less than 17 or 18 ft. water.

NANTUCKET and VINEYARD SOUNDS.—These sounds comprise all the navigation between the *Malabar Point of Monomoy*, on the East, and *Buzzard's Bay* on the West; an extent of 40 miles. The southern boundaries are the islands of *Nantucket, Tuckernuck, Chappaquiddick*, and *Martha's Vineyard*, which are altogether connected by shoal grounds. The eastern entrance (3 leagues broad) is impeded by numerous rips and other shoals, as just mentioned, as are likewise the central and western parts; and the whole presents an aspect of drowned lands which, it is thought, were at some period anterior to history connected with the main.

The intricate navigation of the several channel has been greatly facilitated by numerous lighthouses, buoys, and beacons. On the N.E., or *Sandy Point of Nantucket*, is a fixed light, at 70 ft. above the level of the sea. On the western side of the entrance to Nantucket Harbour are two harbour lights. At 7 miles W.N.W. from the N.E. point of Nantucket is a *floating light*, on the N.E. end of *Tuckernuck Shoal;* and on *Cape Poge*, opposite to the N.E. end of Martha's Vineyard, is a lighthouse, which bears from the floating light W. ½ N. 11 miles, and exhibits a *fixed* light at 55 ft. above the level of the sea.

Martha's Vineyard is now distinguished by three lighthouses, exclusive of that on Cape Poge, above mentioned; the next, on a pier at the entrance of *Edgartown Harbour*, is 3¼ miles W.S.W. from Cape Poge, and another is on the West chop of Holme's Hole, near the North point of the Vineyard.

Gay Head, the western extremity of Martha's Vineyard, is distinguished by a *lighthouse*, having a *revolving light*, at 150 ft. high above the sea; and this constitutes the great mark for the western entrance of the sound.

Upon the West end of *Cuttahunk*, which is the westernmost of the *Elizabeth Isles*, dividing the Vineyard Sound from Buzzard's Bay, there is a *fixed* light. Upon *Nashon*, the fourth island from the West, of the same range, is another. The latter stands on the West side of an indent, called *Tarpaulin Cove;* and from it, at the distance of 5 miles to the East, is another, standing on *Nobsque Point*, Falmouth, at the end of the strait called *Wood's Hole*.

Between the West end of Nantucket and the East end of Martha's Vineyard lie the broken lands or isles called *Tuckernuck, Muskeget*, and *Chappaquiddick*, surrounded by shoals. To the westward of Muskeget is a swash of 2½ fathoms, leading to Cape Poge, the N.E. extremity of Chappaquiddick; and to the N.N.E. of Tuckernuck is a spit of sand, extending 6 miles in that direction. Upon the extremity of the latter is stationed the *floating light* above mentioned, lying in 7 fathoms, with the Great Point light of Nantucket bearing E.S.E. 6 miles; the light at the entrance of Nantucket Harbour, S.S.E. 8 miles; and the centre of Tuckernuck Island S.S.W. ½ W. 7 miles. This lightvessel is, therefore, exceedingly useful to vessels in the Sound, both from the eastward and westward. The lighthouse on Cape Poge bears from it nearly W. ¼ N. 4 leagues, and that of Gammon Point, or Hyannes Harbour, N. by W. ½ W. 4 leagues.

The *different lights* on Martha's Vineyard, excepting that of Gay Head, are *fixed* lights. The lantern of Cape Poge is elevated 55 ft. above the sea, as above mentioned, and its light can be seen over Vineyard land.

NANTUCKET.—The Island of Nantucket is situated between lat. 41° 14′ and

MARTHA'S VINEYARD.

41° 24', and between long. 69° 58' and 70° 15'; its N.W. side forms a fine road for ships, which from the eastward, and under favourable circumstances, may be readily attained.

The soil of Nantucket is light and sandy, but in some parts rich and productive. The inhabitants derive the greater part of their subsistence from the ocean; they hold the land in common, and the greater part are of the Society of Friends. The men are generally robust, enterprising seamen, formerly extensively engaged in the whale fishery, and are as skilful and adventurous as any in the world.

The whale fishery commenced here in 1690; and this place is, perhaps, more celebrated than any other, for the success and enterprise of its people in that species of nautical adventure, which was carried into every quarter of the globe. Indeed, Nantucket was the mother of that great branch of wealth in America.

The **LIGHTHOUSE** on *Great or Sandy Point*, the N..E point of Nantucket Island, a narrow spit running to the N.W., is a whitewashed stone tower 60 ft. high, showing a bright fixed light, elevated 70 ft., visible 14 miles off. A shoal, the *Point Rip*, stretches to the eastward for 3½ miles from the point, and has only 13 or 14 ft. on its outer end. There is good anchorage inside the Lighthouse Point.

SANKATY HEAD LIGHTHOUSE, on the S.E. part of Nantucket, is a tower, 65 ft. high, painted white, red, white, showing a bright light, with a brighter flash of 10 seconds' duration in every minute. It is elevated 150 ft., and may be seen 20 miles off. It is 7½ miles S.S.E. from Great Point lighthouse, and 23 miles S. by W. from the Pollock Rip lightvessel.

Tuckernuck Island lies inside the western spit of Nantucket Island, and is about 2 miles in length. *Muskeget Island* lies on the flat, 2 miles beyond it, and forms the eastern side of the Muskeget Channel, full of shoals.

MARTHA'S VINEYARD, the larger island to the westward of Nantucket, contains about the same number of inhabitants, who subsist by agriculture and fishing. Gay Head, the western part of this island, is a peninsula, separated from the other part by a large pond. Indications of ancient volcanoes exist here, and of those four or five craters are plainly to be seen. The principal harbours are that called Holme's Hole, on the North side, upon which is seated the town of *Tisbury*, and that of *Edgar Town*, or the Old Town, on the eastern side, West of Chappaquiddick Island.

This island is about 15 miles in length from East to West. Its greatest extent, North and South, is about 8 miles. It is divided into three townships—*Edgar Town* on the East, *Chilmark* on the West, and *Tisbury* in the centre. Edgar is the best seaport, and the shire town; and Holme's Hole has water sufficient for large ships. The latter is much resorted to by vessels requiring a wind for proceeding eastward to Boston and other ports.

Martha's Vineyard, like Nantucket, was a great nursery of seamen, and supplies with pilots the numerous vessels with which this part of the United States abounds. Here are to be found the most expert pilots for the two sounds, and the ports in their vicinity. In stormy weather they are at sea, on the look-out for vessels, which they board with singular dexterity, and hardly eve rfail to bring safe to their intended harbour. Gay Head, the western point, distinguished by a *lighthouse*, is also remarkable for abounding with a variety of ochres, with which the inhabitants paint their houses. Hence the coast appears of different colours, as will be noticed hereafter.

Chappaquiddick Island, 5 miles westward of Muskeget, lies against the East end of Martha's Vineyard. Its N.E. point is Cape Poge, distinguished by a lighthouse, hereafter described.

The NANTUCKET SHOALS.—An area, bestrewed with some of the most dangerous shoals in the world, lies to the south-eastward of Nantucket, and which, until late examinations and surveys by the officers of the U.S. coast survey, were very imperfectly known. But the charts now exhibit all that are formidable, and the following descriptions have been taken from the same sources.

But it must be remembered that many of these shoals are so far from land that no marks can be given, beyond that afforded by the lightship on their South extremity. Unless, in case of necessity, no vessel should become entangled in this labyrinth, for the currents and tides are here most devious, the weather thick at times, and the more prominent shoals shown by tremendous breakers, while others are only to be distinguished by ripplings, more or less strong, according to the tide or current, or by a discoloration of the water.

NEW, or DAVIS'S SOUTH SHOAL, the southernmost of the Nantucket Shoals, lies about 20 miles south-eastward of Sankaty light, and is exceedingly dangerous, as close outside it is deep water. It has been surveyed by Commander Davis, who remarks upon it :—The New South Shoal has on it only 8 ft. in some places, and bears from the centre of the Old South Shoal from S. 3° 28' W. to S. 16° 42' E., by compass, being distant 6½ miles. It is 2¼ miles in length from East to West, and its greatest breadth from North to South is nine-tenths of a mile.

Between it and the Old South Shoal there are soundings of from 4 to 18 fathoms, but North and East of it are ridges of only 20 to 24 ft. to the extent of about 3 miles from the New Shoals. Deep water separates these ridges, and the soundings on them are very irregular.

The tide rips showed that two, and perhaps three, lines of shoal water are near each other, in parallel directions. The latitude of the centre of the New Shoals is 40° 57' 50" N., long. 69° 51' 40" W., and it bears from the lighthouse on Sankaty Head, S. ¼ E., 19½ miles.

The tides set regularly round the compass, the main body of the flood running eastward, and the ebb westward, varying North and South of East and West; but the flood begins to turn southward, passing round to the West, and ebb northward, passing round to the East, about 1½ hour before the principal set and strength are attained.

Upon the shoals the tides run across their line of direction, and are much more rapid, which makes an approach on the side to which the tide is setting very dangerous. The tide is never still; at even slack water its velocity is seldom less than half a mile, and on the second quarter of the flood and ebb it sets at the rate of two knots.

From the New South Shoal a ridge of 5¼ to 9 fathoms extends 5 miles in a N.N.E. direction, and has immediately on its edge from 10 to 12 fathoms, deepening very rapidly to 20 and 25 fathoms. On it the sea breaks in bad weather. From the centre of this ridge, the centre of the New South Shoal bears W. by S. 4 miles, and the middle of the Old South Shoal, N. ¾ W. 6 miles.

No part of Nantucket Island is visible from the New South Shoal; but the *revolving* light on Sankaty Head is distinctly visible when the weather is clear, and is a valuable mark to indicate its position.

New South Shoal Lightvessel, at about 2 miles southward of the shoal, is moored in 14 fathoms, and shows two *fixed* lights at 44 ft. above the sea, visible 12 miles off. It is schooner rigged, coloured *red*, and has the name "Nantucket South Shoal" on both sides. A *fog bell and horn* are provided for use in thick weather, and a gun is fired at intervals. A red can buoy is placed in 14 fathoms between the lightship and the shoal.

Old South Shoal.—This shoal lies northward of the New South Shoal, about 6½

NANTUCKET SHOALS.

miles, and has soundingss between of 11 to 12 and 17 fathoms, on an irregular bottom. It is situate in lat. 41° 5', and long. 69° 51', and its centre bearse S. by E. 12¼ miles from the lighthouse on Sankaty Head. It is about 2 miles in extent from N.E. by N. to S.W. by S., and about half a mile broad. The bottom consists of hard white sand, and the sea breaks over it in a tremendous manner, so that, at all times, it must be cautiously avoided, particularly as on some parts there are not more than 3 to 8 ft. water, with 12 fathoms close-to.

The ground northward and north-eastward of the Old South Shoal is broken, dangerous, and marked by occasional strong tide rips. It is probable that there are not any dangers westward of it, as none were found in the examination that was made of the locality. The soundings now become more regular, and it is said that at 20 miles westward of the shoal the depths are 25 to 40 fathoms on black shining mud.

At about 4¼ miles N. ¼ W. from the eastern end of the Old South Shoal, there is a small patch of 8 ft. water, having a depth of 6 fathoms close to it, which lies S.S.E. ½ E. 9 miles from Sankaty lighthouse; and 2 miles north-eastward of this are two patches of 14 and 15 ft. lying 7½ to 9 miles S.E. ½ S. from the same building. There are also some shoals of 8 to 14 ft. between these patches and the Bass Rip, but lying rather nearer to the latter, at the distance of 4 miles S.E. from the village of Siasconset. As there may be other shoals yet undiscovered, it will be prudent when sailing among them to keep a good look-out.

Small coasting vessels from the northward, steering along the shore of Nantucket, and taking the outside way, are advised to follow the East side of Bass Rip, and, passing over the tail of it in 4 fathoms, to haul round under the South side of the Old Man, which, being generally visible, it is best to keep in sight. Here there is a good beating channel of at least 2 miles in width, i.e., from half a mile to 2¼ miles from the Old Man. Vessels making this course with an ebb (or westerly) tide, will clear the shoals in a few hours. They will also have more room, and be more favoured by the prevailing westerly winds than in Nantucket Sound.

Pochick Rip.—This is a rip immediately off the S.E. part of Nantucket Island. It commences at a short distance from Siasconset Village, and runs E.S.E. about 1 mile, where there is a patch of only 6 ft. at low water, between which patch and the island there are a few swatches of from 2½ to 3 fathoms, and therefore deep enough for small vessels to pass. From the patch the Rip runs South 1½ mile, where there is another swatch, half a mile wide, and 7 fathoms deep. There is a very shoal spot of 6 ft. at a quarter of a mile W.S.W. from this channel, which shoal spot runs S.W. by W., one-quarter of a mile, and is succeeded by a swatch 220 yard wide, from which Tom Never's Head bears N.N.W., distant 3 miles. You then come to the East end of the Old Man.

Old Man.—This shoal runs in a W.S.W. direction about 4 miles, and has from 8 feet to 3 fathoms upon it. In about the centre of the shoal there is a narrow passage of 3¼ to 4 fathoms, through which boats may pass into the anchorage between the shoal and Tom Never's Head. On either side of this shoal are 7 to 8 and 12 fathoms. The East end of this shoal bears S. ½ E. from the *lighthouse* on Sankaty Head, distant 3 miles; and its West end S.W. ¼ S. from Tom Never's Head, distant 4½ miles.

The space between the Old Man and Pochick Rip and the shore contains excellent anchorage, which, with the wind at N.W., N.N.E., E.S.E., South, or S.S.W., is considered to be better than any in Vineyard Sound, to vessels bound northward or eastward, particularly in the winter season, provided the cables and anchors are good. The depth is 5 fathoms, coarse sand, with Tom Never's Head bearing E.N.E. ¼ N., and the southernmost land W. by N.; from this to the Old Man the soundings are 5 to 14 fathoms, red sand, which will be about halfway between the two, and from this the depth decreases from 13 to 3 fathoms, fine sand, with black specks.

Bass Rip.—This shoal lies about 2½ miles eastward of Siasconset Village, and is about 2½ miles long in a N. by E. and S. by W. direction, and has from 8 to 10 ft. water upon it, and in some places less. Close-to all round it are 5 to 7½ fathoms. Southward of the shoal there are various patches, of 8 to 14 ft., scattered about. The North end of Bass Rip bears E. by S. from the lighthouse on Sankaty Head, distant 3 miles; and its South end S. by E. ¾ E. from the same object, distant 4¾ miles.

New Shoal.—This is a small patch lying about 2 miles eastward of the Bass Rip, upon which there are only 10 to 14 ft. water, and 7½ fathoms close-to. From it Sankaty Head bears W.N.W. ¾ W., distant 4½ miles, and Great Point light N.W. ¼ N., 10¾ miles.

Northward of the Bass Rip and New Shoal, about 4 miles, there are several patches of 10 to 14 ft. water, situate about 3½ miles from the shore, close to which is a depth of 4½ fathoms. From the northernmost of these shoals Sankaty Head bears S.S.W. ¼ W., distant 4½ miles, and Great Point light N.W. by W. ¼ W. 5½ miles.

M'Blair's Shoals.—These are a cluster of 9 to 18 ft. patches, lying in lat. 41° 24′ N., and long. 69° 49′ W. They have immediately around them 8 to 9 fathoms, and must be cautiously avoided by all vessels approaching Nantucket Island from the north-eastward. From their centre Great Point light bears W. ¾ N., distant 10¼ miles, and Sankaty Head S.W. ¾ W.; nearly 10 miles.

These shoals can readily be perceived by the ripples upon them, caused by the tide, excepting during slack water, at which time there is, of course, no ripple; but in daylight they exhibit the usual discoloration of water.

GREAT RIP.—This is a narrow shoal, lying about 10 miles to the eastward of Sankaty Head. Its northern extremity is about 4 miles to the southward of the M'Blair Shoals, in lat. 41° 21′ and long. 69° 45′, from whence it extends 13 miles to the S. ¼ E. to lat. 41° 8′ and long. 69° 42′ 30″. The soundings over it average 3½ to 5 fathoms, but there is a part near its northern end where for a space of 4 miles there is a depth of not more than 10 to 17 ft., in the centre of which is a spot of 7 ft., named the Rose and Crown; this spot is in lat. 41° 17′, and long. 69° 43′ 30″. In lat. 41° 15′ a small ship might cross the rip, as here for about a mile is a depth of 5 to 6 fathoms, but this depth is not continued, as it soon decreases in proceeding to the southward to 3½ fathoms, with two shoal spots of 17 ft. At 4½ miles from the southern end the rip has only 4 to 13 ft. on it, and there are many shallow spots of 9 to 17 ft. between this and the South extremity of the shoal, which might take up a vessel of heavy draught when attempting to cross it either from the eastward or westward. Upon the whole the rip has a very irregular shape, and as there are many shoal spots about it which may have a shifting character, and the soundings in its immediate vicinity are deep, a vessel should always avoid approaching too near.

DAVIS'S BANK.—This bank extends from lat. 41° 0′ and long. 69° 39′, in a N. ¼ E. direction 4½ miles, being here very narrow, and having a depth over it of 6 to 8 fathoms; thence it runs to the N.N.E. ¾ E. 5¾ miles, and widens to about three-quarters of a mile, but the soundings on it decrease to 5 and 3¾ fathoms. The bank then continues to the N.N.E. 5 miles, and increases in breadth as well as in depth, the soundings over this part being from 6 to 9 fathoms; it thence runs some distance farther northward with a gradually increasing depth, until it is finally lost in about lat. 41° 15′, and long. 69° 33′. The bottom in this latter position is very uneven, there being many spots of 9 to 5 fathoms.

Fourteen-feet Shoal.—Among the many shallows northward of Davis's Bank there is a small patch of 14 ft., situate in lat. 41° 17½', and long. 69° 37½'. It has deep water of 12 and 13 fathoms close to it on each side.

Thirteen-feet Shoal.—This is a little patch 3 miles northward of the Fourteen-feet Shoal, having close around it a depth of 12 fathoms. Its position is lat. 41° 21' and long. 69° 37'.

FISHING RIP.—At about 10 miles westward from Davis's Bank is situate the Fishing Rip, a series of shallows of less than 10 fathoms, but none are sufficiently near the surface to take up a large vessel. They probably extend from lat. 41° 0' and long. 69° 27' to lat. 41° 7½° and long. 69° 23', but thence northward are numerous small banks of less than 10 fathoms, so that it is difficult to define their exact limit. Almost close to the eastern side of these shallows are soundings of 22 and 18 fathoms, and the prevailing depth westward of them, or between them and Davis's Bank, is 15 to 16 fathoms.

Asia or Phelps Bank.—The foregoing are the chief features as explored by the U.S. Coast Survey, but subsequent to that the steam-ship *Asia* got soundings in 11 fathoms, gray sand, in lat. 40° 46¼', long. 69° 24¼' W., or about 13 miles S. ⅛ E. from the South end of the Fishing Rip. A farther examination of this, by Lieut. Phelps, U.S.N., has shown that this bank, with similar depths, extends for 6½ miles to N.N.E., and is 2 miles broad. It is shown upon the chart.

NANTUCKET HARBOUR, on the North side of the island, has a depth of from 7 to 14 ft. water up to the wharves, but at times the entrance has not more than 4 or 4½ ft. at low water on the bars. It is high water on full and change at 12^h 24^m; springs rise 3 ft. 7 inches, neaps 2 ft. 6 inches.

Lights.—On Brant Point, on the West side of the entrance, stands a red lighthouse 42 ft. high, showing a bright fixed light at 46 ft.; visible 11 miles off.

A small fixed light, termed the Old Bog light, is shown from the window of a small wooden house on the South side of the harbour, 1 mile S.E. from Brant Point light, in line with which it clears the Black Flat, leaving that shoal to starboard in entering.

The *Cliff Beacons* are two small red and bright *fixed* lights, 100 yards apart, N.N.E. ¾ E. and S.S.W. ¾ W., on two small pyramidal wooden structures, rather more than half a mile N.W. by W. ¼ W. from Brant Point lighthouse. They are visible 7 miles off.

To enter the harbour, bring the Cliff Beacon lights in line, and run for them, passing near the bell buoy in 3 fathoms. Passing Brant Point within 100 fathoms, steer S.W. for the anchorage in from 2 to 3 fathoms, soft bottom.

The following directions cannot be depended on, as the bar and channels are constantly shifting, and the beacons and buoys are shifted occasionally to suit the altered conditions. It is at all times advisable to take a pilot.

The *Western Channel* is the best, and its fairway is marked by a buoy boat in 3 fathoms. Within this buoy the bar is marked by two buoys, the inner one red, No. 2. There are three more buoys on the Flat within, Nos. 3, 4, 5; No. 6 is the Cliff buoy, and the Flat within this is marked by two more buoys.

Having entered Nantucket Sound by Butler's Hole, and when up with the Handkerchief lightvessel, steer S S.W. towards the harbour, leaving Great Point light 1 or 1¼ mile distant on the port hand. Entering by the Main Ship Channel, proceed till Great Point light comes to the eastward of South, then follow a S.S.W. course. Or, if from the westward, from Cross Rip lightship, steer E.S.E., and as soon as Great Point lighthouse bears S.E. ½ E., distant about 5 miles, haul up S. ½ E. for the harbour's entrance, leaving the *red* buoy on the N.E. extremity of Tuckernuck Shoal 1½ mile westward of you.

A vessel that is to be carried over the bars on the camel will, after passing Great Point light, or Tuckernuck Shoal, run for the town on a S.S.W. or S.S.E. course, and anchor in from 5 to 6 fathoms water, with Brant light bearing S. by E. or S. ¼ E.

A vessel of small draught that can pass the channel will run for the buoy-boat off Nantucket Cliff, which is distinguishable by its mast, and anchor near it in 3 or 4 fathoms water, the square tower of a church showing through a gap in the cliff.

The *Western* or *Best Channel* is marked by eight buoys.

From the inner or No. 8 black buoy continue on the same course a quarter of a mile, then steer S.E. ¾ S. about one-third of a mile, until opening Brant Point enough to haul up S.S.W. ½ W. into the harbour.

Middle Channel.—Find buoy No. 9, by bringing the two small Bugs into range, and run from that in a S.W. ¾ S. course to buoy No. 10. From buoy No. 10 steer S. by E. ¼ E. to buoy No. 6 (or Cliff Buoy), and follow in by the Western Channel as before.

Eastern Channel.—Find the outer buoy of the Middle Channel as before, when the Old Bug will appear a handspike's length to the westward of Brant light; steer in, keeping on this range, which leads into the Western Channel at Buoy No. 7 (or outer black flat).

There is a small shoal to the northward of Brant Point, which will be avoided by shutting in Old Bug light on a house nearly in range to the northward. The best anchorage is near the wharves.

There is a channel eastward of this Eastern Channel, in which a vessel will have a depth of not less than 5 ft. at low water on the bar. Commander Caldwell says, "In coming in, bring Brant Point light to bear South, and run for it, until the two lights (one red and the other white) are in range. Run in on this range until the beacon light at the head of the harbour is nearly in range, but open a little eastward of Brant Point light; then run in on this range, gradually opening the beacon more to the eastward until it shuts in behind the farmhouse; then run southward into the harbour."

In proceeding to sea from Nantucket Harbour, the course from the bar towards the N.E. or Great Point lighthouse will be nearly N.N.E. With the tide setting westward, run for the lighthouse, and pass the point at the distance of about 2 miles, leaving Great Point Rip on the starboard side. Be cautious that a tide setting eastward does not drive you on the Rip. Keep the town of Nantucket open to the westward of the lighthouse on the Great Point, until you are 3 miles to the N.N.E. of that point, when you will be in fair ship channel for proceeding either eastward or westward. An E. by S. course will thence carry you to sea, to the southward of the Great Round Shoal, the *black* buoy on which will be passed at a good distance. With a light wind and southerly tide, there will be a risk of being set too near the Great Point Rip, or on to M'Blair's Shoals; it will therefore be necessary to keep a good lookout for the *red* buoy on the end of the former, and when you are to the eastward of it, to keep Great Point lighthouse bearing southward of West. As soon as Sankaty Head light bears S.W. ¼ W. you will be clear of all **danger**, and may steer to the northward or eastward as desirable.

Muskeget Channel, the passage into Nantucket Sound from the southward, between Nantucket Island and Martha's Vineyard, is mainly occupied by extensive shoals, so much so that the principal navigable passage, which runs along the western side, and parallel to the eastern shore of Martha's Vineyard, is but 3½ cables wide in

EDGARTOWN.

its southern part. This passage should not be attempted at night, and at all times careful attention should be paid to the lead and the set of the currents. Intending to leave Nantucket Sound by this channel, and having followed the directions already given till abreast of Cape Poge lighthouse, steer so as to pass about a mile northward and eastward of it, bringing it in range with Edgartown spire, then shape a course S. ¼ W., steering parallel to, and at the distance of a mile from the shore, leaving the *red* buoy on the S.W. end of Hawes' Shoal on the port, and the *black* buoy on Tom Shoal on the starboard hand. Continue this course for 6 miles, when you will find the water suddenly deepen to about 17 fathoms, and the *red* buoy on Mutton Shoal ahead of you, distant half a mile, with the church on Sampson's Hill, at the same time bearing N.W. ¾ N. Steer from this position S.W. ½ S. to pass between Skiffs Island and Mutton Shoal, leaving the *red* buoy on the latter on the port hand. Keep this course 1 mile, when Wasque Bluff, the S.W. end of Martha's Vineyard, will bear N. by W., and then you may follow any direction between South and S.S.W., and pass out clear of all danger.

Cape Poge Lighthouse stands, as before stated, on the N.E. extreme of Chappaquiddick Island, and on the eastern side of the entrance to Edgartown Harbour. It is a white tower, 35 ft. high, showing a fixed light at 55 ft., visible 13 miles off.

EDGARTOWN.—The harbour of Edgartown, which is 2 leagues to the southeastward of Holmes's Hole, is the best harbour of Martha's Vineyard. It is a port of entry. The harbour is formed by the eastern part of Martha's Vineyard and the western part of the Isle Chappaquiddick, therefore to the West of Cape Poge lighthouse, and is bounded by shoals on each side. The tide runs in strongly, but there is excellent anchorage. The town is situate on the western side, up the harbour.

A pier has been erected at the entrance of the harbour, and a lighthouse placed thereon, which was first lighted on the 15th October, 1828. The light is fixed, and 50 ft. above the sea.

Having followed the directions for Nantucket Sound till off Cape Poge, and coming from the westward, pass to the northward of the outer buoy (*red*), and if from the eastward, give Cape Poge a berth of half a mile. Steer then S. by W. or S.S.W., keeping in not less than 4 fathoms, soft and sticky bottom, until up with the middle buoy (*red*), whence you steer S.S.W. towards the lighthouse. Give the buoy off the lighthouse a small berth on the starboard hand, and enter in mid-channel. If intending to anchor above the first wharf, keep near the wharves to avoid the shoal off the inner point of Chappaquiddick. In the night, after passing the outer buoy, or Cape Poge, make use of the lead, and tack when the bottom changes from soft to hard, especially on the western side, where the water shoals suddenly from 5 fathoms to 12 feet. After Cape Poge bears E. by S., the course changes from S. by W. to S.S.W., and in sailing up you must observe the before-mentioned precautions as to making use of the lead. There is good anchorage off the town in from 3½ to 4 fathoms.

If intending to anchor in the outer harbour, follow the above directions until the harbour light bears W. by S., and Cape Poge light about N.E. by E. ¼ E., when you may anchor in 4½ or 5 fathoms water, good holding ground. When anchoring, be careful, as the bank on either side is steep-to.

Holmes's Hole, on the North side of Martha's Vineyard, is also a place of retreat for vessels during the winter. On the West chop of Holmes's Hole, on the starboard hand as you enter, is a lighthouse, showing a *fixed* light at 60 ft.

If from the eastward, follow the directions for Nantucket Sound, and when abreast East Chop haul to the southward. When coming in from the westward, bring the East Chop well open with the West Chop lighthouse, and it will lead you clear of the Middle Ground. Give the West Chop a berth of half a mile, until you are past the buoy marking the rocks off that chop. You can beat in by the lead with perfect safety, the shores being tolerably bold and clear. You can anchor in 3 fathoms, mud, with the West Chop light just open of the woods on Low Point. Small vessels may anchor farther in, and immediately off the town. If you make the light on the West Chop in the night, bearing S.E., you will be clear of the Middle Ground, and may steer for the East side of it till you get into 4 or 3 fathoms on the flat near the chop, and then steer S.E. by E., taking care not to approach the land nearer than in 3 fathoms; but if, in running S.E. by E., the water should deepen to 6 or 7 fathoms, haul up S. by W. or S.S.W. to 4 or 3 fathoms, as above directed.

NANTUCKET SOUND, North Side.—The harbours described are on the islands which shelter the Sound on the southward. The following are on the South shore of the Cape Cod Peninsula, commencing from the eastward.

The Powder Hole, on the S.W. side of Monomoy Island, has been before noticed. To proceed to this place, steer W. ½ N. from Pollock Rip lightvessel up to the Shovelful lightship and the *black* buoy on the S.W. end of the Shovelful Shoal, leaving in your course a *black and white* buoy on your starboard, and a *red* buoy on your port hand. From the Shovelful lightvessel haul up on a N. ¼ W. course through the narrow but deep channel between the Shovelful and Handkerchief Shoals, leaving the *red* buoy on the edge of the latter on your western side, and as the former shoal is very shallow and steep-to, it will be necessary not to deviate much from this course, and to tack at the first shoal cast (under 4 fathoms) of the lead. When Monomoy lighthouse bears East, steer N.E. till it bears S.E. by E. ¼ E., then steer for the lighthouse, and when past Monomoy Point, which should have a berth of 50 yards, haul in to the southward, and anchor close inside the point in 2½ fathoms, to avoid the flats to the eastward.

Old Stage Harbour lies in the extreme N.E. corner of Nantucket Sound, and is formed by the extensive flats which project from the eastern and northern shores, which make a kind of basin with an entrance above a mile in width, and open to the south-westward, the eastern and western sides of which are marked by two buoys, the *red* to be left to starboard and the *black* to port when entering. Anchorage may be had in this harbour in about 4 fathoms water, good holding ground, but exposed to all winds from the southward and westward.

Bass River, on the northern shore of Nantucket Sound, will itself only admit very small craft. Before its mouth is a well-sheltered roadstead in 15 and 16 ft., except against southerly gales, which bring in a heavy sea, rendering the anchorage insecure. Here there is a small breakwater, behind which vessels anchor in 6 or 8 feet at low water. Those of light draught may run up close under the breakwater to the eastward of it. A *fixed* light is shown from a *white* tower on the keeper's dwelling, situated a mile eastward of the river's entrance, at the height of 40 ft. above the sea, which is visible in clear weather at from 8 to 10 miles off. Vessels approaching from the westward, should bring the light to bear N. by E. to clear the East end of the breakwater, and those approaching from the eastward should bring the light to bear N.W. before running in for the anchorage.

HYANNIS.—This port is 5 miles westward of Bass River, and is rendered of more importance by its breakwater. It forms a portion of Barnstaple township.

Point Gammon, on the eastern side of Hyannis Harbour, is distinguished by a lighthouse of stone, painted white; the light, called the Bug light, is fixed, brilliant, and 36 ft. above the sea.

In the fairway, up to and within the small breakwater, there are from 15 to 18 ft. water, and at the head of the landing wharf from 4 to 6 feet. The deep-water space for anchoring inside the breakwater is, however, very confined, being not more than half a mile in extent, the shallow flats from both shores, especially the Point Gammon side, encroaching upon it and thus limiting its area. High water here, on full and change days, at $12^h\ 22^m$. Springs rise 3 ft. 10 inches; neaps, 1 foot 9 inches.

The dangers in the way of vessels entering Hyannis Harbour are:—the *Bishop and Clerks*, now distinguished by a granite tower on their northern part, serving as a lighthouse, showing a *revolving* light, with a bright flash every half minute, which bears S. by E. nearly 2½ miles from Point Gammon. By giving this lighthouse a berth of a quarter of a mile on the East, North, and West sides, and of 1 mile on the South side, vessels will pass clear of the rocks in not less than 14 ft. A buoy, painted in red and black horizontal stripes, is placed upon a detached rock, which has only 9 ft. water over it, and lies 1¼ mile S. ½ E. from Point Gammon. The *Senator Shoal* and *Gazelle Rock*, which lie off the southern side of Point Gammon, and are both marked by buoys, that on the former lying nearly a mile in a south-easterly direction from the point, the other inside it and nearer the point; both buoys should have a good berth on your northern side. The *Middle Ground*, which is about a mile in extent from N.W. by W. to S.E. by E., has 15 to 18 ft. water on it, excepting on its eastern end, where there is a spot of 12 ft., which lies W. by N. 1⅛ mile from the lighthouse on the Bishop and Clerks; this spot is marked by a *striped* buoy. The *S. W. Ground*, a flat of from 7 to 10 ft. water, running off 1½ mile southward from the West side of the harbour, with several rocks upon it, the outermost group of which, named Gallatin, lies W. ¼ S. from the buoy on the S.E. corner of the ground, and N.W. by W. ¾ W. from the Gangway buoy. The *Gangway Rock*, a patch of 10 feet, is situated on the W.S.W. Ledge, outside the S.W. Ground; the buoy on it bears W. by S. ¼ S. from Point Gammon, and N.W. by W. ¼ W. from Bishop and Clerks' lighthouse. The *Great Rock*, above water, lies on the eastern side of the passage into the harbour, S. ¼ W. 1⅛ mile from the Bug light. And the *Half-tide Rock*, lies S.E. ¼ E. a quarter of a mile from the Great Rock, and N.W. ¾ W. from Point Gammon.

Bound to Hyannis from the eastward, follow the directions given on page 39 for vessels sailing through the North channel of Nantucket Sound, till abreast of Bishop and Clerks' lighthouse. Or, from the Handkerchief lightvessel, steer N.W. towards the said lighthouse, and give it a berth on your port hand of half a mile or more. Or, if from the southward and eastward, and in a position off Great Point, with its lighthouse bearing South, distant about 3 miles, steer N.W. by N. towards the Bishop and Clerks, and round them at the same distance.

To sail through the *North Channel*, or that between the Bishop and Clerks and the Senator Shoal, having proceeded on either of the two latter courses, till the Bishop and Clerks' lighthouse bears W. by N. about three-quarters of a mile distant, steer N.W. ½ W. about 3 miles, until Point Gammon bears E. by N. ½ N., and the Bug light is in one with the West spire of Hyannis; here the East end of the breakwater will be in one with the second small windmill of the salt-works westward of the Bug light, and on with the end of the wharf, bearing N. ¾ E. Run in with this latter mark on (N. ¾ E.) about 1¼ mile, double close round the East end of the breakwater, run N.N.W., a cable's length or so, and anchor in 16 ft. water on a muddy bottom.

If bound into Hyannis by the *Middle Channel* (the one between the Bishop and Clerks and the Middle Ground), pass at least one mile to the southward of the Bishop and Clerks' lighthouse, leaving the buoy on the South extreme of the reef on the starboard hand, and bring Point Gammon to bear N. by E.; run in on that course until the lighthouse on the Bishop and Clerks bear E. ½ S., distant nearly 1 mile, when you steer N.N.W. 2 miles, leaving the *striped* buoy on the Middle Ground half a mile to port, until Point Gammon bears E. by N. ¼ N., distant 1½ mile; you now proceed as before.

If bound in by the *West Channel* (the one between the Middle Ground and the W.S.W. Ledge), proceed from Vineyard Sound up to Succonesset lightvessel by reversing the directions on page 39, and from that lightship steer E. by N. ¼ N., and when Point Gammon bears N.E. by E., distant 2½ or 3 miles, run on that course, leaving the Gangway buoy three-fifths of a mile to the northward and westward, until the Bug light is just open to the westward of the West spire, and the East end of the breakwater is on with the second windmill westward of the Bug light, when you may run N. ¾ E., as before.

DIRECTIONS for Nantucket Sound.—BUTLER'S HOLE.—If intending to enter Nantucket Sound through Butler's Hole, coming from the eastward, and when about 2 miles East of Chatham lights, bring Pollock Rip lightvessel to bear S. by W. ¼ W. and steer for it, leaving the *black* buoy on Pollock Rip on the starboard hand. When up with the lightship, steer West till Monomoy lighthouse bears North; in this course your sounding will not be less than 17 or 18 ft., these depths being found passing over the northern prolongation of the Broken Rips or Stone Horse Shoal, the extremity of which is marked by a *red* buoy, which you will leave a little on the starboard hand. Steer now S.W. by W. for the Handkerchief lightvessel, leaving another *red* buoy about three-quarters of a mile distant on your port side. To ensure a greater depth of water, when up with Pollock Rip lightvessel, steer W. by N. for 2½ miles, or till Monomoy lighthouse bears N.N.W., then proceed on a S.W. ¼ W. bearing for the Handkerchief lightship; on these latter courses you will leave both the foregoing red buoys on the port hand. Although the prominent parts of the Pollock, Shovelful, and Handkerchief Shoals, which form the northern side of Butler's Hole, are marked by *black* buoys, and those of the Broken Rip or Stone Horse, forming the southern side, by *red* ones, yet too great a freedom should not be taken with these directions in tacking towards either side of the channel, because the lead gives but a very indifferent warning of an approach to the shoals.

From Handkerchief lightvessel to Cross Rip lightvessel the course is first W. ¼ S. 8 miles, and then W. by N. ¼ N. nearly 3 miles, passing the latter vessel on its southern side, between it and the red buoy on the North end of Cross Rip. Here the channel is but 300 fathoms in width.

Main Ship Channel.—To enter Nantucket Sound by this channel, keep at the distance of about 4 miles from off Chatham lights, and bring them to bear W.N.W., then steer South for 13 miles, passing 7 miles eastward of Monomoy lighthouse, 4 miles eastward of Pollock Rip lightship, and 2½ miles eastward of the buoy on the outer end of the broken part of Pollock Rip. If this course be made good, then Sankaty Head light will be seen (in clear weather) bearing S.W. ¼ W., and if Great Point light be not brought northward of West you will clear the M'Blair Shoals. Therefore, as soon as Sankaty light bears S.W. ¼ W. distant about 12 miles, haul up W. by N., steering in between M'Blair Shoals on the southern and the Great Round Shoals on the northern side, passing the *red* buoy on the extremity of Great Point Rip, a shoal extending 3¼ miles E.N.E. from Great Point lighthouse, and also the *red* buoy on the N.E. end of Tuckernuck Shoal, on the port hand; and the *black* buoy on the Great Round Shoals on the starboard, giving it a berth of not less than 1 or 1¼ mile. If this course (W. by N.) be followed, when abreast the Tuckernuck buoy, Cross Rip lightvessel will be seen bearing about W.N.W.; steer for it, and leave it almost close-to on your starboard hand, as before directed.

VINEYARD SOUND.

From the Cross Rip lightship steer W. by N. ¼ N. 10 miles, which will bring you up to between the *red* buoys on the East and West extremities of Squash Meadow, and the *striped* buoy on the East of the Hedge Fence Shoal. Shape a course now for Nobska Point light, steering N.W. by W., and give the Squash Meadow buoys, the East Chop and the West Chop lighthouse a berth of at least half a mile on your port hand. This offing, however, should not be increased to more than 1 or 1¾ mile for fear of running on the Hedge Fence, which is long, narrow, and steep-to, with only 4 or 5 ft. on its shoalest part. Its extreme points are distinguished by *striped* buoys. When about 1 mile S.E. by E. from Nobska light, follow the directions hereafter given for Vineyard Sound.

North Channel of Nantucket Sound.—Follow the directions already given up to Pollock Rip lightvessel. From the lightship steer W. ¼ N. up to Shovelful lightvessel, passing the *red* buoy on the North extreme of the Stone Horse or Broken Rip, close on the port hand, and the *black* buoy on the South end of the Shovelful on the starboard. From Shovelful lightvessel haul up to the N. ¼ W., and continue so till Monomoy lighthouse bears East, remembering only that the edges of the Shovelful and Handkerchief Banks, which form the East and West boundaries of this channel, are but 3½ cables' lengths apart, and that in tacking towards them by the lead, you will suddenly shoalen your water from 5 and 4 fathoms to 10 and 6 feet, or even less. When Monomoy light bears East, a N.W. by W. course will clear the North end of the Handkerchief, the *red* buoy on the edge of which must be left to port; by following this direction for 6 miles, Bass River light will be seen bearing North, distant 3¼ miles.

Or, the N. ¼ W. course from Shovelful lightvessel may be continued till Monomoy lighthouse bears S.E. ¾ E., to a black and white *striped* buoy; then steer N.W. ¼ W. for about 2 miles, leaving the buoys on the shoal to the northward on the starboard side, and afterwards W. by N. up to where Bass River light bears North, distant 3½ miles. Proceed then on a W. ¼ N. course, leaving the buoys on the Senator Shoal and Gazelle Rock, which extend southward from Point Gammon, the eastern side of entrance to Hyannis, on the northern side, and the Bishop and Clerks' lighthouse between half and three-quarters of a mile to the southward of you. When this latter lighthouse bears E. by S. ½ S., and the Bug light at Hyannis N.E. by N. ¼ N., at which time the eastern or New Spire at Hyannis will be on, or nearly so, with the middle of the breakwater, put the vessel's head W. by S. ½ S., which will carry you between the *red* buoys on the Middle Ground, the North end of the Horse Shoe, and the Eldridge Shoals, on the port hand, and the *black* ones on the W.S.W. Ledge and Wreck Shoal, on the starboard side, up to Succonesset lightvessel. You will know when you are off the northern end of the Horse Shoe by your water deepening to 9, 10, and 11 fathoms. In turning to windward hereabout do not approach the Horse Shoe nearer than into a depth of 10 fathoms, nor the shore than into 3½ fathoms. Pass close round the South side of this lightship, and steer W. ½ N., leaving the buoys on the Succonesset Shoal to the northward, and those on Loose Shoal and L'Homme de Dieu to the southward, and as soon as Nobska light bears West steer for it, giving the buoy on the West end of L'Homme de Dieu Shoal a berth of 500 yards on the port hand, and Nobska Point a berth of three-quarters of a mile on the starboard. Hence through Vineyard Sound, see directions subsequently given for that channel.

For vessels sailing from Vineyard Sound through Nantucket Sound to the eastward, there will be no difficulty in reversing the foregoing directions. But in all cases a pilot is to be considered a necessary guide.

VINEYARD SOUND.—Gay Head, the westernmost point of Martha's Vineyard, in lat, 40° 20¼', long. 70° 49¾', is distinguished by a lighthouse, already noticed. The land of this head is high, and of various colours, appearing red, yellow, and white, in streaks, not unlike the cliffs in Alum Bay, in the Isle of Wight. It forms the South side of the entrance into Vineyard Sound, the North side of which is formed by the Elizabeth Isles. At the western extremity of the latter is the ledge of rocks called the *Sow and Pigs*, which is very dangerous, but on which a lighthouse is constructing.

The *Elizabeth Isles*, six in number, and famous for their excellent dairies, form the natural division between Vineyard Sound and Buzzard's Bay. The principal isles of the group are Naushon, Pasqui, Nashawina, Pune or Penequese, and Cuttehunk. On the S.E. side of Naushon, upon the S.W. side of a cove called *Tarpaulin Cove*, is the lighthouse, with *fixed* light.

At nearly 2 leagues to the southward of Gay Head is an islet called *Noman's Land*, which serves as a beacon to those approaching the western part of Martha's Vineyard. There is a passage between it and the latter, but it is impeded by a dangerous ledge of rocks, called the *Old Man*, lying nearly in mid-channel, with Gay Head lighthouse N. ¼ W. 4 miles distant.

The Sow and Pigs, a ledge of rocks, some above and some under water, bear N.W. by W. 2¼ leagues from Gay Head, and extend 1¾ miles from Cuttehunk, the westernmost of the Elizabeth Isles, distinguished by the lighthouse. The first of the flood sets strongly over them to the northward, into Buzzard's Bay, the ground of which is very foul. A *lighthouse* is (or was) being erected on the ledge.

The rocks, resting on an irregular reef of hard stones and pebbles, stretch three-quarters of a mile W. by S., then 820 yards to S.S.W., then a quarter of a mile to S.W. by S., the general direction being S.W. by W. ¼ W. 1½ mile from the West point of Cuttehunk Island.

Cuttehunk Lighthouse is white, and stands on the S.W. point of Cuttehunk or Cuttyhunk Island. It shows a bright fixed light, elevated 42 ft., visible 12 miles off. The *Ribbon Reef*, of 15 ft. water, lies 1½ mile N.W. from the light, and is marked by a *striped buoy*.

Vineyard Sound Lightvessel is moored in 13½ fathoms off the S.W. end of Sow and Pigs Reef, with Cuttyhunk lighthouse bearing N.E. by E. ½ E. 2¼ miles, and Gay Head S.E. by E. ¼ E., 7½ miles. The hull of the vessel is painted *red*, with a *yellow* streak, and has the name on each side. There are two *fixed* lights exhibited from the mast-heads, one 34 and the other 23 ft. above the sea, each visible at from 9 to 11 miles. In the daytime one *red* ball is hoisted at each mast-head, and a bell rung and a horn sounded every alternate five minutes in foggy weather.

GAY HEAD Lighthouse is a reddish brick tower, 41 ft. high, showing a bright *flashing* light every 10 seconds at 170 ft., and visible at 20 miles off. Since May, 1874, every fourth flash is to be coloured *red*. The cliff over which it stands, 130 feet in height, is conspicuous and peculiar from the different colours of its stratified rocks.

The Devil's Bridge, a dangerous shoal, stretches off from this cliffy point for half a mile to the N.W., and its extremity is marked by a *red buoy*. Its outer edge is steep-to, and it requires all care in rounding it. A *rocky shoal* lies 1¼ mile N.W. from Gay Head lighthouse.

Menemsha Bight, immediately north-eastward of Gay Head, affords good anchorage in from 5 to 9 fathoms, about 2½ miles eastward of the lighthouse, with the wind from East, round by South, to S.W., but being much exposed to the influence of northerly winds, it should be resorted to only in the summer, or at other times from necessity. There is no danger in the bight, except the flat lining the shore, which may be avoided by giving the land a berth of half a mile, or by not going into less than 5 fathoms.

In the upper part of Vineyard Sound the chief dangers are the Middle Ground and its continuation, Lucas Shoal.

The **Middle Ground**, the eastern end of which lies N.W. from the lighthouse on the West Chop of Holmes' Holes, at a quarter of a mile from the nearest shore, leaving a narrow channel between, extends E. by N. and W. by S. 4½ miles, and has several swatchways through it. The East end, now distinguished by a *striped* buoy, has only from 5 and 6 to 10 ft. over it, and may be avoided by keeping the East Chop open North of the West Chop. About a mile from the eastern end of the bank there are but 2 ft., and on its West end only 14; here there is also a *striped* buoy, lying above a mile from the nearest part of Martha's Vineyard. Both sides are very steep, and should be cautiously approached, 9 or 10 fathoms being sufficiently near on the northern side.

Lucas Shoal may almost be considered as part of the Middle Ground, being separated from it only by a continuous line of soundings varying from 4 to 5 fathoms. It is small, steep-to, has only 14 ft. over it, and on its western side is marked by a *striped* buoy, which bears about S. ¼ E., 2½ miles from Tarpaulin lighthouse, S.W. by W. a similar distance from the *striped* buoy on the West end of the Middle Ground, and 1½ mile off the nearest part of the shore of Martha's Vineyard, with from 5 to 18 fathoms between. There is a small isolated patch of 18 ft. 1½ mile S.W. by W. ½ W. from Lucas Shoal, with 5 and 7 fathoms between.

On running *from the Gay Head light* into Vineyard Sound, if requisite to make a harbour on the North side, bring Gay Head light to bear S.W., and run N.E. 3 leagues, which will carry you up to Tarpaulin Cove light, where you may anchor in from 18 to 4 fathoms; in the deepest water is fine sand, with the light bearing from W. by N. to S.W. On entering the Sound with a southerly wind, the South channel is, of course, the best.

On *advancing from the sea*, you may run for Gay Head light, when it bears from N.N.E. to E.S.E., giving it a berth of 2 miles, in order to clear the Devil's Bridge, which trends from the light N.W. by N. more than half a mile distant. As measuring the distance in the night may be uncertain, you must keep the lead going, and if 7 or 8 fathoms should be found when the light bears S.E. by E. or S.E., haul up to the northward until you have gained 10 or 12 fathoms; then, with flood, steer N.E.; and with ebb, N.E. by E. nearly 3 leagues; E.N.E. will thence be the course of the sound, to the northward of the Middle Ground, a bank on which the shoalest water towards the eastward is 2 ft. When the lighthouse on the West Chop of Holmes's Hole is in sight, run for it, keeping 1 mile distant from the shore until you have the East chop 1 cable's length open. With a flood tide steer directly for it; and with ebb, keep it one point open, till you open a windmill on the West side of the harbour, about 1 cable's length; now run up in the middle of the river till you come to 4 or 3 fathoms, where you may anchor on good ground. The usual anchoring mark is the West chop, bearing from N.N.W. to N.W. by N.; but, for those who may remain any time, the best anchoring is well up the harbour, close to the shore, mooring S.E. and N.W. in 4 or 5 fathoms. In this harbour, which is about 2 miles deep, a vessel is secured from every wind, except a northerly one.

In the night, on approaching the Sound with a strong north-westerly wind, haul to the northward until you find smooth water under the Elizabeth Islands, where you may anchor in from 14 to 10 fathoms. Should the wind be to the southward, it will be best to run down through the South channel or Vineyard side. When Gay

Head bears S.S.E. the course will be N.E. by E. ¼ E. or E.N.E., observing not to approach the land nearer than into 7 fathoms, until abreast of *Lumbert's Cove*, in which is good anchorage with southerly and easterly winds. This place may be known by a high sand-bank, called *Necunkey Cliff*, on its eastern side. In the middle of the cove you may come-to, in from 5 to 3 fathoms, sandy bottom, which is the best ground. The Middle Ground lies about 2 miles without the cove, and has in this part 12 ft. over it.

If, when opposite Necunkey Point, you intend to run for Holmes's Hole, the course will be E. by N., keeping near the land, so as to clear the Middle Ground. You may track the shore by the lead, in from 7 to 4 fathoms, till you come near the lighthouse; but approach no nearer than 3 fathoms, and you may track around the chop, in the same manner as when running down from the North side of the Middle Ground. There is good anchorage alongshore in 6 or 4 fathoms, after passing to the eastward of Necunkey Point, till you come near the West chop.

Quick's Hole, the passage from Vineyard Sound into Buzzard's Bay between Pasque and Nashawena Islands, is but three-quarters of a mile wide, though from 4 to 8 fathoms deep in the fairway. Its eastern entrance is N. ¾ E., 5 miles from Gay Head lighthouse, and distinguished by a *black* buoy on the southern and a *red* buoy on the northern side. Steer in midway between these buoys N.W. by N. till halfway through the Hole, then North into Buzzard's Bay, keeping as nearly as possible the middle of the channel throughout, or, if obliged to deviate at all, approach near the western rather than the eastern shore, following somewhat the bend of that coast. Half a mile northward of the western entrance there is a small and steep rocky patch of 3½ ft., marked by a *striped* buoy, to which a berth should be given on either hand.

Tarpaulin Cove is on the middle of the S.E. side of Naushon Island, and offers good shelter and anchorage; you may ride out a gale with good ground tackle.

Light.—A white tower, 32 ft. high, on the West side of the entrance, shows a bright *fixed* light, with a flash every half minute, at 80 ft., visible 13 miles off.

The soundings in the cove are from 15 to 18 ft., deepening immediately outside to 8 and 10 fathoms, but there are some rocks lying nearly 1¼ cable's length from the shores of the cove which must be avoided. Near the lighthouse there is a rock of 7 feet, marked by a black buoy, to be left to port on entering. This cove is exposed to all winds between East and E.S.E. Vessels when at anchor here should moor in 5½ fathoms, with Gay Head light just open with the lighthouse point.

High water, on full and change days, at 8ʰ 4ᵐ; springs range 2¾, neaps 1¾ ft.

NOBSQUE LIGHTHOUSE.—The lighthouse on Nobsque Point, westward of the town of Falmouth, tends to facilitate, in a material degree, the navigation of the Vineyard Sound, both to the eastward and westward. The light is fixed, and was first exhibited on the 10th of November, 1828. It is elevated 83 ft. above the sea, and is shown from the keeper's house, which stands near the eastern extremity of the passage called *Wood's Hole*. In running through Vineyard Sound from the westward, to pass through the main ship channel bring Nobsque light to bear N.W. ½ W., then run S.E. ¼ E., until West Chop light bears W. by N. ½ N. In passing through the North Channel when Nobsque light bears N.W. ¼ W., and Tarpaulin Cove light W. ¾ S., steer N.E. ¼ E. until Nobsque light bears West, then steer E. ¼ S. for the Succonnesset Shoal lightvessel.

The tide hereabout, on the full and change days, flows at 9ʰ. In the channel, between Elizabeth Isles and Martha's Vineyard, the flood, however, runs until eleven o'clock.

BUZZARD'S BAY extends to the N.E. for 22 miles, being separated from Vineyard Sound by the line of islands before mentioned, of which Cuttyhunk with its lighthouse is the south-westernmost.

There are some detached shoals and dangers in the bay, and also many projecting spits from its numerous points, and the most prominent of these are marked by buoys or beacons, but it requires the utmost caution for its safe navigation, which should not be attempted by a stranger without a pilot.

The entrance to the bay is between the Cuttyhunk lighthouse and the Sow and Pigs Reef and lightvessel on the South side, and the Hen and Chickens Reef with its lightvessel on the North, the soundings between being very irregular, from 5 to 15 fathoms, hard bottom.

The Hen and Chickens and Lightvessel.—The Hen and Chickens is a dangerous reef, extending S. by E., 1½ mile from Gooseberry Neck. On the outermost rock, called the Old Cock, is a spindle. The lightvessel, painted lead colour, is moored in 10 fathoms water, about a mile S.E. of the reef, with the spindle bearing N.W. by N. She shows a *fixed bright* light, elevated 35 ft., visible 11 miles off, and has a fog bell and horn for use in thick weather.

Mishaun Point is to the N.E. of Gooseberry Neck, and, like it, has reefs projecting a considerable distance. On the opposite side of the bay is *Penikese Island*, between which and Cuttyhunk is a deep-water and safe channel to those well acquainted, but embarrassed by shoals.

Dumpling Light.—Off Round Hill, S.S.W. of Clark's Point light and New Bedford, is a white lighthouse with black lantern, on Dumpling Rock, 33 ft. in height, exhibiting, at 42 ft. above the sea, a *fixed* light, visible 12 miles.

Clark's Point Light.—On the West side of the entrance to New Bedford Harbour is a white lighthouse, placed on the N.W. angle of the fort on that point. It is 59 ft. in height, showing, at 68 ft. above the sea, a *fixed* light, visible 12 miles. Cuttyhunk light bears S. 20° W., distant 13 miles.

Directions.—Those acquainted with Buzzard's Bay commonly use the western channel, giving the *Hen and Chickens* a sufficient berth. A league and a half to the north-eastward of these is Mishaun or Mishom Point; and 2 miles N.E. ¼ E. from Mishaun Point is the cluster of rocks, above water, called the *Dumpling Rocks*, which lie off Roundhill Point, and are distinguished by the *lighthouse* described above. The only danger to be avoided is on Mishaun Point, as a rock lies about 1 mile S.W. by S. from it, having over it only 6 ft. of water; there is also a ledge directly South of the point, at the distance of a mile, on which there are not more than 3 fathoms, with common ebbs; it is marked by a *black* buoy.

From a position half a mile South from the Hen and Chickens lightvessel, a N.E. by E. ¾ E. course for 11 miles, leaving the black buoy on Mishaun Ledge, and the striped buoy on Wilkes's Ledge about a mile distant on your port side, will carry you well outside all the dangers before the entrance of New Bedford, and up to abreast the black buoy on the extremity of the ledge running seven-eighths of a mile southward from West Island, and to where Clark's Point lighthouse will be seen bearing N.W. by W. Hence you may steer N.E. towards the head of the bay, passing at a good berth on your port hand, in successive order, the spindle on the Cormorant Rock, the striped buoy on Nye's Ledge, the *black* buoy on *Dobell Rock*, and Bird Island lighthouse; and on your starboard side, when near Bird Island, the *black* and the *red* buoys on the edge of the shoal fronting Scraggy Neck, and Wing's Neck lighthouse. Between these two lighthouses your soundings will be 4 and 5 fathoms, gradually decreasing as you approach the broad and shallow flat occupying the head of Buzzard's Bay, over which are the channels to Wareham

Harbour and Monumet River. A pilot is absolutely necessary to a stranger wishing to enter any of the harbours.

Wood's Hole is in the channel separating Naushon Island from the mainland, and serves as a harbour for vessels either from Vineyard Sound or from Buzzard's Bay, but the passage through is only fit for small vessels.

There are two harbours, both on the eastern side of the channel, and named Great and Little Harbours. *Great Harbour*, on the S.E. side of Long Neck, affords anchorage in from 4 to 8 fathoms, but is open to southerly winds; and its length half and breadth a quarter of a mile; the principal dangers are pointed out by buoys, and there is a landing-place, named Bar Neck Wharf, on its eastern side, nearly close to which are 5 and 6 fathoms water. *Little Harbour*, separated from the Great Harbour by Parker's Neck, has its entrance half a mile north-westward of Nobsque lighthouse, runs in about one-third of a mile to the northward, and is therefore also open to southerly winds, is from 1 to 2 cables' lengths in breadth, and has a depth of from 6 to 10 ft. at low water. Intending to proceed into the Great Harbour by the Ship Channel, when off the harbour in 6 fathoms, bring a yellow house at the head of the harbour to bear N. ¼ W. Steer for it, leaving a *black* buoy on the port hand, and two *red* ones to starboard, and when Bar Neck Wharf bears E.N.E., anchor. Or, steer N.W. for the inner harbour, and bring-to in from 4 to 8 fathoms. *Red* buoys mark the eastern, and *black* the western limits of this channel, in which, if these courses are preserved, there is not less than 18 ft. water, except on a patch lying nearly in mid-channel off the extremity of Parker's Neck, whereon are only 15 feet water, which you will leave a little on your port hand. Continue on this course till the southern point of that neck comes in range with the church to the northeastward, then steer for the eastern part of the breakwater until Bar Neck Wharf bears E.N.E., as before.

NEW BEDFORD.—*The best way to New Bedford*, even to vessels from the westward, is through *Quick's Hole*, the channel between two of Elizabeth's Isles, *Nashawena* and *Pasque*. These are the second and third of the larger isles from the westward. The harbour of New Bedford is on the western side of Buzzard's Bay; and Clark's Point, the western point of the entrance, is distinguished by a lighthouse, before mentioned. Due North from Clark's Point light another *fixed light* is shown on the N.E. extremity of *Palmer's Island*, and on the West side of the entrance to New Bedford inner harbour. The light is elevated 38 ft., and visible 12 miles off. The lighthouse of stone is 34 ft. high, and whitewashed.

The directions are, to bring Gay Head light to bear S. ¾ W., and steering N. ¾ E. to the passage through the islands, named Quick's Hole, which should be entered as near the middle as possible, or keeping rather to the starboard side, so as to avoid a spit or flat, which extends from the S.E. point of Nashawena, on the port. Proceeding thus, you will have from 5 to 6 fathoms, and should then haul in, keeping the port side best on board, and following, in some degree, the bend of the shore. Keep Gay Head light about a ship's length open by the S.E. point of Nashawena, till you are at least 1 mile North of the Hole, and this will carry you to the eastward of a ledge and rock which lie at that distance from it, with only 5 to 12 ft. of water on them, with a good channel to the westward, and 5 fathoms all round. Next steer N. ½ W. till you strike hard bottom in 5 fathoms, on the S.E. corner of the *Great Ledge*, which is on the western side of the channel; then N.E. by N. about three-quarters of a mile, till in 5½ or 6 fathoms, sticky bottom, when the light on Clark's Point will bear N. by W., towards which you advance, and run into the river.

Off *Round Hill Point*, at 2 leagues N.N.W. ½ W. from the outlet of Quick's Hole, is the cluster of rocks before mentioned, called the *Dumplings*, upon which is the

MATTAPOISET.

lighthouse. From this lighthouse that on Clark's Point bears N.N.E., 4 miles distant. It will therefore be seen, on proceeding upon a *direct* course from Quick's Hole to New Bedford, at the distance of between 2 and 3 miles; and when it bears. West, Clark's Point will be about 4 miles distant.

Round Hill Channel.—Running in from the southward and westward, bring Mishaun Point to bear W. by S., and White Rock a ship's length open to the eastward of Dumpling light, and steer to the northward, leaving the red can buoy, No. 4, on Sand Spit, on the starboard hand, and the black spar buoy off Dumpling Rock on the port hand, and keeping the rock more open as you advance, so as to pass a quarter of a mile to the eastward of the light.

When the light bears W. by N. steer N.E. by N., 2½ miles, leaving the red and black buoys on Middle Ledge and Inez Rock on your port hand, until Clark's Point light is in range with Palmer's Island light; then steer for the beacon on Egg Island Flats N. by E., nearly 2 miles, leaving the black buoy on *Old Bartlemy* on your port hand, until Palmer's Island light is in range with the tall chimney of Wamsutta Factory. Steer for them, passing the black buoys on Butler's Flats and Eleven-feet Bank on you port, and the red buoys on Egg Island Flat and Fort Flat on your starboard hand, until up with the southern end of Palmer's Island, then steer for the ends of Fairhaven Wharves, passing a red buoy on the North end of Fort Flat on your starboard hand, until you are halfway between them and Palmer's Island light; then steer for the most northern spire in New Bedford, and anchor near the town.

N.B.—Wamsutta Factory is a large stone building with a very tall chimney on its eastern side; it is in the northern part of the town, and may be seen over Fairhaven Bridge.

Eastern Channel—Bring the white beacon on Fort Point in range with the high dark spire in Fairhaven, and steer for them, until Palmer's Island light and the tall chimney before mentioned are in range, then steer as before directed. On the above course you will pass Hursell Rock and Packet Rock red buoys, and Henrietta Rock striped buoy on your starboard hand, and the black buoy on North Ledge on your port hand.

There are several buoys placed in Buzzard's Bay, but as these are mostly taken up in winter, and may be occasionally altered and shifted, we cannot give a fair account of them; especially would it be needless, seeing that it is entirely in pilots' water.

MATTAPOISET is situated on the North side of Buzzard's Bay, and is a fine harbour, easy of access. On the East side of Mattapoiset Harbour, about a mile S.E. from the village, is *Ned's Point* and *Lighthouse*, showing a fixed light at 43 ft. The tower is of stone, and whitewashed; from it Cormorant Rock spindle bears S. ¼ W., Nye's Ledge buoy S. by E. ¾ E.

Before coming up with West Island, bring Bird Island light to bear N.E. by N., and run for it until Ned's Point light bears N.N.W. ½ W., when you may haul up N.W. ¼ N. In running this course you will pass a white buoy with two black stripes around it, lying on *Nye's Ledge*, in 2½ fathoms water; this ledge is a quarter of a mile across, and has not more than 8 ft. on some parts of it. Continuing this course, you will pass a buoy on your port hand, painted white, with three black stripes around it, lying on the S.E. part of *Mattapoiset Ledge*, in 2⅜ fathoms. Continue the above course, and you will pass two buoys, one on your port hand, and the other to port; the latter is on the East side of the Sinking Ledge, in 3 fathoms, and the former is on the side of the Snow Rock, in 2½ fathoms; the rock has 8½ feet over it. Keep midway until you pass them, when you may steer N.W. by W.

until Ned's Point light bears East, when you may anchor in 3 fathoms water, good bottom.

There are two other buoys not named above; one stands about N.E. from Snow Rock, in 3 fathoms water, by the side of Barslow Rock, the other on the extremity Ned's Point, in 2 fathoms.

Bird Island Lighthouse.—Bird Island is near the N.W. shore of Buzzard's Bay, 8 miles N.E. ¼ E. from the South point of West's Island, and near the mouth of Sippican, or Rochester Harbour; it lies half a mile South from the Great Neck, or eastern chop of the same. It is very small, not covering more than three acres, and is about 5 ft. above the level of the sea.

The light and dwelling-houses are of stone, and whitewashed. The light-tower is 31 ft. high, and the light, elevated 37 ft., seen at a distance of 15 miles off, revolving once in 1¼ minute. The time of total darkness is equal to twice that of light.

From Bird Island Lighthouse the North end of Quick's Hole, between Nashawena and Pasque, bears S.W. by S. 15 miles; that of Wood's Hole South, 9 miles; and the entrance of *Monumet River*, at the head of the bay, N.E. by E. ¼ E. 6 miles.

Sippican Harbour, 3 miles north-eastward of Mattapoiset, has its entrance between Charles's Neck and Bobell Rock on the western, and Sippican Neck and Bird Island on the eastern side. It thence runs in N. by W. ¾ W., 3 miles, the deepest water, 13 to 21 ft., first being found along the eastern, and afterwards along the western shore, passing on the West side of a small island lying nearly in mid-channel, up to Sippican, where are from 7 to 10 ft. To run up to Sippican, a stranger should obtain the aid of a pilot.

Near the head of Buzzard's Bay, on the East side of the entrance to Sandwich Harbour, a *fixed bright light* is shown at 44 ft. elevation.

The COAST westward of Buzzard's Bay, between Gooseberry Neck and Saughkonnet Point, forms a rocky bay, and a ship should avoid drifting within the line joining its outer points. At its head is *Westport,* a small harbour used by coasters, but requiring a pilot. Its West point of entrance is called *Rock Point.*

RHODE ISLAND is the easternmost of the cluster which fills the extensive bay, of which Saughkonnet Point is the S.E. entrance.

Saughkonnet River separates it from the mainland on the East. A shoal flat extends half a mile South, East, and West of Saughkonnet Point, upon which are several large rocks always above water, and there is also a shoal patch of 4¼ fathoms three-quarters of a mile South to S. by E of the point; from Sachuset Point, three-quarters of a mile S. by W., lies the Cormorant Rock, with 6 and 7 fathoms close-to all round; but there is a shallow bank of 3 and 4 fathoms half a mile westward of it, and another W. by S. ¼ S. of it. To avoid these dangers shape a course midway between the two points, steering N. by E.

Brenton's Reef lies off the S.W. point of Rhode Island, and its lightvessel is the guide to the entrance to Newport Harbour on the eastern side, as the Beavertail lighthouse on the South point of Conanicut Island is on the western side of this entrance.

Brenton's Reef Lightvessel, on the East side of entrance to Newport, is moored in 14¾ fathoms. This vessel is painted of a straw colour, with the words " Brenton's Reef" on each side in black letters, and is furnished with a fog bell and horn; she exhibits two *fixed* lights, 40 and 50 ft. respectively above the sea, which are visible about 12 miles. Point Judith light bears S.W. by W. ¼ W.; Beavertail, N.W. by N. ½ N.; Castle Hill Point, N.E. by N. ¼ N.

Beavertail Lighthouse, on the South point of Conanicut Island, entrance to Newport Harbour, is a square granite lighthouse on the S.E. angle of keeper's

NEWPORT, OR RHODE ISLAND HARBOUR.

dwelling, 74 ft. in height, and 96 ft. above the sea, in lat. 41° 26′ 55′, and long. 71° 23′ 59″, exhibiting a *fixed* light, visible 16 miles. Dwelling painted white.

A first-order Daboll trumpet, giving blasts of 6 seconds, at intervals of 10 and 50 seconds alternately, is established here for use in thick weather.

About 300 yards S.S.W. from the Beavertail lighthouse is a sunken rock, named the *Newton*, which becomes awash, and causes the sea to break over it with any swell, and is marked by a *buoy*, moored in 5 fathoms off its southern side.

NEWPORT, or Rhode Island Harbour, is on the S.W. end of Rhode Island, about 3 miles within the entrance points.

The mouth of Newport Harbour, between Rhode Island on the East, and Conanicut Island on the West, is 1½ mile broad. On the western side is the *Newton Rock*, above described; on the eastern side is *Brenton's Ledge*, extending nearly three-quarters of a mile out to the S.S.W., the outer end of which is marked by the *light-vessel*, and there are other rocks near the shore on the same side. Upon the western side, off the Fort Point, at about 3 miles above the lighthouse, are the Dumplings, a cluster of rocks above water, from which the town of Newport bears due East. A *fog bell* is struck every 15 seconds in thick weather.

Before the town is *Goat Island*, with its fort and lighthouse, and having a shoal spit from each end, the extremities of which are buoyed. Brenton's Point, with the South end of this island, form the South passage into Newport. On *Rose Island* a *fixed red* light is shown, elevated 50 ft., as a guide through the East Channel, up the bay, and to Newport Harbour.

Along the northernmost spit a breakwater has been constructed, parallel with the town, for the protection of the vessels lying off it. On the North end of the breakwater is a *lighthouse* showing a bright fixed light.

On one of the *Lime Rocks*, near the South shore of the harbour, opposite the South end of Goat Island, there is a small *fixed* light, 30 ft. high, and visible to the distance of 11 miles in clear weather. It serves as a guide to vessels proceeding to the wharves of the town through the channel between the Lime Rocks and the buoy on the edge of the spit extending from the South end of Goat Island, wherein are from 12 to 18 ft. water.

In coming from the eastward, to clear Brenton's Reef, bring the Beavertail light to bear W.N.W. Run for it until Great Island light can be seen from the deck. The latter will then bear N.E. ¾ E. Run for this light until it bears East (or, continue your course until it bears E.S.E.), at the same time keeping Beavertail light bearing S.W. by W. in 7 to 9 fathoms, good ground.

In coming from the West for Newport, after passing Point Judith, with its revolving light, steer N.E. by N. until you draw up with Beavertail light, to which, giving a berth, run for Goat Island light, and anchor as above directed.

Buoys and beacons in Newport Harbour.—A *spindle on Saddle Rock*, eastward of Rose Island, on either side of which there is a passage; a *spindle with ball* on a rock at the South end of Rose Island, which you can leave to the northward; a *red* buoy with a cross on *Dyer's Reef*, South part of Coaster's Harbour, to be left to starboard; another *red* buoy on the ledge off the Bishop's Rock, called the *Triangle Rock*, on either side of which you may pass, giving it a berth; a *red* spar buoy to the South, and one at the North end of *Gull Rocks*, both of which you pass to the eastward; a spar buoy on Providence Point, which is the North end of Prudence Island, to the northward of which is the main channel.

Providence.—The course to this city from Newport Harbour, between the buoy on the Triangle Rock and Warwick Neck light is N. ¾ W. After leaving Prudence Island 3 miles N.E. by N. from Warwick Neck *fixed* light, you pass on your port hand a spar buoy, which you may go very close to. When Warwick Neck light bears West, steer N.N.E. for Nayat Point, leaving the spar buoy on Providence Point on the starboard hand, and running so far to the eastward as to bring Prudence Island to bear South, by which you leave the Middle Ground, which has a buoy on it, on the port hand. A *fixed light* is shown from the beacon on the shoal extending from Conanicut Point, opposite Nayat Point. Soon after passing this light, you come up with a pyramid directly opposite to the village of Patuxent, the base of which is painted black, with a white top, erected on a ledge of rocks, which you may approach very near, leaving it to the port hand. At a short distance you come to another pyramid, and a stake, both of which you leave to port. One-fourth of a mile from the last pyramid lie Lovely Rocks, having a spar buoy on them, which must be left on the starboard hand, going very near to them. All vessels drawing more than 8 ft. have to wait for the tide below the Crook.

NARRAGANSET BAY lies between Conanicut Island and the main. The course in is about N. ¼ E., taking care to avoid the *Whale Rock*, which may be passed on either side; you may anchor as convenient. At the head of the navigation is the town of Providence, situate at the distance of 9 leagues from the sea.

In the passage between Conanicut Island and the main, on the islet called *Dutch Island*, is a fixed *harbour light* at 56 feet, 3 miles North from the Beavertail, and on the North side of the entrance of Dutch Island Harbour, a harbour in which vessels may lie safely in 4 fathoms. Vessels bound into this place should run within half a mile of the lighthouse, before they haul to the eastward for the harbour, as a shoal lies on the South side. An Anderson's fog horn, worked at private expense, is established near the lighthouse.

Wickford is a small harbour on the western side of Narraganset Bay, opposite the North end of Conanicut Island, and 5 miles within Dutch Island lighthouse. On Poplar Point, the South point of entrance, a *fixed* light is shown from the top of the keeper's dwelling; it is 51 ft. above the level of the sea, and visible to the distance of 12 miles. In sailing towards Wickford the widest channel is on the West side of Dutch Island; thence you may pass on either side of Fox Island up to Poplar Point. Although the rocks and shoals in the bay and off the harbour's entrance are marked by buoys or spindles, still it would be safer to employ a pilot.

There is another harbour light (*fixed*) on *Warwick Neck*, as before described, on the West side of the entrance to Providence River, at 3 leagues to the northward of that on Dutch Island. Warwick Neck forms the eastern side of the entrance to *East Greenwich*, which is half a league broad. The opposite side is called *Long Point;* and on the shoal that surrounds it is a spar buoy, which, on entering, is to be left on the port side.

POINT JUDITH Lighthouse.—About 2 leagues S.W. ¼ S. from the Beavertail lighthouse is another lighthouse, on Point Judith, which is built of stone, 46 feet high, and stands on the S.W. point of the great bay. Its lantern is 50 ft. above the sea, and contains a light, *revolving* every 15 seconds, so that it cannot be mistaken. Point Judith light may be distinguished from Watchhill Point light, by the light not wholly disappearing when within 3 leagues of it. A *steam fog syren* of the first class is sounded in thick weather, giving blasts of 6 seconds at intervals of 40 seconds.

From the S.E. point of Block Island to Newport lighthouse, on the South end of Conanicut Island, the course and distance are N.N.E. ¼ E. 8 leagues. About midway between are 24 fathoms of water, the greatest depth, either to the northward or southward, on the course above given.

If you are on the West side of Block Island, with the body of the island bearing E.N.E., in 8 or 10 fathoms water, your course to Point Judith light is N.E. by E.

about 6 leagues. This point appears like a nag's head, and is pretty bold. Between Block Island and the point there are from 30 to 6 fathoms water, except a small shoal ground of 13 ft. water, called *Squid's Ledge*, bearing about W. by S. from Point Judith light, distant 3 miles.

From a quarter of a mile without Point Judith to the entrance of Newport Harbour, the course and distance are N.E. ¼ E. 7 miles.

BLOCK ISLAND stands as a sentry in the eastern entrance to Long Island Sound. It is about 5 miles long North and South, of moderate height. When made from southward it shows high and round, and if from the S.E. it is like a saddle, the highest point to the southward.

LIGHTHOUSES.—On its North point is a white tower, 50 ft. high, showing a bright fixed light at 65 ft., seen 14 miles off. Towards the South, or between S.E. and S.W. by S. from the light, it is hidden for an arc of 80° by the higher land of the island.

Off the North point of Block Island a shoal extends 1¼ mile North from the lighthouse. It is extremely dangerous, as the tide sets right across it. Point Judith lighthouse bearing N.E. clears this shoal.

On the S.E. end of Block Island is another light, established in 1874. The tower, 67 ft. high, is built of red brick, with granite trimmings, and the lantern painted black. A *fixed bright* light is shown at an elevation of 204 ft. above the sea, visible, in clear weather, 21 miles off.

A first-order *steam fog syren*, giving blasts of 6 seconds at intervals of 20 seconds, in foggy weather, is established just to the S.E. of the lighthouse.

The *S. W.Ledge*, with 5 fathoms least water, lies 2⅛ miles S.W. from the S.W. end of Block Island; it is 1½ mile long in a N.E. and S.W. direction.

With Block Island bearing North, 4 or 5 leagues distant, you cannot see any land to the northward or eastward; but, on approaching the island, you will see Montauk Point, the eastern point of Long Island, with its lighthouse to the westward, making as a long low point.

In sailing to the W.S.W. you will make no remarkable land on Long Island, as its broken land appears at a distance like islands. You will have 20 or 22 fathoms out of sight of land, sandy bottom in some, and clay in other places.

The charts will be the best guide for soundings. To the southward of Noman's Island, near Martha's Vineyard, there is coarse sand, like gravel stones, in 20 and 25 fathoms; and S.S.W. from it, in 28 or 30 fathoms, coarse red sand. S.S.E. from Block Island, in what is termed *Block Island Channel*, there are 30 and 40 fathoms, with oazy bottom; but, shoaling the water to 25 or 20 fathoms, you will find coarse sand.

From the South end of Block Island to Gay Head, distinguished by the lighthouse already described (page 40), the bearing and distance are E.N.E. 13 leagues. From the same end of Block Island to the lighthouse at the entrance of Rhode Island Harbour, the bearing and distance are N.N.E. ½ E. 8 leagues.

U.S.—Part I.

LONG ISLAND SOUND.

Long Island Sound is about 110 miles in length, between Block Island and its western extremity at the East River leading to New York, and is about $17\frac{1}{2}$ miles wide where broadest. Its shores and dangers are well marked by lighthouses and lightvessels, buoys and beacons, so that with ordinary care it affords a safe and easy inland navigation for all classes of vessels up to the important port at its head.

It is, moreover, the outlet of a large portion of the produce of the rich State of Connecticut on the North side, and of Long Island on the South, the latter having no good shelter on its Atlantic shore. Its navigation and the relation of the sea marks erected in it will be best understood by referring to the chart, the result of the elaborate surveys of the United States officers, which leave nothing to be desired.

MONTAUK POINT LIGHTHOUSE.—The eastern extremity of Long Island is also the point of the peninsula which, with the fertile Gardiner's Island, forms the S.W. side of Block Island Sound.

The **LIGHTHOUSE** is a white stone tower 97 ft. high, showing a first-order lens light. It is a *fixed* light, varied by *flashes* once in every 2 minutes, at the height of 172 ft. above the sea. The *fixed* light, between the intervals of flashes, may be seen at the distance of 20 miles, and the flashes from 3 to 5 miles farther. The keeper's house, on an adjacent hill, is painted brown. During thick weather a first-order *Daboll trumpet* gives blasts of 12 seconds at intervals of 50 seconds. A strand of 6 to 18 ft. surrounds the point, and extends off it and the coast to the north-westward, about half a mile, but southward and westward to not more than one-third of a mile; close to its edge are from 4 to 10 fathoms, bottom of sand and specks.

Montauk Shoal lies $2\frac{3}{4}$ miles S. by E. from the lighthouse, is small, and has from 4 to 5 fathoms over it, bottom of hard sand. It is plainly shown by the tide rips, and the sea breaks upon it in heavy gales from seaward. Between this shoal and the point there are from $6\frac{1}{2}$ to 12 fathoms, and from 6 to 12 close-to all round it.

Between Montauk Point and Block Island there are 10 to 15, and for a small space 20 and 23 fathoms; and as you approach the island you will cross the S.W. Ledge. On the N.W. side of this ledge the depth suddenly shoalens from 13 to 6 fathoms, and before a second cast of the lead be obtained, you will be over its shoalest part into 7, 8, 10, 12, and then 14 fathoms. With Montauk light bearing W. $\frac{3}{4}$ S., distant 8 miles, you will be in 7 to 12 fathoms on the western edge of the ledge, from which to the point you will get 12 to 9, 10, and 7 fathoms. Towards the lighthouse, when it bears from W. to S.W. by W., the bottom is strong, consisting of gray sand and gravel; but towards the ledge the bottom is of coarse sand, and over it there is a strong tide and rippling. When rounding Montauk Point, you can go within a cable's length of the surf, and have 17 to 20 ft., but to keep farther off will of course be more prudent.

At $3\frac{3}{4}$ miles N.W. $\frac{1}{2}$ W. from Montauk lighthouse is a small reef, named the *Shagwong*, which has but 5 ft. water on it, and is marked by an iron *bell boat*, painted *black*, with the name in white letters on it. Close to it on all sides there are 4 to 6 fathoms, and between it and Long Island there is a 4-fathom swatch, through which ships may pass, only taking care to avoid the *Washington Shoal*, a shoal of 12 to 18 feet, the shallowest part of which lies five-eighths of a mile from the shore. The Shagwong Shoal is shown by the tide rip.

BLOCK ISLAND SOUND lies, as before said, between Block Island, Gardiner's Island, and the Connecticut shore.

CERBERUS SHOAL—GARDINER'S ISLAND.

The Cerberus Shoal, or *Middle Ground*, is the principal reef to be avoided in it. It is nearly midway between Montauk Point and Fisher's Island, and is highly dangerous, as it consists of pointed rocks, and has but 13 ft. upon it; it is, however, usually shown by the tide rips. It is of but small extent, and bears from Montauk lighthouse, N.N.W. ¼ W., 7¾ miles; from Gull Island light, E.S.E. ⅛ S., 7 miles; and from Watch Hill light, S.W. ⅜ S., 9 miles. On the South and West sides of the shoal the water deepens quickly from 5 to 12 fathoms; and on the North side it is steep-to, there being close to its edge 14 to 15 fathoms. Caution is always requisite in approaching this shoal, the more particularly as little, if any, warning is given by the lead.

It may be marked by a buoy or spindle, but in case that this should not be, then the mark for avoiding the Cerberus Reef is a conspicuous hill with a notch in its centre, at the back of New London, called *Pole's Hill*. This kept a ship's length open, either to the eastward or westward of Mount Prospect (or the sand-hills in the West of Fisher's Island), will lead clear of the shoal, in 10 or 15 fathoms, to the eastward, and in 8 or 9 fathoms to the westward. The tide, as already noticed, sets strongly over the shoal. In scant wind, or a calm, a vessel should anchor before any of the marks or bearings are too near.

Pond Bay, or Fort Pond Bay, is 5½ miles westward of Montauk Point, on the North side of Long Island.

In proceeding towards Pond Bay, or Gardiner's Island, from the eastward, keep the two bluffs, or high parts of the land, to the westward of Montauk Point, open one of the other, until Culloden Point, on the East side of Fort Pond Bay, comes open of Shagwong Point, which is about 2 miles W.N.W. from Montauk Point. These marks will lead safely through, in from 9 to 3 fathoms.

The tides set strongly about Montauk Point; the flood to the N.E., and ebb contrary. At the Shagwong Reef, the flood sets W. by S., and the ebb to the contrary.

On rounding Montauk Point in the night, when the land or light can be seen, and during a westerly gale, you may anchor when the light bears S.W. by S. in 8 or 9 fathoms, coarse sand. Having brought Montauk Point to the southward of West, when the weather is thick, and you cannot clearly ascertain the distance from the point, the lead must be your guide. Steer as high as W.N.W. until you have gained 9 fathoms; then haul off into 13; and if you suddenly shoalen from 10 to 6, steer off E. by N. until you gain 11 or 12, which will soon be; and a good lead kept well going, will prevent your going too near the reefs.

In the daytime, if bound to Gardiner's Bay, and having rounded Montauk Point, steer N. by W. until you clearly discover the points that form Fort Pond Bay, and see the red cliff on the western point open of Culloden or the eastern point. You may then steer W. by S. for the bluff point of Gardiner's Island, passing between the Shagwong and Cerberus Reefs.

A vessel may, if requisite, take shelter in Fort Pond Bay, which is half a league broad, and of the same depth. This place is very convenient for watering; the ground is clear and good, and you may anchor in any depth, from 7 to 3 fathoms, at pleasure. In a large ship you may bring Willis's or the eastern point to bear N.E., and even N.E. by N., and then have in the middle about 7 fathoms of water. Near the shore, at the bottom of the bay, is a pond of fresh water.

GARDINER'S ISLAND is of an irregular figure, and shelters the bay of the same name from the eastward. Its South end is nearly connected with a long island, high shoals forming the head of Neapeague Bay. The Eastern Plain, or N.E. point of the island, is 10 miles W.N.W. from Montauk Point.

A **Lighthouse** stands on the low North point of the island. It is about 200 yards within its extremity, where is a brick-built house, with a circular tower attached to the North end, and painted brown. This tower is 27 ft. high, and shows a *fixed* light at an elevation of 29 ft. above the mean level of the sea, visible 11 miles off. A sandy flat, of 8 to 12 ft., surrounds the island, and runs off the shore in some places about five-eighths of a mile. On the West side of the island is a shoal, named the *Crow*, which lies about 1¾ mile S.W. from the West point of the island, and is connected thereto by a flat of 14 to 18 ft.; this shoal has but 6 ft. water on it, and may be avoided on its western side by keeping Great Gull Island just open North of Gardiner's Point lighthouse.

Neapeague Bay, or the space between the S.E. side of Gardiner's Island and the coast westward of Fort Pond Bay, has a depth of from 8 to 5 fathoms, gradually shoaling towards the sand-banks, which occupy nearly the whole of the passage between the South point of Gardiner's Island and the adjacent shore of Long Island, leaving only a very narrow and winding channel among them, 3 and 4 fathoms deep, into Gardiner's Bay. Neapeague Harbour, a small and almost land-locked basin in the South part of Neapeague Bay, with 6, 8, and 17 ft. water in it, is but seldom frequented.

GARDINER'S BAY is 7 miles long and 6 broad, and is the outer part of the bay which deeply indents the eastern part of Long Island. The principal places in it are Greenport and Sag Harbour.

Its N.E. entrance is between the lighthouse on Gardiner's Point and Plum Island, also marked by a light.

Off the lighthouse on Gardiner's Point is the *Superb's Reef*, the outer part of which is E.N.E. ¾ E. from the extremity of Gardiner's Spit, one-third of a mile; it thence extends S.E. by E. about two-thirds of a mile, and is about 200 yards broad. The depth on the middle is 3 fathoms, 6 close to the N.W. end; 4, 4¼, and 5 fathoms close to the S.E. end; 5 and 6 fathoms close to the East side. The mark for clearing it, when sailing into Gardiner's Bay, is to keep Plum Gut (the channel on the West of Plum Island) a ship's breadth open. You must stand to the northward, until Plum Gut is nearly closing with Oyster Pond Point, or the N.E. bluff of Long Island, or till the South point of Plum Island seems nearly to touch the same; but tack before the points close, or stand over into no less than 7 fathoms.

New London lighthouse, kept a sail's breadth open to the eastward of Plum Island, will run you up into the middle of Gardiner's Bay, in the deepest water, and out of the tide. You may anchor at pleasure in from 5 to 8 fathoms. There is good riding on the S.W. side of the island. A ship from the East side, with an easterly wind, may take shelter here by proceeding as before directed; for it is to be observed, that the channel southward of the island is shoal, and fit for small vessels only. A conspicuous single tree on the S.E. part of Plum Island is a good mark for clearing the Superb's Reef, by tacking before it is brought to touch the South end of the wood on the same island.

Sag Harbour is in the S.W. corner of Gardiner's Bay, on the South side of Shelter Island. Extensive sand-banks bar the approach to it, over which from 12 to 15 ft. water can be carried, but the channel up to Sag is narrow and winding, and, though buoyed throughout, it is advisable to employ a pilot. When in, excellent shelter can be had in a moderate depth, and supplies of all descriptions can be obtained at the village. About one mile inside the bar, and on the port hand in entering, is *Cedar Island*, with a *white* building on it, on the top of which a small fixed light is exhibited, at the height of 34 feet, visible to the distance of 10 miles.

PLUM ISLAND AND GUT.

Greenport is a place that has become of some importance, in consequence of its being the termination of the Long Island Railway; the distance hence to Stonington, the southern end of the railway from Boston, being by sea 24 miles.

Light.—On the shoal extending from Long Beach Point a pile lighthouse is constructed in 5 ft. water. From it a *fixed red* light is shown, elevated 54 ft. In thick weather a cast-steel bell is sounded at intervals of 15 seconds. Vessels rounding this point, should pass at least 160 ft. outside the buoy placed on the extremity of the shoal.

Vessels bound to Greenport from the Plum Gut, just described, may make their course S.W., and run 3 miles, which will carry them up to *Ben's Point*, or *Long Beach*. This beach is 3½ miles long, and covered with low cedar trees, which you leave on your starboard hand going up to Greenport. You will have, from Plum Gut to Ben's Point, from 4 to 4½ fathoms water, and then your course is W.S.W. 3½ miles. In running this course you will shoal your water to 3 fathoms, and if you get any less water, haul to the southward; and as soon as you get 3 fathoms, keep your course, and run on until you, by heaving your lead, from one heave will have from 3 to 7 fathoms water. As soon as you get 7 or 8 fathoms water, your course is W.N.W. 1 mile, which will carry you to Hay Beach Point, on Shelter Island, which you will leave on your port hand. Haul close round Hay Beach Point, and your course is W.S.W. 1½ mile to Greenport; then you may come to an anchor in a good harbour.

From off Gardiner's Point to Greenport is 12 miles, and the course is W. by S. Running this course, you will shoal your water gradually from 6 fathoms to 3 fathoms on Long Beach side, and then you follow the above directions to Greenport. Five fathoms can be carried into Greenport.

Oyster Pond Point is the N.W. point of Gardiner's Bay, and off it is Plum Island, the channel between being called Plum Island Gut.

PLUM ISLAND Lighthouse stands on the West point of the island. It is 34 feet high, which shows a light *revolving* once in every 30 seconds at 63 ft. above the sea, visible 12 miles off. A cast-steel *fog bell* is struck at intervals of 15 seconds in foggy weather.

Along the S.E. side of Plum Island there is a sandy flat of 8 to 12 ft. water, upon the edge of which there is a rock nearly awash at low water. There are 12 ft. inside this rock, and 3½ fathoms close-to outside. To avoid it, go not into less than 6 fathoms, when approaching the East side of the island. The northern shore of the island should have a berth of at least half a mile, as there are a 6 and a 9 ft. rock lying off the middle of that side, with deep water close-to.

PLUM GUT, between Plum Island and Oyster Pond Point, is the channel commonly used by vessels bound to the western part of Long Island Sound. In this Gut is a rock, on which the British frigate *Loire* once struck; but it is so very small, that it is difficult to strike soundings on it; it is nearer to the reef extending from Oyster Pond Point than to Plum Island.

This shoal consists of rocks and large stones with 16 ft. of water over them, having 16 and 17 fathoms on the N.E. side, 20 on the N.W., and 6 and 7 on the South side. It is marked by a stone beacon 12 ft. high, surmounted by a shaft and cage of iron, 20 ft. in height. It stands E. ¼ N. half a mile from Pond Point. Plum Island lighthouse bears N.E. ¼ N. three-quarters of a mile from it.

There is another rock, having 24 ft. over it, about 400 yards from the rocky or bluff point of Plum Island.

In advancing towards Plum Gut, the *Gull*, or *Bedford Reef*, is to be avoided. This reef lies to the south-westward of the Great Gull Island, and has 16 or 17 ft. over its shoalest part at low water; and its outer part is about half a league to the S.W. by S. from the Gull lighthouse. It is about 30 yards broad and 400 long, lying S.E. and N.W. The shallower part lies with a house on Plum Island, standing about one-third of the way between the middle and the N.E. end, on with the northernmost of the two trees which appear beyond the house; the West end of Gull Island N. by W. ¼ W., and the South end of Plum Island on with Oyster Pond Point, or the N.E. point of Long Island.

The marks formerly given are—1. The N.E. end of the northernmost grove of trees on Plum Island touching the South declining end of the southernmost of the white sand-hills on Plum Island. These sand-hills are the two next South of the houses in the bay. 2. A large notch or gap in a wood on the main land, to the westward of Black Point, a sail's breadth open to the northward of a remarkable single black rock, which is between the South end of Great Gull Island and the N.E. end of Plum Island N.W. by N. The rock appears nearly in form of half a semi-circle, with its perpendicular side to the East.

In order to avoid this reef, be sure to keep Oyster Pond Point open to the South end of Plum Island, whilst the house on Plum Island is on with the northernmost of the two trees above mentioned. There are several trees, but they appear, when seen from a distance, as two only.

Plum Island Road is on the S.E. side of Plum Island. In this road a vessel may anchor, with Mount Prospect, or the high white sand-hills of Fisher's Island, touching the Gull lighthouse, and bearing N. 62° E.; and the N.E. part of Long Island in one with the S.E. end of Plum Island, bearing West; or the East bluff points of Gardiner's Island in one with the low beach extending from the North side of the island, S. 45° E. With these marks are from 7 to 8 fathoms, soft mud, and quite out of the tide, at not more than three-quarters of a mile from the shore of Plum Island, where there is very convenient and good water.

LITTLE GULL ISLAND LIGHTHOUSE.—The Gull Islands lie to the westward of Plum Island. They are two in number, of but small extent, are surrounded by a rocky reef, especially off their eastern and western extremities, and should, therefore, not be approached nearer than 3 or 4 cables' lengths. Upon the eastern and smaller island, on the South side of the main entrance to Long Island Sound, is a gray granite lighthouse, 74 ft. high, showing a *fixed* light at the height of 92 ft. above the sea, visible 17 miles off. A *steam fog syren*, giving blasts of 5 seconds at intervals of 25 seconds, is sounded in thick weather.

The channel between Gull Islands and Plum Island has a width of 1¼ mile, and a depth of from 3¼ to 6 fathoms, but as there are several dangers in it, this passage is better avoided. In the middle of the channel there is a black rock, named the *Old Silas*, close to the westward of which is a sunken ledge of 5 to 13 ft.; and about half a mile S. by W. of the Old Silas is a reef named the *Bedford*, before mentioned, upon which there are 13 ft. The stream of flood in this channel during the second and third quarters sets N.W., at a rate of from 1¾ to 2¼ miles an hour, but in its early part it runs N.W. by W. 1½ mile, and during the latter portion N. by W. ½ W. three-quarters of a mile an hour; the ebb preserves nearly the same direction throughout, namely, S.E. by E. ½ E., running with a velocity of 2½ to 2¾ miles, except in its latter part, at which time its strength is only about half a mile an hour.

The RACE, or the channel between the western end of Fisher's Island and the Gull Island is the one principally used by vessels bound into and out of Long Island Sound, as it is both wider and deeper than the channel between the Gull Islands and Plum Island, or than that between Plum Island and Oyster Pond Point, named Plum Gut. The depth varies from 7 to 40 fathoms, and the width is 3¾ miles, but

THE RACE ROCK—DIRECTIONS.

there are two dangerous rocks in the way, named the Race and Valiant Rocks, the position of which should be avoided.

On the days of full and change high water takes place at $9^h\ 38^m$; spring tides rise $2\frac{3}{4}$ and neap $2\frac{1}{4}$ ft.; the average duration of the flood or rising tide being $6^h\ 1^m$, and that of the ebb or falling tide $6^h\ 21^m$, allowing 37 minutes for still water. During the first quarter the flood runs by compass in a N.W. direction, at the rate of $2\frac{1}{4}$ miles an hour; during the second, N.W. by W., $3\frac{1}{4}$ miles; in the third, W. by N. $\frac{3}{4}$ N., $3\frac{3}{4}$ miles; and during the last quarter, N.W. by W. $\frac{1}{4}$ W., $1\frac{3}{4}$ mile per hour. For the first quarter of the ebb the tidal current sets S.E. with a velocity of rather more than 2 miles an hour; in the second quarter nearly in the same direction, but with a rate increased to $3\frac{3}{4}$ miles; during the third quarter, S.E. by E. $\frac{1}{4}$ E., 4 miles; and in the fourth quarter, about E. by S., $1\frac{3}{8}$ mile per hour.

The Race Rock lies S.W., half a mile from the West end of Fisher's Island, and has but 4 ft. on it, with 14 to 18 fathoms close-to, and 5 and 7 fathoms between it and the island. It is marked either by buoys or a spindle. The mark to clear it on the western side is Mistic lighthouse open to the northward of North Hill. A *lighthouse* is building on it.

The *Valiant Rock* lies in the middle of the Race Channel, and has but 17 ft. upon it, with 5 to 13 fathoms close-to all round. It bears from Little Gull Island N.E. by E. $\frac{3}{4}$ E., distant 2 miles, and from New London lighthouse S. $\frac{1}{4}$ E. $5\frac{3}{8}$ miles.

The marks for this rock are, 1. New London lighthouse in one with two conspicuous trees, which stand on the declivity of a hill, at the back of New London, being remarkable for a gap on its summit, N. 40° W. 2. The western side of the South Dumpling, within Fisher's Island, just touching with the North hill or point of that island, N. 41° E. 3. The East bluff of the Great Gull Island in one with the western lower extreme of Little Gull Island, or the Gull lighthouse a small sail's breadth open to the eastward of the East part of Great Gull Island, S. 64° W. 4. The North part of Long Island just shut in with the N.W. point of Plum Island, S. 76° W.; Gull Light, S. 63° W.; and Mount Prospect, or high white sandhills on Fisher's Island, N. 60° E.

Directions.—To run for the Race Channel from the south-eastward, bring Montauk lighthouse to bear N. by W. $\frac{3}{4}$ W., distant $1\frac{3}{4}$ mile, when you will be in 8 fathoms, sandy bottom. Steer N. $\frac{3}{4}$ E. $3\frac{1}{4}$ miles, until the lighthouse bears S.W. by S., distant 2 miles, when you will be in 7 fathoms, gravelly bottom; haul now to the N.W. $\frac{1}{4}$ W., and run 13 miles, which will take you into the Race Channel, 1 mile E.N.E. from Little Gull Island lighthouse, leaving the Shagwong Reef 1 mile to the southward and westward, and Cerberus Shoal 1 mile to the northward and eastward.

If wishing to pass to the eastward of the Cerberus Shoal when Montauk lighthouse bears S.W. by S., distant 2 miles, steer N.W. by N. $\frac{1}{4}$ N., $7\frac{1}{4}$ miles, until Montauk lighthouse bears S. by E. $\frac{3}{4}$ E., $8\frac{1}{4}$ miles, and Gull light W. by N. $\frac{1}{4}$ N., when you will be in 25 fathoms, gray sand and black specks. Steer now W. by N. $\frac{3}{4}$ N., $6\frac{3}{4}$ miles, leaving the Cerberus Shoal $1\frac{1}{4}$ mile to the southward and westward, when, if these courses are made good, you will be in the Race Channel as before, and southward of the Valiant Rock.

If you are off the South end of Block Island, give it a berth of 1 mile, passing between it and the S.W. Ledge in 7 and 8 fathoms, and steer W.N.W., 18 miles, and when Gull light bears W. $\frac{1}{4}$ N., steer W. by N. for about $3\frac{1}{4}$ miles, you will then be at the entrance of the Race Channel as before. In this course you will go to the northward of the Cerberus Shoal.

With the flood tide safest course is to give Gull lighthouse a berth of from half to

1¼ mile; or if bound to New London follow the suggestions given on page 59, taking care, however, not to bring Gull lighthouse to the southward of W. by S. till New London light is in range with the highest steeple in the town, bearing North a little westerly; a W. by N. course will then carry you through the Race clear of the Valiant Rock. Passing through the Race between Valiant and Race Rocks, keep the highest point of Great Gull Island open South of the lighthouse, till New London lighthouse is well open to the westward of the gap in Bolle's Hill, N. by W.; keep it on this bearing until up with the harbour's mouth; or, if bound up the Sound, you may steer to the westward as soon as South Hummock appears northward of North Hill, on Fisher's Island. Should you be compelled to enter between Race Rock spindle and Fisher's island, you must be careful to avoid a reef running off a quarter of a mile from the West point of that island, the edge of which is usually marked by a buoy. When leaving the Sound for the eastward with the ebb tide, the reverse of these instructions will answer the same purpose.

The **NORTH COAST** of Block Island Sound extends between Point Judith lighthouse before mentioned and Watch Hill Point. Westward of Judith Point, and separated from it by soundings of 4 and 5 fathoms, is *Squid's Ledge*, a narrow rocky shoal, extending three-quarters of a mile in a N. ¼ W. and S. ¼ E. direction, with 13 feet at each end, the southern being 1½ mile West from Point Judith lighthouse, and the northern end half a mile from the shore, between which the depth is 3¼ fathoms. To clear it on the South side, do not bring Point Judith light eastward of E. by N. Hence to Watch Hill Point, at the entrance to Fisher's Island Sound, the coast trends W. ¼ S. 18 miles, and consists of a low sandy beach, enclosing several lakes or ponds, which have communication with the sea by means of very narrow and shallow outlets; there is, however, no outlying danger, and a depth of 3, 4, and 5 fathoms will be found a quarter of a mile off the land, so that at night time, or in thick weather, soundings of 10 and 12 fathoms and upwards should be maintained.

FISHER'S ISLAND and SOUND.—Fisher's Island Sound is the northern entrance to Long Island Sound, and is perfectly safe with local knowledge or with a pilot, and with the following directions; and is to be preferred, if bound eastward on the flood, or West with an ebb tide, to going through the Race, or to the South of Fisher's Island; but it should not be attempted without a leading wind by strangers, and great attention should be paid to the lead.

It is about 8 miles in length, but the fairway or main channel through it is not over three-quarters of a mile in width where narrowest, though the sound itself has an average breadth of 1¾ mile. In it there are a great number of rocks and shoals above and under water, a correct knowledge of the positions of which can only be obtained by a reference to the chart, the result of the survey made by the officers of the United States Navy. Upon several of the most dangerous reefs there are spindles or buoys to mark their situation, but there are many dangers which are not so marked, hence great caution must be taken in proceeding through, or to any place in it.

Tides.—At Watch Hill Point it is high water on the days of full and change at 9^h; springs range 3 ft., and neaps 2¼ ft.; the average duration of the flood is about $6^h\ 35^m$, and that of the ebb $5^h\ 56^m$. The stream of flood comes in from the eastward, and continues through the sound with a velocity not exceeding 1½ mile per hour, and the ebb the contrary, its greatest rate being 1½ mile per hour.

Lights.—On Watch Hill Point, at the eastern entrance of Fisher's Island Sound, there is a *fixed* light shown at the height of 62 ft. above the mean level of the sea, from a granite tower 40 ft. high, standing at the S.E. corner of the keeper's dwelling, which latter is built of brick, and whitewashed; in ordinary states of the atmosphere the light can be seen at the distance of 14 miles. Within the sound, on the northern shore, and on the South end of the promontory which forms the eastern side of the harbour, and whereon is built the town of Stonington, is a *white* building serving as the keeper's dwelling, from the top of which, at the height of 50 ft., a *fixed* light is exhibited, visible to the distance of 12 miles. About 4 miles W. by N. from Watch Hill Point, nearly 2¼ miles W.S.W. from Stonington light, and on the South side of Eel-Grass Ground, is a lightvessel moored in 4 fathoms, which shows a *fixed* light at an elevation of 32 ft., visible 10 miles in clear weather; a bell is rung and a horn sounded in foggy weather every alternate 5 minutes; the main ship channel is southward of it. Morgan's Point lighthouse on the northern shore of the sound, and on the West side of entrance to Mistic River, is 34 ft. high, and coloured *white*; its light, a *fixed* one, may be seen about 11 miles off, being shown at the height of 44 ft. The light on the North Dumpling, an islet in the western entrance to the sound, W. by S. 3½ miles from Eel-Grass lightvessel, is a *red* fixed light, 70 ft. high, exhibited from a *white* tower 25 ft. high, and is therefore visible at a distance of 12 miles; a bell is rung in foggy weather at intervals of 15 seconds.

Directions.—At the eastern entrance to Fisher's Island Sound a chain of isolated reefs, with from 3 to 6 fathoms between, forms a kind of curve from the East point of Fisher's Island to Watch Hill Point. There are many channels through it, but the three principal are the Watch Hill Point, Lord's, and East Point Channels. When approaching, therefore, great caution should be exercised, particularly as the tide sets over the rocks with considerable strength. If to the eastward of Watch Hill Point, and bound *through* the sound, steer so as to give the point a berth of 2 cables' lengths to avoid the Gangway Rock, with only 2 ft. water over it, which lies 300 yards S. by W. from Watch Hill light, and is marked by a buoy; you will thus leave the spindle on Watch Hill Reef 3 or 4 cables on the port hand; a W. ¾ N. course should now be followed, giving the next point to Watch Hill, namely, Napatree Point, a berth of 3 cables on your starboard side, in case the buoy marking the reef running from it should be driven from its position; as you proceed on this course, the two spindles marking the rocks on each side of Lord's Channel will be left to port, and that on Latimer's Reef should have a berth of a quarter of a mile on your starboard hand. A rock lies a quarter of a mile E. by S. from Latimer's Spindle, with only 3 feet upon it, which is marked by a buoy on its eastern side. When nearly abreast Latimer's Reef, you will have on the opposite side of the channel the Wicopesset Reef, Seal, and Young's Rocks, consequently you should not approach the shore of Fisher's Island hereabout nearer than 3½ or 4 cables' lengths, though Young's Rock has a buoy off it. Continue on the above (W. ¾ N.) course, leaving East Clump Islet on the port, and the buoy and spindle on Ellis' Reef on the starboard side. As soon as Ellis' Spindle, which is about 1¼ mile westward of Eel-Grass lightvessel, bears North, distant 3½ cables' lengths, steer W. ¾ S., passing on the North side of Dumpling lighthouse; this will carry you out to the lightvessel off the South end of Bartlett's Reef, and a fresh course can then be shaped up Long Island Sound. But if bound to New London, continue as before—that is, W. ¾ N., and you will probably pass over an 18-feet hard spot, just before you come abreast of Groton Long Point. Give this point and the buoy on the edge of the off-lay from it a good berth, and also the point next westward of it, off which there is a rock, with only 1 foot over it, at the distance of 2 cables' lengths. When the spindle on Seaflower Reef bears S.W. by W., and the North and South Hummocks or Dumplings are in range, the first will be distant 4 cables' lengths, and the buoy on the Horseshoe Reef will be a similar distance off on your starboard side. From this position the New London lighthouse will appear just open North of Smith's House N.W. by W. ¼ W., a course that, when followed, will lead up to the former through Pine Island Channel.

In following these directions, notice that between Watch Hill Point and Latimer's Reef, the last of the tide sets across the reefs which lie between Watch Hill Point and the East end of Fisher's Island. This set, on the ebb particularly, must be allowed for. On the flood it is not so strong.

Lord's Channel, on the eastern side of Wicopesset Islet, should not be attempted by a stranger, unless the leading mark, namely, Stonington lighthouse, open a sail's breadth to the eastward of the white hotel in the northern part of the town, can be clearly distinguished. When such is the case follow that direction, passing between the two spindles, giving the eastern one a berth of 1¼ cable's length, and when Watch Hill Point lighthouse bears E. ¼ S., haul up W. ¾ N., and proceed as before directed.

East Point Channel, between Wicopesset Islet and Fisher's Island (East point), cannot be recommended to a stranger; in it there are only from 15 to 18 ft. water. The leading mark is Latimer's spindle in line with the centre and highest part of a wood on Mason's Island, bearing about N.W. ¾ N.; this leads over or very near a sunken rock of 4 feet, which has a buoy on it to be left on the port hand going in. Having followed this line of direction till within 3½ cables of the spindle, steer W. ¾ N. as before.

Coming in from the *westward*, when the lightvessel off Bartlett's Reef bears North, distant nearly half a mile, steer E. ¾ N., and pass almost close-to on the North side of North Dumpling lighthouse up to where the spindle on Ellis' Reef bears North, distant 3½ cables' lengths. An E. ¾ S. course will then lead out between Watch Hill Point and Reef, and by reversing the foregoing directions for passing through from the eastward, a vessel will be enabled to get out by one or other of the channels clear of the reefs at the eastern entrance of Fisher's Island Sound.

STONINGTON lies on the North side of the eastern entrance to Long Island Sound, and is built principally on a rocky point of land which projects half a mile into the sound. It has a good harbour, protected by a breakwater, constructed by the United States Government at an expense of 50,000 dollars. It is on the termination of the railroad running to Providence and Boston, and will, with the Long Island railway, which terminates at Greenport, on Long Island, form the most direct route between New York and Boston, a distance of 211½ miles.

Light.—The entrance to the harbour is marked by a *lighthouse*, showing a fixed light, elevated 50 ft., which bears from Watch Hill Point lighthouse N.W. ¼ W. 2 miles distant; Latimer's Reef N.E. ¼ E. 2 miles; and the North Dumpling E. by N. ¾ N. 5¼ miles.

Bound into Stonington from the eastward, and having followed a W. ¾ N. course from the Gangway Rock buoy, lying 300 yards off Watch Hill Point, then as soon as Napatree Point bears N.E. by N., steer N.W. by W. towards the highest part of the wood on Mason's Island, until the beacon on the end of the breakwater, which is a *white* conical stone with a *black* barrel on the top, comes on with a large circular building (an engine-house) at the inner end of the steam-boat wharf, bearing N. by E. ¼ E. Haul up on this bearing, turn in close round the breakwater, and anchor just far enough in to swing clear of it in 2 fathoms, mud.

Smaller vessels can, when Napatree Point bears N.E. by N., run in with the breakwater beacon in line with the easternmost *white* house on the N.W. side of the harbour, N. by W. ¾ W., passing over a sandy bank in 9 and 10 ft. at low water, close to the

NEW LONDON.

West side of Bartlett's Reef, half a mile S.S.E. ¼ S. from Stonington light, and giving the lighthouse point a berth of a cable's length or more.

If from the southward, and resolved to enter the sound by Lord's Channel, bring the hotel before mentioned open a sail's breadth westward of Stonington lighthouse, which will carry you through Lord's Channel in 6 to 3½ fathoms water. Steer now north-westerly, so as to clear the shoal water extending from Bartlett's Reef until the light bears N. by E., when you may steer directly for the beacon on the end of the breakwater, into the harbour.

Bound to Stonington from the westward, steer to where the spindle on Ellis' Reef bears North, distant 3½ cables' lengths, continue on an E. ¾ N. course, passing about a cable's length southward of Eel-Grass lightvessel, and when Stonington lighthouse bears N.E. ¾ E., run for it, until the beacon on the breakwater is on with the enginehouse, then proceed as before. At night haul in for the anchorage when half a mile from the lighthouse, steering N. by E. ¼ E.

Mistic River flows into Fisher's Island Sound at 3½ miles westward of Stonington. There are two channels into it, one for vessels of 8 ft. draught, the other for vessels drawing not over 10 ft. They are buoyed, but are too narrow and crooked to be taken by a stranger without the aid of a pilot. There is a *fixed* light on Morgan's Point, on the West side of the entrance to Mistic River.

NEW LONDON.—The lighthouse on the western side of the entrance to New London bears from the *Race Rock*, off the West end of Fisher's Island, N. by W. ¾ W. 4¾ miles. It is a white tower, with the keeper's dwelling painted a drab colour. The *light* is *fixed* and *bright*, at 90 feet above the sea, and visible 15 miles off. A third class fog-trumpet is sounded in thick weather, giving blasts of 6 seconds at intervals of 14 seconds.

A vessel bound to this port, after passing the Race Rock and S.W. end of Fisher's Island, should keep the light bearing between N.N.W. and N.N.E., if beating to windward; but with the fair wind, bring the light to bear North, and run directly for it; leave it on your port side when running in. When in you may find good anchoring in 4 or 5 fathoms water, clayey bottom.

White Rock and *Powder Island* are on the West side, about halfway up to the town. *Fort Point*, on the same side, is half a mile above White Rock. In New London are three remarkable buildings—the Court House, the Presbyterian Meeting House, and Church. The Meeting House is the middle one. *Pine Island* is an islet three-quarters of a mile without the harbour, on the eastern side.

There are reefs on both sides, without the entrance; but particularly the *Sea Flower*, the *S.W. Ledge*, and *Black Ledge*, both marked by buoys, on the eastern side, at three-quarters of a mile both from the eastern and western shores. On the Sea Flower Reef, 2¾ miles S.E. by E. from New London lighthouse, is a stone beacon, 12 ft. high, surmounted by an iron mast and cage. At 1½ mile N.W. by W. from it is another, on the northern part of Black Ledge. *Frank's Ledge*, of 13 ft., lies midway between S.W. Ledge and Black Ledge. New London is 2 miles up the harbour, from the lighthouse; and on the opposite shore is the town of *Groton*.

High water at 12ʰ 30ᵐ. Common spring tides rise 3⅓ ft.; high spring tides 5 ft.

Having brought the Gull light to bear W. by N., or the light on Watch Hill Point N.E., steer so as to bring New London lighthouse open of Fisher's Island, and when the spire of New London Church, bearing N. 8° W., is in one with the gap on Bolle's Hill, steering with it in that direction will carry you between the Race Rock and Valiant's Rock, or you may bring New London lighthouse a sail's breadth to the eastward of the church spire, bearing N. 5° E., which will carry you to the westward of the Valiant's Rock, or between that rock and the Gull lighthouse. Thence steer for New London, as hereafter directed.

In case the weather should be thick, and New London church spire is not to be seen when bound to the westward through the Race, steer for the Gull lighthouse, keeping it to the northward of West, until New London lighthouse bears N. ¼ E.; then steer for it, leaving the Gull lighthouse at half a mile on the West or port side. When the Gull lighthouse bears S. by W., you may steer N.N.E. for the roads, making proper allowance for the tide, which is very strong.

In the winter season, when bound to or from New London, keep well to the West, should the wind be at N.E. and stormy. Your course, under such circumstances, for a good anchorage, is W.N.W. from the Gull, about 5 miles; then haul up, should the wind continue at N.E., and steer N.W. until you get into 10 fathoms of water, muddy bottom. Anchor as soon as possible. Here you will be to the westward of Black Point, between it and Sarah's Reef. This is the best place to ride in, with a N.E. gale and thick weather, when the harbour of New London cannot be attained.

To run into and up the harbour in the deepest water, through the *Western Channel*, bring the lightvessel off Bartlett's Reef to bear W. by S. ¾ S., and New London lighthouse N. ¾ W., distant about 1¼ mile, and steer N. ¼ E., and it will carry you up in mid-channel in from 4¼ to 6 fathoms. In this course you will leave on your port hand the Rapid Rock and Goshen Reef, the Mercer's Rock, and Eleven-feet Rock, the Hog's Back, Melton's Ledge, and also several others close in, but which can be avoided by not running nearer than 250 yards to the shore; and on the starboard hand S.W. Ledge, Frank's Ledge, and the Black Rock. Most of them are pointed out by buoys. Vessels, after passing the lighthouse, are often embarrassed by light winds, and, after rains, by a strong surface current setting out on the flood-tide.

To make up with a *head wind*. When outside the S.W. Ledge, keep the lighthouse between N.N.W. and N.N.E., but do not bring the lighthouse to the eastward of N. ¼ E. When up with the White Rock, before reaching Fort Trumbull, keep the Presbyterian spire open of Fort Point, by which you will clear Melton's Ledge, which lies 150 yards to the eastward of Powder Island, and is marked by a buoy.

To run through *Black Ledge Channel*, you may bring the Presbyterian spire on with Fort Point, N. by W., or the eastern point of the harbour in one with Ocean House, N. ¼ E., as either of these marks will lead through clear of Frank's Ledge.

From the eastward, keep the lighthouse just open to the northward of Smith's House, bearing N.W. by W. ¼ W., and it will take you through the Pine Island Channel in from 4½ to 3 fathoms. When to the eastward of Seaflower spindle, keep the lighthouse open to the southward of Pine Island, and it will clear the Horseshoe and Groton Long Point. When up with Pine Island, which is bold-to, there being 16 feet immediately off it, keep Long Rock open to the southward of a large stone house to the westward, and you will clear the North point of Black Ledge.

Between Goshen Reef and the shore is the *Middle Channel*; it is narrow, but has a depth of from 13 to 18 feet. When running from the westward after passing Two-tree Island Channel, bring the large *black* rock, South of Two-tree Island, on with the first large tree to the northward of the house on Black Point, and you will go through the channel in 13 feet. When up with the buoy on Mercer's Rock, you may steer for the lighthouse, and pass into the harbour.

To go through the *In-shore Channel*, the one between the Middle Channel and the shore, which lies about one-eighth of a mile from Goshen Point, and amongst the rocks bordering the coast, follow the above range (the large *black* rock South of Two-tree Island on with the first large tree, &c.), until Middle Rock is on with the *black* rock, near the East point of the harbour, which latter mark will take you through the channel in 8 to 10 ft. water. Pass 20 yards to the southward of Middle Rock, and then steer for the *black* rock until Fort Griswold Monument is open to the eastward of the lighthouse, when you may haul up the harbour, giving Quinnipeag Rock (the rocks near the lighthouse) a berth of 100 yards. This channel is only to be followed when the wind is from the northward, and with a vessel drawing under 10 ft.

BARTLETT'S REEF, the South point of which is $3\frac{1}{4}$ miles S.W. from New London lighthouse, and the same distance E. by S. $\frac{3}{4}$ S. from the extremity of Black Point, extends thence N.N.W. $1\frac{1}{4}$ mile, or to within one-third of a mile of the shore, and afterwards curves round W.N.W. half a mile to the buoy on its north-western extremity, where there is also an inlet named Two-tree Island; its greatest breadth is about a quarter of a mile. In many parts the reef dries at low water, and there are narrow swatchways between these parts with $2\frac{1}{2}$ fathoms and upwards in them. Close-to all round the reef are from 4 to 7 fathoms water, and you will find 13 fathoms, fine sand and mud, at less than half a mile off its southern extremity.

A **lightvessel**, with "Bartlett's Reef" painted in *white* letters on each quarter, lies off the South end of the reef, in 11 fathoms water, on rocky bottom, and exhibits two *fixed* lights at the heights of 28 and 35 ft., which are visible at a distance of 10 miles; during foggy weather a bell is rung and a horn sounded every alternate 5 minutes.

Two-tree Island Channel, between the North end of Bartlett's Reef and the shore, has a breadth of one-third of a mile, and is from $4\frac{1}{2}$ to 13 fathoms in depth. When passing through it do not stand into the bay to the northward, as there are several sunken rocks scattered about in it, which would prove dangerous to a vessel striking thereon.

Niantic Bay, between Black Point and Millstone Point, is said to be one of the best harbours of refuge on the northern shore of Long Island Sound, while the wind is northward of West and East. When between Bartlett's Reef and Black Point run for a small island, named White Rock, near to which is a buoy, which lies half a mile westward of the eastern point, and as it is bold-to you may pass it on either side, and anchor to the North of it in $3\frac{1}{2}$ fathoms.

Black Buoy Reef, to the westward of Black Point, has only 9 feet water over it at nearly half a mile South of the Black Bay Rock. It is marked by a *red* spar buoy.

Hatchett's Reef lies off Hatchett's Point, its eastern extremity being $2\frac{3}{4}$ miles about W. by S. $\frac{1}{4}$ S. from Black Point; here it is shoalest (5 ft.), and is about half a mile broad, with a *red* spar buoy on its S.E., and a black buoy on its N.E. extreme, thence it extends W.S.W., and joins the extensive sands fronting the entrance of Connecticut River, the water over it varying from 10 to 15 ft. in depth. It should not be approached nearer than into a depth of 12 fathoms.

The Connecticut River, which enters Long Island Sound to the westward of Hatchett's Reef, has thrown up such a formidable bar 2 miles to seaward, that no one, unless well and recently acquainted with it, should attempt to enter. The outer S.W. point of these flats is marked by a red spar buoy.

The greatest depth that can be ensured at low water over the bar is from 5 to 7 ft., but to maintain the latter depth up to Lynde Point requires the aid of a skilful pilot. The wharves of Saybrook are $1\frac{1}{4}$ mile within the bar, and on the north-eastern side of Saybrook Point. On the days of full and change, high water takes place at 10ʰ 17ᵐ; springs range 5 ft., and neaps 2¾ ft.; the duration of both flood and ebb is about 6 hours each, allowing 36 minutes for still water.

Saybrook.—As a guide to vessels running for this place, a *fixed* light is exhibited from a *white* building erected on *Lynde Point*, on the West chop of the river; it is 80 ft. above the mean level of the sea, and may be seen at a distance of 15 miles. But the marshes to the westward of it raise so much mist that it is frequently obcured. A bell is rung in foggy weather at intervals of 12 seconds.

The old S.E. channel, which was abandoned in 1853, was found to have 7 feet water through it in 1873, when three spar buoys, painted with perpendicular stripes, were placed to mark it, and the following directions issued:—

From the entrance buoy, which is about three-quarters of a mile N.E. ¾ E. from can buoy No. 8, in the sound, bring Saybrook lighthouse to bear N.W. ¼ W.; steer in on that course (passing close to the outer and middle buoys), keeping the beacon open to the South of the lighthouse, and bringing the latter nearly in range with, and a little to the South of, the Congregational Church in Saybrook village. When up with the inner buoy, placed about half a cable's length from the beacon, which will then be in range with Fenwick Hall, take a direct course (N.N.W.) for the railway depot at Saybrook.

For vessels bound in from the eastward, and for all vessels entering the Connecticut during north-easterly and south-westerly winds, the use of this channel offers superior advantages.

There is good anchorage by bringing the lighthouse to bear from N.E. by E. to N.N.E. 1 mile distant, in 3 and 4 fathoms water, soft bottom; and by hoisting a signal can always procure a pilot, which is imperatively necessary.

Long Sand Shoal, to the westward of Saybrook bar, is narrow, and has but from 6 to 15 ft. over it, the shallowest part being near the middle. Its eastern end (15 ft.) lies 1¾ mile S.S.E. ¼ S. from Saybrook lighthouse, and has a *buoy*, red and white in horizontal stripes, whence it extends about W. ¼ S. 5 miles to the similar buoy on its western extremity, from which Saybrook light bears E.N.E. 5 miles.

Cornfield Point, or *Long Sand Lightship*, is on its South side, near the centre of the Long Sand shoal, and about one-eighth of a mile from it, in 7½ fathoms, sandy bottom; she is sloop-rigged, and shows a *fixed* light 40 ft. above the water, seen at a distance of 10 miles; has a square cage-work day-mark at the mast-head, and is painted *red*. In foggy weather a bell is rung and a horn sounded every alternate 5 minutes; and from it Saybrook light bears N.E. ¾ N., Bartlett's Reef lightvessel E. by N., Little Gull Island light E. by S., Falkner's Island light W. ½ S., and Plum Island light E.S.E.

A too near approach to Long Sand Shoal may be dangerous, as it is steep-to, and probably increasing so as to become connected at the N.E. end with the bar of Connecticut River. It is also the more dangerous because the tide sets athwart it to the N.W. and S.E.

Should the lightvessel be off her station, to avoid the shoal the Falkner's Island light should not be brought to bear to the southward of W. ¾ N., or the lightship on Bartlett's Reef to the southward of E. ¾ N.

Between the western part of the Long Sand Shoal and the shore bank are several detached banks, the *Cornfield Reef*, *Hen and Chickens*, and *Crane Reef*. They are all marked by buoys, and lying out of the ordinary track of vessels, they need not be further particularized.

FALKNER'S ISLAND and Lighthouse.—Falkner's Island is 2¾ miles southward from the nearest point of the main at the small and shallow harbour of Guildford, and bears from Little Gull Island light W. ⅞ N. 24½ miles, and from Stratford Point light E. ¼ N. 20½ miles. A narrow reef of rocks extends from it nearly half a mile northward, the extremity of which has a black buoy upon it, and around *Goose Island*, a mile westward of Falkner's Island, there is likewise a dangerous reef running northward also about the same distance. The South side of Falkner's Island and the West side of Goose Island are steep-to, but on all others they will require to have a good berth given them. The *white* building on Falkner's Island, which has an elevation of 44 feet, exhibits a *fixed* light, varied by *flashes*, every 1½ minute, at the height of 98 feet above the mean level of the sea, and visible 15 miles off. A fog-bell is struck at intervals of 15 seconds.

Kimberley's Reef, on which there are only 10 feet, is very small and steep-to, with 5 and 8 fathoms a short distance off all round. It lies 1¼ mile E. ¼ N. from Falkner's lighthouse, and 3 miles South from Hogshead Point, the nearest part of the shore.

The Thimbles, a cluster of islets against the North shore, are 5 miles W.N.W. of Falkner's Island. One-third of a mile south-westward of the Outer Thimble is *Wheaton's Reef*, with a buoy on its northern end. *Brown's Reef* is southward of Wheaton's, and *East Ledge* south-eastward; the latter bears S.W. by S. ¼ S. three-quarters of a mile from the Outer Thimble.

Branford Reef has a gray granite beacon on its northern part, and is dry at very low tides; it is not of very great extent, but deep water of 7 and 8 fathoms is found at a short distance off it all round. Falkner's Island bears from it E. by S. nearly 7 miles distant, and New Haven light N.W. by W. ½ W., 4¾ miles. Therefore, to pass clear on the southern, or outside of these rocks, do not bring Falkner's Island lighthouse southward of E. ½ S., or decrease the depth below 8½ fathoms.

NEW HAVEN is about 12 miles westward of Falkner's Island. The harbour, open to the South, is exposed in that direction. The entrance is between Five Mile Point on the East, and Oyster River Point on the West.

A Lighthouse stands on Five Mile Point, showing a fixed light at 93 ft., visible 15 miles off. It has a fog-bell.

At 1¼ mile North of the lighthouse is *Fort Hale*, on the eastern side of the harbour, and off this is the *bar*, having 20 to 11 ft. least water; within it deepens 13 to 17 ft., but shoalens gradually to the extremity of the Long Wharf, which projects two-thirds of a mile south-eastward from the town; on the end of the Long Wharf is a *fixed light* at 21 ft.

The flats extend for above a mile and a half south-westward of Five Mile Point, and near their outer edge, and also near the leading mark given on the U.S. survey, on the port hand are the *Luddington Rocks*, 1¼ mile S.W. from the lighthouse, consisting of two sharp-pointed rocks 13 yards apart, with 12½ ft. upon them; around them are 17 and 19½ ft. Nearly three-quarters of a mile N.N.W. from the Luddington Rocks is a hard patch of 11 ft., and between this patch and the western shore are several others of 5 and 6 ft. water.

On the starboard hand are the S.W. Ledge, Quixe's Ledge, Adam's Fall, &c.; therefore the lighthouse, which appears very conspicuous, should not be approached too near while bearing to the northward of N.E. by E. The *S. W. Ledge* is marked by a buoy, bearing from the lighthouse S.W. by S. ¼ S., one mile, and from the spindle on Quixes' Ledge W.S.W. half a mile. From 5 to 10 feet is the depth on this ledge at low water, and there are from 10 to 18 feet between it and Quixes Ledge. A *lighthouse* is building on S.W. Ledge. *Quixes' Ledge* bears from the lighthouse S. ¼ E., distant about five-eighths of a mile, and is marked by a spindle. *Adam's Fall*, a shoal of 4 to 5 ft., is distant about half a mile from the lighthouse point, and is marked by a buoy, which bears from the lighthouse S.W. ¼ W., and from the spindle on Quixes' Ledge N.W. ¼ W. about half a mile.

To enter, bring the lighthouse to bear E.N.E., and run for it until Fort Hale is in range with the larger of two church spires next each other in the village of Fair Haven. You will then be about half a mile from the light in 3 fathoms water, and but a short distance to the westward of the buoy on Adam's Fall Ledge. S. ½ E. you will see the buoy on the S.W. Ledge, and still further to the eastward, the spindle on Quixes' Ledge.

Run into the harbour upon the above-mentioned range, Fort Hale and the Spire, until the lighthouse bears S. by E., when you will be in 2 fathoms, soft bottom. Then steer up a little to the westward of the head of Long Wharf, and you will soon deepen into 2¼ and 2¾ fathoms. A little above Fort Hale is a buoy which you leave to the eastward, and five-eighths of a mile further up, another, which you leave to the westward. Soon after leaving this last buoy, you will shoal to 8 and 7 feet, carrying this depth up to the head of Long Wharf.

STRATFORD POINT Lighthouse.—This point is 8½ miles south-westward from New Haven entrance; the coast between offering no interest to shipping, except that a good berth should be given to it. The lighthouse is striped *black* and *white*, showing a light *revolving* once in every 1½ minute, at an elevation of 53 ft. above the mean level of the sea; and being visible at a distance of 12 miles, is of great use to all vessels beating up or down Long Island Sound. A *fog-bell* is struck, in thick weather, 4 blows at intervals of 10 seconds, then a rest of 30 seconds, and then 4 blows repeated.

The coast immediately westward of Stratford Point is fronted by an extensive hard sandy flat, the 3-fathom edge of which is in some places nearly 1½ mile off; therefore vessels should give the shore a good berth, more particularly as there are some 9-feet patches upon the bank, the outermost of which is marked by a *red* spar buoy.

Middle Ground and Lightvessel.—Nearly in the middle of the sound S. ¾ W., 5½ miles from Stratford Point light, is the Middle Ground, a dangerous shoal, with but 2 feet water on it. It extends two-thirds of a mile in a N.E. and S.W. direction, and is buoyed on its North and South sides; it is also marked by a lightvessel, moored in 11 fathoms water, one-eighth of a mile S.W. of the shoalest part. She is painted straw colour, with "Stratford" painted in white letters on each side. She shows *two fixed bright lights*, elevated 32 and 40 ft. above the sea, and is also provided with a *fog-bell* and *horn*. A *lighthouse* is *building* on the Middle Ground.

BRIDGEPORT is at the entrance of a small river, 3½ miles north-westward of Stratford Point, having the shore flat on the starboard hand. On the opposite side of the bay, in which is also Black Rock Harbour, is Fairfield Bar, a long, narrow spit, terminating at the Cows, on which is a beacon, 5½ miles westward from Stratfort Point.

Light.—In the entrance to Bridgeport, on the outer bar, is a white pile lighthouse showing a *red* fixed light at 56 ft., seen about 13 miles off. It is to be left to port in entering. The harbour is narrow and difficult to enter, but is much used by coasters. There is an outer and an inner bar, the least depth on which is 6 and 7 feet. It is necessary to have a pilot, but the channel up is marked by buoys and beacons. A *bell* is struck at intervals of 15 seconds in foggy weather. The lighthouse must be passed to the eastward, and not be approached within 200 ft.

It is high water, at full and change, at $11^h 2^m$. Springs rise 8 feet 9 inches, neaps 5 feet 2 inches.

The entrance to this harbour is obstructed by two bars, the outer one of which has been deepened by dredging, and the cut, which is three-eighths of a mile long, is in-

BLACK ROCK HARBOUR—PENFIELD'S REEF.

dicated by a buoy at each end in line with the deepest water. The inner or northern buoy bears from the outer buoy N. ¾ E. distant three-eights of a mile.

To run in, keep these buoys in one, passing the lighthouse on your port hand and the inner buoy close upon the starboard bow, to pass the outer bar; then keep a couple of cables' lengths south-easterly, or outside of the line of the N.E. and S.W. beacons upon the edge of the western flats, standing on across the inner bar in from 6 to 10 feet water. Haul up round the N.E. beacon, deepening to 16 feet, when a buoy which marks the N.E. point of the western flats, will bear N.W. by N., five-eighths of a mile distant. Run up through the channel for the town, keeping this buoy a little on the port bow.

BLACK ROCK HARBOUR is 2 miles westward from Bridgeport. It is to the westward of Fairweather Island, and is used by small vessels as a place of refuge, there being from 10 to 12 feet least water within shelter.

Light.—Fairweather Island, which is low and narrow, has upon the South of it a lighthouse, 35 ft. high, showing a *fixed* light at 52 ft. above the sea, visible 12 miles. A reef, partly awash at low water, runs about a quarter of a mile to the southward from the lighthouse, and has on its extremity a red spar buoy. When you have rounded this buoy, on your starboard hand, the harbour will be farely opened, and you may run up N. ½ E., in 8 to 10 ft.

At 1¼ mile S. ¾ W. from Black Rock lighthouse is the outer end of the Fairfield Bar, a reef running off 1¼ mile in a S.E. ¾ E. direction from Shoal Point, and being dry at low water serves as an efficient protection to Black Rock Harbour against heavy seas from the southward.

PENFIELD'S REEF and Lighthouse.—At the extremity of this reef there are some rocks awash at low water, named the *Cows*, and near them is another cluster, named *Penfield's Reef*. These rocks lie just within the 18-feet line, and have from 4 to 6 fathoms at a quarter of a mile to the eastward of them. There are two buoys on the south-eastern and southern sides of this danger, which will assist a vessel in ascertaining its limits.

The *lighthouse* on Penfield Reef bears S. by W. ¼ W. from Black Rock light, and S.W. 3 miles from Bridgeport Harbour light. The tower is white, and a *red light*, *flashing* every 5 seconds, is shown from it at an elevation of 54 feet. A cast-steel *fog-bell* is sounded, two strokes in quick succession every 30 seconds.

If coming into Black Rock Harbour from the eastward, when abreast of Stratford light (which pass at a distance of 2 miles to avoid a shoal spot South of it), bring Black Rock light to bear W.N.W., and steer W. by N. ¼ N., keeping it on the starboard bow.

Enter midway between the light and beacon, passing the light until it bears N.N.E., then haul up N. ¼ E. into the inner harbour. Give the lighthouse a berth of from one-eighth to one-quarter of a mile, and anchor in 2 fathoms, soft bottom, with the light bearing anywhere from East to S.S.E.

If coming from the westward, keep in not less than 4 fathoms, to avoid Penfield's Reef, to the southward of the beacon, and the Cows to the northward. After passing the beacon, steer East until you bring Black Rock light to bear N. by W., then run for it until midway between the light and beacon, when you may steer as before.

There is *safe and good anchorage* between Bridgeport entrance and Fairweather light, 1¾ mile westward, in all winds from W.S.W., by the North, to E.N.E. The shore on the eastern side of the light is bold, having 3 fathoms almost close to it, and deepening gradually outwards.

The **NORWALK ISLANDS**, which are 5 miles in extent, and connected by shoals with each other and the main land, are 7 miles westward of Fairfield Bar. Shoal water stretches out for 1¼ mile to the East and S.E. of *Cockenoe's Island*, the easternmost; the outer point of these is marked by a *red* spar buoy.

SHEFFIELD ISLAND and Lighthouse.—The island is the westernmost of the Norwalk Islands, and the lighthouse near its western end is about 16 miles westward of that on Stratford Point. It shows a *fixed light* varied by *red flashes* every minute, 40 ft. above the sea, visible 11 miles off, by which it may readily be distinguished from the light on Stratford Point.

A shoal with several sunken rocks upon it, some awash at low water, runs off from the lighthouse point 1¼ mile in a W. by S. ¾ S. direction, and has a buoy upon its extremity. There is likewise a detached shallow patch of 4 fathoms, lying at 1⅜ mile S.W. ¾ S. from the lighthouse, which bears the name of *Budd's Reef*.

An excellent harbour exists on the northern side of Sheffield Island, where shelter in all weather may be had by vessels drawing 19 ft. of water and under. To run in, pass midway between the buoy on the extremity of the ledge extending from the West end of Sheffield Island and Fish Island (a small low island covered with cedars lying near the main shore), from which the buoy bears S.E., distant about three-quarters of a mile. Steer E.N.E., shoaling gradually from 4 fathoms to 12 ft. on a rather irregular bottom, and anchor in 12 or 13 ft., soft bottom, with the light bearing S. by W.

CAPTAIN'S ISLANDS are two in number, named *Great and Little*, and lie above a mile off shore, at about 10 miles westward of the Norwalk Group. The islands are low, situated on a shallow flat, and between and around them are many rocks above and under water, especially on the north-eastern side of the East island, where they extend off 4 cables' lengths. High water at 11ʰ 1ᵐ on full and change; springs rise 8¼ ft., and neaps 7 ft.

Lighthouse.—The *white* lighthouse on the eastern end of the Great or West Island is 34 ft. high, and shows a fixed light at an elevation of 62 ft., visible in clear weather at the distance of 12 miles.

On the North side of the East Island there is excellent anchorage in from 2 to 4 fathoms, good holding ground, and shelter from all but south-easterly winds, which, when heavy, send in some swell. The channel to it, between East Island and Flat Neck Point, is from 4 to 8 fathoms deep, and half a mile wide. When running in, steer N.W., keeping midway between the two. When well within the line of the island and Flat Neck Point, with the lighthouse bearing S.W. ¼ W., haul up to the westward, and anchor in 18 ft., sticky bottom, with the hummock on East Island bearing S.S.E.

Hence to Execution Rocks, the northern shore of the sound should be avoided, particularly by strangers, for numerous rocks and reefs detached and extending from the land, to distances varying from one quarter to three-quarters of a mile, render it advisable to give it a good berth.

The SOUTH SHORE of Long Island Sound.—For the distance of 55 miles from its eastern point, the North shore of Long Island offers few points of interest to the sailor, and is entirely without harbour or shelter. The shore is tolerably bold-to for the first 4 miles westward of Oyster Pond Point, when a narrow sandy isthmus, *Truman's Beach*, is reached, which connects the eastern extreme, called the Oyster Ponds, to the rest of Long Island. A slender bay between *Terry's Point* and *Rocky Point* has a 6-ft. shoal off its entrance, three-quarters of a mile off the beach.

Horton's Point and Light is 5¼ miles beyond Rocky Point. It has a brick tower, cemented and whitewashed, 30 feet high, on its summit, which shows a *fixed* light, elevated 110 feet, visible 18 miles off. To the westward of this a line of

HUNTINGTON BAY. 67

banks, with large patches nearly awash, consisting of hard sand, stretches along the shore for 6 miles. The outer edge of them is two-thirds of a mile from the beach. As the water shoalens rather quickly towards this bank, caution should be used, and a large ship should not come into less than 12 fathoms when passing this part; but further westward this depth will not lead clear, as off *Roanoke Point* and the *Friar's Head*, the latter 14 miles beyond Horton's Point light, a projecting shoal extends 2¼ miles N.E. by N. from Friar's Head, and 1¾ mile from shore, having 12 feet water near its extremity, and 6 feet at three-quarters of a mile from shore; off the outer point of this shoal the depth is 19 fathoms within one-third of a mile.

At 4½ miles westward of Friar's Head is *Herod's Point*, and a shoal off this point extends nearly 2 miles from the land, with 6 feet least water on its outer point. To the East of this the depth is 14 and 15 fathoms within the line of its projection, so that vessels should not venture into less than 15 fathoms when near it.

The shore bank to the westward reaches to from three-quarters to 1¼ mile off the beach, and near the shore are *Sill's Rock*, the *Old Sow Rock*, and others, all out of the way of larger vessels passing through the sound. *Mount Misery Point* is 1¾ mile eastward from Old Field Point light, and a shoal extends three-quarters of a mile northward of it, having only 6 feet water on its outer point. The Mount Misery Shoal has a spar buoy, black and white striped, on its outer edge, which deepens suddenly from 2½ to 13 fathoms on the North, and from 3 to 18 fathoms on the N.E. part. The Stratford Point lighthouse is 4 miles N. ¼ W. from this buoy.

Old Field Point Lighthouse is a white tower, 34 feet high, with two dwellings adjacent on the low bluff. It shows a fixed light, elevated 67 feet, seen 13 miles off.

Eastward of Old Field Point, between it and Mount Misery Shoal, is the entrance to Setauket Bay, wherein are the villages of *Port Jefferson* and *Setauket;* but the channel over the bar is both shallow and intricate.

Smithtown Bay lies to the westward of *Crane Neck Point*, which is 2 miles westward of Old Field Point. Here the coast runs in 2¼ miles to the southward to the entrance of *Stoney Brook Harbour*, the bar of which is shallow. The bars of *Nissequaque River* lie 4 miles W. by S. from that of Stony Brook, the intervening coast being fronted by a broad and shallow flat. Hence to Eaton's Neck Point the coast trends N.W. by W. ¼ W. 7½ miles, and should not be approached nearer than 1 mile, for a flat of hard sand extends off to nearly that distance in several places. Crane Neck and Eaton's Points are the East and West extremities of Smithtown Bay, distant 11 miles from each other.

HUNTINGTON BAY runs in 2 miles to the southward, between Eaton's and Lloyd's Necks, is above a mile in width, and in the fairway there are soundings of 5 and 6 fathoms, decreasing as you advance inwards to 4 and 3 fathoms. Good anchorage may be had in any part, except with northerly winds. Its shores are lined with sandy flats. In the S.E. corner of the bay there is a narrow channel, about 60 fathoms in width, and 3 and 4 fathoms deep, leading in between the sand-bank extending southward from East Beach Point and that fronting the mainland, into *Cow Harbour* or *Northport Bay*, wherein are from 9 to 4 fathoms, gradually shoaling as you proceed eastward round Little Neck Point towards the village of *Northport*, where there are only 4, 5, and 6 ft. water, or southward into *Centreport Inlet*. In the S.W. corner of the bay are the entrances of two shallow inlets; that running in southward, and named Huntington Harbour, has 10, 8, and 6 ft. in it, but the channel way is not more than 50 fathoms in width; and that running in westward, named Lloyd's Harbour, is much frequented by coasters, and may be entered by bringing the point of West Beach to bear West or W. ¼ N.; stand in on that direction, keeping the point close aboard, and anchor when within it.

Upon *West Beach*, and just within the extremity of this point, is a brick tower 34 feet high, showing a *fixed* light at 48 feet, visible 10 miles off; it is of much service to vessels seeking refuge in the night time.

High water on the days of full and change at 11ʰ; spring tides range 9¼ ft., and neaps 6¼ ft.

Eaton's Neck Point and Light.—On the eastern side of the entrance to Huntington Bay, there is a *white* lighthouse 56 feet high, showing a *fixed* light at an elevation of 142 ft., visible 18 miles off. In thick weather a *steam fog syren* is sounded, giving blasts of 9 seconds duration at intervals of 35 seconds. From the shore of the lighthouse a reef stretches out 4 cables' lengths north-eastward, with only 2 ft. of water on its outer part, the extremity of which is marked by a buoy moored in 14 feet; from this spot shoal water of 16 and 18 ft. extends nearly three-quarters of a mile further in a N.N.Westerly direction, the northern end being also pointed out by a black spar buoy, and half a mile still further north-westward, with from 4 to 7 fathoms between, lies a small rocky patch of 19 ft., with the lighthouse bearing from it S. by E. ¼ E., distant 1½ mile; this has likewise a buoy, striped horizontally, on its northern side.

Lloyd's Point, the N.W. point of Lloyd's Neck, is the western entrance point of Huntington Bay. A rocky shoal extends three-quarters of a mile beyond it, the outer end of which is marked by a black spar buoy, which makes a near approach to it dangerous; keep in 10 fathoms and upwards.

Oyster or Syosset Bay lies to the westward of Lloyd's Neck, its western part being *Hog* or *Centre Island Point*, off which there also runs a reef three-quarters of a mile beyond the point. A buoy lies just outside the rocks, but a sand spit projects some distance further.

Across the entrance to Oyster Bay a spit extends from Hog or Centre Island to within 1½ cable of the eastern side against Lloyd's Neck, there being a depth of 8 to 11 fathoms in the narrow channel, which is thus close to the eastern side of the bay.

When inside the spit there is plenty of room and a good depth of water, which shoalens very gradually as you proceed southward up Cold Spring Harbour. In this harbour from 14 to 17 feet over a sticky bottom will be found to within 100 or 150 fathoms of either shore, but it is quite exposed to northerly winds, whereas *Oyster Bay Harbour*, an arm of the bay running in to the south-westward, forms a spacious and safe retreat from all winds, with good anchorage in 7½ or 8 fathoms, soft sticky bottom; smaller vessels may go further in and anchor in what depth they please. It is high water on full and change days of the moon at 11ʰ 4ᵐ; springs range 9½ feet, and neaps 5½ feet.

At *Oak Neck Point*, the next westward of Hog Island Reef, commences a broad flat, which continues along the coast thence to Matinicock Point, the eastern point of entrance of Hempstead Bay, where its extremity is marked by a *black* buoy.

Hempstead Harbour is 6½ miles westward of Oyster Bay, and runs in nearly 5 miles in a southerly direction, gradually narrowing and shoaling as you proceed towards the village of *Hempstead* or *Roslyn*, at its head. Being quite open to the northward it affords no shelter from wind or sea from that direction, except to such small vessels as are capable of entering Mosquito Cove on the eastern shore, or Hempstead Harbour in its upper part. In the outer part of the bay the depths are 4 or 5 fathoms, near the middle 3 and 2½ fathoms, and just before you enter the latter harbour 4 and 3 fathoms. When sailing in give both shores a moderate berth, and bring-to where convenient. Near the eastern shore there is excellent anchorage.

Prospect Point is the western point of Hampstead Harbour; it may be known by a remarkable rock on the shore, named the *Pulpit*, which, while it bears between S.E. southward, and S.W. by S., should not be approached nearer than to have Sand's Point light bearing S.W. or S.W. by S., so as to avoid the Old Hen Rock, and the shallow ground surrounding it and the point.

Sand's Point Lighthouse is two-thirds of a mile westward of Prospect Place, and exhibits a light *flashing* once every half minute, at an elevation of 53 ft., visible 13 miles off. When off this point you should make but short tacks, on account of the Execution Rocks, and also on account of the rocks which surround Sand's Point and the adjacent coast.

The **EXECUTION ROCKS** occupy a position right in the fairway of the sound, and extend N.E. by N. and S.W. by S. about a mile, and are one quarter of a mile across in the broadest part, where the lighthouse is placed, near the middle of the reef.

Lighthouse.—The light on Execution Rocks is a *fixed white* light, and being 54 feet above the sea, may be seen at a distance of 12 miles in a clear atmosphere. A Daboll *fog trumpet* is sounded every 10 seconds in foggy weather. From this light that on Sand's Point bears S. by E. ½ E. nearly a mile. On each end of these rocks a buoy is placed, which, with the lighthouse, ought to guard vessels from running on them.

From midway between Sand's Point and Execution lights the course is S.W. 2¼ miles for the South end of Hart Island, leaving the black buoy off Sand's Point and the Gangway Rock *black buoy* and Success Rock red buoy on the port hand. These rocks lie opposite the middle of Hart Island, and seven-eighths of a mile south-westward of Sand's Point lighthouse, the former, which is the outermost, having but 6 feet over it, and lying right in mid-channel. The South point of Hart Island has, or had, two single trees on it, and is bold-to.

Hence to Throg's Point the course and distance are S.S.W. 2½ miles, passing the black buoy on the end of the *Stepping Stones Reef* on your port hand, and stand over to the western side into 3 fathoms, being guided by the lead. Should the buoy on the Stepping Stones have drifted from its position, take care, when about halfway towards Throg's Point, not to bring the South point of Hart Island northward of N.N.E. At the extremity of Stepping Stones Reef the flood runs S.W. by S. about half a mile an hour, and the ebb in a contrary direction, not quite 1 mile. Give Throg's Point a berth of 2 cables' lengths when rounding it, and steer W. by N. towards Whitestone Point. A *lighthouse* is building on Stepping Stones Reef.

THROG'S POINT Light is *fixed*, elevated 66 ft., shown from the N.E. side of Fort Schuyler, and visible 10 miles off in clear weather. A bell is struck four times per minute in foggy weather, which should be heard from 1 to 1½ mile off.

EAST RIVER.—From Throg's Point westward vessels should maintain a midchannel course, for, from the eastern point of Flushing Bay, a deep inlet on the port hand, a reef named *Lawrence*, extends nearly one-third the channel over, but this, as well as the other prominent dangers in this passage, has a buoy on its extremity. Keep along by the main or northern shore, and pass round to the northward of *Riker's Island* and the *North Brother*, and when between Lawrence's Point and the *sunken meadow*, you will cross over the Middle Ground, whereon are soundings of 20 21, and 22 ft., rocky bottom, but deeper water nearer the island. Still continue in mid-channel up to the South point (Negro Point) of Ward's Island; you will now have arrived at *Hell Gate*, and very great care will have to be exercised to go clear of the many rocks and shoals which are here scattered about.

HELL GATE.—This proverbially difficult channel should not be attempted except by those well acquainted with its complicated tidal currents. These and its other features have been well examined by the U.S. surveying officers, and the following are the general directions given by them. These and the chart must suffice. Since they were written some of the rocks have been lowered by blasting.

Previous to entering Hell Gate, the anchors should be got ready for letting go, and chains ranged and stoppered at 10 or 12 fathoms.

From the Southward.—Flood Tide.—The channel East of Blackwell's Island is the best. Vessels standing through the West channel run great danger of being carried by the current on to Middle Reef (extending N.W. from Flood Rock. With a head wind, vessels may beat through Hell Gate, either by the East Channel, or with a commanding breeze, go round to the northward of Great Mill Rock. In the latter case, a stretch very near Hog's Back may be made with safety. With a fair wind, small vessels may keep in the East Channel, and in the main body of the current. Large vessels must go through the Main Ship Channel. In the Main Ship Channel, steer with the Great Mill Rock well open on the starboard bow, and stand past it far enough to avoid the eddies, which extend about 30 yards to the northward of the rock; steer then with the ripple of the Frying Pan one point on the port bow. After passing the Frying Pan, haul up for Negro Point, passing clear of it about 60 yards, then if a vessel keeps in the middle of the channel, the current will take her to the westward of the Middle Ground off Lawrence's Point.

In entering Hell Gate from the East side of Blackwell's Island, take the middle of the channel, avoiding the eddies about Bread and Cheese, and those about Hatter's Dock, which show very plainly; pass Astoria Ferry about 50 yards off (on the starboard hand) and steer for the centre of Flood Rock; this will put a vessel in the true flood tide when she is abreast Flood Rock. From Flood Rock steer for an old house on Ward's Island (then bearing about N.E. ¼ E.) with poplar trees in front of it, until nearly up with the ripple of the Frying Pan, when haul up or keep away for Negro Point, and proceed as before directed.

Approaching Hell Gate through the West channel of Blackwell's Island, do not attempt to pass over to the Eastern Channel, unless the wind is fair and fresh, then stand across past Flood Rock until the old *white* building on Ward's Island opens to the right of it, when proceed as before directed.

With a light wind from the westward a vessel is at the mercy of the current, and her only chance to avoid being drifted over on Cram's Bank (S.E. of and opposite Negro Point), is to hug the Frying Pan, passing only one length to the southward of it, and tack in towards Negro Point when it bears North, stand on only long enough to get headway on the vessel, tack again and keep the mid-channel.

Entering Hell Gate (with no prospect of wind), anchor in Hallet's Cove (southeastward of Blackwell's North point) to the northward of Thornburn's Dock, taking care not to let go the anchor with any headway on, as the ground is very rocky, and many anchors are lost at this place. In getting under weigh from Hallet's Cove, stand out due West from Thornburn's. Vessels frequently stand too near Hatter's Dock, when they invariably strike on Bald Headed Billy, a round, smooth rock, dry at low water. In case a vessel is caught in the eddies of Bread and Cheese, the only chance of avoiding the rocks is to stand through between Bread and Cheese and Blackwell's Point, a good 7-ft. channel at low water, and about 50 yards wide.

When, owing to light westerly or N.E. winds, vessels are drifted within the influence of the Pot eddies, they must inevitably go over on Cram's Bank, and get on

HELL GATE. 71

shore to the North of Woolsey's Bath House; to avoid this, run into Pot Cove, and anchor. The current turns into Pot Cove opposite Woolsey's Bath House, and will enable a vessel to reach good anchorage.

Slack Water.—With a fair wind, take the East Channel; with a head wind, allow room for tacking when near Flood Rock, as a slight under-current often makes vessels miss stays when they go upon the Gridiron. The longest tacks can be made by going to the northward of Great Mill Rock, but a vessel this way is in danger of losing the slack water, which never lasts more than 10 minutes, and generally not more than 6 minutes.

Ebb Tide.—With a fair wind, keep along the shore near Hallet's Point, to avoid the strength of the currents; but after passing this point, keep mid-channel to avoid the rocks off the southern extremity of Ward's Island. Unless the wind, however, is very fresh, it is not advisable to attempt to pass through Hell Gate from the southward, after the ebb tide has been running 20 minutes. Abreast of Hallet's Point, vessels meet the strong current which sets them back over on the Gridiron, and they must either go on shore or anchor at great risk.

From the Northward.—Ebb Tide.—The Main Ship Channel is the best at all times, as having deeper water and less current. Vessels must not give the Hog's Back too wide a berth, which might set them on Mill Reef (extending S.E. 130 yards from Great Mill Rock), or compel them to run the middle channel. Always stand close to Negro Point, about 50 yards off.

With a fair wind.—Stand close to the Frying Pan Ripple, and give Great Mill Rock a good berth to avoid the eddies which extend out 3 or 4 vessels' lengths; open the Little Mill Rock until Horn's Hook (the projecting point of Manhattan to the S.W.) and Gallows Hill, on the North end of Blackwell's Island, are nearly in range; steer for Bread and Cheese (the rocks extending from the North point of Blackwell's Island) a little open on the starboard bow, this will bring a vessel into the Middle Channel tide; take the eastern side of Blackwell's Island when the wind is light, and to reach it, when abreast of Negro Head, steer for Hatter's Dock (on the shore eastward of and opposite Blackwell's North point); if the tide is strong, take the western channel.

With the wind S.W., or dead ahead.—In entering the Gate, tack near Negro Point Bluff, and stand towards Scaly Rock (on the opposite side) so as to tack again one vessel's length outside the eddy; the next tack will bring a vessel to windward of Negro Point; make a short tack, which will clear the eddies of Pot Rock; stand directly through the Main Ship Channel over towards the meadows, keeping Horn's Hook and the white house on Gibb's Point open; the next tack will fetch between Great Mill and Little Mill Rocks, on the edge of the eddies; tack with the Bread and Cheese and Gibb's Point in range, make a short tack towards Rynlander's Reef; tack again off Rynlander's Reef, when a vessel, meeting the Middle Channel tide, will be forced up into the wind, the current drifting her to windward clear of all danger.

With a good breeze, vessels may pass through the Middle Channel, having 19 ft. at low water, save two tacks, and avoid the danger of Rynlander's Reef and eddies. After passing the Frying Pan, stand for the North end of Little Mill Rock, until within 60 yards of it, when steer for the South end, and pass within 20 yards of it, tacking before Horn's Hook and the white house on Gibb's Point are in range.

Vessels passing through either the Main Ship Channel or Middle Channel, take the channel *West* of Blackwell's Island, the winds being more steady in that direction. Go pretty close to Horn's Hook, always avoiding the eddies. After passing

Horn's Hook, keep as near the middle of the channel as possible, and never shut in one point of land with another.

Take the same course with a southerly wind, but with a northerly wind cross over to the *East* side of Blackwell's Island, giving the Bread and Cheese a wide berth. The greatest danger from the eddies of Bread and Cheese is on the ebb.

The Eastern Channel is only safe with the wind northward and westward, the line of true current being very narrow. Shave Hallet's Point very closely, and steer with Flood Rock open on the starboard bow; a vessel will apparently be setting upon the rock, but when her bow gets within the influence of the true current, it will put her head directly through the channel. Vessels always get on the Gridiron from those on board not making up their mind in time which channel to take; in light winds steer for Hallet's Point when abreast of Pot Rock, and for the Main Ship Channel when abreast of the Frying Pan.

With the *flood tide* and a fair wind go either around Great Mill Rock or through the Middle Channel.

Tides.—There is a difference in the tides and tidal currents between Governor's Island and Negro Point (Ward's Island), at the eastern entrance to Hell Gate, of about $2\frac{3}{4}$ hours. Between this point and Throg's Neck, near which the easterly and westerly currents meet, the change is small.

At *Hell Gate* it is high water on the full and change days of the moon at $10^h\ 10^m$; springs range $6\frac{1}{4}$, neaps $4\frac{1}{4}$ ft. At *Throg's Neck* at $11^h\ 20^m$; springs range $9\frac{1}{4}$, and neaps 6 ft. And at *New York* (Governor's Island) at $8^h\ 19^m$; springs range $5\frac{1}{4}$, and neaps $3\frac{1}{4}$ ft.

The main body of both tides passes on the East side of Ward's Island; off Negro Point Bluff the change from ebb to flood takes place suddenly. With the ebb, which runs to the westward, the tidal current passes close to Pot Rock; the slack water lasts only a few minutes. South-eastward of the Flood Rock the current of ebb, which is deflected from Hallet's Point, and recoiling from the Gridiron, makes numerous eddies affecting its velocity; its force is lost in the whirls, but the westward motion of the main body is uniform; its greatest velocity is very close to Flood Rock—too close for a vessel to lie safely. Between Great Mill Rock and Ward's Island the ebb current runs a direct course, but that of the flood has numerous, though not violent eddies; the direction of the ebb from Pot Rocks is on to the Gridiron; the current of the flood tide is very weak, the main stream passing to the southward of the Flood Rock. Off the edge of Rynlander's Reef the slack water lasts 20 minutes; the flood tide is very weak, and the eddies frequent; the ebb is both direct and strong. In the Middle Channel of Hell Gate the current of ebb is broad and rapid, with numerous eddies. In the channels of Blackwell's Island, the currents of both flood and ebb are strong and direct.

GENERAL DIRECTIONS for Long Island Sound.

In sailing from Newport, Rhode Island, to a proper berth off Point Judith, your course and distance will be S.W. by S. for 3 leagues; and from thence towards the Little Gull Island lighthouse, W. by S. 8 leagues, and W. by N. 2 leagues; thus, when you get about 6 miles to the S.W. of Point Judith, you will bring the lighthouse at the North end of Block Island to bear S. $\frac{1}{2}$ W., and in the direction of the reef which runs from the northern part of the island. Proceeding thence about 6 leagues, you will leave Watch Hill Point lighthouse and Fisher's Island on your northern side, but be careful to avoid the rocky reef which extends from the S.W. end of the island, outside which you will see the Race Rock, to the S.W. of which is the Valiant Rock; the Little Gull Island will be on your port side; having passed these you will fairly have entered the Sound. The distance from the Race Rock to the Little Gull light is 3 miles; but nearly in a line between Fisher's Island and the Little Gull is the Valiant Rock, which must be carefully avoided.

In proceeding from the Gull Island light up the Sound, steer W. $\frac{1}{2}$ N. for about 8 leagues, and it will bring you up within a mile to the southward of Falkner's Island lighthouse; observe, in running the above course to give the Long Sand Shoal a berth; it lies south-westward of Saybrook, 2 miles from the land, and is a narrow shoal of 4 miles in length, marked by a buoy at each end. From thence a W.S.W. course for 8 leagues, will carry you to a berth off Old Field lighthouse; here steer W. $\frac{1}{4}$ N., 5 leagues, and having passed Eaton's Neck lighthouse, a W. by S. $\frac{1}{2}$ S. course will take you up to Sand's Point light; then leave this light on your port side, and the Execution Rocks lighthouse on your starboard. In steering the above W. $\frac{1}{4}$ N. course from Old Field Point to Eaton's Neck, be careful when making the latter point of the shoals lying to the northward; that stretching from the point has a buoy upon it, at about three-quarters of a mile from the point. The next is a detached shoal of 3 ft. and marked by a buoy, about $1\frac{1}{2}$ mile from the point; between these two buoys there is a channel of 8 fathoms depth. N. by E. $2\frac{1}{4}$ miles from the point, is a shoal of $3\frac{1}{2}$ fathoms, with 8 and 14 fathoms between it and the former shoal of 3 ft. If when up to Falkner's Island you should prefer going to the northward of the Middle Ground, steer as recommended elsewhere; and you may, if you think more prudent, adopt the courses given to the southward of the Middle Ground.

If a ship could have a fair departure from the middle of the Race, and is obliged to run in a dark night or thick weather, the best course would be West, 15 leagues, towards Stratford light, as it would afford the largest run on any one course, and if made good, will carry you 2 miles South of Stratford Point light in 6 fathoms water, and $3\frac{1}{4}$ miles North of the Middle Ground; on this course you will leave Saybrook, Falkner's Island, and New Haven lights on your starboard hand, and Plum Island on your port hand; you will pass 3 miles South of Falkner's Island in 17 fathoms water. When up with Stratford light, and it bears North, 2 miles distant, your course to Sand's Point light is W.S.W. $\frac{1}{4}$ W., 11 leagues.

Should you wish to anchor under Falkner's Island, there is good holding ground on the East or West side in $2\frac{1}{2}$ or 3 fathoms, but the best place, with the wind from the West, is close to the N.E. point of the island, the lighthouse bearing S.W. by S., in $2\frac{1}{2}$ fathoms North from the island a narrow shoal puts off a quarter of a mile, and is bold-to; but you are to the North of it when the centre of Goose Island bears S.W. by W., and when the light bears S E. by E. you may run for it and anchor.

The course from Sand's Point light to Hart Island is S.W., and the distance about $2\frac{1}{4}$ miles; to the West of this there is good anchorage for vessels of any size. If a ship, in making these courses good, should be under the necessity of turning to windward, they must be careful to avoid two rocks, one called the Gangway Rock, the other the Success Rock; the former bears W. 28° S. from Sand's Point lighthouse, distant a mile, having a black spar buoy floating perpendicularly, in 19 ft. water, upon it; the other bearing N.W. by N. from the East bluff of Cow Bay, distant half a mile, on which an iron spindle is erected. On Gangway Rock, which tapers to a point, there is only 6 ft. water, making it very dangerous; but Success Rock is

U. S.—Part I.   L dry at low water. Between the two is a channel with 2¼ fathoms in it; they bear from each other N. 40° W. and S. 40° E., being distant one-third of a mile.

The course from Hart Island to Throg's Point light is S.S.W., about a league; taking care to avoid the Stepping Stones, which lie on your port hand, and have a black spar buoy upon them, in 19 ft. water; they are steep-to, while the soundings on your starboard side are regular to 3 fathoms. , In passing Throg's Point light, do not haul up until you have passed it at least one-eighth of a mile; and when the light bears N.W. steer West, which will carry you in mid-channel. A *shoal* of 17 feet extends S.S.E. from Throg's Point ; but, by following the above directions, that will be easily avoided. From Throg's Point to Hunt's Harbour the course is West, observing to keep in mid-channel.

From Old Field Point light to Eaton's Neck light the bearing and distance are W., northerly, 13 miles; Crane Neck is 2 miles to the westward of Old Field Point, and the land between it and Eaton's Neck forms Smithstown Bay, in which the water shoals gradually from 12 to 3 fathoms. There is a *reef* running from the northern part of Eaton's Neck, to the distance of half a mile, as noticed previously, near the edge of which are 6 and 5 fathoms. From Eaton's Neck the northern sandy point of Lloyd's Neck bears W. ¼ S., distant 4 miles ; between them lies the deep bay of Huntington, where a ship of any size may obtain anchorage, only keeping the eastern shore on board ; the entrance is easy, and the ground good.

Within Lloyd's Harbour on the West, and Cow Harbour on the East, are from 4 to 3 fathoms water, with a bottom of mud. Here N.E. winds, blowing fresh, frequently swell the rise of the tides, which commonly average from 7 to 12 ft. On the western side of Lloyd's Neck is Oyster Bay, the entrance to which is narrow; when going in here, keep nearer Lloyd's Neck until you have passed the tail of the Middle, this being a sandy flat, which runs from Hog Island, on the western side, to the distance of 180 fathoms; when fairly within it the bay is clear, and the anchorage good throughout.

From Lloyd's Point to Metinicook Point, the course and distance are W.S.W. ¾ W., 7 miles; and from Metinicook Point to Sands Point light, the course is nearly W.S.W., and the distance 5 miles; between these two last points is Hempstead Bay, in which is good anchorage, keeping the eastern shore on board. At three-quarters of a mile to the northward of Sands Point lighthouse are the Execution Rocks.

LONG ISLAND.—South Coast.—When Block Island bears North, distant 4 or 5 leagues, you cannot see any land to the northward or eastward, but as you approach the island you see Montauk Point to the westward, making a long low point, on which is the lighthouse. In sailing W.S.W., you will make no remarkable object on Long Island, its southern shore from East to West appearing at a distance like islands, except Shinnicock and Fire Island lighthouses. From Fire Island light a shoal extends South three-quarters of a mile, and joins the bar, which is very dangerous, as it shoals suddenly from 8 to 6 fathoms, then directly on the shoal, when the flood tide sets very strong. It is not safe to approach the shore nearer than 2 miles, when the light bears to the E. of N. To the eastward of the light the shore is bold; the bar is subject to change, and has 7 ft. of water on it. When Fire Island light bears North in 10 fathoms water, you may steer W. by S., which will carry you up with Sandy Hook light.

Shinnicock Bay.—There are a few inlets on the South side of the island. The first one of any importance is Shinnicock Bay, about 34 miles to the westward of Montauk Point.

The LIGHTHOUSE is erected on Pondquogue Point on the North side of the bay, in lat. 40° 50' 57", and long. 72° 29' 55". The building is of brick, 150 ft. in

FIRE ISLAND LIGHTHOUSE.

height, and 160 ft. above the sea, exhibiting a *fixed* light, visible 20 miles. This light is 1 mile North of the outer or ocean beach, 35 miles to the eastward of Fire Island lighthouse, and 32½ miles to the westward of Montauk Point lighthouse.

Fire Island Inlet.—The next place is Fire Island Inlet. Fire Island Inlet is navigable for vessels drawing 9 ft. water; it is subject to change, and those who are acquainted with its entrance are guided by the breakers when entering. The *shoal* off Fire Island lighthouse extends about a mile from the shore, and a mile from where the lighthouse stands. It is bold-to on the eastern side, having 6 fathoms close to it.

FIRE ISLAND LIGHTHOUSE is on the E. side of the inlet, in lat. 40° 37' 53", and long. 73° 12' 51". The tower is built of yellow brick, 150 ft. in height, and 166 feet above the sea, and exhibits a *revolving* light every minute, visible 22 miles. This lighthouse is 37 miles from the highlands of Navesink lights, 31 miles from Sandy Hook lightvessel; 35 miles from Great West Bay light, and 67½ miles from Montauk Point.

Gilgo, New, and *Hog Island Inlets* are all barred harbours, having very little water. The channel of New Inlet, into South Oyster Bay, is marked by a *spar buoy,* painted with *white* and *black perpendicular stripes,* and surmounted by a cage, placed outside the bar, in 5 fathoms at low water; and a spindle on shore, in range with the cupola on Woodsburgh Hotel, painted with *red* and *black horizontal stripes,* and having a day-mark on top in the shape of a barrel.

Rockaway Inlet is about 9 miles N.E. of Sandy Hook. This bar is subject to change, and extends 2 miles from shore; the depth on the bar is about 12 ft. at low water. A striped spar buoy is placed outside, and one inside, to mark the channel over the bar, which, owing to its shifting nature, should only be used by those experienced.

Should you make Block Island, bearing North of you, distant 5 or 6 leagues, as before observed, you cannot see any land to the northward or eastward; but as you near the island you will see Montauk Point to the westward, making a long low point, running out eastward, on which is the lighthouse; steering from hence about W.S.W. ¼ W., Long Island will, when at a distance, appear broken, like islands; and when you bring Fire Island light to bear North, in 15 fathoms, a W ¾ N. course will carry you up to Sandy Hook. The quality of the bottom is various, viz., yellow, red, brown, blue, and grey sand, within short distances.

You will see the Highlands of Navesink before you come in sight of Sandy Hook. On the Highlands, which is the most remarkable land on that shore, two lighthouses are erected.

When bound to New York, should you happen to make the land to the southward, and fall in with Cape May (on which is a lighthouse, exhibiting a revolving light), the greatest caution is necessary, to avoid the shoals near the cape, as well as the 5-fathom bank lying in the parallel of the cape, and 15¼ miles to the eastward of it, having only 12 ft. water on its shoalest part. In thick weather, come no nearer this part of the coast than 20 or 19 fathoms; but when to the northward of 39°, you may safely approach to 13 or 14 fathoms.

As a number of vessels have been lost, bound to New York, from heaving-to with their heads on shore, we cannot too strongly urge on the ship-master the necessity, *if he is in doubt of his position,* of heaving-to with his head off shore.

NEW YORK HARBOUR.

The **CITY of NEW YORK**, one of the chief commercial places in the world, is situated on the South end of Manhattan or New York Island, at the confluence of the Hudson or North River, and a strait called the East River, which connects Long Island Sound with the harbour of New York. It is the capital of the State of New York, and in population, commerce, and wealth, the largest city in America.

The first perfect chart of the harbour was published in 1845, by the U.S. Coast Survey. New editions of this chart show extensive changes in the banks and channels in the entrance.

The system of lighting and beaconage is complete, and is quite sufficient to ensure safety with ordinary caution, but it must be evident that exact bearings and directions cannot be depended on for any length of time. Therefore what follows refers to the existing condition of the channels and buoys, and must be received with some caution in the future.

Lights, &c.

The HIGHLANDS OF NAVESINK are frequently the first land discovered on arriving on the coast, and may be seen 8 leagues off. When first seen they appear like an island, rather level on the top, except some irregular risings on the West or inland side. The highest point is Mount Mitchill, 282 feet. They form the S.E. angle of New York Harbour. Tompkins Hill, on Staten Island, near the Narrows, is 307 ft. high, and Hempstead Hill, on Long Island, East of the entrance to New York, 319 ft.

HIGHLAND LIGHTS.—The elevated lighthouses which stood on the Highlands of Navesink, were first lighted up in the evening of the 21st June, 1828. The two lighthouses are built of reddish gray granite, situated 100 yards apart, the northern one being in lat. 40° 23′ 45″, and long. 73° 58′ 51″. They are each 53 ft. in height, and 248 ft. above the sea, exhibiting *fixed* lights, visible 25 miles each. The bearing and distance between the northern or fixed light and the lighthouse on Sandy Hook are N. ¼ W. 4 miles.

SANDY HOOK, extending in a N. by W. direction nearly 5 miles from the Navesink lights, has towards its North end a lighthouse 77 ft. in height, and showing a *fixed* light at 90 ft. above the sea. At about 2 cables' lengths W.N.W. from it is the *telegraph*, a small white tower. The light may sometimes be discerned from aloft at the distance of 10 leagues. It is generally visible 15 miles. This light is intended to mark the entrance to the channel.

Beacon Lights.—In addition to the above light, there are two beacon lights on Sandy Hook. The N.E. beacon light is situated on the North point of the Hook, two-thirds of a mile N. by W. from the principal light, and the S.W. beacon on the bay side of Sandy Hook, at a quarter of a mile N.W. of the principal light. These two lights are elevated 35 ft. each, visible 10 miles. The lighthouses are coloured white, and there is a fog horn at the northern one. When the West beacon light is obscured by the screen, it marks the outer edge of the bar; and when just clear to the northward of Sandy Hook lighthouse it marks the turning-point round the S.W. spit into the Main Ship Channel.

FLOATING LIGHT.—Off Sandy Hook is a lightship of about 360 tons burden, showing *two lights*, which were changed to *red lights* in 1873, each elevated

NEW YORK HARBOUR.—LIGHTS, ETC. 77

45 feet above the sea. In 1868 the berth of this float was 6¾ miles W. by S. from Sandy Hook light, and the same distance W.N.W. from the Highlands lights, in 14 fathoms water. She is also provided with a bell of 800 pounds weight, to be tolled in thick weather, alternately with a fog horn.

A *lightvessel* was placed, in September, 1874, on the South side of the South channel, to mark the wreck of the *Scotland*. She was placed in 7 fathoms water, W. ½ N., 4 miles from Sandy Hook lightvessel.

Within the harbour of New York there are six leading lights, intended as ranges for the different channels.

Gedney's Channel Lights, situated near Point Comfort, 5 miles West of Sandy Hook. These lights are two in number; the front one, Bayside beacon, on the Jersey shore, is on the keeper's house in a turret, and is of a white colour, with the top of the lantern black, being 45 ft. above the sea. The rear light, Wilson's beacon, is in a tower 76 ft. above the sea. These are both *fixed* lights, visible 12 and 14 miles respectively, and form a range W. by S. from the inside of the bar to the S.W. spit.

Swash Channel Lights.—These lights are on Staten Island, one near Elm-tree Station, and the rear one at New Dorp. The front light is elevated 62 ft. above the sea. This lighthouse is painted with two white and one red horizontal bands, with the roof of the lantern red. The rear light is on the keeper's dwelling in a turret, 180 ft. above the sea, and is painted red. These lights form a range to N.W. for the Swash Channel from outside the bar to main channel, above Romer stone beacon; both *fixed* lights, visible 14 miles each.

Main Ship Channel Lights are two in number, and situated on the Jersey shore, near the beach, and Chapel Hill, N.W. by W. 3½ miles from the Highland lights. The northern light, or Conover beacon, bears from Sandy Hook light S.W. 3½ miles, to be used after turning the S.W. spit buoy. The front light is in a tower 60 ft. above the sea, and is painted with two white and one red horizontal bands; roof of lantern red. On each side of this, to distinguish it when the ground is covered with snow, black frames are placed. The Conover beacon is 3½ miles from the S.W. spit buoy.

The rear light is shown on Chapel Hill at 224 ft. above the sea. The front of the dwelling, which supports the light-tower, shows from the direction of the main channel of the bay a surface of 25 ft. by 40 ft., painted *white*. Frames of the same dimensions, each 25 ft. by 40 ft., and covered with boards, are shown on each end of the dwelling, and are coloured *black*.

The surface of the entire front is therefore 25 ft. by 120 ft., and shows *white* between two *black* surfaces. The distance from the S.W. spit buoy to Chapel Hill beacon is 5 miles.

These two lights are situated 1½ mile apart, and are both *fixed* lights, visible 12 miles each. After turning the S.W. spit, by keeping these two lights in range, you run in mid-channel until Robin's Reef light is open with the light at the Narrows; keeping them open clears the West Bank. Especial attention is called to the distances of these day-marks from the S.W. spit buoy, and the difficulty of distinguishing them unless the day is moderately favourable.

Fort Tompkins Light, *Staten Island.*—There is a white lighthouse near to Fort Tompkins, which marks out the western point of the Narrows; it has a *fixed* light, 89 feet above the level of the sea, and visible 15 miles. There is a very strong fort and barracks in the rear of Fort Tompkins.

At *Fort Lafayette*, on the opposite side of the Narrows, a fog bell is established, sounding alternately one blow and two blows at intervals of 20 seconds.

Robins Reef Light stands 3¼ miles northward of Fort Tomkins Light. It is a white stone tower built on the reef, and marks the western edge of the channel up to the city, and into Newark Bay through Kill Van Kull. It is a *fixed* light, visible 12 miles, 66 ft. above the sea. It has a fog bell.

Princes Bay Light.—This lighthouse, which is painted white, stands near the S.W. end of Staten Island, on the West side of Princes Bay, bearing from Sandy Hook light W.N.W., distant 10 miles, and West from the Knoll buoy, and is intended to guide vessels to Perth Amboy and Raritan River, and will serve as a guide to vessels from mid-channel buoy at the entrance to Gedney's Channel to the line of main channel range lights on Point Comfort, and to the line of Swash Channel range lights at Elm Tree and New Dorp on Staten Island. The lighthouse is 33 feet in height, and at 106 feet above the sea exhibits a *fixed* light, varied by a flash every two minutes.

At *Fort Columbus*, the N.W. point of Governor's Island, a *fog bell* is sounded.

ROMER BEACON.—A stone beacon, 25 ft. high, is erected on the N.W. point of the Romer Bank, and 9 ft. above the water. It was intended as a guide for the Swash Channel; but being placed at the wrong end of the shoal, vessels bound in will infallibly get on shore if they run for it. It bears from the light at the Narrows S. 15° E., and from Sandy Hook N. 10° W. There is an iron beacon S.E. of it.

The channels leading into the harbour are as follow:—

The FALSE HOOK CHANNEL, running along the shore of Sandy Hook on the West, and the outer Middle Ground, the Oil Spot, and the False Hook Shoals on the East. The direction is to the West of North, and it is marked by *spar buoys*.

The SOUTH CHANNEL lies outside the above-named shoals. It leads up to the Swash Channel, and the leading mark through both is the two lights on Staten Island in one, as above mentioned. It is marked by *can buoys*.

GEDNEY'S CHANNEL, discovered by Lieut. T. R. Gedney, U.S. N., is to the North of the last, and is marked by *nun buoys*.

The SWASH CHANNEL, a continuation of the South Channel, as before mentioned, runs between Flynn's Knoll and the Dry Romer, marked by the stone and iron beacons, and is marked by *can buoys*.

The EAST CHANNEL, to the northward of the Dry Romer, is marked by *spar buoys*.

The FOURTEEN-FEET CHANNEL, still farther North, is but seldom used.

The MAIN SHIP CHANNEL, into which these lead, is marked by NUN BUOYS.

Tides.

	H.	M.
It is high water, on the full and change days, at Sandy Hook (Corrected Establishment) at..	7	20
But the stream of tide continues to set in, at the rate of 2 knots, until ..	9	0

	FT.	IN.
Mean rise and fall of spring tides...	6	3
——————— neap tides...	3	9
Rise of highest tide, observed May 30, 1836, during a heavy E.N.E. gale .	9	1

	H.	M.
At New York, at Governor's Island, the Corrected Establishment is	8	19
Mean rise and fall of spring tides	5	8
——————— neap tides	3	8

The vertical rise of tide is sometimes checked by the westerly or north-westerly winds, so as to lower the water on the bar to 3¼ fathoms. Easterly or north-easterly winds frequently raise it to 5 fathoms.

GEDNEYS CHANNEL. 79

The flood sets strongly to the westward from the S.W. spit, until above the Upper Middle, whence it runs up in the channel-course to the Narrows.

The tide, during the last quarter-ebb, sets from North or Hudson's River, around Fort Point, and flows up the East River, at the rate of 3 knots; whence, with a like velocity, it returns two hours before the North River high water time. This affords great convenience to ships in shifting their berth from one river to the other. Ships of war may, during the summer season, ride in either river, in the stream; in the winter they haul-to, or moor between the wharfs. The *twelve-feet ledge* off the town, and the sunken wrecks and *chevaux-de-frize*, are shown by the ripple of the tide.

Variation of the compass in 1875 is 7° W.

The times of high and low water are very nearly the same all the way from Delaware River to Block Island and South of Nantucket. Consequently, vessels bound to New York, and making the land in the vicinity of either of these places, and in sailing thence in the customary routes towards Sandy Hook, they will have the same succession of tides, within some 15 minutes, as if they remained off these points. As the flood tide sets in generally to the northward and on shore, and the ebb the contrary, they will know by the time that elapses from their departure, and the period of tide at which they started, what tidal currents they may expect to meet with as they approach New York.

Anchorage may be had in Sandy Hook Bay. When as far in as the point of the Hook where the East beacon stands, haul into the bay S.W., giving the Hook a berth of half a mile, until the lighthouse bears East or E. by N., when you may anchor in from 4 to 6 fathoms, muddy bottom.

Pilots.—New York pilots generally board vessels from the southward between Delaware River and Barnegat Inlet, at from 10 to 80 miles off shore; and those from the eastward between Nantucket Shoals and Fire Island lighthouse, at from 10 to 15 miles from shore. Boats having pilots on board are always found near Sandy Hook. In approaching New York Bay in thick weather, or in the night time, without a pilot, you should bring-to in 12 or 15 fathoms, unless the weather is threatening from the eastward, when it is most prudent to avoid a lee shore.

Directions.—Having made the lightvessel, which should be the object sought for, especially by a stranger, and still without and waiting for a pilot, be careful when tacking towards either the Jersey or Long Island shores not to decrease your water below 10 fathoms. Should no pilot be obtainable and it becomes advisable to run in, then the following directions will be found of service, bearing in mind that the only channels recommended to those ignorant of the navigation are Gedney's and the Main Ship Channel, in which are 23 ft. at mean low water, or the South and Swash Channels, with 21 and 17 ft. respectively.

Gedneys Channel.—Entering by Gedneys* and the *Main Ship Channels*, steer N.W. ¼ W. from the lightvessel for the *black* and *white* perpendicular-striped nun buoy at the entrance of the former, then W. by N. 1¼ mile, or till the two range lights near Point Comfort come in line, bearing about W. by S., when you must haul up for them on that bearing, and continue till the two Main Channel lights, just westward of the Highlands of Navesink, are brought in range, nearly S. by W., which will also be shown by the main light on Sandy Hook being open South of the

---

* A stranger, when up with the buoy at the entrance of Gedneys Channel, may cross the bar in 24 feet water by bringing the East Beacon on Sandy Hook in line with the inner (or Wilson's) light at Point Comfort, nearly W. ¾ S. When the water deepens again to 4 fathoms, steer to the northward, so as to bring Gedneys *range* lights on, to pass the Hook.

West Beacon. Steer now, with these latter lights in line over the stern, about N. by E., which will lead up towards the Narrows, clear of West Bank and Cravens Shoal. As soon as Robins Reef light bears N. by W., shape a course for it, passing in mid-channel through the Narrows, and when about three-quarters of a mile from the lighthouse haul up N.E. by N. for the city.

South Channel.—Entering by the South and Swash Channels, steer for the light-vessel W. by N., until the Elm Tree or Swash Channel range lights on Staten Island, which can be seen outside the bar, come in a line bearing about N.W. ¼ N., then steer towards them till the *red* can buoy (No. 8), which marks the "Upper Middle," is passed, or till the Main Ship Channel range lights (in one, nearly S. by W.) is on, when haul up on that range towards the Narrows, and proceed as before. Vessels drawing more than 17 feet should not be taken through the Swash Channel on the above range at low water.

Having proceeded on the line of the Elm Tree lights from the South Channel bar to where the Point Comfort lights are in one, the direction of the latter may be followed, and the Main Channel lights brought in line as before, if drawing too much water to pass through the Swash Channel.

The False Hook Channel, safe though narrow, runs along the eastern side of Sandy Hook, between it and the Outer Middle, the Oil Spot, and False Hook Shoals. From 15 to 18 ft. of water can be carried through at the distance of one quarter of a mile or so from the shore; but as no good ranges can be given, this passage should only be attempted by those acquainted. The shoalest part of the shoals, namely 12 feet on Oil Spot, lies three-quarters of a mile off shore, and S.E. by E. ¼ E. from the main lighthouse on the Hook.

The East Channel has its entrance about one mile northward of Gedneys, and runs in nearly parallel to that and Swash Channel, being separated from them by the Dry Romer, &c.; it is safe for vessels of light draught, but is very little used, as the ranges are distant and uncertain, and the East Bank shoals up very suddenly.

The Fourteen-Feet Channel, about 2½ miles from the shore of Coney Island, is narrow, winding, and without leading marks or buoys. It is the northernmost of the channels into New York Bay, and but very seldom used.

GENERAL DIRECTIONS.—The Gulf Stream, by its high temperature, gives the first warning of an approach to the coast. In lat. 38¼° N. it is nearly 360 miles from the land, measuring on a parallel of latitude, and immediately after passing through it the temperature will be observed to fall. There is also a fall of temperature on striking soundings, which will indicate the time when the deep sea lead ought to be used. With the decrease of soundings the colour of the water will change,—as from a dark blue in a depth of 150 fathoms the colour alters to a light blue in 50 fathoms, which again becomes of a greenish tint as the coast is approached.

Soundings.—Up to the 20-fathom curve or line they follow the general form of the shore, and between 80 and 100 fathoms the water suddenly deepens. The 20-fathom line is 31 miles from Cape May, in an East by South direction, but less than 7 miles from Montauk Point. A depth of 20 fathoms off the East point of Long Island is therefore too near the land, unless with a commanding wind; while 20 fathoms off Cape May is at a safe distance from the shore.

The latitude of a ship's place is usually better known than the longitude, but the latter is most important on approaching this coast, and can be determined approximately from the latitude, in connection with the distance, curves, or lines of depth.

East of the entrance to the Delaware, the bottom in 100 fathoms is mostly dark

SOUNDINGS. 81

gray sand mixed with broken shells. To the North of this parallel it is mostly green and blue mud mixed with sand.

Eastward of Delaware Bay, the bottom, between 100 and 40 fathoms, is most frequently sand and broken shells; inside of 40 fathoms, gray or yellow sand with black specks. North of this parallel the bottom is as often mud as sand, the mud being more frequent going to the N.E. until off Block Island, where the bottom from 100 to 20 fathoms is mostly green mud or ooze, known as the Block Island soundings. Green mud or ooze cannot be found within 15 miles of Block Island, and seldom to the West of the meridian of Montauk Point in less than 30 fathoms water.

Between 40 and 20 fathoms off the coast of Long Island and New Jersey, the character of the bottom changes so often between these depths, that constant reference must be made to the descriptions on the chart.

The 5-fathom bank off the Delaware has 13 feet on it. A lightvessel is stationed 3 miles to the S.W. by S. of this bank, which vessels from sea will leave on the starboard hand when bound into Delaware Bay, and on the port hand when bound to the northward. In an E.S.E. ⅜ S direction from Barnegat Inlet the 20-fathom curve or line extends as far out as 45 miles.

There are other banks from 2 to 4 miles N. by W. and N. of this 13-ft. bank, least water 3½ fathoms; another southward 3 miles, and another directly eastward of Townsend Inlet, both with 4 fathoms.

In general the soundings decrease regularly and more or less gradually from 100 or 80 fathoms to the shore, but there are some remarkable exceptions, among which may be mentioned the Five Fathom and other banks at the entrance to the Delaware. The principal exceptions are, however, the *mud holes*, which extend in a S.E. direction from Sandy Hook, and form a very remarkable gorge. When passing over them, the least distance from New York, at which a depth of 100 fathoms is found, is 100 miles.

The Mud Holes.—The first holes met with after leaving New York are the *Twenty-three, Twenty-one,* and *Thirty-two Fathom Holes,* which lie at the distance of 11, 12¼, and 17¼ miles from Sandy Hook lighthouse, in a south-easterly direction. They are not very extensive, but you may know when you are over them by the lead dropping suddenly into them from a depth of 16, 13, or 17 fathoms. Between these holes and the New Jersey coast the soundings decrease from 15 to 13 and 7 fathoms, the latter depth being close to the shore.

The next hole, that with which seamen are particularly acquainted, is called the *First Thirty-seven Fathom Hole.* It is about 8 miles long and 1¼ mile wide, and has 22 fathoms immediately outside it, with soundings of 20 and 19 fathoms close to its south-western extremity. Its centre is distant from Sandy Hook lighthouse 28 miles in a S.E. ¾ S. direction.

The *Second Thirty-seven Fathom Hole* lies 7 miles to the south-eastward of the First, with Sandy Hook bearing N.W. ½ N., distant 39 miles. It is about 5 miles in extent, and has 27 fathoms outside it in a N.E. direction, but only 21 fathoms in a southerly direction.

The *Thirty-eight Fathom Hole* lies 11 miles to the S.E. by E. ¼ E. from the Hole last mentioned, in lat. 39° 55' N., and long. 73° 10' W. Its length is 8½ miles from North to South, and its width 2½ miles. From it Sandy Hook bears N.W., distant 50 miles. Close to it are 25 to 29 fathoms, and near its northern end are 25 and 24 fathoms.

U.S.—Part I. M

At 11 miles South (true) from the Thirty-eight Fathom Hole is another of *Thirty-five Fathoms*, which is about 4 miles in extent, and lies with Sandy Hook bearing N.W. by N. 63 miles. It has 27 fathoms close to it outside, which deepen rapidly to 30 and 34 fathoms.

The *Fifty Fathom Hole* lies in lat. 40° N., and long. 72° 30' W., at about 50 miles from the shore of Long Island. It is 4 miles in extent, and has 35 and 38 fathoms close-to all round. From it Sandy Hook bears N.W. by W. ¼ W., distant 74 miles.

The ninth and last of the mud holes is the most extraordinary of the whole series, as the lead at once falls from 55 to 60 fathoms into a depth of 145 fathoms. It is situated about 12 miles within the edge of soundings of 100 fathoms, and lies in lat. 39° 38' N., and long. 72° 23' W. Its extent is not more than 2⅓ miles, and from it Sandy Hook bears N.W. ¼ W. distant 89 miles.

It has been observed that in approaching Sandy Hook, the soundings to the southward are full of black specks, between the depths of 10 and 20 fathoms; in the true channel they are of mud; while to the northward, near Long Island, they are of black and white sand.

Foggy Weather, &c.—The instructions deduced from the foregoing observations will doubtless be of considerable service to vessels in the night time or in thick and hazy weather. Therefore, when coming from the eastward and striking soundings in more than 35 fathoms, green mud, steer to the northward of West, shoaling the water very gradually on that course. If beating against a westerly wind, do not stand into less than 18 fathoms on the northerly tack, till nearly up with Fire Island lighthouse, for the soundings inside of 25 fathoms decrease very rapidly towards the Long Island shore, but very slowly towards that of New Jersey, a distinction that should be carefully borne in mind.

When coming from the southward a depth of 15 fathoms and upwards should be preserved, for to the northward of Barnegat Inlet 10 or 12 fathoms is found within 1¼ mile of the beach. When the water has decreased to 15 fathoms, the lead should be kept constantly going and the bottom examined; gravelly bottom indicates too near an approach to the land.

Remarks on approaching the land.—The appearance of Long Island is generally low and level, excepting a few hills, which lie 40 miles to the westward of Montauk Point. Along the South side of the island a flat extends all along the shore, which at the mouths of some of the inlets, especially those westward of Fire Island, runs off about a mile. Your course from Montauk Point to Sandy Hook is S.W. by W. ¾ W., 60 miles, and then W. ¼ N., 45 miles. At 12 miles southward of Montauk Point there are 26 and 23 fathoms, coarse gray sand and gravel, with black specks, which depth is maintained at the same distance from the land until you get to about 20 miles eastward of Fire Island lighthouse, when you will meet with soundings of 20 to 18 fathoms, thence decreasing to 16, 15, 14, and 13 fathoms, and again deepening to 16 fathoms as you approach the harbour of New York. Within this distance from the shore it is not safe for a large ship to approach without a commanding breeze, because the coast of Long Island is steep-to, having 6 and 7 fathoms immediately off the edge of the flat, and the line of 20 fathoms approaches Montauk Point to within 7 miles, the soundings between decreasing very rapidly. In the vicinity of Fire Island Inlet, the depth is shoaler, there being 12 to 15 fathoms at 8 miles from the shore. Outside the depth of 20 and thence to 40 fathoms, the character of the bottom changes so rapidly that constant reference must be made to the chart, as no general description would be at all applicable. The difference in latitude between Montauk Point and Sandy Hook is only about 37 miles, but there will be no difficulty in determining

SOUNDINGS.

which of the two you are approaching, as the character of the lights and that of the soundings affords an infallible distinction.

In passing the Nantucket shoals between latitudes 39° and 39° 29', you should take notice, if possible, when you have crossed the Gulf Stream; as, at the distance of 10 leagues, within it, you may expect soundings; so soon as you obtain which, you will possibly experience a S.W. current.

Should you now be running for the New Jersey coast, to the northward of Great and Little Egg Harbours, you may suddenly strike one of the Mud Holes previously mentioned as existing in a south-easterly direction from Sandy Hook. In that case it will be necessary to take particular notice of your position, because many ship-masters have been deceived, especially by those near Sandy Hook, and fancying themselves at a greater distance from the coast of New Jersey than they really were, have run on and put themselves to considerable inconvenience, and even danger. It should be remembered that the coast of New Jersey is steep-to, there being 6 to 10 fathoms immediately off it.

In beating to windward of Sandy Hook, in from 12 to 15 fathoms, when waiting for a pilot or a wind, either by day or night, when the lighthouse bears nearly West, you will be sufficiently near to Long Island.

Should you fall in so far to the southward as to approach *Cape Hatteras*, be very cautious of its shoals, and bear away to the N.N.E., so as to obtain soundings on the Jersey shore. When you have gained 28 or 26 fathoms in latitude 40°, haul in to make the land.

It has been remarked that ships from sea, approaching any part of the American coast between Long Island and Cape Hatteras, if in doubt about their reckoning, should take notice of what is commonly named the Gulf Weed, which is more plentiful, and in larger clusters to the eastward of the Gulf Stream than in it, where the sprigs are but small and few. Within the stream there is no weed, unless in rare instances, and there, as before observed, the colour of the water changes to a still darker and muddy colour.

If you fall in to the *northward* of the *Chesapeake*, approach the Chincoteague Shoals no nearer than into 15 fathoms; from this steer N. by E. until nearly up with Great Egg Harbour, keeping the lead going. You may advance towards this place, and to the northward, to the depth of 15 fathoms. From Great Egg Harbour to lat. 39° 30' the shore trends about N.E. by N., and thence to the high lands of Navesink nearly N. by E.

Should you fall in so as to make the *Capes of the Delaware*, keep above 6 leagues off the land, or in not less than 15 fathoms, in order to avoid the bank named the Five Fathom Bank, which lies 15 miles E. by S. from Cape May lighthouse, and is marked by a lightvessel moored in 12 fathoms S.E. $\frac{1}{2}$ S. from its shoalest (13 feet) spot, which exhibits two *fixed* lights, and is provided with a bell and fog-horn. After passing the bank, which is steep-to, you may haul up N.E. for 45 miles, which will lead into 15 fathoms, off Little Egg Harbour, and by altering the course to N.N.E. for 18 miles, will reach Barnegat. Here the soundings will be coarse gray sand, with a few shells and gravel; and having these soundings, you may steer along in the direction of the land North by East, on which course you will have from 16 to 18 fathoms. In the day time you will notice the Woodlands, between Barnegat and Sandy Hook, which is a remarkable part of the coast, resembling, it is said, no other land between Cape May and the high lands of Navesink. It is in this part of the coast of New Jersey, between Barnegat and Shrewsbury Inlets, that so many fatal shipwrecks occur from approaching too near the land; they principally take place on Squan and Long Branch Beaches.

Barnegat may be readily known in the day time, even when the breakers are not seen, as there is a long grove of wood, back in the country, apparently 3 or 4 miles long, directly within the inlet named the Little Swamp. With the North end of this land directly abreast, you will be to the northward of Barnegat.

There is another grove, directly in the rear of Egg Harbour, which is known by the name of the Great Swamp; this is much higher than the former, the Little Swamp, and is 8 or 10 miles in length. These swamps cannot be seen at one time, as the distance between Egg Harbour and Barnegat is 6 leagues.

Barnegat lies S. by W. $\frac{1}{4}$ W., 43 miles from Sandy Hook. When hauling in for the Woodlands, already mentioned, with the wind off shore, you may, in a small ship, and exercising great care, keep within a short distance of the coast, until up with the Highlands; and, should your vessel not draw more than 10 feet, may continue your course until up with the northernmost part of the cedars on Sandy Hook; after which steer according to the subsequent instructions. When approaching Sandy Hook there are some shoal spots of 10 and 20 feet, about 2½ miles before reaching the entrance of Shrewsbury Inlet; and also along the shore of Sandy Hook there are some banks of 10 to 17 feet, named the Middle Ground, Oil Spot, &c., all of which must be cautiously avoided.

On the southern side of the entrance to New York Harbour are the Highlands of Navesink, the highest part of which, Mount Mitchell, is estimated to be 282 feet above the sea. This high land of Navesink is a very important mark when approaching the coast, as it can be seen from the First Thirty-seven Hole, when you are 8 leagues off, and in a depth of 30 or 36 fathoms water. It appears at first like an island, being pretty level on the summit, excepting some irregular risings towards Point Comfort, on the West end or inland side. As you approach nearer to the harbour, you will see some other high land, situated more at the back of the bay, the first of which may be Hempstead Hill in Long Island, the summit of which is about 320 feet above the sea level. On Staten Island is Tomkins Hill, at the back of the small village of Tompkinsville, which is estimated to be 307 feet high. Both these hills will be seen after you have made Navesink

SECTION II.

SANDY HOOK TO CHARLESTON.

To the valley at the foot of the Highlands of Navesink succeeds a tract of low table land, and southward of this is a considerable and remarkable tract of woodland, which terminates at 6 leagues S. by W. from the Navesink lighthouses; next follows an extensive lagoon, named *Barnegat Sound*, which is fronted by a narrow strip of low land. The coast, from the Highlands of Navesink to the elbow of an island called *Barnegat Long Beach*, trends nearly S. by W. 16 leagues, and the soundings regularly decrease toward the shore from 12 to 7 and 5 fathoms.

Barnegat Inlet.—At 12 leagues to the southward of New York Harbour is the Inlet of Barnegat, or the entrance of Barnegat Sound. A shoal bar extends outward from this place to the distance of 2 miles, and the bottom is an admixture of mud, shells, and gravel. The outer edge of the shoal is steep-to, and you may pass it in 6 fathoms within a short distance from the outer breaker; but during night keep at least in 9 or 10 fathoms. The soundings more to the northward in these depths are fine white sand, with very hard bottom.

BARNEGAT LIGHTHOUSE.—On the South side of the inlet is a lofty tower, the upper part of which is red, the lower half white; it is 150 ft. high, and shows a bright revolving light every 10 seconds, at an elevation of 165 ft., seen 22 miles and upwards; lat. 39° 46′ N., long. 74° 6′ W.

Barnegat also may be readily known in the day, even when the breakers are not seen, as there is a long grove of wood, back in the country, apparently 3 or 4 miles long, directly within the inlet, and commonly called the *Little Swamp*. With the North end of this land directly abreast, you will be to the northward of Barnegat.

When advancing from the *southward* for New York Harbour, and hauling in for the woodlands above described, you may, with the wind off shore, keep within a cable's length of the coast until up with the Highlands; and should your vessel not draw more than 10 ft., you continue your course until up with the northernmost part of the cedars on Sandy Hook, whence you proceed for the harbour according to the preceding instructions.

Between the elbow of Barnegat Long Beach and Cape May, at the mouth of the Delaware, the coast forms a gentle concavity, but its general trend is nearly S.W. ¼ S., and the distance 18 leagues. The land is generally low and broken, forming several islets and inlets. The soundings are regular, commonly 8 to 10 fathoms at 2 leagues from shore; but there is a sand bar at every inlet, several of which extend off to a considerable distance.

LITTLE EGG HARBOUR, in the parallel of 39° 30′, long. 74° 19′, is a small harbour formed by low islets or beaches on the East, and by salt marshes on the West. It is also known as the port of *Tuckerton*. To a stranger this harbour cannot be recommended, unless as a retreat in case of emergency, several shoals about the entrance being dangerous; yet it has frequently served as a place of *refuge* in the winter, when violent N.W. winds have prevented vessels from entering the Delaware or New York Harbour.

The shoals form three channels, of which that called the *Sod Channel*, next the shore on the North side, appears to be the best. The next is the *Middle* or *East Channel*, but it has only 6 ft. at low water, and the third the *South Channel*, which has 9 ft. water. The Sod Channel lies in a S.W. direction; the Middle Channel in a W.N.W., and the South Channel in a N.N.W. direction.

On the North side of the entrance is *Tucker's Beach*, with Tucker's House, a remarkable house with two chimneys upon it, having a cluster of three single trees at some distance to the N.E., and a smaller house to the S.W., and a lighthouse to S. by E. When advanced to this part you will come up to the buoys which mark the northern or Sod passage.

The Lighthouse is a red structure, and shows a fixed light with a *flash* every minute, visible 12 miles off.

The buoys are as follow:—

The outer buoy is at the middle of the Sod Channel, a little inside of the bar of breakers.

The middle buoy is at the inner part of the same channel, off Sod or Small Point, and upon the North side of the main channel into the harbour. The latter bears S.W. ½ S., nearly half a mile from the outer buoy, and both lie in 2½ fathoms of water.

The *inner buoy* lies in mid-channel at two-thirds of a mile N.N.W. from the middle buoy in 8 fathoms water.

Sod Channel.—Coasters bound to the northward will generally make this harbour when caught by a north-easter, after having passed to the northward of it, and before being able to make Sandy Hook. In running down within sight of the land, pass the boarding-house near the point of Long Beach, giving the breakers off the Old Inlet (which is to the North of Tucker's Beach) a berth of half a mile, and keeping in 24 feet of water, until the boarding-house on Tucker's Island bears N.W. by W.

The boarding-house on Tucker's Island is distinguished from that on Long Beach by having three small trees close to the northward of it, and a thick undergrowth on the hillocks on the northern extremity of the island; whereas the sand-hills in the neighbourhood of the boarding-house on Long Beach are bare.

Being in 24 ft. water, fine black sand, with the boarding-house on Tucker's Island bearing N.W. by W., steer W. by S. for the outer buoy near the middle of the entrance of Sod Channel.

While abreast of Tucker's Island, and before reaching the outer buoy, there will not be much tide, and the least water will be 10 feet at low water. When up with the outer buoy, the S.W. point of Tucker's Island being 900 ft. distant to the westward, steer S.W. ½ S. for the middle buoy, keeping on the outside. Strong tide will here be met; the flood-tide setting over the point of Sod, and the ebb setting over towards the Round Shoal, for which allowance must be made. Turn the middle buoy in 19 feet water, and steer for the inner buoy. With a scant wind and ebb tide vessels will be obliged to anchor here, or even before reaching this point. With a change of tide a better anchorage will be found further up, between Anchoring Island and the marsh to the northward. This part of the harbour, from the N.W. extremity of Anchoring Island to Hatfield's Store, is 1½ mile long, and a quarter of a mile broad.

Vessels coming from the southward, and wishing to enter by the Sod Channel, will bring the boarding-house on Tucker's Island to bear N. ¼ W., and steer for it, giving the Round Shoal a berth. When the hillock on the South end of the island bears

ABSECUM INLET AND LIGHTHOUSE. 87

W. ¼ N., haul up W. by S. for the outer buoy, and afterwards follow the directions given before.

South Channel.—Vessels coming from the southward will give the Brigantine Shoals a good berth, keeping in 4 fathoms water, until the northernmost house on Brigantine Beach bears N.W. by N., then steer N. by W. ¾ W. if the weather be clear. Hatfield's Store, on the marsh, will be seen ahead 4½ miles distant; keep on this course until the northern house on the Brigantine Beach bears N.W. by W. ¼ W., when you will be between the breakers on the South point of the Round Shoal and those on the beach; then haul up N.E. ¾ N., and continue on that course six-tenths of a mile, until the northern house on Brigantine Beach bears West, and the S.E. point of the sand-hillock, on the South end of Tucker's Island, bears N. ¼ W.; haul in then N. ¾ W., and steer for the hillock until nearly up with the middle buoy, after which proceed as before directed.

High water, full and change, at Little Egg Harbour, at 7ʰ 10ᵐ; mean rise of tide 4 ft. In this harbour there are about 15 ft. at high water.

ABSECUM INLET, at the distance of 10¼ miles S.W. from the lighthouse at Little Egg Harbour, is another harbour which affords shelter to vessels of easy draught.

ABSECUM LIGHTHOUSE, a lofty brick tower, 150 ft. high, painted in three horizontal bands, white, red, and white. It stands on the South side of the inlet, and shows a brilliant *fixed* light at 167 ft., which may be seen 22 miles off.

Off the inlet are some dangerous shoals. One discovered in 1867, called the *Round Shoal*, with 11 ft. water, bears S.E. ¼ E. 1¾ mile from the lighthouse. Vessels not bound into Absecum should give the shore a berth of 3 miles; the course parallel to the shore is N.E. ½ E. and S.W. ½ W. The course from this to clear the Brigantine Shoals to the southward of Little Egg Harbour, is N.E. by E. The shoals have several spots of 10 ft., with 4 or 5 fathoms between them.

There is a depth of 8 ft. on Absecum Bar. To run in, bring the lighthouse to bear N. ¼ E., and run for it; this will lead to the outer buoy of the bar, distant 1¼ mile S. ¼ W. from the light. Keep that course until up with the second buoy, when you steer N. by E. ¼ E. for the other buoy until past the lighthouse. The ordinary rise of tide is 5 ft.

In approaching this inlet you must carefully avoid the shoal which lies 2¼ miles E.S.E. from the entrance, having near it, within and without, a depth of 5 fathoms, increasing to 10 fathoms, at 6 miles from land. The bell beacon which formerly marked the shoals has been removed.

Great Egg Harbour.—The shoal entrance of the inlet of this name, with about 12 ft. of water, is 3¼ leagues S.W. from Absecum Inlet. Should you, when abreast of this place, be in the depth of 6 or 5 fathoms, you will find white and black sand, intermixed with broken shells. In the rear of Egg Harbour is the grove known by the name of the *Great Swamp*, by means of which this place may be found. Having passed Great Egg Harbour, at the distance of 4 miles, a course of S.W. by S. for 25 miles will bring you up to Cape May.

In sailing between Great Egg Harbour and Cape May, on the course above mentioned, you will pass the inlets called Corson's, Townsend's, Hereford, Turtle Gut, and Cold Spring, each of which has a bar at its entrance.

Hereford Inlet and Lighthouse.—Hereford Inlet is frequented by the Delaware pilots, who have no other harbour to the northward between this and Great Egg Harbour.

The *lighthouse*, established in 1874, on the North end of Five-mile Beach, 11 miles North of Cape May lighthouse, is built of wood, attached to the keeper's dwelling, and both are painted straw colour. It is surrounded by trees. The light is a *fixed red* light, elevated 51 ft. above the level of high water, and in clear weather should be seen from a distance of 13 miles.

In sailing between New York and the capes, if the wind should be in the N.W. quarter, with which, in general, is clear weather, keep no further off than to 10 fathoms; the nearer in-shore the stronger the current, which sets about 1 mile in an hour. The tide of flood runs W. by S., and the ebb E. by N., but you will have no tide further off than in 8 or 9 fathoms.

If you are turning, with the wind to the westward, stand off no further than to 18 or 20 fathoms of water. You may venture to stand in-shore into 6 fathoms, until you advance towards Hereford Creek, or about 2 leagues to the northward of Cape May.

The soundings opposite to the entrance of the Delaware are very unequal. At 15 leagues eastward from Cape Henlopen are from 25 to 30 fathoms, decreasing at half that distance to 15 and 16 fathoms. In the channel, near Cape Henlopen, there are from 14 to 16 fathoms; but at 5 leagues East from the cape there are only 9 and 10 fathoms. The greatest danger to a ship cruising hereabout is the shoal called the *Five Fathom*, or *Cape May Bank*, and lying at the distance of 17 miles East to E.S.E. from Cape May.

The **FIVE FATHOM BANK** lies, as above said, at 17 miles E. by S. from Cape May lighthouse. The shoal, within the 5-fathom line, is about 10 miles from North to South, the shoalest spot of 12 ft. least water is about in the centre. It extends N. by E. ½ E. and S. by W. ¼ W. about three-quarters of a mile, and is half a mile broad, bold-to on its eastern edge, there being 7 fathoms at half a mile distant. A *black* nun buoy marked F F is usually moored on its N.E. edge. The bank is about 1½ mile broad, and between it and the land is a safe channel of 6 or 7 fathoms depth, but strangers should not attempt it, especially in large vessels, on account of M'Cries shoal, which is in its southern part.

The **LIGHTVESSEL** is moored in 12 fathoms near the S.W. part of the Five-Fathom Bank, with Cape May lighthouse bearing W. by N. ¼ N., distant 16 miles, and Cape Henlopen light W. by S. ⅛ S. Her position is in lat. 38° 53′ 30″, and long. 74° 39′ 0″; she is painted straw colour, with "Cape May" on each side, and exhibits two *fixed* lights at the respective heights of 45 ft. and 40 ft. above the sea, visible about 10 miles each. A fog bell and horn. The dangerous shoal of 12 ft. lies N.W. ⅜ N., 2¼ miles, and should be approached cautiously.

M'Cries Shoal, a dangerous patch, with 16 ft. least water, lies 12 miles westward of the lightvessel, and 7 miles S.E. ¼ S. from Cape May lighthouse. Within the depth of 18 ft. it is a mile in extent, and within 24 ft. 2½ miles. Off its S.W. end a *red* nun buoy No. 2 is usually moored in 5 fathoms water.

DELAWARE BAY AND RIVER.

The extensive estuary or arm of the sea into which the Delaware River falls is 33 miles long from between the capes to Cohansey, and 22 miles in its greatest breadth, and the river is navigable for large vessels for 55 miles further up to Philadelphia, the channels being marked by lights, beacons, and buoys throughout. These channels are generally separated by narrow banks running in parallel lines in the direction of the main stream of tide which runs outward chiefly towards the southern entrance point.

The entrance between Cape May and Cape Henlopen is 10 miles in width, and on

DELAWARE BAY.—SHOALS, ETC.

the N.E. side, for nearly half that distance, is much filled with shoals, which, however, leave some entrance-channels between them.

CAPE MAY LIGHTHOUSE, on the northern cape, is in lat. 38° 55' 50" N., long. 74° 57' 36' W. It is a gray tower, 145 ft. high, on the low extremity of the cape, and shows a bright revolving light every half minute, at 152 ft. above the sea level, visible 18 miles off. It is not seen up the estuary beyond the bearing of S. 31° W. At 1⅞ mile East of the lighthouse is a cluster of houses on the low beach, one of which is called the Congress Hall.

CAPE HENLOPEN LIGHTHOUSE is 10¾ miles S.W. by S. from Cape May lighthouse. It is a white tower 82 ft. high, 1 mile from the North pitch of the cape, near some large white sand hills, and shows a bright *fixed* light, elevated 128 feet, visible 17 miles off.

A Beacon Light, on black screw piles, stands 1 mile North of the main light on the low sandy point. This also shows a *fixed* light, elevated 45 ft. above the ground and sea, between W. ¼ N. and E. ¼ S. by the North, and may be seen 10 miles off.

Delaware Breakwater.—The estuary of the Delaware for 70 miles from the sea has no safe natural harbour, and to remedy this defect, the General Government of the United States has constructed a magnificent breakwater within Cape Henlopen, forming a safe artificial harbour.

This work consists of a stone dyke or pier, similar to that in Plymouth Sound, 1,200 yards in length, forming an angle to the W.N.W. and West, the nearest point being less than a mile West from the point of Cape Henlopen. To the westward of this is another similar pier of 500 yards long, forming an angle with the former, and across the line of the downward current, intended to keep off the floating ices from the harbour within. These works consumed 900,000 cubic yards of stone, each weighing from one-quarter to three tons each, at the estimated cost of 2,216,950 dollars. Entering Lewistown Roads, you will observe the depth of water at low tide, on the piers of the breakwater, is reduced to 12 ft., and that in order to mark the situation of these piers, twelve spar buoys have been anchored around them.

Breakwater Light.—On the N.W. end of the main breakwater is a house, from the top of which a harbour light is shown. It is a fixed light, varied by a *flash* every 45 seconds. It is elevated 47 ft., seen 11 miles off between East and W. ¼ N. A bell is sounded in fogs.

The foregoing are the principal marks on the entrance capes, the low land within offering but few points of recognizance to strangers. A pilot is therefore to be considered as indispensable. A few brief directions for entering will be given, but every caution must be used, as the shoals and channels are liable to alter, and the buoys to drift away.

It is high water, on full and change days, at Cape May at 8ʰ 33ᵐ. Mean rise of spring tides 4¼ ft., of neaps 3 ft.; at Cape Henlopen at 8ʰ 0ᵐ; springs rise 6¼ ft., neaps 5¼ ft. The first quarter of the flood tide sets to W.N.W., from the second to the last quarter N.N.W. The first quarter of the ebb sets to the E.S.E., second to last quarter S.S.E., but they are much affected by the winds.

SHOALS *on the North side.*—At 1¼ mile S.E. from the Congress Hall on Cape May there is a shoal 1 mile in extent, on which there is only 6 ft. water. It is called *Uncle Eph* or *Old Eph*, and there is a narrow 3½-fathom channel inside it. There is a *spar buoy*, painted black and white in horizontal stripes, at the East end, and a similar buoy at its West end, each in 2 fathoms. They are numbered 1 and 2.

U. S.—Part I.

At half a mile S.W. of Cape May lighthouse there is a 10-ft. shoal a quarter of a mile in extent.

The **Overfalls** extend 5¼ miles southward from Cape May lighthouse, their southern edge bearing S. by W. ¼ W., and 6¼ miles N.E. ¼ E. from Cape Henlopen lighthouse. They consist of broken ground to within a mile of Cape May, with shoal spots of 4 and 6 ft water; in many places breakers and strong tide rips. On the S.W. point a *red* nun buoy with staff and triangle is moored in 7 fathoms.

Inside the cape are the following shoals:—

Round or *N.E. Shoal* lies W. by S. ¼ S., 2⅛ mile from Cape May lighthouse; least water 3 ft.

The *Mummy Shoal*, between it and the Crow Shoal, separates Ricords and Blunts Channels.

On the South end of the Mummy Shoal is a *black* spar buoy.

Crow Shoal South point lies W. ⅛ N. 1½ mile from Cape May lighthouse, and extends 4 miles North, nearly parallel to the shore; least water 7 ft. The Ricord Channel lies West of it.

The Shears eastern point lies N. by W. ¼ W., 3 miles from Cape Henlopen lighthouse; least water 6 ft. On the tail of this shoal is a *black* nun buoy in 3 fathoms.

Brown Shoal southern edge lies W. by N., 7¼ miles from Cape May lighthouse; least water 8 ft. A *black* can buoy marks it, in 6 fathoms.

Brandywine Shoal southern edge lies W.N.W. ¼ W., 7 miles from Cape May lighthouse; least water 1 foot. A *red* nun buoy with flag lies on its N.W. part in 6 fathoms.

The **Brandywine Shoal Lighthouse,** an iron screw pile tower, painted red, 46 feet above the sea, showing a *fixed* light, visible 13½ miles. Situated on the South end of the shoal in lat. 38° 59' 7" and long. 75° 6' 28". It has a fog bell A red nun buoy marks the N.W. part of the shoal as above mentioned.

The **Hen and Chickens Shoal,** on the *South* side of the entrance, lies in a S.E. direction from Cape Henlopen lighthouse, and is 3 miles in length, North and South, least water upon it 5 ft. Southern point lies S.E. ⅛ S.; northern point N.N.E. three-quarters of a mile from Henlopen lighthouse, and 4 cables' lengths East of the beacon light.

The southern point, on which there is 13 ft. water, bears S.E. by S. 2½ miles from Cape Henlopen lighthouse. On this southern part is a *spar* buoy, red and black horizontal stripes, No. 1, in 4 fathoms. Inside the shoal, and parallel to the shore, there is a 4½ and 5-fathom channel, which is used by coasters following the beach around the cape.

The **Shears** is the first shoal within the point on the South side of the Main Ship Channel. It is a prolongation of the broad shore bank which lies on the S.W. side of the Delaware. Its *S.E. tail* is marked by a *black* nun buoy, No. 3, in 3 fathoms.

The **CHANNELS** through the northern shoals are the *Coasters'* or *Cape May Channel*, South of Eph's Shoal, between it and the North part of the Overfalls. The *Through Channel* is a continuation of the foregoing, between the Overfalls and the South end of the Round Shoal; *Blunt's Channel* between the Round and Mummy Shoals, and Ricords or Rickards Channel, between the Mummy and Crow Shoals.

DIRECTIONS.—The following are given by Lieutenant-Commander B. Bache, U.S.N. :—

Having the lightvessel near the Five-fathom bank bearing N., distant 1 mile, steer for Cape Henlopen lighthouse W. ¾ S., the soundings on the line varying from 7 to 9 fathoms. When they deepen to 10 fathoms or over, Henlopen lighthouse 3½ miles distant, steer N.W., to bring Henlopen lighthouse and the beacon on the cape in one,

DELAWARE BAY.—DIRECTIONS.

being careful, particularly in light winds and on the flood, which sets to the westward, not to cross much to the westward of the range, the *Shears* being near. Steer up the bay on this range (the lighthouse and beacon in one), which passes to the eastward of the buoy of the Brown; soundings shoaling gradually from 15 to 8 fathoms, until the screw pile lighthouse on the Brandywine Shoal bears N. by W., when steer N.N.W. ¼ W. to the lightvessel on the Cross Ledge, at 12 miles distance, thus passing about half a mile to the westward of the Brandywine Shoal and to the eastward of the buoy at the South end of the Flogger Shoal.

Bound into Breakwater Harbour from the Southward.—Pass the Hen and Chickens at a safe distance, 2 miles from the shore, then haul in to the shore, keeping as close to Cape Henlopen, which is bold, as convenient.

From the Eastward.—Bring Cape Henlopen lighthouse to bear W. ¾ S., and stand in; enter the harbour at either end, or between the breakwater and Ice Breakwater, according to the wind and tide, and to the berth selected. Do not anchor in the gap, as the best anchorage is close to the Main-work Breakwater lighthouse, bearing N. by W. The holding ground is excellent in every part of the harbour.

Chains and anchors can be procured on the Breakwater, and ship's stores generally at the town of Lewes, which has a landing pier.

RICORDS' CHANNEL.—Vessels drawing 15 ft. water can pass through this channel at ordinary low water, smooth sea.

BLUNTS CHANNEL is not yet buoyed.

THROUGH CHANNEL TO BREAKWATER.—Vessels drawing 15 ft. can pass through this channel at ordinary low water, smooth sea.

The rise of tide may be estimated at 5 ft. Strong tides running, an allowance of two points must be made in the course steered, crossing the direction of the tides. The lead is a guide. The shoals, although pretty steep-to, can be avoided by constant and true soundings.

When off the boarding-houses on Cape Island, in the Coasters' or Cape May Channel, buoy No. 1, on Eph's Shoal, will be seen W. by N. ½ N.; steer for it, leaving it close on board on the starboard hand when passing. When up with buoy No. 1, buoys Nos. 2, 3, 4, 5, and 6, in clear weather, will be in sight.

ᵻ TO PASS THROUGH THE THROUGH CHANNEL TO BREAKWATER.—This channel is narrow; on the S.E. side is a shoal, with 7 ft. water upon it, and the Round, or E.N.E. shoal is to the northward, and has 4 ft. water upon it, and the breakers show plainly in any breeze. When abreast of No. 1 buoy on Eph's Shoal, stand W. ¾ N. towards buoy No. 3, keeping it open on the port bow a point, and gradually hauling up for it. When up with No. 3, leave it on the starboard hand, and steer S.W. by S. for No. 2, which leave close on board on the starboard hand, and continue on S.W. by S. for the Breakwater.

TO PASS THROUGH RICORDS' CHANNEL.—This channel lies between the Crow and Mummy Shoals; the Crow Shoal having on it 7 ft. water, and the Mummy Shoal 6 feet water. After passing buoy No. 4, it is a good beating channel.

From buoy No. 1, steer N.W. ¾ W. for No. 4, which will leave No. 1 on the starboar hand, at a short distance, and steer N.N.W., westerly, for No. 5, which pass on either hand and haul up N.W. ¼ W., westerly, for No. 6, which pass on either hand, and shape your course W. ½ N., which brings you between the buoy of the Brown and the lighthouse on the Brandywine Shoal, in the Main Ship Channel.

The following directions are taken from the chart published by the U.S. Coast Survey, and must be taken with some caution, as the shoals and buoys are subject to change, and it is moreover very undesirable that a stranger should venture up the estuary without a pilot.

In running up the bay, Henlopen light bearing S. ¼ E., steer North a little West, for the black can buoy, No. 5, on the Brown Shoal, which bears N. 40° W., 9¼ miles distant from the light, which you leave to the westward. Keep on that course until up with the Brandywine lighthouse, from which you steer toward the lightboat on the *Cross Ledge* or *Upper Middle*. She shows one fixed light, and lies on the West side of the Main Ship Channel. Your course on the flood is N.W. by N. ¼ N., and on the ebb N.N.W., the distance 11¼ miles, in soundings of 4½ to 8 fathoms. You leave the red nun buoy with a flag on the N.W. end of the Brandywine Shoal to the eastward, and the black nun buoy, with circular mark on the Fourteen-feet Bank, to the westward, the former being 1¾ mile, the latter 5 miles, from the lightboat.

The tides in this course are influenced very much, in direction and strength, by the winds; but as the channel is well defined by the lighthouse and lightboat, which lie in a line with its direction and in connection with the buoys, there can be no difficulty in clear weather.

You make *Egg Island fixed light*, bearing about North, soon after leaving the Brandywine light. It is on a dwelling-house, elevated 45 ft., seen 12 miles off. There is also a small *fixed light* at the entrance to Maurice River, on Hogstack Island, about West from Egg Island light. At 1½ mile N.W. by W. from the buoy on the Fourteen-feet Bank, is the South extremity of the *Joe Flogger* (or Folger) *Shoal*, a narrow ridge running N.N.W. 15 miles, nearly dry in places, and forming for that distance the western side of the main channel. In beating up do not stand to the westward into less than 4 fathoms. In thick weather the Joe Flogger may be safely tracked along the whole extent, hauling on to 4 fathoms hard, and deepening off to 5 and 6 fathoms soft.

The *Cross Ledge Lightboat*, as before mentioned, shows a single *fixed* light, elevated 45 ft., visible 9 miles off, has a fog bell and horn, and is moored about mid-channel between Joe Flogger and the *red nun buoy* with cross on the lower end of the Cross Ledge, which is a narrow ridge of hard sand on the East side of the channel, 4½ miles in length, and nearly dry in places. On it a *pile lighthouse* is constructing, E. by S. 7¼ miles from Mahon River light. Leave the lightboat to the westward, keeping well in the Main Ship Channel to avoid the foundation of the lighthouse, and the course then to the Middle is N.W. by N. ¼ N. on the flood, and N.N.W. on the ebb tide, distance 4 miles, soundings 7½ to 5 fathoms. These courses carry you in about mid-channel between Joe Flogger and the Cross Ledge. From the buoy on the Middle to Bombay Hook bar, the *Thrum Cap* (the lower of two small insulated clumps of trees on the western shore) bearing S.W., the course is N.W. ¼ W. on the flood, and N.W. by N. on the ebb, distance 9 miles, depths 5 to 6½ fathoms. Bombay Hook Bar is very bold; the soundings in the channel off it are 6 to 6½ fathoms. It should not be approached nearer than 5 fathoms.

Cohansey Light, on the New Jersey shore, is in sight from the buoy of the Middle, bearing N.N.W. ¼ N.; it is upon a dwelling-house, elevated 40 ft., seen 10 miles off. *Mahon River light, fixed*, is on the West side of the bay, bearing about W. by N. from the Cross Ledge lightboat, distant 7¼ miles, and bears from Cohansey light S. by W.

Ship John Shoal Light.—A light is constructing (1874) to the South of this shoal, in about 8 ft. water, 2½ miles S. by W. from Cohansey lighthouse. While in progress a *red light* is shown when the weather permits.

When nearly up with the northern end of Joe Flogger, Bombay Hook light, *fixed light*, will be made just open with Bombay Hook Point, and bearing N.W. When up with Bombay Hook Point, *Reedy Island light, fixed, white* for 1 minute, with five *red flashes* during the next minute, at 55 ft. elevation, will be made bearing N.W. by N. A fog bell is sounded here, six blows at intervals of 21 seconds.

The harbour of *Reedy Island* is much used, particularly in winter, while ice is running. A small spit makes South from the lower end of the island half a mile; being clear of this, your course is North. Anchor off the piers in 4 to 6 fathoms water, muddy bottom.

Bombay Hook Roads is an anchorage much used by vessels waiting for the tide or wind. Bring Bombay Hook Point to bear S. by E., the light W. by N., and anchor in from 3 to 4 fathoms, sticky bottom.

Blake's Channel, to the westward of Joe Flogger, was discovered during the progress of the U.S. Survey in 1844-5. It cannot be considered available until it is properly buoyed.

The following directions are given because it has sometimes been entered by mistake, and considerable embarrassment experienced in working back to get into the main channel again. This channel is as direct as the main channel, though not so wide. The red and black striped spar buoy on the tail of Joe Flogger, as already observed, bears N.W. by N. 1½ mile from the buoy on the Fourteen-feet Bank. Entering with the latter buoy bearing East 1½ mile, steer N.W. by N. ¼ N., which course will carry you along the western side of the shoal in not less than 4 fathoms, until Mahon light bears W. by N., when you strike a middle ground 1½ mile long, least water 13 ft., having passed which you drop into 4 fathoms again.

When the buoy of the Middle Main Channel bears E. by N. ½ N., and Mahon light W. by S. ½ S., steer N.W. by N. ¼ N., and you may pass through into the Main Channel a little below the Thrum Cap, and in not less than 3¾ fathoms. This swash is marked by a *black nun buoy*.

The following directions will also serve for this channel with a head tide more safely than the foregoing. Entering as before directed, track the West side of the channel, shoaling to 3½, and deepening to 4 and 5 fathoms, until Mahon light bears W.N.W., when you take your soundings from Joe Flogger cautiously (not shoaling to less than 3 fathoms, for the shoal is very bold), and carry 3½ to 4½ fathoms through, between it and the Middle Ground. When past the Middle Ground, track the West side of the channel along as before.

Above this point the Delaware River is lighted and buoyed with numerous marks, but as the winding channel to Philadelphia cannot be well verbally described so as to be of use in piloting a vessel, the directions given on the large charts are here omitted, a few remarks only are appended.

REEDY ISLAND TO PHILADELPHIA.—In passing Reedy Island, be cautious of a long shoal extending to the North of that island, and 1½ mile in length. When passing it, keep the port side best on board. You will next make a small low island, the *Pea Patch*, on the starboard, which is the site of Fort Delaware; on its South point a fixed light is shown. A shoal, the *Bulk Head*, extends to the northward of it, which must be avoided by keeping the port side on board, until the river bears N.E. or N.E. by N., when you may stand up for *New Castle*, which is 10 leagues below Philadelphia.

From the distance of 2 miles above New Castle, give the port shore a berth, to avoid a flat extending nearly half a mile from shore, leaving the *fixed light* at the entrance to *Christiana River* leading to *Wilmington* on the port hand. With a fair wind, you may then keep up the middle of the river, which winds upwards to Marcus Hook from N.E. to E.N.E., whence the course to Chester Island is N.E. by E. 4 miles.

Chester Island and a long low point, which lies W.S.W. from it, is to be left on the starboard, giving it a good berth, and thus keeping the port shore best on board until arrived at *Billingsport*, a high sandy bluff point; next haul up for *Fort Mifflin*, on the pier opposite to which, a *fixed* light is shown; in sailing towards which you may pass close to a black buoy which lies in the channel. Run directly for the fort, giving it a berth; when abreast of it you will see two small islands, between which you must pass; and, having passed them, may haul up N.E. by N. for Gloucester Point, to the distance of a mile from it. In sailing hence, upon a northerly course, for 3 miles, keeping the port side best on board, you will arrive off Philadelphia.

Philadelphia, one of the finest cities in the world, and the second in size and population in the United States, is regularly laid out in the narrowest part of the peninsula included between the *Rivers Delaware* and *Schuylkill*, at 5 miles above their confluence. Its wharves are commodious and spacious, and the water so deep as to allow a vessel of 500 tons to lay her broadside to it. The warehouses are large and numerous, and the docks for ship building well adapted to their purposes.

The COASTS of DELAWARE and MARYLAND.—At 15 miles N.W. of Cape Henlopen a lighthouse is erected near the mouth of Mispillion River; a *fixed white* light, 48 ft. above the sea, is shown from a wooden frame tower, connected with the dwelling of the keeper, both coloured gray, with the exception of the lantern on the tower, which is black.

Between Cape Henlopen, in lat. 38° 47', and Cape Charles, in 37° 8', the coasts are very low, broken into islands, and bordered with shoals. From a comparison of the old with the modern charts, it appears that the sea must have encroached very considerably upon these coasts within the last half century, and that the shoals generally have increased. The position and figures of the latter can be best understood by reference to the chart.

At $14\frac{1}{2}$ miles S.E. by E. $\frac{1}{4}$ E. from Cape Henlopen, and E. by N. $\frac{1}{4}$ N. 12 miles from Indian River Inlet, is a small *shoal* of $4\frac{1}{4}$ fathoms. This shoal is the farthest out to sea of the dangers of the River Delaware, southward of the capes, and should be guarded against by large vessels, especially at low water.

Fenwick Island Shoal.—The centre of this shoal is in lat. 38° 27' 30", and long. 74° 56' 9". It is in length about 2 miles S.W. to N.E., and has 15 ft. water on its shoalest part. It bears S.E. by S. $\frac{1}{4}$ S, 11 miles distant from Indian River Inlet, and E. $\frac{1}{8}$ S. to E. $\frac{3}{4}$ N., 5 miles from Fenwick Island lighthouse. On approaching the shoal from seaward the soundings suddenly decrease from 10 to $2\frac{1}{4}$ fathoms, and on the West side of the shoal there are 10 fathoms, at the distance of about 2 miles. This part of the shoal appears to be extending, as does also the northern portion.

Bell Boat.—Off the N.E. part of Fenwick's Shoal an iron bell-boat is moored in 10 fathoms water, close to the outer edge of the shoal, with Fenwick Island lighthouse bearing W. $\frac{3}{4}$ S., distant $6\frac{3}{4}$ miles. The hull is painted *black*, the mast *red*; the bell is rung by the action of the sea.

FENWICK'S ISLAND Lighthouse, at 20 miles to the South of Cape Henlopen, in lat. 38° 27' 9", and long. 75° 2' 49"; a white brick tower 82 ft. in height, exhibiting a *fixed* light, varied by a flash every 2 minutes, 86 ft. above the sea, and visible 15 miles off.

Isle of Wight Shoal.—On this shoal there are but 3 fathoms water, and it bears S. $\frac{1}{4}$ W., $4\frac{1}{2}$ miles from the centre of Fenwick Island Shoal; East from the Isle of Wight Woods, and is nearly $6\frac{1}{2}$ miles from the beach. Within a mile of the shoal there are 10 fathoms water on either side.

About midway between Fenwick's Island and Isle of Wight Shoals there is a spot with 3½ fathoms water upon it.

Little Gull Bank lies S.W. ½ W., 7 miles West from the Isle of Wight Shoal, and has 12 feet water on it.

Great Gull Bank lies 10 miles S.W. ¾ S. from the Isle of Wight Shoal, and has 3½ fathoms on it.

The Sinepuxent Shoals are several shoals near the shore, near the lighthouse, and inside of Fenwick's Island Shoal, having 3½ fathoms on them at low water.

WINTER QUARTER SHOAL and LIGHTVESSEL.—The centre of this shoal bears E. by N. ¼ N., distant 11¼ miles from Assateague lighthouse, and is 1 mile long, and one-third of a mile wide, running in an E. by N. ¾ N. and W. by S. ¾ S. direction, and has not more than 3 fathoms water upon it, and in several places only 12 ft. at low tide. On the seaward side the soundings change suddenly from 9 to 4 fathoms, and then to 2 fathoms. There are 10 fathoms between it and the nearest land, from which it is distant 6¼ miles. In clear weather the lantern of Assateague lighthouse is visible from it. The sea breaks upon this shoal in heavy weather, and it was very dangerous before the placing of the lightvessel, as the soundings change suddenly, and it lies just in the track of vessels.

The *Lightvessel*, painted red, lies E. by N. from Assateague lighthouse, and S.E. by E. ½ E. 2 miles from the centre of the shoal in 11 fathoms water. She shows a fixed white light at 15 feet above the sea, visible 11 miles off in clear weather.

Buoy.—An iron nun buoy, painted *red*, with W. Q. S. in white letters, has been placed in 8 fathoms water E. by S., one quarter of a mile from the shoalest part of the shoal. Green Run bears from the buoy N.W. ¾ N., 5½ miles, and Cape Chincoteague W. by S. ¼ S.; but it is liable to go adrift.

Between the Winter Quarter Shoal and the Gull Banks there are several spots of 3½, 4, and 5 fathoms, which will be best understood by the chart.

ASSATEAGUE ISLAND LIGHTHOUSE, near the S.W. point, is a brick tower, 125 ft. high, and shows a bright fixed light at 150 ft., visible 19 miles off.

Black Fish Bank is a long narrow ridge, running in a direction N.E. ½ E. and S.W. ½ W., 5 miles long, with an average width of a mile and distant 4½ to 6 miles from the land, with from 3¼ to 5 fathoms upon it. Its North end bears E. by S. ¼ S., distant 7¼ miles, and its South end S.E. by S., 5½ miles from the Assateague lighthouse.

The CHINCOTEAGUE SHOALS lie within the Black Fish Bank, and are the outer shoals from the Assateague lighthouse, and bearing from it S. ½ W. to S.E. by E. ¾ E., comprising six points of the compass, and at the distance from it of 3½ to 4¼ miles. They have from 9 to 17 ft. water upon them.

In the immediate neighbourhood of these shoals, and especially within 12 miles range of the Assateague light, the bottom is exceedingly broken and uneven. The general set of the current along this part of the cost is to the southward and westward; and vessels from the southward have sometimes been set in-shore among these dangers by it; so that this part of the coast should be avoided by large vessels, unless well acquainted with the district. Should the mariner suspect himself approaching the land in this vicinity, he should keep the lead going, and after striking soundings in 11 or 12 fathoms should keep a good look-out. In day time large vessels should not approach the land nearer than 10 miles, with the trees just in sight from the deck; and at night, even in clear weather, when coming from the southward, no nearer than to get the light just in sight.

Assateague and Chincoteague Inlets are to the south-westward of the lighthouse. The bar and entrance to the latter are marked by several buoys; but neither entrance should be taken without being acquainted. To the southward of Assateague bar there is anchorage in 3 fathoms for small vessels, partially sheltered from the N.E. and East by the Ship and Chincoteague Shoals.

From Chincoteague to Cape Charles the land trends S.S.W. ¼ W., with several barred inlets; and the land is low, sandy, and marshy.

Metompkin Harbour is 17½ miles southward of Assateague light, and is said to have 12 ft. water on its bar at spring tides, and 8 ft. at low water. The outer bar buoy is a red nun buoy, No. 2, in 10 ft. water; the inner bar buoy is *black*, No. 1. To cross the bar, keep the two buoys in one. The inlet is dangerous within, being filled with oyster beds.

The whole of the above inlets afford but dangerous harbours in a gale of wind, but you may ride along shore with the wind from N.W. to S.W. Should it blow hard from the N.E. or E.N.E., and you are in sight of Assateague light, your only chance of safety is to stand for the southward, as you cannot claw off the land to the northward, neither can you get into the harbour of Chincoteague; and when the wind is to the eastward, there is generally found thick weather on this coast. The current generally sets in the direction of the land, or about S.S.W.

Porpoise Bank.—This is a bank of 6 fathoms sand and shells, of small extent, but lying considerably off the land; it bears from Assateague lighthouse S. ¼ W., 15 miles, and 19 miles from the nearest land, in lat. 37° 39′.

Paramore Bank.—This is a more extensive bank than the former, lying E. by N. and W. by S., 4½ miles. The easternmost end has 4 and 4¼ fathoms water upon it, while there are 3¼ fathoms about the centre, and also at the West end, the latter bearing S.E., 4¼ miles from Wachapreague Inlet.

Hog Island Light is on the West point of the island, and North side of Great Machipongo Inlet, in lat. 37° 23′ 16″, and long. 75° 41′ 55″, is white, and 45 feet in height, exhibiting a *fixed* light, 60 ft. above the sea, visible 13 miles off. This light serves as a guide to coasters, and for entering *Great Machipongo Inlet*; the shoalest water on the bar of which is 9 ft. at low water. *Little Machipongo Inlet* is about 7 miles to the northward, and of similar depth.

These are very dangerous harbours in a gale of wind; but you may ride along shore with the wind from N.W. to S.W. When the wind blows hard at N.E. or E.N.E., and you are in sight of Chincoteague Shoals, your only chance for safety is to stand to the southward, for you cannot clear the land to the northward, or go into the harbour of Chincoteague. The weather is generally thick, with easterly winds.

To the southward the low, swampy land, broken into islands, takes a S.W. by S. direction for 18 miles to Smith's Island lighthouse, or the lighthouse of Cape Charles. In this extent there are several smaller inlets, only navigable to small coasters, and the shoal water, to 5 fathoms, extends to 3½ miles from the land.

Smith's Island Shoal and Shark Shoal.—Nearly in the latitude of Cape Charles, 4 and 5 miles off the land, are the Smith's Island and Shark Shoals. The former lies E. by S. ¼ S., 7 miles from Smith's Island lighthouse, and has 3¼ fathoms upon it. The latter lies S.E. by E., a little under 5 miles from the same, and has but 2¾ fathoms upon it. These shoals are small in extent, but the surrounding depths are but moderately greater, and towards the sea deepen gradually, so that at 11 miles from the land you will only find about 10 fathoms.

DIRECTIONS.—*Vessels bound from the Delaware to the Chesapeake*, should, in order to avoid the *Hen and Chicken*, &c., steer out with the lighthouse of Cape Henlopen E. by S., to the distance of 10 miles (the beacon light in range with the light on the breakwater will lead you on the edge of the Hen and Chicken). They may thence, with an off-shore wind, pursue a S. by W. course for 13 leagues, which will clear the Gull Banks on the West. Thence S.S.W. ¼ W., 20 leagues, leads to the parallel of the light on Smith's Island; and the same course continued, 8 leagues farther, brings you in sight of the light on Cape Henry, presently described, and bearing W.N.W.

A course S.S.E. ¼ E., 23 miles from off Cape Henlopen, will clear the Cap, and lead well to the eastward of the Fenwick Shoal; and when you get the Bell-boat, riding off that shoal, to bear about West, you may alter your course to S.S.W.; this course for about 30 miles will bring you nearly abreast of Winter Quarter Shoal, about the parallel of 38°; then a long course of 60 miles S.W. by S., if your vessel will lie well up, will bring you abreast of Smith's Island Shoal, with Smith's Island light bearing W. by N.; from hence a S.W. by W. course for 18 miles will take you to Cape Henry.

In pursuing the course of the land from Cape Henlopen southward, you will see an opening at the distance of 11 miles. This is *Indian River Inlet*, and leads to Indian River Bay, and another large lagoon called *Rehoboth Bay*; but this is generally shallow, and fit only for vessels drawing not more than 6 ft. water.

There is good anchorage within the Chincoteague Shoals, which is frequently used by coasting vessels; some, however, make Matomkin Harbour; but this place should only be taken by those acquainted with it; and, as previously observed, the harbours are all dangerous along this coast in gales of wind, and should not be attempted.

Approaching the Chesapeake on the above course to the southward of Chincoteague, you will have from 12 to 9 and 8 fathoms up to Smith's Island Shoal. Coming in for the entrance from the E.N.E. and steering W.S.W., at the distance of 50 miles, you will have 25 fathoms, and at 30 miles from the entrance 18 fathoms, decreasing to 12, 9, and 7 fathoms off Smith's Island Shoal. Coming in due West for the entrance, you will have 27 fathoms at 55 miles distance; at 25 miles distance 13 fathoms, coarse sand and shells, decreasing gradually to the flats. Steering W.N.W. for the entrance, you will find 22 fathoms about 45 miles off, shoaling towards the entrance to 10 fathoms at 12 miles from the flats. Approaching N.W. there are 14 fathoms coarse sand, at 40 miles from the entrance, and 10 fathoms at 20 miles, thence gradually lessening in depth to the 5-fathom line of the flats of the Middle Ground, where a *red buoy* is moored.

In coming from sea and falling into the northward of the Capes of Virginia, you might make the light on Hog Island, which has a shoal off the East side, and also Machipongo Island; the latter is the smaller island. Smith's Island, on which is a lighthouse, is about 6 leagues S.W. by S. from Hog Island; the latter is longer than Smith's Island, and the trees stand more open, and are not so thick as on Smith's Island. In proceeding southward from this you will make the sand hills, which lie between Hog Island and Smith's Island, which is a sure mark that you have not passed Smith's Island. Do not come nearer than 7 fathoms when off the sand hills, as within that depth the ground is broken.

In proceeding along these coasts, during easterly winds, great caution is requisite; as with such winds the weather is generally hazy, and the coast obscured. The current will generally be found setting to the S.S.W., in the direction of the shore.

On the courses above prescribed, the soundings will be found to vary from 11 to 15 and 16 fathoms, until approaching Cape Charles, where from 9 to 8 fathoms may be found. At 10 miles E.S.E. from Cape Henry are from 10 to 12 fathoms, which depths continue in a W.N.W. direction to the cape.

Those bound to the Chesapeake from the ocean eastward should observe that the greatest extent of soundings from shore is to the eastward of Cape Henry; it being, in that part, between 23 and 24 leagues, with various depths.

The **CAPES of VIRGINIA**, which form the entrance points of the Chesapeake, are 11 miles apart. *Cape Charles*, on the North, is very undefined, as shoals and dry patches extend for 2½ miles southward of the point of the peninsula. *Cape Henry*, on the opposite side, is nearly bold-to, and thus the entrance of the Chesapeake is similar to that of the Delaware, in having the northern side of the entrance much embarrassed by dangerous shoals, which apparently drift down from the northward in an opposite course to the great Gulf Stream in the offing; but in accordance with that inner Arctic Current which sets southward along the coast within the warmer waters of the Gulf Stream.

In coming from seaward to the northward of the entrance, Hog Island, with its lighthouse, just described, is longer than Smith's Island, which forms the outer point of the northern cape, and the trees stand more open, being not so thick as on Smith's Island. Between the two islands are some sand hills, which are a good guide.

The ground off Cape Henry is in general coarse sand, with some gravel; but thence southward, to Cape Hatteras, it is commonly fine sand, with ooze.

Ships falling in with the land to the northward of the entrance should not stand inwards to a less depth than 7 fathoms, until they come into the latitude of Smith's Island and Cape Charles, whence they may stand with safety into 5 fathoms. In coming along shore from the southward, 7 fathoms will be a proper depth to keep in, until up with Cape Henry; whence, falling into 8 or 9 fathoms, with a stiff or sticky bottom, you will be in the channel-way.

When you come in towards the land, to the southward of Cape Henry, you will have deeper water than when you are in the same latitude; as 21 fathoms, reddish sand, and pretty large; 9 leagues off it there are 35 and 40 fathoms, fine gray sand.

The land is low and sandy; you cannot see it above 7 leagues off. Cape Henry is low, but bluff, with a few trees to the sea side, at a little distance from the water; it is moderately steep-to, excepting that a small shoal stretches about 2 cables' lengths from the shore East of the lighthouse.

When coming in from sea, in the latitude of Cape Henry, 36° 59', you will meet with soundings, as above described. You may readily ascertain when in soundings by the muddy colour of the water. In clear weather, the land of Cape Henry may be seen from the depth of 10 or 11 fathoms, regular soundings, which extend 5 or 6 leagues to the southward of the cape; more to the northward the soundings are irregular and coarser, as above described.

CHESAPEAKE BAY AND RIVERS.

The **CHESAPEAKE**, one of the finest estuaries on the globe, being 160 miles in extent from North to South, is the recipient of many important rivers, which fall into it on all sides, but especially on the North and West. At its head is the *Susquehanna*, which pervades Pennsylvania; on the N.W. the *Patapsco*, falling from Baltimore; at a degree farther South is the *Patuxent*; then the *Potomac*, which passes the federal city of Washington; the *Rappahanock*, running downward from Fredericsburg; *York River*, on which are situated York Town and Gloucester; *James River*, on which stands the town of Richmond; and, in the South, *Elizabeth River*, on the right bank of which stands Norfolk.

In advancing towards the Chesapeake from the Ocean, the Gulf Stream is commonly crossed from the south-eastward, in its narrowest part, near the parallel of Cape Hatteras, or 35° 10′ N. In crossing it thus, the water of the stream will be found in September, of the temperature of 83 degrees, and thence diminishing to the shore. Even in December, over soundings of 19 fathoms, in latitude 35° 19′, with the air at 45°, the water has been found at 68°, after leaving the dark blue ocean for the green water on soundings. The water of the stream, quite warm, had previously sparkled, like fire, along the ship at night.

Within the stream, upon the soundings, you will come into the cold southerly current, the prolongation of the currents passing over the Newfoundland Banks, as described in our "North Atlantic Memoir."

The elevated lighthouse on Cape Henry, in lat. 36° 55½′, more particularly noticed hereafter, is an excellent mark for the Chesapeake. Having passed this cape, in sailing upward, in the main stream, low banks, fringed with trees, are all that is to be seen of the country, excepting here and there a house near the shore.

Lighthouses and Lightvessels in the Chesapeake Entrance.—The numerous lights in the Chesapeake tend very much to facilitate the navigation of this arm of the sea.

CAPE CHARLES LIGHTHOUSE stands on the N.E. end of *Smith's Island*, or at nearly 5 miles eastward of the cape whose name it bears. It is a round white tower, 150 ft. high, with an old tower near it, and shows, at 160 ft., a *bright fixed* light, varied by a *bright flash*, every three-quarters of a minute. This light may be seen at 19 miles off.

CAPE HENRY LIGHTHOUSE, on the South side, is a white tower, 82 feet high, and shows a *fixed* light, elevated 120 ft., seen 12 miles off. A *striped* buoy is placed in mid-channel, to the N.E. of the lighthouse. There are high white sand-hills in the vicinity of the lighthouse.

Cape Henry and Lighthouse, W.N.W. ½ W. 9 miles.

The Thimble Shoal Pile Lighthouse, painted of a drab colour, stands in 11 ft. water, on the shoalest point of the Thimble, 3¼ miles E. by N. ¼ N. from Old Point Comfort light, and on the North side of the entrance to Hampton Roads. The light is *fixed*, varied by *red* and *white flashes*, at 45 ft. above the sea. A 10-foot patch lies 700 yards westward of the lighthouse. *Fog-bell* struck at intervals of 5 seconds. A *black buoy* takes the place of the Willoughby Spit lightvessel. Vessels entering Hampton Roads pass southward of the Thimble light, and between it and the Willoughby black buoy.

Old Point Comfort Lighthouse is on the North side of the channel to Hampton Roads, 15 miles W.N.W. of Cape Henry light. It is a white tower, 40 ft. high, showing a *fixed* light, elevated 48 ft., seen 11 miles off. A *fog-bell* is sounded at intervals of 10 seconds.

Back River Light, on the Point of Breakers, is 5 miles N.E. of Old Point Comfort light, and immediately in front of the main channel to the Chesapeake. It is a *revolving* light, visible every 1½ minute to the distance of 10 miles. Plum Tree

Point, on the North side of the entrance to Back River, lies N.N.W. 2½ miles from this light.

York Spit Screw-pile Lighthouse, established in 1870, in place of the lightvessel formerly marking the York Spit shoal, shows a *fixed red* light, elevated 37 ft. above high water, and visible 11 miles off. The lighthouse stands in 11 ft. water at low water springs, and is painted yellow; from it, Point Comfort lighthouse bears N. by W. 5½ miles, and Back River lighthouse S. by W. 7¼ miles. A *fog-bell* will be sounded at uniform intervals of *fifteen seconds.*

Vessels drawing 24 ft. water should not approach the lighthouse on the eastern side within half a mile, but vessels not drawing over 18 ft. water may approach within a quarter of a mile in the same direction, and on the South and S.W. within three-quarters of a mile; those drawing under 14 ft. may pass over the shoal to the north-westward of the lighthouse within a quarter of a mile, but not farther distant than 2½ miles.

These are the lights which have reference to the entrance of the Chesapeake. Those adapted to its inner navigation will be described presently.

Shoals in the Entrance of the Chesapeake.—As before mentioned, the principal collection of shoals is on the North side, Cape Henry being nearly bold-to. The following is a brief enumeration of them. Their form and character being much better understood from the chart. They extend, generally, from 2 to 3 miles S.E. from Smith's Island light, (except the outlying shoals before described), and 10 miles to the south-westward, or within a radius of 6 to 8 miles from the true Cape Charles.

The principal are the Nautilus, Middle Ground, and Inner Middle, besides the small low *Isaac* and *Fisherman Islands*, which lie within 2 miles of Cape Charles, and to the S.W. by W. of Smith's Island. *Shark's Shoal* and *Smith's Island Shoal* are described on page 96.

The Nautilus Shoal lies to the S.E. of Cape Charles, about 4 miles distant, and has 1½ and 2 fathoms upon it. It lies in a direction parallel to Smith's Island, or N.E. by E. and S.W. by W., curving round the entrance of the bay, and nearly joining the Middle Ground.

The Middle Ground commences about 6 miles South of Cape Charles, and then curves round to N.N.W. ¼ W. up the Chesapeake to the extent of about 9 miles, and within about 6 miles of the shore. It is a narrow strip of shoal ground, having 1¾ fathoms least water upon it, and 2½ and 3 fathoms on other parts.

The Inner Middle Ground is within the former, and may also be said to be within the bay, commencing about 2 miles W.S.W. of Fisherman's Island, and extending in the same direction as the land and the Middle Ground, 5 miles. The shoalest parts of this sand have but half a fathom, which are nearly abreast of Fisherman's Island; at other parts, ¾, 1, 1½, 2, and 3 fathoms upon it. It is separated by a gateway running N.N.W. ¼ W. and S.S.E. ¼ E., which has 5½ and 7 fathoms in it; and between the main body of the shoal and the coast there is a shallow channel of 3½ and 4 fathoms, called the North Channel.

False Channel.—Between the western edge of the Inner Middle and the eastern part of the Middle is a channel 2 miles in width, with 4, 4½, and 5 fathoms, called the False Channel; from the northern entrance of which flats stretch off to the northward and W.N.W., having 4½ and 5 fathoms upon them.

False Approach.—Between the Nautilus Shoal and the Middle Ground, at the entrance of the bay, there is what is termed the False Approach, a narrow way of 3½ fathoms, leading to the False Channel; and off this False Approach flats stretch off to the southward and S.E., 4 miles, to within 3 miles of Cape Henry. These flats carrying 4, 4½, and 5 fathoms, extend north-eastward to the Shark and Smith's Island Shoal, and to the shoal water along shore to Hog Island, &c.

At the S.W. elbow of the Middle Ground there is a *red buoy*, placed in 2½ to 3 fathoms, at about 5 miles N. by W. ¾ W. from the striped buoy in mid-channel. This buoy lies with Cape Henry lighthouse bearing nearly South, distant 5¼ miles; and Smith's Island lighthouse N.E., 9¼ miles.

HORSE-SHOE SHOAL.—Within the cape is the Horse Shoe, stretching eastward from Old Point Comfort, and dividing the navigation between the James River and Chesapeake Bay. On the tail of the Horse Shoe there is a *black* nun buoy, with the name "Horse Shoe" in large white letters, in 29 ft. water; it lies about 4½ miles N.W. by N. from Cape Henry lighthouse, and 12 miles E. ¼ S. from the lighthouse on Old Point Comfort; the least water at the buoy is 4 fathoms hard sand, with broken ground. The southern edge of this shoal, extending in a westerly direction for 6 miles, connects with the main shore, a little to the North of Old Point Comfort, forming the northern side of the channel into Hampton Roads. The N.E. side extends in a N.W. direction until it connects with the *Pocosin Flats*, nearly up to the entrance of York River, and forms the western side of the bay channel. There is good anchorage on the Horse Shoe, from the tail to within 3½ or 4 miles of the shore, and smaller class vessels may run further in.

On the southern edge of the Horse Shoe are two other *red* buoys, one on the point of the sand, at 6 miles W. by N. ¼ N. from the red buoy of the Tail, the other on the Thimble.

The **Thimble**, marked by the pile light before described, is a small lump lying E. 15° N. from Old Point Comfort lighthouse, distant 3¼ miles, and on the North side of the channel leading to Hampton Roads, with about 9 ft. water on it. A buoy lies in 5 fathoms water, with the name "Thimble" on two sides, in black letters. There are 7 fathoms close to this shoal, but it is small in extent, and therefore quickly passed. Between it and Willoughby's Point the channel is about a mile wide.

LYNHAVEN ROADS.—The coast within Cape Henry forms the slender bay called Lynhaven, or *Lynn Haven Roads*, extending 7½ miles East and West, in which there is anchorage under the shelter of the cape for vessels waiting for a pilot, or weather bound.

HAMPTON ROADS is that part of the estuary of the James River, which is inside the strong fortresses of Fort Monroe, on the North, and Fort Wool on the Rip Raps, on the South. The name is derived from the town of Hampton, 2 or 3 miles to the northward, an old place possessing much historic interest. It became a fashionable and much frequented bathing place for the Southern States.

If bound into Hampton Roads, bring Cape Henry lighthouse to bear South, distant 1¼ mile, and steer W. by N. ¼ N., passing to the southward of the Thimbles lighthouse, between it and the black buoy on the Willoughby Spit, in not less than 5 fathoms water. If the tide is flood, steer half a point more to the southward; if ebb, half a point more to the northward. When the Thimbles lighthouse bears N.E. by E. ¼ E., distant 1 mile, the course up is then W.S.W.; or, when Old Point Comfort lighthouse bears W. ¼ S., alter the course gradually for it. When the East end of Rip Raps is on with Sewall Point, steer midway between the Rip Raps and Old Point Comfort lighthouse for Hampton Roads, and anchor in from 7 to 10 fathoms water, the lighthouse bearing from N.E. ¼ N. to N.E. ¼ E., distant 1, 2, or 3 miles; moor with open hawse to the northward and eastward.

From Fortress Monroe, at Old Point Comfort, a *telegraph cable* is laid to Sewall's Point, passing round the East end of the Rip Raps. Vessels are warned not to anchor in its vicinity.

SANDY HOOK TO CHARLESTON.

Keeping Thimbles lighthouse to the northward of W. by N. clears the 18-feet shoal on the tail of the Horse Shoe. Vessels may anchor on the tail of the Horse Shoe in 5 fathoms water, fine sand, at about 5 miles to the N.W. of Cape Henry lighthouse.

Bound up Elizabeth Roads to *Norfolk*, about 8 miles distant, on the right bank, the channel being buouyed, the chart and lead will be the best guides. Strangers should not attempt this river without a pilot. Least water 21 ft.

Craney Island pile lighthouse stands on the western side of the entrance to Elizabeth River, showing a fixed light. *Fog-bell* at 12 seconds interval.

At *Lambert's Point*, 2 miles below Norfolk, and S.S.E. 1¼ mile from Craney Island light, a pile lighthouse is placed, about 600 yards West of the point, and on the eastern side of the channel. A *fixed red* light is shown from it, elevated 38 feet, visible 10 miles off. At 50 yards South of this lighthouse a stone pile is nearly bare at low water. *Fog-bell* at intervals of 10 seconds. At the wharf of the Naval Hospital, in Elizabeth River, a *fixed light* is also shown. On the opposite shore is *Gosport*, with its navy yard and a graving dock, 350 ft. in length, with 25 ft. water over the sill.

James River falls into Hampton Roads from the N.W. At about 100 miles from its entrance are the towns of Richmond and Manchester. Vessels of 18 feet draught can navigate this river for about 70 miles to the junction of the Appomatox, and vessels of 7 ft. draught, up to Warwick Bar, within 5 miles of Richmond.

Tides.—The flood tide runs in round Cape Henry and Lynhaven Bay until 8 o'clock, on the full and change, in mid-channel; and out of the way of the Chesapeake stream it flows at 8 o'clock; in Hampton Roads at $8^h 22^m$; rise 3 ft. As the tide varies considerably in its direction, according to the tide from ebb to flood, and is influenced by the wind, attention should be paid to the bearings of the lights, as well as to the soundings, when running up either to Willoughby's Point or New Point Comfort, for fear you cross the channel. The ebb from James and York Rivers sets over the Middle Ground to the eastward, which renders the navigation dangerous in the night or thick weather. In 1872, Staff-Commander Dathan observed the flood tide run up in mid-channel until very nearly low water by the shore.

DIRECTIONS FOR ENTERING THE CHESAPEAKE.—In coming from the southward, and intending to round Cape Henry, care should be taken to avoid a small shoal that stretches about 2 cables from the shore, East from the lighthouse; when round this, the rest of the point is moderately steep.

In turning to windward for the entrance, you may stand to the southward until the lighthouse bears N.W. by N., and to the northward till it bears W.S.W. On either of these bearings you will have about 6 fathoms at 6¼ miles from the lighthouse; but within that distance on the former bearing you will be approaching the shoal water of the shore, and where you will have to make shorter boards. In rounding Cape Henry you will have 12, 11, and 10 fathoms, mid-channel, and 7 fathoms well in with Cape Henry and the Flat of the Middle Ground. Within Cape Henry, on standing into Lynhaven Bay, the water shoals from 7 to 4½ and 3½ fathoms in the Roads. A striped mid-channel buoy lies off Cape Henry.

If you intend anchoring in Lynhaven Bay, when you are in the channel with the light W. by S. in 8 or 9 fathoms sticky bottom; you can take your soundings from the South shore, by keeping in towards the lighthouse, and when within a short distance of it you may haul round the point into the bay, and anchor in from 3½ to 4¼ fathoms.

Having brought Cape Henry lighthouse to bear S. by W., distant nearly 2 miles,

CHESAPEAKE BAY AND RIVERS. 103

or just shut in the beach to the southward of it, steer N.W. by N. till Back River lighthouse bears W. by S. ½ S., then a N. ¼ E. course will lead 1¼ mile to the eastward of the 18-feet edge of the Wolf Trap Spit, and over a spot with 26 ft. water on it, at 2 miles N.E. of the Wolf Trap.

On the Horse Shoe side of the entrance the bottom is of hard sand; the midchannel has a soft bottom, but Willoughby's Bank, again, is of hard ground. From the South side, where the bottom is soft, you may therefore always know when you are approaching Willoughby's Bank, by the change in the soundings.

Vessels drawing more than 25 ft. water should not approach the Wolf Trap lighthouse on the eastern side nearer than three-quarters of a mile. Vessels drawing under 18 ft. should not approach the lighthouse on the North and South sides within 1½ mile.

Having passed to the eastward of the Wolf Trap at a distance of 1¼ mile, on a N. ¼ E. course, continue on the same course until Smith Point lighthouse bears N.W. by W. ½ W., distant 2¼ miles, then steer N. by W. ¾ W. for about 10½ miles, and when in 7 fathoms water, with Look-out Point lighthouse bearing West, distant 4 miles, steer N. by W. until Cove Point bears West, distant 1½ mile. Vessels drawing 20 ft. can go up Chesapeake Bay as far as Annapolis Roadstead.

As the main channel into the Chesapeake around Cape Henry is so clear and well marked by its lights and buoys, there will be no need to enter into any further description of, or directions for, the winding channels between the banks on the North side, the more so, as it is certain that these banks and channels are liable to change, and, therefore, in the absence of any good marks, it would be very hazardous for a stranger to get entangled here, except under the most favourable circumstances and extreme caution, with which the chart must form the best guide.

CAPE HENRY OR LYNNHAVEN BAY TO YORK RIVER.—In sailing from this bay for York River, you may safely bring Cape Henry S.S.E., which leads over the tail of the Horse Shoe, in 5 or 6 fathoms. This is marked by the buoy previously mentioned. This part of the shoal lies in ridges, so that you will frequently find more than a fathom difference at a cast, but without danger. The ebb tide down the bay sets over it to the southward.

On the tail, and along the N.E. side of the Horse Shoe, the shoalings are gradual, but the western side of the Middle Ground and York Spit is steep. In proceeding onward, you should not steer from the cape to the northward of N.N.W., allowing for tide and wind, lest you get upon the latter.

Toos Point Light is shown from a brown pile lighthouse on the South point of entrance to York River. The light (first lighted in August, 1875), is *fixed*, elevated 40 feet above the sea, and visible 11 miles off. York Spit light is described on page 100.

If bound into York River, when in 6 fathoms water, with the lighthouse on York Spit bearing N.W. ¼ N., distant about 5 miles, steer in for the mouth of the river on a N.W. by W. course. Vessels drawing under 12 ft. may pass over the shoal to the north-westward of the lighthouse, not within half a mile, but not further distant than 2¼ miles. When in 8 fathoms water, with Toos Point light bearing S.W. by S., steer W. by S. ¼ S. When Gloucester Point bears W.N.W., steer up midway between it and the opposite point to York Town. The deepest water is in the middle of the river; vessels of 15 ft. draught can go up to West point, 35 miles from the entrance; and vessels of 21 ft. draught to 2 miles below West point. H.M.S. *Royal Alfred* anchored in 7½ fathoms water, South of York Spit lighthouse.

Close to the extremity of York Spit there is a depth of 7 fathoms, close to the middle of it there are 10 fathoms, and close to its N.W. part, near the York Isles, there are 13 fathoms, being all steep-to. Within this, the flat from the North shore extends nearly one-third over the river, and should not be approached nearer than in 9 or 8 fathoms.

CAPE HENRY TO MOB JACK, OR NEW COMFORT BAY.—You may proceed from Cape Henry, over the tail of the Horse Shoe, &c., as above directed, for sailing towards York River.

A shoal spit extends to the S.E. 2 miles from New Point Comfort. Its outer point is (or was) marked by a *black* buoy, No. 1. At nearly 2 miles further out in the same S.E. directon is a shoal of $2\frac{3}{4}$ fathoms, with 4 and $5\frac{1}{2}$ fathoms between it and buoy No. 1. Its outer ridge is marked by a *black* buoy, which is $2\frac{1}{2}$ miles S.E. from No. 1, and 4 miles N.N.E. from the York Spit lightvessel, the channel lying between the two.

New Point Comfort Lighthouse is a white building on the low spit, showing a *fixed* light, visible 13 miles off.

Between the New Point Shoal and York Spit you may run in, and anchor under the point, in 4 or 5 fathoms, fine bottom, and lie securely from northerly and N.E. winds.

The four rivers which empty themselves into Mobjack Bay, namely the *Severn, Ware, North River,* and *East River,* are navigable to vessels of 50 or 60 tons burthen, and are, or have been places of considerable trade.

The direct bearing and distance from Cape Henry to the lighthouse on *New Point Comfort* are N.N.W. $\frac{1}{2}$ W. $8\frac{1}{2}$ leagues. The passage by night is dangerous, owing particularly to the tide of ebb, which sets irregularly over the Horse Shoe, and sometimes deceives those best acquainted with this navigation.

In *Mob Jack Bay* vessels at anchor are exposed to winds blowing in any direction between E.S.E. and S.S.E.; but, when thus incommoded, they may go into the River Severn, on the West, where they will lie safely. On sailing in, bring the lighthouse of New Point Comfort E. by S., and steer W. by N. until the entrance of the river bears W.S.W.; you may then steer in W.S.W. or S.W. by W., and be land-locked from all winds.

In running for the river, you descry two clumps of trees on the port hand, which, at first, make like islands, but on a nearer approach the difference will be found. Keep in the middle, and with the lead going; thus passing between two points of marsh, you will carry 3 fathoms all the way over a muddy bottom. Vessels for sea may pass from this river with the wind from any point between N.W. and S.W.

NEW POINT COMFORT TO THE RAPPAHANNOCK AND POTOMAC RIVERS.—You may avoid the spit, which extends to the S.E. from New Point Comfort, by not running into less than 4 fathoms of water.

The main channel of the Chesapeake is from 8 to 10 miles wide between the shoals from the York to the Rappahannock Rivers on the West, and the peninsula on the East. The eastern side of the channel is marked by a *white screw pile lighthouse,* on the western side of the entrance to *Cherrystone Inlet.* It has a *fixed* light, elevated 36 feet, seen 10 miles off, and lies 12 miles E. by S. $\frac{1}{4}$ S. from New Point Comfort lighthouse.

At $6\frac{3}{4}$ miles N.E. $\frac{1}{2}$ N. from New Point Comfort lies the *Wolf Trap Rock,* over which there are only 12 ft. at low water. There are 7 fathoms near the rock. From the spit, extending off the point, to the entrance of Rappahannock River, the mid-channel course is N. $\frac{1}{2}$ W., and the distance 17 miles; thence to a flat, extending to the south-eastward from Smith's Point, the course and distance are North above 5 leagues.

The Wolf-trap Shoals Lighthouse.—The *lighthouse* stands near the East end of the shoals in 12½ ft. water. The iron piles are painted red, and the house itself of a lead colour. The light, elevated 38 ft., is *bright*, revolving every half minute. A *fog-bell* is sounded at intervals of 15 seconds; if the bell is out of order a fog-horn will be sounded.

The **RAPPAHANNOCK RIVER**, which leads up to Fredericksburg, is 18 miles northward of New Point Comfort. Its entrance is between the spit which runs off to the E.S.E. of Windmill Point for above 4 miles on the North side, and *Stingray Point* on the South side, on which is a screw pile *lighthouse*, lying 10¾ miles N. by W. ¾ W. from Wolf Trap lighthouse, and showing a *red* light. A *fog-bell* is sounded at intervals of 5 and 30 seconds. The entrance, which has 4½ to 10 fathoms depth, is quite clear, and the channel up the river is (or was) beaconed and buoyed.

Windmill Point, just half-way between New Point Comfort and Smith's Point, is remarkable, and it appears, when bearing W. ¼ S., 7 miles distant, as represented beneath.

View of Windmill Point, at the North Entrance of the Rappahannock.

Rappahannock Spit Lighthouse.—On the North side of entrance to Rappahannock River is a screw pile lighthouse in 12 ft. water, off Windmill Point, painted straw colour; a *fixed* white light is exhibited from it, at an elevation of 38 ft. above the sea, which can be seen at a distance of 12 miles. A *fog-bell* is sounded every 10 seconds.

The Windmill Reef now extends 4 miles from the point to the S.E. by E., and forms a broad shelf of 2½, 2, and 1½ fathoms, thence shoaling to the dry shore. A *black buoy*, No. 9, marks the eastern extremity of the spit.

Should the weather render it necessary to take shelter in the Rappahannock, when in 6½ fathoms water, with Rappahannock Spit lighthouse N.W. by W., steer into the middle of the river, on a W. by N. ¼ N. course, 10 miles, leaving the black buoy which marks the eastern extremity of Rappahannock Spit about two-thirds of a mile on the starboard hand, and the buoy off Hunting Creek about 3 cables on the port hand. Vessels drawing 18 ft. water, or upwards, should not approach the Rappahannock Spit lighthouse on the eastern side nearer than 2½ miles; but vessels under that draught may approach the lighthouse on its North or South side to three-quarters of a mile. The spit is steep-to on the South side.

POTOMAC RIVER.—In sailing from off *New Point Comfort*, on the course N. ½ W., you may run along in 5 or 6 fathoms; afterwards passing Windmill Point, in from 5 to 7 fathoms. Towards Smith's Point you should not, however, approach to less than 7 fathoms.

The River Potomac separates Virginia from Maryland; its entrance being formed by Smith's Point on the South side, and Point Lookout on the North. The distance between the two points is more than 3 leagues.

Smith's Point, N. by W. ¾ W.

Lights.—A white pile lighthouse is placed in 12 ft. water, on the shoal extending off Smith's Point. It shows a bright light, *revolving* every half minute, at 38 feet above the water. A *fog-bell* is struck every 15 seconds.

On Point Lookout a *fixed* light is shown at an elevation of 37 ft. from a white house. The *fog-bell*, on a red frame, detached from the house, is struck at intervals of 10 seconds.

The River Potomac is navigable for large vessels as high up as Washington, which is 90 miles above Point Lookout; but the navigation is extremely intricate, and nature has done much for the protection of the country, by placing about one-third of the way up (between the Wycomico and Cedar Point) very extensive and intricate shoals, called the *Kettle-bottoms.* They are composed of oyster banks of various dimensions, with passages between them.

If bound into *St. Mary's River*, within the North side of the Potomac, give Point Lookout and the shore about it a good berth. Smith's Point has 4 to 6 fathoms at 150 yards N.E. of the lighthouse, but in a S.E. direction is only 21 ft. at 1½ mile. On approaching St. George's Island (8 miles above Point Lookout), keep nearer to the main on the port than to the shoal extending from that island. The course into the river is nearly N.W., and you may anchor where you please in 5 or 6 fathoms, the river being all open.

If bound to Wicomico, 5 leagues higher up the Potomac, the course and distance from the East end of St. George's Island, past *Pincy Point*, on which a light is shown, and Ragged Point, are N.W. ¼ W., and the distance nearly 3 leagues. On the South side flats extend from the shores, in some places to the distance of a mile, and should be approached no nearer than in 6 fathoms. In the mid-channel you will find 11, 10, 12, 10, and 8 fathoms. In passing Ragged Point, you must give it a good berth, in order to avoid the shoal, which stretches from it. Above Ragged Point, in the middle of the channel, there are 6, 5, 4½, and 7 fathoms of water. You will next advance on a W. ¼ N. course to *Clement's* or *Blackstone's Island*, where a fixed light is shown, passing Nominy Bay on the port hand. From abreast of Clement's Island you may steer W.N.W. in 6, 5, and 4 fathoms, until you have Wicomico River open; then pass pretty near to the island, which is on the East side of the entrance, in order to avoid the shoal stretching from the point on the western side. Steer into the river about North, and anchor on the South side of *Newton's Point*, in 5 or 4½ fathoms.

The distance from Ragged Point to the city of Washington is about 24 leagues; and to those unacquainted with the river a pilot is indispensable.

POTOMAC RIVER TO THE RIVER PATUXENT.—In sailing from the entrance of the Potomac to that of the Patuxent, you must be careful to avoid the flat already described, which extends from Point Lookout, by not going into less than 6 or 7 fathoms. Opposite to this point the flats from the *Tangier Islands* extend so far to the westward as to narrow the Chesapeake Channel to a breadth of about 5 miles. This part of the eastern flats is steep-to, having 12 fathoms close to it.

Tangier Sound, &c.—On the opposite shore of the Chesapeake is a series of islands and channels, of which no verbal description can be of use. The southern portion of them is the entrance to *Tangier* and *Pocomoke Sounds.*

Watt's Island and *Lighthouse* lie in their South entrance. The lighthouse is 40 ft. high, and shows a fixed light with flashes every 2 minutes, at 50 feet, seen 12 miles off.

If you wish to go into Tangier Sound, bring the lighthouse on Stingray Point to bear S.W. ¾ W., and steering N.E. ¾ E., soundings will be found on Tangier Bar in 6 fathoms; the cluster of pine trees and buildings on the southern Tangier Island will then be seen bearing N.E., and you may then edge off on the southern part of the bar in what depth you please, from 3 to 13 fathoms, bottom hard and sandy; but it is not advisable to come nearer Tangier Bar than 6 fathoms, as it shoalens from 6 to 2 fathoms in 200 yards. Should you wish to anchor, when the cluster of trees bears West, haul up to the northward and westward, where there is good anchorage for small vessels, secure from westerly winds, in a bay called Croket's Bay, about S.E. from the houses in the middle of the island, and N.E. of the cluster of trees. In proceeding up the sound, it is proper to get soundings on the Watts Island side, as it is rather more gradual, steering parallel with the islands on your starboard hand North, and keeping in mid-channel. Above this the channel is lighted and buoyed, but it is not navigable by any descriptive directions; and if not locally acquainted, a pilot is necessary.

Fog Point Light, on Smith Island, opposite the Potomac entrance, marks the Kedge's Strait entrance of Tangier Sound. The light is fixed, at 35 feet, visible 11 miles off.

Hooper's Strait.—Below the Patuxent, on the eastern side of the Chesapeake, is the inlet named Hooper's Strait, an entrance to Tangier Sound, formed by the bank of *Bloodsworth Island* on the South, and that of *Hooper's Island* on the North. Within this strait is a *pile lighthouse*, showing a *fixed* light. It is close on the edge of deep water. If running upward, bring the light to bear E. by N., and stand for it, which course will take you across Hooper's Island bar in about 4 fathoms of water. Continue on until you deepen into 7 fathoms; then steer E.N.E. until the light bears East, and run for it. Pass the light on your starboard hand, which will carry you into the harbour. A *fog-bell* is sounded at intervals of 12 seconds.

If coming down the Chesapeake, bring the light to bear N.E., and steer for it, when you will gradually shoalen your water on the South side. You may, with safety, course round the bar or shoal in 3 fathoms, until you bring the light to bear East, then steer as above.

In sailing between Point Lookout and the entrance of the Patuxent, a good depth to keep in is 7 and 8 fathoms. On the eastern side, near the flat, there are 10, 12, 9, and 10 fathoms.

Patuxent River.—*Cedar Point*, the S.E. point of the Patuxent, is low and sandy, and has some straggling trees upon it. A flat extends about the point to the eastward and northward. The North side of the river may be known by the high lands called the *Cliffs*, having trees upon them; from this side, as well as from the other, there is a flat, but the shoalings on each side are gradual, and the bottom soft. In mid-channel there is a depth of 8 to 10 fathoms. At 4 miles to the North is *Cove Point*, on which is a lighthouse, showing a *flashing* light every 1½ minute. A *fog-bell* is sounded at intervals of 10 seconds.

Within Cedar Point, on the South side, is *Rously's* or *Hog Point*. On the North side of the entrance is *Drum Point*. The latter is low and sandy. Without these points yo may anchor; or, passing between them, proceed further up the river.

Having arrived at the *eastward* of Point Lookout, with the wind ahead, you will have a good channel to beat in up to the Patuxent, and may stand to either side into 4 or 5 fathoms; but observe that, when standing to the eastward, it is proper to tack when you have gained 9 or 10 fathoms, and the ground suddenly shoalens to 5 or 4 fathoms, and thence to 2 fathoms, hard sand. On the western side the soundings are more regular.

The course and distance from Point Lookout to the entrance of Patuxent River are N. by W. ¼ W. 5 leagues. The depths 7 to 8 fathoms up to Cedar Point. Should it be requisite to anchor, and you cannot get into the Patuxent, which frequently happens with northerly winds, you may run in under Cedar Point, and anchor in 3 or 4 fathoms, good ground.

The entrance of the Patuxent is remarkable from its having very high land on the North side, with red banks or cliffs. You may enter the river by the preceding directions; or, give Cedar Point a berth, and stand to the northward until you have the river open, when you may run in for Drum Point on the starboard side, which is sandy and bold, with some bushes on it. Double this point, and come-to in 3 or 2½ fathoms, where you may lie securely.

In beating in or out of the Patuxent, you may stand towards the North side, against the high cliffs, into 3 fathoms, and towards the South side to 5 fathoms, of water. In the channel there are 7 fathoms. When standing towards the South shore, you will perceive some building on the North side, above Drum Point; so soon as these buildings come on with that point you must tack, in order to avoid the shoal which extends from the South side at the entrance.

RIVER PATUXENT TO ANNAPOLIS AND BALTIMORE.—On leaving Patuxent, and being bound up the Chesapeake towards Annapolis, you must give a wide berth to the cliffy land southward of Cove Point, as a flat extends from it to the distance of half a league. On the edge of this flat there are 2½ and 3 fathoms; but there are 10 fathoms at no great distance. On sailing out run eastward into the main stream until you have 9 or 10 fathoms water, when you will be near mid-channel; the course and distance hence up to Poplar Island are N. ⅛ W. 9 leagues. In running thus, you will have 10, 9, 8, 7, and 10 fathoms.

In proceeding as above you will pass *Sharp's Island*, lying off the eastern shore at the entrance of *Choptank River*, and 8 miles to the southward of Poplar Island. Sharp's Isle is 3 miles long, and surrounded by a shoal more than a mile broad; but with an adverse wind good anchorage under it may be found. A *pile* lighthouse stands on its North point, showing a fixed light, which comes in sight soon after passing Coal Point. The similar isle, called *James Island*, lies 5 miles S. by E. from Sharp's Island, and is likewise surrounded by a shoal. To gain the anchorage under Sharp's Island, after passing James Island Point, steer to the N.N.E., which will carry you under Sharp's Island, when you may anchor at about half a mile from the island, secure from northerly and N.W. winds. There are pilots who may be engaged at this place. A fixed light is shown from a pile lighthouse in Choptank River, 9 miles within Sharp's Island light.

From the channel West of *Poplar Island* a N. by E. course to the distance of 4½ leagues will carry you up to the Severn, or Annapolis River. Should the wind oppose you when up with the South end of Kent Island, you may run in under it, to the north-eastward of Poplar Isle, and anchor in 6 fathoms, secure from all winds, except those from the south-westward.

From the *River Patuxent* to that of *Annapolis*, the western side of the bay is rather high; but the soundings are generally gradual. In running from Poplar Island to Talley's or Annapolis Point (the southern part of the entrance to Annapolis), you will have from 7 to 8 fathoms; but you must observe to give a good berth to Talley's Point, as well as to Thomas Point, lying more to the southward, as there is a long spit from each.

Upon *Thomas Point*, on the North side of South River, at 4 miles below Annapolis, there is a lighthouse, with *fixed* light. From the shore hereabout the shoal extends outward to the distance of 2 miles.

Annapolis.—Besides the Thomas Point light, marking the South side of the entrance of this port, there is a *fixed light* on Greenberry Point, on the North side. A light, revolving every 1½ minute, is shown on Sandy Point, 4 miles N.E. of Greenbury Point, and a *fog-bell* is struck at intervals of 10 seconds. In running from abreast of Poplar Island to Annapolis Roads, steer N.N.E. about 9 miles to abreast of Thomas Point (on your port hand, and on which is a lighthouse). From this point a dangerous shoal runs off in a S.E. direction, which must be carefully avoided, and which is marked by a *black* buoy, lying about 1¾ mile from the lighthouse. From abreast of Thomas Point you may steer N. by W., 3 miles for Annapolis Road, past the spit marked by a *black* buoy off Tally Point, on the port hand.

When abreast of Poplar Island, should the wind prove contrary, run into Eastern Bay, between Kent and Poplar Islands, anchoring in 7 or 8 fathoms. Here you will be safe from all winds but those that blow from the south-westward.

The land from the Patuxent to Annapolis is high, and the soundings towards the shore gradual; and in this space are several small bays. In running from Poplar Island to Tally's or Annapolis Point (the southern point of the entrance to the Severn River or Annapolis), you will have 5½, 6, 11, 14, 8, and 7 fathoms. Give a good berth to the Horse-shoe, Thomas, and Tally Points, steering well to the eastward, as there is a long spit from each.

If bound into the river, after having given Tally Point a berth, haul in to the westward for the mouth of the river, taking soundings from the South side, in 3 or 4 fathoms. You will thus pass between Tally's and Greenbury Points (on the latter of which is a lighthouse), keeping nearly midway between them. On the northern side of the entrance, on a spit that runs South from Hacket's Point, is a *red* buoy, about a mile from the point; and a *red* buoy is also placed to the southward of Greenbury Point. Just above Greenbury Point you may anchor in 3 or 4 fathoms, secure from all winds.

The best anchorage for a large ship in the Outer Roads, is with the Poplar on Horn Point in one with the State House, in 8 fathoms, mud, and Thomas Point lighthouse bearing S.W. by S. about 4 miles from the city. The State House at Annapolis is very remarkable, by its having a large steeple, and may be seen from abreast of the head of Poplar ,Island.

CHESTER RIVER.—To enter Chester River, which lies to the N.E. of Annapolis, on the East side of Chesapeake Bay: when up with the lower 5 fathoms buoy, the black buoy on the South end of Swan Point bar bearing East, and the red buoy on the N.E. end of Kent Island Spit (the spit extending from Love Point), E.S.E., steer E. by S. ½ S., passing between these buoys. When past the buoy on the Kent Island Spit, steer S. by W. ¼ W. until the tall poplar tree on Love Point bears N.W. ¼ W., and anchor on the West side of the channel in 30 ft. water, soft bottom. Small vessels, if the wind is North, can run up and anchor off Hail Point.

Love Point pile lighthouse, on the shoal running off from the upper end of Kent Island, painted white, exhibits, at an elevation of 38 ft. above the sea, a *red* light, with *red flashes every* 20 *seconds*, having elipses between the flashes. The light is visible for 11 miles. Vessels drawing more than 9 ft. should not pass between the point and lighthouse. A *fog bell* is struck at intervals of 8 *seconds*.

Bound to Baltimore, and not intending anchoring in Annapolis Roads, continue your course N.N.E. from off Thomas Point, 12 miles, through a depth of 8, 9, 7, 6, and 5½ fathoms, till you come to a buoy painted in perpendicular stripes. In this part of the Chesapeake the channel narrows to 3 miles, leaving the navigable passage between the shallow water on either side, only 2 miles in width. Here, on the port side of the channel, in lat. 39° 1', is Sandy Point with its lighthouse, and off which at a mile to the eastward, is a *black* buoy. When up with the first perpendicularly *striped* buoy, which lies N.E. by N., 5 miles from Sandy Point lighthouse, steer N. by E., 2¼ miles for the second, and North, 1½ mile for the third. Here you will come abreast of the buoys that mark the approaches to the Patapsco or Baltimore River, and the navigation becomes too intricate for directions to be of much service to a stranger.

From the middle of the channel, East of Annapolis, the course and distance are N.N.E. and N. by E., 4½ leagues. This leads up to the entrance of the Patapco, or Baltimore River.

· In sailing as above, between Annapolis and Baltimore River, you will find from 4 to 9 fathoms of water. You should go no nearer to the western side than in 4½ or 5 fathoms, until the river comes open, and Swan's Point bears about E.S.E., when you may haul in for the river.

PATAPSCO or BALTIMORE RIVER.—The entrance of this river is shoal, and its navigation rather intricate. *Baltimore* is 3½ leagues above the North point of the entrance. It is the third city in population, having 267,354 inhabitants in 1870, and the fifth in consequence, in the United States. It stands on the North side of a basin formed by a narrow arm of the Patapsco, which constitutes a safe and convenient harbour. The entrance is defended by a fort and battery. A rivulet, *Jones's Falls*, divides the city into two parts, called the *Town* and *Fell's Point*, which are connected by bridges.

The port of Baltimore is particularly well situated for carrying on a large foreign commerce. The city is built upon the shore of a bay, or estuary, which extends about 2½ miles inland from the North side of the Patapsco River, about 12 miles from its entrance into the Chesapeake Bay. The city, by ship-channel, is about 200 miles from the ocean. It is 38 miles by railroad N.E. from Washington, and 98 miles S.W. from Philadelphia.

Having a spacious and secure harbour, being in a central position as regards the Atlantic portions of the United States, and having direct communication with the West by the Baltimore and Ohio Railway; with the North and N.E. by the Pennsylvania Northern and Central, and the Baltimore, Philadelphia, and Wilmington lines; and with the South by the Baltimore and Potomac, and the branches of the Baltimore and Ohio. Besides the foregoing lines of railways, Baltimore is in direct communication by steam-ships with Norfolk, Wilmington, Savannah, Charleston, and New Orleans, also with Philadelphia, Boston, and New York.

In 1873, a company was chartered to connect Chesapeake and Delaware Bays by means of a ship-canal, to admit the largest class of vessels frequenting Baltimore; thus decreasing the distance to Europe.

Lights.—At the mouth of Patapsco River, between the Main and Swash Channels, is a black pile lighthouse, on the *Seven Foot Knoll*, showing a fixed light at 43 feet. A *fog bell* is struck at intervals of 12 seconds. On Fort Carroll, on the North side of the channel, another fixed light is shown, and a fog bell sounded.

Leading lights for Brewerton Channel are established on the South side of Patapsco River, at Hawkins Point and Leading Point. At Hawkins Point white pile lighthouse an upper and lower *fixed bright* light are shown at 70 and 28 ft. On Leading Point, at an elevation of 70 ft., one *fixed bright* light is shown from a brown structure 1½ mile from Hawkins Point light. They bear from each other W.N.W. ¼ W. and E.S.E. ¼ E.

A *red light*, to distinguish it from the flame of a blast furnace near by, is shown on the North side of Baltimore Harbour, on Lazaretto Point, opposite Fort McHenry, at an elevation of 35 ft. A fog bell is struck at 10-second intervals.

To enter Patapsco River.—Having passed the lower and upper 5-fathom buoys, the water deepens to 7½ fathoms; then steer N.N.W. for the entrance buoy in 4 fathoms water. Leave this buoy to the northward, and when it bears E. by N. ½ N.,

CHESAPEAKE BAY AND RIVERS.   111

distant about 3 cables, steer W. by N. ¾ N. for the red buoy off the 16-ft. knoll, leaving it a little on the starboard hand; bring the lighthouse on Leading Point on with the lighthouse on Hawkins Point, and proceed up the Brewerton Channel with them in line, leaving the red buoys on the starboard hand, until Fort Carroll bears N.N.W. ¾ W., when Fort McHenry flagstaff should be slightly open to the southward of Washington Monument, which may be known from the shot-towers by its being white, and standing to the westward of them; steer N.W. ¼ N., passing between the buoy off Hawkins Point and the buoy on the spit that extends 2 cables off from Fort Carroll. This course leads over the tail of the spit that runs off from between Hawkins and Leading Points, in 18 ft. water, up to the Narrows. When abreast of Lazaretto lighthouse, having passed to the westward of a buoy on a spit below the Lazaretto, stand on in mid-channel, passing to the eastward of a buoy on a spit extending from Fort McHenry, then haul up for the anchorage in the basin, keeping to the southward and westward of the middle ground.

Craighill Channel and Lights.—Leading lights for Craighill Channel were established in 1873, the near lighthouse painted black and straw colour, showing one fixed light at 106 ft., and the front light in 15 ft. water off the Patapsco River, two fixed lights at 30 and 17 ft. are shown, and a *fog* bell sounded at intervals of 5 and 30 seconds. These two lights are designed as leading or range lights for the Craighill Channel. The one near Miller's Island is distant from North Point, in a northeasterly direction, about 3½ nautical miles; and the other, 2¼ nautical miles E. by S. from North Point. The two lights are 2½ nautical miles apart, bearing due North and South (true) from each other, and they are exactly in range with the axis of the Craighill Channel. The front (or low) lighthouse will show as a cast-iron cylinder, surmounted by the keeper's dwelling and lantern. The lower light is a range light, and will be seen in the axis of the channel only. At present (1875) the structure is in an unfinished condition, and is surrounded by a wharf, on wooden piles, so that the cylinder is not seen. The rear (or high) lighthouse is a open-frame pyramid, of four sides, the lower portion being painted straw colour, and the upper part black. The lens of the rear (or high) light is a range lens, and will be seen only in the direction of the axis of the Craighill Channel. They should both be distinctly visible below the South end of the channel, in ordinary states of the atmosphere. When a vessel is on the true course, going up or down stream, the two lights will show one directly over the other, a slight change to either side producing a corresponding change in the relative position of the lights.

In consequence of vessels, drawing over 20 ft., not being able to reach Baltimore, the work of making a straight channel from the deep waters of Chesapeake Bay up to Baltimore by dredging away the shoals was undertaken; and in 1873, from the lower end of Craighill Channel, 18 miles below Fort McHenry, to a point opposite Fort Carroll, a distance of 13 miles, a channel had been opened 24 ft. deep at mean low water, and 235 ft. wide through all soft bottom, and 400 ft. wide through the hard shoals crossing the line of the Craighill Channel. An appropriation of about 50,000 dollars a year will keep the Craighill and Brewerton Channels with an uniform depth of 24 ft.

Havre de Grace, at the mouth of Susquehanna River, can only be reached by vessels of from 6 to 8 ft. draught; vessels drawing more, have to load or unload at Spesutic Island. The terminus of the Tidewater Canal is here.

Lights.—Pool Island lighthouse, on West side of the channel, off the mouth of the Gunpowder River, is white, and exhibits, at 35 ft. above the sea, a *fixed* white light, visible 10 miles. A bell is sounded during foggy weather at intervals of 12 *seconds*.

On *Turkey Point*, the bluff separating the mouths of the Elk and Susquehanna Rivers, at the head of Chesapeake Bay, is a white lighthouse, 30 ft. high, which exhibits, at 65 ft. above the sea, a *fixed* white light, visible 12 miles. The tower is partially hidden by foliage, but the light can be seen above it.

Fishing or Donoho Battery lighthouse, about 3 miles southward of Havre de Grace, rises from the keeper's dwelling, is red, and exhibits, at 36 ft. above the sea, a *fixed* white light, visible 10 miles.

On Concord Point, the West side of entrance to the Susquehanna, is a white lighthouse, which exhibits, at 40 ft. above the sea, a *fixed* white light, visible 10 miles.

BOUND UP CHESAPEAKE BAY TO SUSQUEHANNA RIVER from the upper 5 fathom buoy, keep the lead going, steer N. by E. ¾ E. until Swan Point bears East, distant 1¾ mile, and the Seven-foot Knoll lighthouse bears W. by N., distant 4 miles; when steer N.E. by N. until the South point of Pool Island bears N. ¾ W., distant 3½ miles, giving Mitchell Bluff a berth of five-eighths of a mile. Thence the course is N.N.E. ¼ E., passing 1½ cable to the westward of Worton Point buoy. With Worton Point bearing S. by E., distant 1½ mile, and the walnut tree E. by S. ½ S., distant 1¼ mile, steer N.E. by E. ¼ E., giving Howell Point a berth of half a mile. Having passed the mouth of the Sassafras River, with Grove Point bearing S.E. by S., distant 1½ mile, and Turkey Point lighthouse bearing N.W., distant 3½ miles, steer N.N.E. ¼ E.

When Turkey Point lighthouse bears East, distant 1¼ mile, the course is N.N.W. ¾ W., until Locust Point bears W. ¾ N., distant five-eighths of a mile, and Turkey Point lighthouse S.E. ¼ E., distant 2¾ miles; then steer N.W. ¾ W. for nearly a mile, until Locust Point bears S. ¼ E., distant three-eighths of a mile, then W. ¼ N. until the Persimmon tree is on with two poplar trees at Webster's house, bearing S. by W. Stand to northward and eastward with this mark on until the Susquehanna River opens, and the Havre de Grace lighthouse on Concord Point bears N.W., distant one-third of a mile, when anchor, or follow the buoys up the river.

From Patapsco River up the bay.—In Brewerton Channel and abreast of North Point low lighthouse, bearing N.N.W., steer N.E. by E. ½ E., until Martin's house on Hart Island bears N.W. by W. ¾ W., distant 2¼ miles; thence, if intending to pass to the eastward of Pool Island, steer E.N.E. until abreast of the black buoy on the S.W. spit of Pool Island; from here the course is N.E. ¼ E. When abreast, and 1 cable to the westward and northward of the buoy on the Middle Ground, steer E. ½ N. until Worton Point and the walnut tree are in line. Steer with this mark until Pool Island lighthouse bears W. ¼ S., when follow the directions given above.

If intending to pass to the westward of Pool Island.—With Martin's house on Hart Island bearing W. by N. ¼ N., distant 2¼ miles, steer N.E. ¼ N. until Pool Island lighthouse bears E. ¼ S., distant half a mile. Thence the course is N.E. by E. ¼ E., passing one-third of a mile to the northward and westward of the buoy off Worton Point, when follow the directions previously given. The channel to the westward of Pool Island should not be attempted by strangers.

Devil Island Bank, opposite Concord Point, is nearly dry at low water. The channel leading towards Havre de Grace lighthouse is narrow and crooked. Strangers must be guided altogether by the lead, and not run in the night.

(113)

COAST FROM CAPE HENRY TO CHARLESTON.

Southward of Cape Henry the coast presents but few features by which it can be recognised by passing vessels, and has no maritime interest whatever. For a distance of 270 miles to Cape Fear, it mainly consists of a narrow belt of low beach or sandhills, enclosing the extensive sounds or lagoons which form the sea face of North Carolina. *Caution* is necessary not to mistake the higher inland for the coast.

The soundings decrease regularly towards the shore as far as the Wimble Shoals, or for a distance of 85 miles, except in one spot 22 miles South of Cape Henry, where a projecting 15-ft. shoal stands 1¼ mile off the beach. For the rest the 10 fathoms line is about 6 or 8 miles off, and 5 fathoms at 2 miles off the shore. The chief marks are the *Wash Wood*, abreast of the above-mentioned detached breakers. At 30 miles South of Cape Henry is *Currituck Inlet*, now closed; 13 miles farther is *Baum's Windmill*, in lat. 36° 15¼'. Some sandhills are seen farther South, and a larger one, the *Nag's Head*, in lat. 35° 55', is almost the only noticeable feature.

Currituck lighthouse, to show a light at an elevation of 150 ft., visible 18 miles off, is building on Currituck Beach, midway between Cape Henry and Body Island lighthouses.

Oregon Inlet, once of use, is now nearly closed. Six feet of water can be found there at smooth times, but the "bulkhead" inside affords but 3 or 4 ft. It is so dangerous that the smallest craft dare not use it. The new "Body Island light" stands upon the North point of the beach.

BODY ISLAND and LIGHTHOUSE.—Body Island forms the South side of *Oregon Inlet* into Roanoke Sound. The lighthouse, erected in 1847, was destroyed during the war, and a fine new lighthouse, 150 ft. high, was completed in 1872, 2¼ miles North of the old light, and 1½ mile North of Oregon Inlet. The tower is painted in bands, 22 ft. wide, alternately white and black. The light is a *fixed bright light*, elevated 156 ft., and visible, all round the horizon, 18 miles off. From it Cape Hatteras light bears due South 35 miles, and Cape Henry light, N. by W. ½ W., 70 miles.

At the South end of Body or Bodie Island is *New Inlet*, having only 4 ft. of water in 1869, 6½ miles from the white tower; and 3½ miles farther is *Loggerhead Inlet*, with only 5 feet of water in 1869 into Pamplico Sound. From this the coast assumes a more southerly direction, trending S. ¾ W. for 23 miles to Cape Hatteras lighthouse.

Wimble Shoals, in the vicinity of which many wrecks have happened, lie off the coast of North Carolina, between lat. 35° 37' and 35° 30'. On and around the shoals the bottom is very uneven, varying suddenly from 8 to 10 fathoms, and from 4 to 5 fathoms. The least water found on the shoals 3½ fathoms, at two places. Their outermost limit is nearly 4 miles from the coast. No vessel drawing more than 18 ft. should pass in less than 11 fathoms water, either around the Wimble, or around Hatteras Shoals.

The *currents* hereabouts are governed by the wind, and are very strong, making heavy rips, which have every appearance of shoals to those who are not familiar with them. Sometimes the current begins to run quite strong twenty-four hours in advance of the wind at the same place. The storm, which is sure to come, always sets in from the direction in which the current has started.

CAPE HATTERAS is a singular projection, the northernmost of the three apparently formed by the same cause, probably the conflict between the Gulf Stream

U. S.—Part I.   Q and the Arctic current within it, which flow in opposite directions. Cape Hatteras is the S.E. extreme of that narrow spit, or line of banks, which enclose Pamplico and Albemarle Sounds, and from its extremity a series of very dangerous shoals extend for a distance of 9 miles south-eastward. In former years, on this account, this cape was very much dreaded, and its dangers were also much exaggerated, but the U.S. coast survey, in 1850, made us acquainted with its true character. But its changing nature will not allow of any permanent marks being given for its shoals and channels, for between 1845 and 1857 the S.W. spit, on which the beacon light stands, had increased nearly half a mile, and the lighthouse built on its extremity, in 1798, is now above 2 miles from its extremity.

The **LIGHTHOUSE**, in lat. 35° 15′ 8″ N., long. 75° 30′ 57″ W., is a tower 140 feet high, painted in spiral bands, alternately black and white. It has a lens apparatus of the first order, which gives a bright flash every 15 seconds, at 150 ft. above the sea, and may be seen more than 20 miles off.

A **Beacon Light**, bright and *fixed*, is shown from an open framework structure, painted red, at above a quarter of a mile, within the extremity of the point, and at 1½ mile *South true* from the high light. It is elevated 25 ft., seen 7 miles off. In one with the high light it leads clear to the westward of the shore.

The **HATTERAS SHOALS**, according to the survey, consist of the *Spit*, extending for about 1¼ mile from the dry land to S.S.E., and has very irregular depths of from 9 ft. to 5 or 6 fathoms.

The *Diamond Shoal or Stone* lies within 3 miles of the point, and has about 12 ft. least water. It is about 2 miles in extent. The *Outer Shoals* lie 3¼ miles outside the Diamond, and are 9 miles from the beacon light, and have patches of 9 ft. least water.

The sea breaks over all these shoals tremendously, and the roar of the surf and breakers may be heard at a considerable distance, and should be a warning in thick weather.

The following directions are taken from the survey; but, as the shoals and channels are liable to shift, they must be received with some caution.

Cape Hatteras Light bears N. 37° W., distant about 8½ nautical miles from the south-eastern edge of the 9 ft. or Outer Shoals.

To clear the *Outer Shoals*, in approaching them from the northward and eastward, bring the lighthouse to bear West in 12 to 10 fathoms water, when run South, keeping in not less than 10 fathoms water, until the lighthouse bears N.W. ½ N., when any course South of West may be steered with safety.

In coming from the southward and westward, keep in not less than 10 fathoms water, until the lighthouse bears N.W., when any course eastward of North may be steered. The beacon light and the high light in one clears all to westward.

In bad weather, and especially at night, do not approach the Outer Shoals nearer than 15 fathoms water from the northward and eastward, and 12 to 11 fathoms from the southward and westward.

It is necessary to watch the bearings of the lighthouse, and keep the lead going in beating around or between the shoals. In approaching the shoals at night, or in bad weather, if the lights have not been seen before night, it will not be prudent to run for it.

As 10 or 11 fathoms may be found to the westward of the shoals, in going outside of them from the southward and westward, do not approach the land to the southward of the cape nearer than 8½ to 10 miles.

To pass between the Diamond and Outer Shoals, from the northward and eastward, bring the lighthouse to bear West in 10 to 9 fathoms water, about 4¼ miles from it, and run South until the water shoals to 7 or 8 fathoms, and the lighthouse bearing N.W. ¼ W., when run S.W., carrying not less than 4 fathoms through the channel, and deepening gradually to the south-western edge of it, until in 7 or 8 fathoms, with the lighthouse bearing North.

In approaching this channel from the southward and westward, bring the lighthouse to bear North in 8 to 7 fathoms water, about 4¼ miles distant from it, and run N.E. until in 8 or 9 fathoms water, and the lighthouse bearing N.W., when the shoals will be cleared.

To pass between the Diamond and Cape Hatteras Spit from the northward and eastward, bring the lighthouse to bear N.W. by W. ¼ W. in 8 to 7 fathoms water, 2½ miles distant, and steer S.W., giving the end of the Spit and breakers a berth of half a mile. On this course not less than 3 fathoms will be found. When the lighthouse bears North in 5 to 6 fathoms water, the Diamond will be cleared, and when the lighthouse bears N.N.E. ¼ E., in 6 to 7 fathoms water, the Spit will be cleared, and the anchorage in the cove open.

To pass between the Diamond and the Spit from the southward and westward, bring the lighthouse to bear North in 5 fathoms water, 2 miles from the breakers and point, and run N.E. until in 9 to 10 fathoms water, when the shoals will be cleared.

HATTERAS COVE, which lies on the western side of the projecting spit of the cape, marked by the beacon light, affords protection from all winds, except those from the southward and westward, being exposed from South to W.N.W.

To enter from the southward and westward, bring Hatteras high light to bear N.E. by N. ¾ N., and run for it. Anchor, when in from 5 to 4½ fathoms water, muddy bottom, with the breakers on the S.W. spit bearing South, and the low light to eastward.

To enter from the northward and eastward, pass round or between the shoals, as above directed, and when the low light comes in range with the main light, you are to westward, and may bear up for the anchorage. Vessels beating in should go about on approaching the western shore, or in standing towards the spit, on getting into less than 4 fathoms.

The greatest rise and fall of tides in Hatteras Cove is 5½ ft.; the mean, 3 ft. 3 inches, and the least 2¼ ft.

The bottom is hard sand, with an occasional small spot of blue mud. The currents over and in the vicinity of the shoals have a velocity of 3 to 5 knots per hour, and are greatly influenced in direction and force by the winds. The surface water of the Gulf Stream extends to within a short distance of the Outer Shoals for some time after a continuation of northerly and easterly winds.

WEATHER NEAR CAPE HATTERAS.—Gales from the eastward are more severe in the vicinity of Cape Hatteras than on any other part of the coast, and they give very little warning; but the first indication is hazy weather, with small rain. When these come on, it is, consequently, proper to get an offing as quickly as possible.

In the summer season, dangerous thunder storms are very frequent here, and about the inner border of the Gulf Stream. The first indication of these storms is a black heavy cloud, the weather sultry, little wind, and variable. It is advisable, at the appearance of these warnings, not to stay to reef, but to clew up every sail, except the fore-sail and foretopmast stay-sail, and your ship will be ready to veer; if you have time to have the sails clewed up, do it; but it seldom happens that you have, as these gales come on suddenly.

This uncertainty and violence of the wind hereabout is owing to its being on the northern limit of the tropical calms in the summer season, when there is a conflict between the trades to the South, and the anti-trade winds to the North of it.

SANDY HOOK TO CHARLESTON.

HATTERAS INLET is 12 miles W. by S. ¾ S. from Cape Hatteras. It may be known by a low sand island on its eastern side, which was formerly a round hummock, covered with trees. The breakers seldom extend entirely across the entrance, but rise on each side of the entrance, leaving the channel between.

Oliver Reef Lighthouse.—Within and on the North side of Hatteras Inlet is a white pile lighthouse, from which is shown a *red flashing light* every half minute, elevated 38 ft., and visible 11 miles off. From it Fort Clark bears S. ½ E. 5 miles, and Cape Hatteras light E. ¾ S. 11 miles. A *fog bell* is struck at 8-second intervals.

Hatteras Inlet has from 17 to 20 ft. upon the bar, but there is a bulkhead with but 11 ft. on it just inside the points of the beach. Above that there is good anchorage in from 3 to 4 fathoms. Below the bulkhead there is little or no shelter, and the current frequently reaches 6 and 7 knots.

The bar should be approached from the northward and eastward. Keep in from 4 to 5 fathoms water along the breakers, until up with the opening. The course in is, or was, N.W. by W. half a mile, keeping the southern breakers aboard until well up with the point of the beach on the western side of the entrance; then steer E.N.E. for the sand island on the eastern side, and up with it, anchor, and wait for a pilot.

The entrance is buoyed by a *black* cask, and three *black* spar buoys, which are to be left to the port hand; and by a *red* spar buoy and *red* cask on the starboard side, with a black and white striped cask in the channel. As the channels are always shifting, these buoys cannot be further described, and no one should attempt to enter with a vessel drawing above 8 or 9 ft. without a pilot, or compelled to do so by stress of weather, in which case anchor between the first and third buoys, and await a pilot. A weather tide frequently gives a deceptive appearance, which would deceive a stranger. The bottom is generally of hard sand.

ALBEMARLE and PAMPLICO SOUNDS.—These extensive but shallow lagoons, which form a large proportion of the seaboard of North Carolina, are separated from the ocean by a line of narrow sandy islands or banks thrown up by the motion of the sea, through which there are but few communications. They receive the numerous rivers which drain the eastern portion of the state, and consequently their water is nearly fresh. The means of ingress to these waters are several, viz.: from Chesapeake Bay through the Chesapeake and Albemarle or Dismal Swamp Canals, or from the Atlantic Ocean through either Ocracoke or Hatteras Inlets. The canals afford 6 to 6¼ ft., and the inlets 6¼ and 8 ft.

The tides scarcely affect their level, except near to Ocracoke Inlet, and they are shallow throughout, scarcely exceeding 20 ft. in any part, and have many extensive shoals; the channels are marked by numerous lights. But as this navigation does not belong to over-sea ships, we need not further allude to it.

OCRACOKE LIGHTHOUSE, in lat. 35° 6' 28" N., long. 75° 58' 51" W., stands near the entrance to the inlet on the West end of the island. It is a white tower 65 feet high, showing a bright fixed light at 75 ft., visible 15 miles off.

Ocracoke Inlet, which is limited on the East side by the West end of the long island or spit, was the principal ocean entrance to the extensive sounds. Twenty years ago from 9 to 7 ft. was found upon its "swash." It has now but 6 or 7 ft., and is only used by the corn fleet or such light draught vessels as are bound to southward. The bar has 16 ft., and the harbour inside is excellent, being completely sheltered. As may be well supposed, its banks are very liable to change.

The *bar buoy* is a black and white striped cask, in 15 ft. Within this are other black and red or striped buoys, which mark the limits of the channels, but no directions can be given to a stranger that would be of service. A pilot is indispensable.

CAPE LOOKOUT—BEAUFORT.

CAPE LOOKOUT.—A long line of narrow beach extends from the village of *Portsmouth*, which stands on the S.W. side of Ocracoke Inlet, for 40 miles to the extremity of the low spit, projecting and extending to the S.S.W., and called Cape Lookout, an expressive term. The land is very low, and cannot be seen at more than 3 or 4 miles off from the deck.

The **Lighthouse** stands at more than 2¾ miles from the extremity of the dry spit forming the cape. It is in lat. 34° 37′ 16″ N., and long. 76° 31′ 28″ W. The tower is 150 ft. in height, painted in black and white chequers, and exhibits a *fixed* light, 156 ft. above the sea, visible 19 miles off. The house is surrounded by a small growth of trees, from which a bold sand beach extends in a S.E. direction, about 3 miles, in the centre of which are small hillocks of sand. This light, although seen clearly all night, until near the approach of day, cannot then be discerned, owing, it is thought, to a mist that rises between the vessel and the lamps. It is judged imprudent to approach the shoals of Cake Lookout in the night nearer than 9 fathoms on the East, and 10 fathoms on the West side.

CAPE LOOKOUT SHOALS.—A line of very dangerous banks project to the S.S.E. from Cape Lookout, in a similar manner to the reefs off Capes Hatteras and Fear, showing a similarity of origin. They are most probably of a very changeable character; but the following is the description by the U.S. coast surveyors.

The breakers make S. by E. ¼ E., 7½ miles from the lighthouse, which are constant with the exception of a space of 2½ miles, where, in moderate weather, the sea does not break; and this space is reported to be used by vessels drawing less than 9 ft.

From the South point of the constant breakers, the shoal continues in the same direction 3 miles farther, or 10¼ miles S. by E. ¼ E. from the lighthouse. This part of the shoal is indicated by light green water, varying to a yellow tinge on the shoalest lumps, and is also very "lumpy," the water over it varying in depth from about 9 to 18 ft.; and it is on this point, South of the constant breakers, that vessels have recently grounded.

About 1½ mile to the S.E. of the above shoal is one on which there are 5½ fathoms water; and still farther in the same direction, and S.E. by S. ½ S., 13½ miles from the lighthouse, lies another shoal, on which there are 5½ fathoms of water. Beyond this no indications of shoals were discovered.

With the eye elevated 12 ft. above the water, and 10¼ miles from the lighthouse, just clear of the dangerous shoal, the ground on which the lighthouse stands is below, and the lower red stripe of the *old lighthouse* is half its width above the horizon. The constant breakers are plainly in sight 3 miles distant. The lower red stripes well on the horizon will carry a vessel around the dangerous shoal in 6 to 8 fathoms water.

On the 5½ fathoms shoal the breakers are in sight, with no horizon showing beyond; and when on the outer shoal in 5½ fathoms, the lower edge of the upper red stripe of the old lighthouse is a little above the horizon, and there are no breakers in sight. With the top of the old lighthouse just discernible above the horizon a vessel will be clear of all the shoals, and 15 miles from the lighthouse.

In from 7 to 11 fathoms the colour of the water is a dark green; in 5 fathoms a pale green, and in 3 fathoms and less a very light green, varying according to depth.

Lookout Bight, an anchorage on the western side of the cape and banks, is also analagous to that of Cape Hatteras. There is a depth of 4½ to 6 fathoms close to the beach, with the lighthouse bearing to the southward of East. It may be run for when the light bears eastward of N.N.E.

BEAUFORT.—This harbour is said to be the best in the State of North Carolina, and from its commanding a large extent of inland navigation, through Pamplico and Coro Sounds, its commerce would be considerable if its staple products were flourishing. Its commerce, however, has been far eclipsed by the neighbouring port of Wilmington.

The entrance, which used to be called *Old Topsail Inlet*, lies between the East end of the Shackleford Banks on the East, and the Bogue Banks on the West. At the extremity of the latter is Fort Macon, which commands the entrance. The space between these points, nearly a mile wide, is almost filled up with a bank of hard sand, nearly awash, but which leaves a channel close to either point, that around Fort Macon being called *The Slue*, the other being the main channel.

This harbour is accessible with all winds, except those from the North and West, and affords safe anchorage.

The buoys which marked the bar and channels are doubtful.

Directions.—The following are taken from the U.S. Survey of 1857:—On making the flagstaff of Fort Macon keep in 6 fathoms water, until the white square tower in Beaufort bears N.N.W. ¼ W.; stand in upon this bearing for the Outer Bar buoy, which bears S.E. ¼ E. from Fort Macon flagstaff. Leave the outer buoy a few yards on the starboard hand, crossing the bar by running directly from buoy to buoy. The buoys are in the best water, and must be kept close aboard. When abreast of the third or inner striped buoy steer N.W. by W., and when Fort Macon flagstaff bears N.W. ¼ N., change the course to N.N.W., leaving the red buoys off Shackleford Spit and the southern extremity of the Middle Ground 30 yards on the starboard hand. Fort Macon Point must not be approached nearer than half a cable's length. When off the Government Wharf anchor at will in 3 or 4 fathoms, muddy bottom. Generally the outline of the channel-way is clearly indicated by the shoal water and breakers on both sides.

When entering on the flood, keep nearer to the Bar breakers than those on the starboard hand, and reverse of this when entering on the ebb. The channel is narrow and subject to frequent changes, but the buoys are carefully attended to, and kept in position for the best water. No stranger should attempt to enter Beaufort Harbour at night.

The Slue or Point Channel is not buoyed, and no stranger should attempt it; 15½ feet can be carried through the Main Channel, and 7 ft. through the Slue at mean low water.

The beacons cannot be clearly distinguished from the outer buoy, and consequently afford no assistance in crossing the bar.

It is high water at $7^h\ 27^m$. Mean rise and fall of tide, 2 ft. 8 in.; least depth on the bar, 15 ft. 5 in.

The harbour of Beaufort may be taken with care, and affords perfect shelter from all winds. The outer bar buoy is a black and white striped iron nun buoy, in 31½ ft. water, with Fort Macon light bearing N.W. ¼ W.

Pilots can be obtained by hoisting a signal at the fore. Vessels should heave-to when off the S.E. spit, in 4 fathoms, convenient for entering, as soon as a pilot is on board.

To the westward of Cape Lookout, about 10 leagues, is *Bogue Inlet*, leading to Swansboro', and forming a communication with Pamplico Sound. Over the bar of this inlet there is 8 ft. water. W.S.W. ¼ S. from Bogue Inlet, distant 3½ leagues, is New River Inlet, on which there are also 8 ft. water.

At 18 miles from New River Inlet lies *New Topsail Inlet*, with 10 ft. water; 9 miles farther is Deep Inlet, with 7 ft. water; S.S.W. 18 miles from this lies New Inlet, with 7 ft. water. All these are of very uncertain and changeable character.

WILMINGTON, the principal port of North Carolina, has been much increased

NEW INLET—FRYING PAN SHOALS.

in importance since the development of the railway system which terminates here. The following directions must not be considered absolutely correct, in consequence of the many improvements which are now taking place, the chief of which is described below under the heading of Cape Fear River.

NEW INLET is the northernmost entrance to the Cape Fear River, leading to Wilmington, and enters between Federal Point and the North end of Smith's Island.

Federal Point Lighthouse, on the North side of the entrance, is a white tower, 45 ft. high, showing a *fixed* light at 50 ft., seen 12 miles off.

The *outer* buoy, black and white stripes, lies outside the bar in 5 fathoms. Black buoys Nos. 1 and 3, on the N.E. end of Carolina Shoals, mark the southern edge of the channel, and should be passed on the port hand close to in coming in. The passage between Zeek's Island and Federal Point is called the *Rip* or *Swash*. A *red* nun buoy is placed at its turn off the South end of Federal Point, and a *red* spar buoy on its eastern edge, marking the best water across it.

The channel to the southward and westward of Zeek's Island has not yet been developed.

When in 5 fathoms water, with Federal Point light bearing N.W. ¼ W., and the large house on Zeek's Island W. ¾ S., stand in on a W. by N. ½ N. course, passing a few yards to the northward of the bar buoy, until Federal Point light bears N. ¾ E., when you may steer W.S.W., passing within 50 or 100 yards to the northward of the wharf on the N.W. end of Zeek's Island; then alter the course to S.W. ¾ W., leaving the buoy 10 yards to the northward. When halfway between this last-named buoy and the site of the light-boat, anchor; or, if bound up the river, steer N. by E. ¼ E., until abreast of the N.E. point of the Marsh Islands; the course is then N. by E. up the channel-way. The shoalest water in crossing New Inlet Bar is 8 ft. by the bar at mean low water. Both the western and New Inlet bars are subject to frequent changes, and should not be attempted without a pilot.

CAPE FEAR is the southern point of the low, swampy tract called Smith's Island, the eastern coast of which, trending in a straight line N. by E. and S. by W., is 6½ miles long from Zeek's Island on the South side of the New Inlet. From it the Frying Pan Shoals extend for 13½ miles to S.S.E. ¼ E. The western point of Smith's Island is called *Bald Head*, and has extended much to the westward, so that the lighthouse erected on it in 1795, a black tower 90 ft. high, is now two-thirds of a mile E.N.E. from the point it was meant to indicate. The light is therefore discontinued, and the leading lights are placed on the other side of the inlet.

The FRYING PAN SHOALS are exceedingly dangerous. They stretch out S.S.E. ¼ E., 15 miles from the point of Cape Fear, and the shoal water across, within the 5-fathom line, is 3¼ miles in width, East and West. The water within this space is very shallow, in some places not more than 7 to 8 and 9 ft. to the distance of 12 miles from the cape, and breakers may be observed at 10 and 12 miles from the same, in a depth of 7½ and 9 ft. Beyond these breakers there is a flat of 4, 3, and 2½ fathoms, the last forming the South point of the shoals, and the position of which has already been given. Near to the cape, within 1½ mile, the water is much shoaler, and the bottom nearly dries. These shoals are marked by a lightvessel and four buoys.

The Lightvessel is schooner-rigged, the hull painted yellow, with the words "Frying Pan Shoals" painted in large black letters on each side; lower masts yellow; top masts white; one black day-mark on each mast-head. She is moored in 10 fathoms water, off the end of the Frying Pan Shoals, 1 mile beyond the outer 18-feet shoal. She exhibits two *fixed* lights, one on each mast, at 40 ft. above the sea, which are visible 11 miles off. The vessel is furnished with a fog bell and horn. Lat. 33° 50′ 0″, long. 77° 50′ 0′.

The eastern side of the Frying Pan Shoals is (or was) marked by two buoys; these lie in a S.S.E. ¾ E. direction from the cape, the first at 4 miles distant, the second at 7½ miles. Two other buoys mark the western side of the shoals; the first lies S. by W. ¼ W., 3 miles, and the second S. ¾ E., 8½ miles from the point of Cape Fear; or both these buoys may be said to bear S.S.E. from Oak Island lighthouse of the main channel, the one 7 miles, the other 12¼ miles distant. All four of these buoys lie within the 5 fathoms line of depth.

The soundings, in approaching the Frying Pan Shoals from the eastward, are regular, but from the westward are irregular.

Vessels of heavy draught, in passing these dangerous shoals, should be careful to get casts of the lead at short intervals of time, and never run into less than 10 fathoms water, if in a steamer, and 15 and 18 fathoms in a sailing vessel.

CAPE FEAR RIVER.—The principal entrance to Wilmington is on the western side of Smith's Island, and, like all the rest of the inlets on this coast, is much encumbered with sands. The southernmost bank is called the *Fingers*, which is connected by *Marshall's Shoal* with the *Keepers*, three-quarters of a mile outside Bald Head. A middle ground lies North of this, and to the southward of the Western Bar Channel around Oak Island Point. The entrance points are 1¼ mile apart.

To enable vessels of 16 or 18 ft. draught to reach Wilmington, extensive operations have been carried on for increasing the depth of the bar of Cape Fear River. To effect this the whole outflow of Cape Fear River will be turned into the ocean by one outlet. A breakwater is constructed 3,600 ft. in length. From a report, dated the 19th of January, 1875, we learn that vessels of 15½ ft. draught can pass in and out at high-water spring tides; and ordinary vessels below 12 ft. draught may beat through at will, and need not be detained by tides anywhere between Wilmington and the ocean. We have recived no information to enable us to state the new character of the channel with confidence, so the following directions must be received with caution.

Oak Island Lights.—On the shore to the westward of the entrance, at two-thirds of a mile West of Fort Caswell, which stands on the West point of the river, are two brick towers, the front one painted brown, 30 ft. in height, the rear one white, 40 ft. From these are shown *fixed* lights, at 33 and 45 ft. respectively. These two towers are surrounded by sandhills, and the lights are designed to serve as a range for crossing the bar at Oak Island.

The bar is buoyed; the outer one is a *red* conical iron buoy, No. 2, in 9 ft. water, Oak Island light bearing N.E. ¼ N., Bald Head, E. by S. Further inwards there are other buoys on the prominent points of the shoals.

At *Price's Creek*, which is 1¾ mile north-eastward of Smithsville, a town lying opposite to the entrance, are two lighthouses, the front one a brick tower, the other on the keeper's house, which show fixed lights. In one they lead through the Horse Shoe Channel to the north-eastward.

Western Bar Channel.—When in 4 fathoms, bring the high and low lights on Oak Island in range, and keep that range N.E. ¼ N., passing either side of the buoy, until Bald Head bears E.S.E. and Cape Fear is open about two ships' length to the southward of the South end of Bald Head Point, when steer East until Bald Head bears S.E. by E., and the citadel in Fort Caswell N.N.E. ¾ E., then N.E. by E. ¼ E. until reaching 5 fathoms. When Bald Head bears S.S.E. ¼ E. steer N.N.W. ¼ W., which will clear the spit of Battery Island. Having cleared the point of Battery

Island and opened the river, anchor at pleasure in mid-channel, abreast of Smithville. Eight feet can be carried in over the Bulk Head at mean low water.

The Marshall Shoal is now connected with the Fingers, and has obliterated the Old Channel, over the main bar. The buoys have consequently been removed. High water, full and change, at Oak Island, about $7^h 30^m$; rise about 4 ft.

Above the bar the river is buoyed and lighted up to Wilmington, but a pilot is necessary.

The Currents on the coast between Cape Fear and Cape Hatteras vary with the winds. During the summer, when the prevailing winds are south-westerly, the current sets in the direction of the coast to the eastward; but, when the southerly wind ceases, the current suddenly changes, and this change frequently appears before the change of wind.

When sailing towards these coasts, it is prudent to keep nearly a degree to the southward of the latitude of the place you intend to make, until you reckon yourself on the edge of the *Gulf Stream*, when you must be directed by judgment, according to circumstances. Do not, if possible to avoid it, sail to the northward of 33° 20', or at the highest, 33° 25' until you attain 10 fathoms of water. In this depth you will be within the South or outer end of the Frying-pan Shoal. In approaching the coast in 33° 20', your first soundings will be from 30 to 35 fathoms; in this depth you will be very near to the inner edge of the Gulf Stream. You will have fine grey sand, with black spots, when you get into 17 fathoms; there is a long flat in this depth of water. In steering West you will, for the first 5 or 6 leagues, shoalen the water very little. When you come into 14 fathoms, you shoalen your water quicker, but gradually. You will see the land from 10 fathoms of water, if the weather be clear, and may then be sure that you are within the Frying-pan, from the outside of this shoal. To the westward of N.W., no land can be seen, when without the shoals.

From Cape Fear River to the entrance of Georgetown, or Winyah Bay, the bearing is S.W. ¾ W., and the distance 23½ leagues. The bight formed by the coast between these points is called *Long Bay*. *Little River Inlet* lies 8½ leagues to the westward of Cape Fear lighthouse, and divides North from South Carolina; and *Lockwood's Folly* lies about 13 miles westward of the cape. The land appears broken, and affords no safe harbour.

The *North Inlet* of George Town is 7 miles to the northward of the lighthouse, and forms the northern boundary of North Island, on the South point of which the lighthouse is situated. The bar of this inlet has formed into the shape of a crescent. It cannot be attempted by a stranger, as it varies considerably, according to the prevailing winds, and cannot, under any circumstances, be recommended. On the North end of North Island is a village of about thirty houses, which may be distinctly seen from sea; there are also several houses on an island opposite to this point. This is a summer residence, and has often been mistaken for the houses on Sullivan's Island, near Charleston. To small vessels this inlet affords an occasional harbour; there are two passages leading from it up to George Town, but fit for boats only.

WINYAH BAY, an estuary formed by the confluence of the *Peedee*, *Sampit*, or *Black*, and *Waccamaw-Rivers*, at a short distance above Georgetown, affords a ready means of access to large vessels for that place.

GEORGETOWN HARBOUR entrance is 9 or 10 miles to the southward of the northern channel into Winyah (or Winyaw) Bay.

The Lighthouse, which is coloured white, stands on a low sandy point at the South end of North Island and East side of the entrance to Pedee River, and harbour of Georgetown. It is in lat. 33° 13' 21", long. 79° 11', being 82 ft. in height, exhibiting a *fixed* light, 85 ft. above the sea, visible 14 miles.

The light bears N. by W. ¼ W. from the entrance of the S.E. Pass, 4½ miles distant. From the south-easternmost part of Cape Roman Shoals, to the entrance of the South bar, the course is N.N.E., and the distance 12½ miles.

In approaching Georgetown Bar from the northward, the harbour is shut out from view by North Island, and the lighthouse appears to be situated in a low wood.

Vessels at sea will find deep water, and, with southerly or westerly winds, good anchorage near the land, about 1½ or 2 miles to the northward of the lighthouse. In passing the light, either northerly or southerly, vessels will find 5 fathoms water within 5 miles of the land. S.S.E. ¼ E., 4½ miles from the lighthouse is the East Bank, of 9 ft. to 2½ fathoms.

There are several buoys placed on the best water on the bars and in the channels. In the Bottle or Northern Channel the outer buoy is a *red* can, in 14 ft. water, the lighthouse bearing N.W. ¼ W.; the middle buoy *red* can, W.N.W.; the inner buoy also a *red* can, lies N.W. from this.

The S.E. Pass outer buoy is a *conical* black with white stripes, in 17 ft. water, the lighthouse bearing N. by W. ⅜ W.; middle buoy *black* nun, N.W. ¼ N.; the inner buoy, also a *black* nun buoy, bears S. by E. from the lighthouse, and N.W. from the middle buoy.

The soundings in approaching Georgetown Bar are irregular, the land low, and unmarked by any distinctive scenery, consequently the lighthouse is the only guide for approaching the channels, and avoiding the East Bank Shoal. The changing character of the channels, and the total dependence on buoys, renders it unsafe for strangers to attempt the passage without a pilot.

There are but two channels in use, the S.E. Pass and the Bottle Channel; the former has 8 feet at mean low water, is the widest, safest, and most generally used by the pilots. The Bottle Channel is a recent washing of the ebb current, and for the last three years has continued to improve in depth and directness; 7 feet at mean low water can be found in it.

To use the S.E. Pass.—Coming from the northward, keep in 5 fathoms water to avoid the East Bank, till the lighthouse bears N.N.W. and is in range with a large whitewashed chimney on the point; then stand in on this course and range till up with the outer buoy, and keeping it on the starboard hand, steer N.W. for the middle buoy, which leave 20 yards on the starboard hand, and continue the same course till abreast of the inner buoy. Leaving the inner buoy on the port hand steer N.N.W., passing about 10 yards to port of the buoy on the Fishing Bank, then steer N. by W. ¼ W. till the lighthouse bears S.E. by E., where there is anchorage in 4 and 5 fathoms water, about 150 yards from North Island beach.

To use Bottle Channel.—In 4 fathoms water, bring the lighthouse to bear N.W. by W. ¼ W., and steer W.N.W., which brings up with the outer buoy; pass it close on either hand, and continue the course until up with the middle buoy, which must be kept close on the starboard hand in passing; then steer W. by N. till up with the inner buoy, passing a few yards to the starboard of it. The course will then be N.W. by W. ¾ W., till abreast of the buoy on the Fishing Bank, which leave about 80 yards to the southward, and steer N. by W. ¾ W. for the anchorage. Due allowance must be made for the flood and ebb tides.

Tides.—It is high water, full and change, at South Island, at $7^h\ 56^m$; springs rise 4 feet 7 inches, neaps 2 feet 7 inches; at Georgetown at $8^h\ 40^m$, springs rise 4 feet 5 inches, neaps 2 feet 5 inches.

Between Georgetown entrance and the outer shoal of Cape Roman lie the entrances

CAPE ROMAN AND LIGHTHOUSE.

of Santeo River. Of these, the southern one, which is the best, is about 2½ leagues S.W. from the entrance of Georgetown River, and 3 leagues N.E. from Cape Roman.

The ebb tide of the numerous rivers which fall into the estuary of Georgetown, with that of the next great river, called the *Santee*, have formed the extensive flats originally called the Shoals of St. Roman. These flats border the coast in a S.S.E. S.W., and West direction, not less than 11 leagues, taking the extent of their outer edges; and off the mouth of the Santee, the extent from the shore is not less than 7 miles. Vessels passing should not approach them, in the vicinity of Georgetown, nearer than into 4 fathoms; nor towards the isle called *Cape Roman* into less than 7 fathoms. The muddy appearance of the water hereabout may frighten strangers, but no real danger is to be apprehended. The land is an extensive assemblage of low islands, and is scarcely discernible from the outer extremity of the bank.

CAPE ROMAN (or *Romain*) is very improperly called a cape, it being a very low land, without either tree or bush, and appears, at a distance, like a sand left dry by the tide.

The **LIGHTHOUSE** of Cape Roman is erected on Raccoon Cay, about 6 miles from the extremity of the shoals off the cape, and 10 miles S.W. of the South entrance of the Santee River. This is a red brick tower, 150 ft. high, in lat. 33° 1' 8", long. 79° 22' 23', exhibiting a *revolving* light every minute, elevated 154 ft., and visible 18 miles off. The light from this tower should be seen 17 miles outside the shoals off Cape Roman.

The old tower stands near the new lighthouse. Its elevation is 65 feet, and it is painted with red and white horizontal stripes.

The **SHOALS** off Cape Roman run S.E. about 6 miles from the light, and are about 1½ mile in width, and have but 6 ft. water on them; the outer point has only 7 ft., with a Swash Channel of 2½ fathoms between that and the cape, nearly 2 miles in width. Off the point of the shoals the water shoalens from 7 to 5 fathoms, then directly on the breakers.

There was formerly a nun buoy, painted in perpendicular *black* and *white* stripes, with a black flag on staff, placed in 15 ft. in the Slue Channel of Cape Roman Shoals, with Cape Roman light bearing N.W. by W. ¼ W., point of Cape Island N.W. by N. This buoy was passed close on either side. Courses from the buoy out of the Slue, S.W. by W. and N.E. by E.

Vessels of heavy draught should not approach Cape Roman within 8 fathoms water, there being a 5-fathom bank outside of the shoals.

Vessels of light draught coming from the southward, and intending to run inside the shoals, will, when in 4½ fathoms water, bring Cape Roman old lighthouse and the old mill in range, the South point of Cape Island bearing N. by E., then steer N.E., passing directly through the Slue.

These shoals are of a dangerous character, lying directly in the track of coasters. With moderate winds from N.E. or West the sea does not break upon them, but with winds from S.W. around by South and to East, they are shown by the breakers on the seaward side. A 6-feet channel extends from the S.W., leading to the harbour inside the cape. There is good anchorage during northerly winds S.W. of the lighthouse, with not less than 3 fathoms water.

From the South entrance of Santee River, to 6 miles S.E. of Cape Roman, the shoal extends to a considerable distance from the land; the S.E. point of it lies about 15 miles S. by W. from Georgetown lighthouse. Close to this dangerous shoal there are 4 and 3 fathoms, and the land is so low that you cannot even see it from the deck of a ship at the extremity of the shoal.

Raccoon Cay, on which the lighthouse is erected, as before observed, is to the westward of Cape Roman. It is a long, narrow island, and not visible until a near approach to it. Being abreast of Cape Roman Shoals, with the lighthouse bearing N.W. by W., distant 7 miles, your course clear of all the shoals off the coast to the Bell-boat at the entrance of Charleston Harbour will be S.W. ¾ W., 34 miles. In this course you will pass the wide opening of Bull's Bay, and clear of all the breakers and shoals off Bull's Island.

Bull's Bay lies between Raccoon Cay and Bull's Island, and is about 19 miles North of Charleston; 13 feet can be carried across the bar at low water spring tides; the rise and fall of which is 5¾ ft.; the harbour is round near to Bull's Island, where you may anchor in 2½ fathoms water.

At 25 miles N.E. of Charleston, on the North end of Bull's Island, stands a lighthouse, built of brick, and painted white, and shows a *fixed light* at 45 ft. above the level of the sea. The back ground of the lighthouse is woods.

A *can buoy*, with *black* and *white* perpendicular stripes, in 2¼ fathoms low water, is (or was) placed off the bar at Bull's Bay; the North point of Bull's Island bearing N.W. by W.; Bull's lighthouse, W.N.W.; South point of Raccoon Cay, N.W. by N. ¼ N. To be passed close on either side.

The *South Breaker* has a buoy on the East end in 12 ft. water, and in the middle of the channel is a buoy with a small *white* flag upon it, in 18 ft. water, low tide, on either side of which you may go in rounding in. These buoys are uncertain.

This is a safe anchorage, and the channel way is clearly marked by the breakers on either hand. In leaving the bay, keep away until the outer spit is cleared, which bears S.E. by S. from the bluff part of Bull's Island distant three-quarters of a mile.

When clear of the bar and bound to the northward, steer West from the light, full 15 miles, before you haul up to the north-eastward; you will by this means be well clear of Cape Roman Shoals, with a sufficient offing from the shoals off Charleston Bar. If bound southward from the anchorage of Bull's Harbour, steer E.S.E. from abreast of the light, full 5 miles past the buoy, into 5 fathoms water, when S.S.W. ¾ W. 9½ miles, will bring the light on Bull's Island to bear North. You will then be in the former track as from off the shoals of Cape Roman, and may steer S.W. ¾ W. past the Rattlesnake lightvessel to the bell boat and round her as before.

From Cape Roman to the entrance of Charleston the bearing and distance is S.W. ½ W. 34 miles. The land between is alluvial, and forms numerous low islands, the principal of which are named Bull's, Capers, Devies, Long, and Sullivan's Islands. Flats extend from all these isles, along which the soundings are regular. *Bull's Island* appears very bluff, with red sand-hills, and a spit from the outer end of it extends eastward, about 3½ miles.

RATTLESNAKE SHOALS.—A spit, called the *Rattlesnake*, extends to the distance of 3 miles E. by S. from Sullivan's Island, which forms the North side of the entrance to Charleston, and you will be on the edge of it in 5½ fathoms.

When Charleston churches are seen to the northward of Sullivan's Island, you will be on the edge of the Rattlesnake; and when the churches are open to the southward of Sullivan's Island, you are clear of that shoal. You should approach no nearer to this bank than in 5 fathoms of water.

A **Lightvessel** lies off the Rattlesnake Shoal, and opposite the North end of Sullivan's Island in 5⅙ fathoms water. The hull of this vessel is painted white; masts yellow, and top-masts black, with two oval day-marks, painted black. Rattlesnake Shoals East end bearing N. by W. 2¼ miles; red beacon on Morris Island, W. by S. ½ S.; and Fort Sumter, W. ¾ N. This vessel is furnished with *fog-bell* and *horn*, and exhibits *two fixed lights*, visible 12 miles. Lat. 32° 44′ 0″, long. 79° 43′ 45″.

There are *two black buoys* on the Rattlesnake Shoal, one on the East, the other on the West end of the shoal, $2\frac{1}{4}$ miles distant from each other, in a W. $\frac{1}{4}$ S. and E. $\frac{1}{4}$ N. direction. On the shoal on the South side, midway between the buoys, there is 8 ft. water. The eastern one bears from the lightship N.E. $\frac{1}{4}$ N. 6 miles, and is 3 miles from the nearest point of land; the western one bears from the lightship N.N.E. off Charleston $4\frac{7}{8}$ miles.

CHARLESTON is the principal seaport and town of South Carolina. It is on a low tongue of land at the confluence of the Wando, Cooper, and Ashley Rivers,* about 6 miles up the harbour, which is entered between Sullivan's Island on the North, and Morris Island on the South, the opening between them being $1\frac{1}{2}$ mile wide. The banks across which are the entrance channels, are 3 miles broad outside the line of coast. Nearly in the middle of the entrance is the famous Fort Sumter.

Operations are now being carried on for the improvement of Charleston Harbour. Mons. Maillefert, the engineer, who began the work in 1872, had at the end of 1874 removed twenty-three vessels, sunk during the American war, all of which impeded the navigation.

Lights.—On the South end of *Morris Island* stand two range beacons, the front one being a pyramidal wooden tower, 15 ft. high, painted red; the rear one, a black framework, 35 ft. high, which is to be superseded by a first order lighthouse, 150 ft. high. From these, *two fixed lights* are shown, at 20 ft. elevation, from the front beacon, and 40 ft. from the rear. Kept in line W. by N. $\frac{1}{4}$ N. they lead through the Pumpkin Hill Channel until Sullivan Island lights are in line.

On *Sullivan Island two fixed red lights* are shown, the rear light elevated 57 ft., and the front light 34 ft. They show in full brilliancy down the Main Ship Channel, from S. by E. to S. The beacons from which these lights are shown are coloured white, the front one situated on the N.E. angle of Fort Moultrie, and the near beacon 600 yards to the northward.

At *Fort Sumter*, on the opposite side of the channel, and W.S.W. of Fort Moultrie, a *fixed light* is shown from a brown wooden frame on the N.W. face of the fort, elevated 57 ft., visible 12 miles off.

At *Castle Pinckney, a red* light is shown from a yellow tower, elevated 41 ft.

Buoys.—Red buoys mark the starboard side of the channels entering, and black the port. Black and red in horizontal stripes are danger buoys. Black and white vertical striped are channel buoys.

The Channels are constantly shifting. In the survey, published by the U.S. Hydrographic Office, in 1871, four channels are shown as leading into the Main Channel from the eastward. The northernmost of these is called the *Beach Channel*, which passes close along the South side of Sullivan's Island. By the recent removal of Bowman's Jetty, formerly extending from Sullivan's Island into the channel, there is now a depth of 17 ft. through. From the buoy at its eastern end the distance is $1\frac{1}{4}$ mile to its junction with the Main Ship Channel off Fort Moultrie, the narrowest part, where the channel is not a cable wide. Two buoys mark its eastern end.

Swash Channel.—The outer buoy of the Swash Channel is 2 miles S.S.W. from the outer buoy of Beach Channel. It has a least depth of $12\frac{1}{2}$ ft. at its western end, and is marked by a striped mid-channel buoy at its eastern end. After passing this buoy,

---

* In a letter addressed to the Board of Trade, and published in the "Mercantile Marine Magazine," December, 1870, pages 367-8, shipmasters are warned against going up these rivers for the phosphate rock, and especially against spending a night there, from June 1st to the end of November, because of the danger of an almost certain attack of malarial fever.

with Fort Sumter bearing about W.N.W., you leave first a black buoy close on the port hand, and then two red buoys on your starboard hand; the last of them is on the eastern side of the Main Ship Channel.

Pumpkin Hill Channel.—The principal entrance lies 3½ miles southward of the Swash Channel. It is to be kept dredged to a depth of 20 ft. Early in 1875 Mons. Maillefert reported that a depth of 18 ft. already existed, the operation only having been begun in October, 1874.

To enter by this channel, get the lights on Morris Island, before described, in range when you are in 5 fathoms water, and steer for them, passing sea buoy (black and white perpendicular stripes) and outer bar buoy (black and white perpendicular stripes) on either hand, and leaving middle buoy (No 1 black) and inner or junction buoy (black and white perpendicular stripes) on the port hand, soon after passing which the beacon lighthouses on Sullivan Island are in line N. ¼ W.; with these in line, proceed through the *Main Ship Channel* until Fort Sumter beacon bears West, when a N.W. ¼ W. course will lead into Rebellion Road; and a W. ⅛ N. course will lead through the South channel, keeping the buoys that mark the South side of the shoals off Fort Ripley on the starboard hand, when Castle Pinckney bears N.N.E. steer for the wharves.

Another channel, with 13 ft. least water, lies S.W. 1 mile from Pumpkin Hill Channel. The leading mark in is with the front Morris Island beacon bearing N.W. ¼ N.

Good holding ground in 5 fathoms, at mean low water, with a soft, sticky bottom, will be found outside the bar, with the leading lighthouses on Morris Island in line.

It is high water, on full and change, at the city, at $7^h\ 24^m$. Springs rise 6 feet, neaps 5 feet.

Strong or long-continued westerly winds reduce the water on the bar from 1 to 2 feet. The flood and ebb set across the sailing line over the bar, and should be allowed for. Large vessels should cross the bar during the last quarter of flood, and *should not wait for high water.*

REMARKS ON THE WINDS., ETC., ON THE COAST OF SOUTH CAROLINA.

When the wind blows hard from the N.E. quarter, without rain, it commonly continues so for some time, perhaps for three or four days; but if such winds are attended with rain, they generally shift to the East, E.S.E., and S.E.

S.E. winds blow right in on the coast, but they seldom blow dry, or continue long; in 6, 8, or 10 hours after their commencement the sky begins to look dirty, which soon produces rain. When it comes on to blow and rain very hard, you may be sure that the wind will fly round to the N.W. quarter, and blow hard for 20 to 30 hours, with a clear sky.

N.W. winds are always attended with clear weather; they sometimes blow very hard, but seldom last longer than 30 hours.

The most lasting winds are those which blow from the S.S.W. and W.N.W., and from the North to E.N.E. When the wind is in any of these quarters the weather is the most settled.

Thunder storms are very common on this coast in summer time; they always come from the N.W. quarter, and are sometimes so heavy, that no canvass can withstand their fury; they come on so suddenly, that the greatest precaution is necessary to guard against the effects of their violence.

The first appearance of these storms is a black heavy cloud, and the weather sultry, with little wind and variable. It is advisable at the appearance of these warnings to stand by, to clew up and be ready to wear, as these gales come on so suddenly, as scarcely to allow of time to do more.

When the wind backs against the sun, with a drizzling rain, you will generally perceive the sea rise before the storm begins; then be prepared for a gale, which will often last 50 or 60 hours. If you should be in the vicinity of Charleston or St. Augustine, and obliged to cut or slip, your best way will be to carry all the sail you can, and get out to sea before it acquires its fury, for otherwise you will not be able to carry sails at all: and observe, the flood tide will carry you out no further than 12 fathoms, and there you will have the advantage of the southern current, until you get into 45 fathoms, or about the distance of 15 leagues from the land; you will then be in the Gulf Stream, which runs strongly along the edge of soundings.

SECTION III.

CHARLESTON TO HAVANA AND THE MISSISSIPPI.

The whole of the coast of South Carolina, South of Charleston, and all of Georgia, is low, and bordered with extensive shoals, consisting of a range of islands called the "Sea Islands," which give their name to the famous cotton grown on them. From off Charleston Bar, in 5 fathoms of water, to North Edisto Inlet, the course is S.W. by W. ¼ W., and the distance 5¼ leagues. This course will carry you clear of the shoals which lie off Stono Inlet; and which lie farther out than any other that are in your way to Edisto.

PILOTS, &c.—" On the South coast of Carolina, for St. Helena Sound and all rivers connected, principally Bull River and Coosaw, there are twelve opposition pilots, having five boats, two of them at sea all weathers. District runs 30 miles to the South, and 30 miles to the North of the sea buoy at the entrance of St. Helena Sound, and they often board ships as far off the land as the inner edge of the Gulf Stream. They are fine large craft fore-and-aft rigged with two masts; no distance money charged. There is also a Ship Chandler's Store at Coosaw, where a ship can get what stores she requires at a reasonable rate. Good water can likewise be obtained at Coosaw."—*James Cheesman*, Master, barque *Gipsey Queen*, February, 1879.

Stono Inlet is 7 miles from the South Channel of Charleston; there are two islands between Morris's Island and the island called the *Folly* or *Coffin Land*. You may know where the shoal is by the breakers, unless the sea be smooth. There are 9 or 10 ft. at low water in Stono Inlet.

North Edisto.—From Stono Inlet to North Edisto Inlet the course is S.W. by W. ¼ W., and the distance 11 miles; the soundings between are regular, and shoalen very

ST. HELENA SOUND.

gradually as you come from the offing towards shore. The bar of North Edisto, and the shoals which are near it, lie off about 4 or 5 miles from the land; there are 3 and 4 fathoms of water close to the bar and shoals, and on the bar 10 to 12 ft. at low water.

South or Main Channel.—Off the entrance is a *black* and *white* buoy in 2¼ fathoms, which bears S.E., distant 2¾ miles from the southern point of the entrance. It is 34 miles N.E. ½ N. from the lightship at Port Royal, and 12 miles N.E. from the entering buoy at St. Helena. From this buoy steer N. by W. 2½ miles, passing *red nun* buoy close-to, and keeping inner *black* and *white* buoy on with large gap in wood on Seabrook's Island.

When within 100 yards of inner buoy in 3 fathoms at low water, haul up N.W. by N. for large pine on northern side of entrance; continue on that course until the water deepens to 5 fathoms, when you may keep the middle of the river up to the anchoring wharf at "Point of Pines."

Least water over the bar on above ranges, 12 ft., which will be found close to the red buoy. Mean rise and fall of tide, 5 ft. 10 in.

East Channel.—Bring the southern side of the inlet to bear N.W. ¾ W., and run in on that bearing, keeping inner black and white buoy on with tripod on Botany Bay Island, and both in middle of avenue cut through the woods behind the tripod. This course is about 60 yards South of *red* spar buoy on bar, and carries 9 ft. over the bar at low water. When up with inner buoy, leave it on the port hand, and steer N.W. ½ W. up the middle of the river.

It is high water, full and change, in North Edisto Harbour, at 7ʰ 10ᵐ; springs rise 7 ft. nearly, neaps 5½ ft. The tide here is very rapid. In the harbour, 4 miles West from the anchorage, you may get good water.

South Edisto lies 2½ leagues W.S.W. from North Edisto. The shore off the islands between may be approached by the lead without danger, as the shoalings are gradual. It is not prudent to enter without a pilot.

ST. HELENA SOUND.—Between South Edisto Island and the northernmost Hunting Island, lies the entrance of St. Helena Sound, which is about 2 leagues wide. Six navigable rivers empty themselves into the Sound, viz., South Edisto, Ashepu, Combahee, Chehaw, True Blue, and Coosaw, some of which extend 200 miles up the country.

Light.—On the North end of Hunting Island, at the western entrance point of St. Helena Sound, stands a fine conical lighthouse, 121 ft. in height, painted white from the base to the level of the top of the foliage in the background, and black above that line. From the tower is shown a *revolving light*, exhibiting a bright flash every half minute, elevated 132 ft. above high water, and visible 17 miles off in clear weather. The position of the lighthouse is lat. 32° 23′ 26″ N., long. 80° 25′ 10″ W.

Combahee Banks Beacon, from which, previous to 1876, a light was shown, stands on the S.E. point of Combahee Banks.

Directions.—The following sailing directions were issued in 1857:—

The shoals of St. Helena Bar extend 6 miles to seaward. The land is low and difficult to distinguish. The Sound being so full of shoals, no stranger should attempt its navigation without a pilot (see p. 1). After the prevalence of a strong north-westerly wind the bar is usually 2 and 3 ft. less than the general average.

The outer buoy is an iron can buoy, painted in *black* and *white* stripes, and moored in 15 ft. water, with the North point of Hunting Island bearing W.N.W.; South point of Otter Island, N.W. ½ N.

. A large black and white nun buoy is placed in 4½ fathoms water at the entrance of the *South-East* or *Main Channel.* It is 21 miles N.E. ¾ N. from the lightvessel at

Port Royal, and 7 miles S. by E. ¼ E. from the sandhills on the northern side of the entrance to South Edisto River. From it steer W. by N. 2½ miles to a *black nun* buoy, passing a *black* can buoy midway on the course, and steering for the middle of the opening in the wood on Hunting Island; then N.N.W. ¼ W., 1½ mile to a smaller black can buoy in 4 fathoms inside the bar; thence 4½ miles N.W. ¼ W. to Otter Island anchorage; or N.W. by W. ½ W. 8 miles to the junction of Coosaw and Combahee Rivers at the head of the Sound. A small black can buoy lies in 20 feet on the tail of the Combahee Bank on the former site of the lightvessel.

From the entrance of St. Helena Sound, along the Hunting Islands, to the entrance of Port Royal, the course is S.W. ½ S., ann the distance about 5½ leagues. Here you will find 5 or 6 fathoms water, with regular soundings.

PORT ROYAL.—"A very fine natural harbour, capable of holding a large fleet of ships at anchor. It is situated between Savannah and Charleston; has 31 feet of water on the bar, and at high water spring tides there is 7 ft. rise and fall. Vessels carry 26 ft. of water from inside the bar right up to the wharf, a distance of 15 miles. The harbour is well protected from all winds. The town itself is comprised of about forty wooden houses, occupied mostly by negroes. There is good wharfage for about a dozen vessels, but there is a great want of sheds and proper protection in case of fire. There are no facilities in the neighbourhood for repairing vessels; the nearest blacksmith's shop is at Beaufort, distant about 2 miles.

"The nearness of this port to Savannah will prevent its being of any great importance for some years yet, and its success will probably be ruinous to Savannah as a shipping port.

"The bulk of the cotton shipped at this port for Europe is compressed at Augusta, distant from here 112 miles, from whence it is brought down to the ships by rail. There is one small steam press close to the wharf. Vessels loading cotton for Europe are generally chartered by lump sum, the charterers paying compressing, stowage, and other charges. Coasting steamers call weekly and take the cotton from the interior uncompressed on to New York."—Captain Stark, *Nautical Magazine*, January, 1878.

Hilton Head is on the South side of the harbour of Port Royal, and is a higher bluff point than any hereabout. Range lights were exhibited on the head previous to 1869.

Coles Care is the shoal stretching 3 miles from the point of St. Philip's Island, on the northern side of the entrance.

The *North Breakers* are 4½ miles from the same point, and in the same direction; then the S.E. Breakers at 7 miles from the point, and the shoal called Martin's Industry, between the S.E. Breakers and the lightvessel. Some parts of the latter shoal have but 6 ft. over them at low water.

Gaskin Bank is on the western side of the South entrance, and has even less water than Martin's Industry, and is very dangerous, having continual breakers at low water. The flat to the northward of Gaskin Bank is termed the South Breakers, and forms the western side of the entrance, to where it joins the Joiner's Bank, which stretches about 3½ miles from Hilton Head, and is about 4 miles S. by E. from St. Philip's Point. From this, the East end of the bank, it extends W.N.W. about 2½ miles and has 3½ fathoms on it at low water.

The three channels of Port Royal entrance are about 10 miles from the headlands of the mouth of the bay. The most seaward part of the bar is called Martin's Industry, upon which, in several spots, there are but 6 ft. at mean low water, and less than 4 ft. at low spring tides. The breakers are generally constant, and when fairly entered in either channel, afford an excellent guide. The sands fronting the entrance to Port Royal Sound are subject to change, especially after strong easterly gales.

The entering buoys in both channels are black and white in vertical stripes, and the buoy at the South-east channel carries a staff and cross with the letters S.E. on it. There are four red buoys in the South channel, and two black buoys in the S.E. channel; and a large black buoy lies in 5 fathoms on the S.E. side of the Gaskin Bank.

Martin's Industry Lightvessel, painted red, is moored about 1¼ mile off Martin's Industry Shoal, in 8 fathoms water; with Tybee lighthouse, W. by S. ¾ S. 15 miles; South channel entering buoy, W. by S. ¾ S. 2 miles; and the S.E. channel entering buoy, N.N.E. ½ E. 2½ miles. She exhibits two *fixed* white lights, each at a height of 44 ft. above the sea, which should be visible in clear weather, from a distance of 12 miles.

A *Fog-bell* and *horn* are sounded in thick weather.

Vessels bound to Port Royal are advised to make Tybee Island, as Tybee lighthouse serves as a good object to distinguish the coast by. Hereabout the land is low, with high trees upon it.

The *South-east Channel* carries 19 ft. at low water. Vessels from the northward, steering for the lightvessel, should make the entering buoy on the starboard hand, when steer for it and pass it on either side; then steer W. ¾ N. 2½ miles, passing the black buoys on the port hand. From the inner black buoy steer N.N.W. ½ W., 5 miles to Fishing Rip buoy, having the lightvessel astern and the house on Bay Point ahead, passing at 2 miles on the course the upper red buoy of the South channel at the junction of the two channels. From Fishing Rip, follow the directions for the South channel. One of the red buoys is in line with the black buoys, or about W. by N. ½ N. from the inner buoy, but is not to be steered for when up with the inner black buoy.

The *South Channel* carries 19 ft. at low water. Vessels coming from, or going to the southward, should not pass westward of the Gaskin Bank buoy. From the lightvessel steer W. by S. ¾ S. 2⅛ miles for the entering buoy, and then N.N.W. ½ W. 1 mile for the first red buoy, then N. by E. 2½ miles for the third red buoy, passing the second buoy midway between the first and third, and all the red buoys on the starboard hand, and North 1¾ mile to the junction of the South and S.E. channels. From the upper red buoy to the black buoy on the S.E. end of Fishing Rip steer N.N.W. ½ W. 3 miles; this course will bring the lightvessel astern, and the large house with a platform on the roof, at the West end of Bay Point, ahead. If bound into Beaufort River, steer from Fishing Rip buoy N.W. ½ N. 3 miles, until the house on Bay Point bears E.N.E., after which the chart will be the best guide up the river. If bound to Hilton Head, steer N.W. by W. 3 miles from Fishing Rip buoy, and anchor off the piers.*

It is high water, full and change, at Beaufort, at $8^h\ 2^m$; springs rise 8½ ft., neaps 7½ ft. At Hilton Head, at $7^h\ 16^m$; springs rings 7½ ft., neaps 6½ ft.

TIDES.—It is observed on this coast that N.E., easterly, and S.E. winds cause higher tides than other winds, and also somewhat alter their course. At Port Royal entrance the tide flows, on the full and change of the moon, at a quarter past eight o'clock. About 6 leagues from the land, in 12 fathoms of water, the flood sets strongly to the southward, and the ebb to the northward; at a great distance from the shore there is no tide at all. Near the entrance of the harbour there is a strong in-draught during the flood tide, and an out-set with the ebb.

---

* Chas. O. Boutelle. United States Coast Survey, 1862.

SAVANNAH.

TYBEE INLET, the entrance of Savannah River, lies 5 leagues S.W. ¼ W. from the entrance of Port Royal South Channel. Between is Trench Island, from which the Gaskin Bank extends outward about 6 miles; at the broadest part you may proceed along, in 5 fathoms of water.

Tybee Lighthouse is on Tybee Island, at the mouth of the river. The lantern shows a *fixed* light at 108 ft. above the sea, visible 18 miles.

The Beacon Light, which in line with the high light serves as a leading mark over the bar, is 600 yards from the light, in an E. ¼ S. southerly direction. It stands on the N.E. point of Tybee Island, and the present structure, completed in 1877, consists of an iron skeleton framework, painted white, and erected 40 ft. S.E. by S. (approximately) from the old beacon. It shows a *fixed bright light*, elevated 28 ft. above the sea, and visible 10 miles off.

It has been recommended by those bound to Port Royal to make the land about Tybee, as the lighthouse makes that part of the coast more distinguishable than any other. Ships which draw 14 or 15 feet of water may go in at Tybee, and proceed through land to Beaufort, in Port Royal Island; and thence, in vessels that draw 8 or 9 ft. of water, may go through land to Charleston; and from Charleston, in vessels of 7 or 8 ft. of water, may go through land to the River Medway, in Georgia.

Calibogue Sound, northward of Tybee Inlet, has its entrance between Daufuskie Island on the West and Braddock Point on the East.

Two leading lights were established on the N.E. end of Daufuskie Island in 1873, for the purpose of assisting vessels in passing up from Tybee Roads to Calibogue Sound. The lights are *bright* and *fixed*: the front light near the shore (shown from a red lantern on a white tower) being elevated 15 ft. and visible through an arc of 90°. The rear light (shown from a red lantern on the keeper's dwelling) is elevated 65 ft. stands 750 yards to the northward of the front light, and shows through an arc of 270 degrees.

Vessels coming up from Tybee Roads will bring the beacons in range, when Tybee main light bears S.W. by W.; the course is then N. ¼ W., keeping the beacons in range until Braddock Point is passed, then haul up N. by E. in mid-channel. Shoals lie in close proximity to the range line near the South end, and a strong current sets directly across it; 8½ ft. can be carried through the channel where it crosses the shoal at low tide.

SAVANNAH * is seated on the S.W. bank of the river, at 17 miles above Tybee. The city is built on a sandy plain, about 40 ft. above the level of the tide, and is laid out in the form of a regular parallelogram; several of the streets are bordered with the elegant Pride of India, and other trees. It was formerly more unhealthy than now, from the rice being grown on wet grounds, instead of the dry cultivation now used.

The following general description of Savannah is taken from a more detailed

---

* GEORGIA was founded in the year 1733, as a British colony by General Oglethorpe, when Savannah received its first instalment of white inhabitants. During the early years of its colonial life, the city had enough to do to maintain its existence, and it was not until 1749 that exports from the colony were made, when 10,000 dollars' worth were sent out.

In 1776, when the Declaration of the Independence of America was promulgated in Savannah, her position as a British colony may be deemed to have ceased.—*Mr. Consul Tasker-Smith.*

description given by Capt. Stark, of the Salvage Association of Liverpool, in the "Nautical Magazine" for January, 1878:—

This port is considered to be the second cotton port in the United States. The sea approach is one of the easiest on the whole southern coast, the depth on the bar at mean low tide being 19 ft., with a rise of 7 ft., so that vessels can carry 26 ft. of water to a safe anchorage inside the bar; 24 ft. to Tybee, and 17 ft. to the town, which is distant from Tybee 18 miles. Vessels load alongside the wharves until they draw 16½ or 17 ft., when they proceed down the river to Venus Point—distant from Savannah 9 miles, where they load up to 19½ ft. draft, and they then proceed to Tybee, where they complete their loading.

About 1 mile from Savannah are the wrecks or obstructions, over which there are 18 ft. of water at top of springs. Many vessels take the ground at this place in going down the river, but the bottom being soft mud they take no harm. When vessels are becalmed outside the bar at Tybee, the ebb tide carries them to the S.E. and the flood tide to the southward, so that there is no danger of their being driven on shore.

There are five cotton presses in all, situated on the wharves and close to the shipping. The cotton being taken by hand-trucks direct from the press to the gangway is hoisted by steam tackles and lowered into the holds of vessels lying alongside the quays, so that no carting is required, thus sparing the inevitable expansion caused by jolting, which would occur if being conveyed in drays. The upper hydraulic press has quay space for six ships of 700 tons register, with a draft of 17 ft.

A *Dry Dock* is established on the other side of the river capable of receiving a sailing ship of the largest size; its dimensions are 315 ft. long and 70 ft. wide, and will take vessels drawing 16 ft. of water. There is also a large *patent slip*, capable of hauling up a vessel of 1,000 tons, drawing 16 ft. of water; the length of the cradle is 250 ft. Steam pumps and other appliances are attached to this slip.

Depth of water at Tybee is 24 ft., and Venus Point 19 ft., and to the city 17½ ft.

The amount of cotton exported from Savannah during the last four years has averaged over 600,000 bales, it will therefore be seen how important a port it is, even although deep-drafted ships have to float down the river to complete their loading.

This completes the remarks by Captain Stark.

The Bar at the mouth of Savannah River is the deepest and most accessible of any on the southern coast. The average depth is 19 ft. at low water; and hence, with a full tide, a large ship may pass in safety. But, although thus favoured at the entrance, these advantages are soon lost in ascending the river. Farther up the shoals are frequent, and have less water; and the river, at first brackish, becomes fresh; and hence being surrounded by marshes, it is in summer unhealthy. Dredging operations have, however, materially improved the navigation of the port.

Tybee Island is a pleasant island to the southward of the bar. The lighthouse above mentioned is on the N.E. part of the island; it is about 13 miles from Savannah. On the bar there are 19 ft. at low water; on the South breaker not more than 7 or 8 ft., and at a mile and a quarter from the lighthouse the ground is uncovered at low ebbs. On the North breaker there is not less than 12 ft. of water, to the distance of a mile.

Besides the lights above mentioned on the N.E. point of Tybee Island, and the leading lights on Daufuskie Island, the following are established.

Tybee Island Knoll Lightvessel.—Off the knoll North of Tybee Island a red lighthouse exhibiting a *fixed* light, 30 ft. above the sea, visible 10 miles. A *Fog-bell* and horn.

SAVANNAH.

Cockspur Island Beacon Light.—On a knoll connected with the eastern end of Cockspur Island, a white lighthouse, 35 ft. above the sea, showing a *fixed* light, visible 9 miles.

Oyster Beds, Beacon Light.—On the Oyster Beds, opposite to Cockspur Island, to mark the South Channel, a white lighthouse, exhibiting a *fixed red* light, elevated 35 ft., visible 9 miles off. A fog-bell.

Tybee Knoll Leading Lights have, since November, 1878, been exhibited from two beacons, erected at the East end of Long Island, about 1 mile W.S.W. of Oyster Beds Beacon light.

The low light is a fixed bright light, elevated 21 ft. above high water, and shown from the upper part of the keeper's dwelling, which is of one story, and painted white. *The high light* is a fixed bright light, elevated 44 ft. above high water, and shown from a frame tower, which is painted white, and situated W. ¾ S. from the low light, distant 717 yards. These lights in line lead through the dredged channel from Tybee Road into Savannah River.

Fig Island Beacon Light.—On the East end of Fig Island, a white wooden building, 21 ft. in height, and 26 ft. above the sea, showing a *fixed* light, visible 9 miles. To guide vessels going up to the city at night.

The following directions have been given, but it should be premised that they must be taken with the greatest caution, as the marks and buoys will probably be altered and no stranger should attempt to enter.

The course from the Light Boat off the Ship Channel of Charleston to off Port Royal lightvessel will be S.W., and the distance 52 miles. In this track you will have from 5 to 7 fathoms; and as you pass the lightvessel to the eastward you will clear the dangerous shoal called Martin's Industry. This shoal lies 8 miles from the South side of the entrance to Port Royal, which is the North side of Hilton Head Island, the highest land in sight; come no nearer than 7 fathoms, keeping your lead going; and in the night, or thick weather, do not approach nearer than 10 fathoms. The tide of flood sets boldly in. In rounding the lightvessel, a S.W. by W. ¼ W. course, 12 miles, will take you to the bar buoy of Savannah or Tybee entrance. When you get to the southward of Hilton Head you will see the lighthouse on the northern point of the island of Tybee. If in the night, be careful after rounding the lightvessel not to go nearer the Gaskin Bank than 5 fathoms. In fresh winds you take a pilot abreast of the lighthouse, and in moderate winds just without the bar. In clear weather you might expect to see Tybee light at the distance of 16 miles. Shoal ground, with 6 or 7 fathoms, lies S.E., 14 or 15 miles from Tybee light.

Buoys.—There are two buoys on the bar, the outer one bearing E. ¾ S., 3½ miles from Tybee lighthouse, and several others inside of Tybee Island point; but these are of use only to the pilots and those acquainted, and best understood by a reference to the chart. No stranger should attempt the bar without a pilot.

If intending to anchor under Tybee Point, steer W. ¼ N. till the lighthouse bears S.S.E, when anchor in from 4 to 5 fathoms, muddy bottom. But if bound higher up having crossed the bar with Tybee lighthouse and beacon in line, and being near the position of Inner Bar buoy (*black*), No. 3, steer N.W. by N. until Tybee Knoll lightvessel bears W. by N. ¼ N., and which may then be steered for till Tybee Knoll beacons are in line.

Strangers should not attempt the navigation of the river.

In beating over the bar, when to the eastward of the Inner buoy, and standing to the northward, tack when Square Beacon opens to the northward of Tybee Point, or before the buoy ranges with Tybee light. To avoid the shoals between the buoys, the southern tacks can be kept (while eastward of the inner buoy) till the lighthouse bears W. ¼ N. When westward of the buoy, the port tacks can be kept on board till the outer buoy bears E.S.E., and the starboard tacks till the Square Beacon is open but two ships' lengths to the northward. The lead is a safe guide, as the soundings are regular in the channel way, except just to the eastward of the inner buoy. The Southern Breakers should not be approached nearer than in 3 fathoms water.

At Savannah wharves, ships can load to 13½ ft.; 2 miles below it, or the Five-Fathom Hole, to 15 ft.; and at Four-mile Point (4 miles below), to 16 ft.; at Venus Point, 4 miles above Tybee, to 17 ft.—*R. Leighton.*

It is high water, full and change, at Cockspur Island, at $7^h\ 20^m$. Springs rise 8 ft. neaps 7 ft.

OBSERVATIONS ON THE WINDS, ETC., ON THE COASTS OF SOUTH CAROLINA.

If the wind blows hard from the N.E. quarter, without rain, it commonly continues so for some time, perhaps three or four days; but if such winds are attended with rain, they generally shift to the East, E.S.E., and S.E. South-east winds blow right in on the coast; but they seldom blow dry, or continue long. In 6, 8, or 10 hours after their commencement the sky begins to look dirty, which soon produces rain. When it comes to blow or rain very hard, you may be sure the wind will fly round to the N.W. quarter, and blow hard for twenty or thirty hours, with a clear sky.

North-west winds are always attended with clear weather; they sometimes blow very hard, but seldom for longer than thirty hours. The most lasting winds are those which blow from the S.S.W. and W.N.W., and from the North to the E.N.E. The weather is most settled when the wind is in any of these quarters.

In summer time thunder gusts are very common on this coast; they always come from the N.W. quarter, and are sometimes so heavy that no canvass can withstand their fury; they come on so suddenly that the greatest precaution is necessary to guard against the effects of their violence.

To these difficulties, which are encountered in the navigation of these parts, may be added, contrary currents in approaching the coasts, and the almost constant haze on the low land, and bad horizon near it, which renders it difficult to distinguish the land, or to ascertain the latitude.

Great Warsaw Sound.—At the southern end of the Island of Tybee is Warsaw or Wassaw Inlet, with only 10 ft. water on the bar; but it is too intricate for strangers.

The BAR is 8¼ miles S.W. ¼ S. from Tybee Bar, and 19¾ miles S.W. ¼ W. from the lightship at Port Royal.

A large *black* and *white* buoy is placed in 5 fathoms off the entrance. Bring it on with the large sand-hill at the N.E. end of Great Warsaw Island, and steer on that range:—W. by N. ¼ N., five-eighths of a mile to 1st *red* nun buoy; then N.W. ¾ N., 1 mile to 2nd *red* can buoy, carrying staff and red ball; then W. by N. ¼ N., 1¼ mile to 3rd *red* spar buoy; then W. by N., 2 miles to anchorage above the site of former earthworks on Great Warsaw Island.

OSSABAW SOUND—ST. CATHARINE'S SOUND.

OSSABAW SOUND forms the entrance of the River Ogeechee, and its bar, which extends a league out to sea, bears S.W. by S. about 5 leagues from Tybee lighthouse, its latitude being 31° 50'. The bar has over it about 17 ft. of water. There is an isle up the river, called *Green Island*, which serves as a mark; its land being higher, and its trees taller than any other in the vicinity. The latter are of pine, and their general verdure gives name to the spot.

There are two channels over the bar at the entrance. The North Channel, leading into the mouth of the Vernon River, through which 8 ft. of water can be taken; and the South Channel, leading into the mouth of the Ogeechee River, through which 17 feet can be taken. Through this channel 19 ft. could be taken by a series of buoys carefully placed. Both these last depths can be taken up only to an anchorage inside of the bar, and the great North and East Banks.

North Channel to Vernon River.—When in from 3½ to 4 fathoms of water, bring the South end of Great Warsaw Island to bear N.W. ¼ N., and the N.E. point of Ossabaw Island W. ½ N., and the course over the bar is W.N.W. ¼ N. To go further up, a local knowledge is required.

South Channel.—Buoys.—The outer buoy of the South channel to Ogeechee River is a first-class buoy, painted in *black* and *white* perpendicular stripes, and is moored in 5 fathoms, 19 miles S.W. by S. from Tybee bar, and 28 miles S.W. ¼ S. from the Light-ship at Port Royal entrance.

On the southern point of entrance to the river and N.E. point of Ossabaw Island, is Fort Seymour, with a flagstaff.

In proceeding for the southern entrance bring the above buoy on with the flagstaff, which will be on a N.W. ¼ N. bearing, steer 1¼ mile to a *black* buoy; thence North, 2¼ miles to a *black* and *white* buoy, passing a *black* buoy midway on the course, and steering for a gap in the woods of Great Warsaw Island, having a tall tree upon the right side, and a white sand-hill on the left side of the gap. From the last *black* and *white* buoy steer N.W. ¼ W. 1¼ mile for another *black* and *white* buoy, keeping it on with the easternmost edge of wood on Racoon Island. This buoy is moored in 7 fathoms, ond is at the forks of the channels. From the Fork buoy you may steer W. ½ N., 1½ mile to a *black* buoy, keeping it on with the flagstaff at Fort Seymour, and crossing the bar of Ogeechee River in 14 ft. at mean low water. Be careful in steering the latter course, to make allowance for the tide, which sets diagonally across it.

If bound to Fort Seymour, anchor about half a mile above the black buoy in 4 fathoms near the shore. From the sea up to the forks of the channels the least water is 17 ft. Mean rise and fall of tide 6½ ft.

ST. CATHARINE'S SOUND, or the entrance of the Port of Sunbury, lies about 30 miles to the south-westward of Tybee Inlet, or the entrance of Savannah River. It has a bar, but the harbour is capacious and safe, and has sufficient water for large ships. The entrance is, howeuer, difficult, for the bar, which is a mile South of the North point of St. Catharine's Island, has only 8¼ ft. at low tide, while the channel is not more than 200 yards wide, and the shoals on each side are commonly uncovered. Vessels bound to Sunbury, &c., have therefore been directed rather to enter at Ossabaw, to the North, or Sapelo, to the South, and go by the inland passage, than to attempt St. Catharine's Sound.

From the outer striped buoy of Ossabaw, in 5 fathoms water, steer South, 3 miles, then W. ¼ S., until you get off the South point of Ossabaw Island, 1½ mile distant. On this course you will carry 10 ft. at low water, then W.S.W. for St. Catharine's Island, and anchor in 5 fathoms; rise of tide 6 ft.

DOBOY OR DARIEN INLET.

There is a *red* can buoy, No. 2, in 16 ft. water, outside the bar at Beach Channel, inner point of St. Catharine's, bearing S.W. by W. ¼ W.; inner point of Ossabaw W. by S. ¼ S. Leave this buoy on the starboard hand, and steer S.W. by W. 2¼ miles to *red* can buoy, No. 4, inside the bar in 10 ft. water.

Buoy No. 4 is on the point of a shoal running from Ossabaw Island, and must be left on the starboard hand entering, inner point of St. Catharine's, bearing S.W. by W.; inner point of Ossabaw, W. by S. You cannot well go farther without a pilot, indeed you ought to be acquainted to take the bar.

Sapelo Inlet.—This inlet is between St. Catharine's and Sapelo Islands, and carries about 18 ft. at mean low water. On the southern part of St. Catharine's Island are two mast-beacons with large barrels on top.

To enter the inlet, get the outer beacon open about three handspikes' lengths to the North of the inner one, and steer nearly for the North end of Blackbeard Island, or W. ¼ S., leaving both buoys on the port hand. Between the points of the island the water is deep.

DOBOY or Darien Inlet.—Ships of heavy burthen can enter the Port of Darien; the mean low water depth being 15 feet 6 inches, high water 22 ft.; but it is unsuitable to naval purposes by reason of its unfavourable locality, being surrounded by swamps and morasses, having a fresh water river, and is consequently unhealthy. It lies immediately along the South side of Sapelo Island; and its bar, which is 4 miles to the eastward of the nearest land, lies in lat. 31° 20'. The Pelican Shoals, which stretch from Sapelo Island, border the channel on the North side.

Darien was one of the earliest settlements in the State of Georgia. It was occupied soon after General Oglethorp founded the settlement of Savannah by a party of Scotch Highlanders, and is situated on the Altamaha River, about 10 miles above the Island of Doboy. The chief trade of Darien is timber and lumber.

Doboy Island, which is about 7 miles from the mouth of the river, and 10 miles from Darien, forms the port, which affords a perfectly safe anchorage, completely sheltered by Sapelo and Wolfe Islands. Vessels drawing 22 ft. have passed out on spring tides, and vessels drawing 19 ft. can pass out on any ordinary tide. Trade chiefly timber and lumber.

Lighthouse.—On the South end of Sapelo Island, in lat. 31° 23' 28", and long. 81° 17' 6", is a lighthouse, 65 ft. in height, and 74 ft. above the sea, painted red and white in horizontal stripes, which exhibits a *fixed* light, varied by *flashes* every 40 seconds, and visible 14 miles off.

Beacon Light.—A little to the S.E. of the main light is a beacon, painted brown, 50 ft. above the sea, showing a *fixed* light.

Wolf Island Beacon Lights.—These beacons are erected near the North end of Wolf Island, and S.S.E. of Sapelo Island light. In connection with Sapelo Island light, these are intended to be used as ranges in crossing Doboy Bar and into the Sound. The front light is a *fixed bright* light, placed on a skeleton frame tower, painted brown, 31 ft. above the level of the sea. The rear light is also a *fixed bright* light, placed on the keeper's dwelling, painted white, 38 ft. above the level of the sea, and 480 ft. distant from the front light. Both lights are visible 10 miles off.

Keep in 5 fathoms water till the lighthouse of Sapelo bears N.W. by W. ¼ W., when you discern the outer buoy, which is moored in 3 fathoms water. To run in, bring the beacon light in range with the main light of Sapelo, and run for them until the outer or East beacon on Wolf Island bears S.W. by W. ¼ W., when steer N.W. by W. ¼ W., and keep in not less than 4 fathoms water to the anchorage abreast of the Sapelo lighthouse. The water shoals gradually on the South side of the channel, but on the North side the breakers are steep-to.

ST. SIMON'S.

Chimney Spit is bare at half-tide, and is a good guide to the anchorage.

The following are, or were, the depths of water, bearings, and distances of the buoys in Doboy Inlet.

Outer bar buoy is an iron nun buoy, painted black and white stripes, with flag on staff, in 17 ft. water, just outside the bar, Sapelo light bearing N.W. by W. ¼ W.; Wolf Island beacons, W. ¾ N.

Second bar buoy is a *red* iron nun buoy No. 2, with a white flag on a staff, in 13 feet water, on the South edge of the North Breaker. Give this buoy a berth of 50 yards, and leave it on the starboard hand entering. Wolf Island beacons bear W. ¾ N.; Sapelo light N.W. by W.

Third bar buoy is an iron nun buoy, with a black flag on a staff, painted *black* and *white* stripes, in 17 ft. water, with Sapelo light bearing N.W. ¾ W.; Wolf Island beacons W. ¾ N.

Fourth bar buoy is a *black* iron nun buoy No. 1, with palmetto branches on a staff in 18 ft. water, near the outer edge of the Knuckle, Sapelo light bearing N.W. ¾ W.; Wolf Island beacons W. by S. ¼ S. Leave this buoy on the port hand, giving it a berth of 100 yards.

Alatamaha or *Little St. Simon's Sound* lies about S.W. by S. ¼ S. from the entrance of Savannah, distant 47 miles; and from the lightvessel at the entrance of Port Royal, S.W. by S., 64 miles.

ST. SIMON'S.—In proceeding from Tybee for St. Simon's Bar, bring Tybee lighthouse to bear N.W., in 10 fathoms of water; a course S.W. by S. 24 leagues, leads to St. Simon's Bar. The shore of the several islands between these places is flat, and the soundings towards it are gradual.

Lighthouse.—A lighthouse is situated on the North side of entrance to St. Simon Sound, on the southern point of St. Simon Island. It is a conical brick tower, with a two-story keeper's dwelling, of brick, attached, both of which are painted white; the tower is painted black. The light is *fixed* and *flashing*, a fixed bright, being varied by *red* and *bright flashes* alternately every minute; elevated 108 ft. above the sea, the light is visible 16 miles off. From the lighthouse, Amelia Island light lies S. ¼ W., distant 28 miles, and Tybee Island light N.N.E. ¼ E. 60 miles.

The waters forming the port of Brunswick are generally designated *Turtle River*, an arm of the sea entering between St. Simon's and Jekyl Islands, and flowing upward for more than 20 miles, thus forming a wide, deep, and rapid stream. As no fresh water falls into this basin, rain excepted, it is always salt, free from freshes and alluvial deposits; and hence from an early period of time, no change whatever has been perceptible in the soundings or general character of the port.

From St. Simon's and Jekyl Islands project extensive banks of sand, to the distance of 6 miles eastward from the lighthouse. At low water portions of them are laid bare; and unless the sea be unusually smooth, they form in nearly their whole extent, lines of continuous breakers. Between these lines of surf lies the channel, which is three-quarters of a mile between the spit heads, and which enlarges to a mile soon after entering. Between the spit heads are about 22 ft. at low water. Proceeding toward the land by traversing the whole breadth of the channel, the soundings gradually shoal to 18 ft., the least water found in the channel way.

At about 1 mile within the spit heads is the *Middle Ground*, a bank of sand resting on the Jekyl or southern spit, and jutting about 200 fathoms into the channel way; but leaving a passage of 18 ft., toward the St. Simon or northern spit, sufficiently wide for a large ship, even with an adverse wind. The Middle Ground has but 14 ft. at low water. Entering still farther up, the soundings gradually become deeper; so that, whan between the islands, it has an increased depth of 12 fathoms. The vessel is now in safety.

Here, on the right, is St. Simon's Sound, which together with similar watercourses farther North, affords a safe internal navigation to steam-boats and craft to Savannah and Charleston. To the left is the arm of the sea, called *Turtle River*, from which, by Jekyl and Cumberland Sounds, is a southern internal navigation to St. Mary's.

The course from sea to the mouth of the harbour is nearly W.N.W., keeping the northern breakers on board; the channel then runs South and south-westerly, and making a short turn to the N.W. we arrive at the town of Brunswick. The average rise of the tide is 6 ft., which gives on the bar, at high water, 24 ft. The country hereabout is healthy.

St. Simon's Sound is between St. Simon's and Jekyl Islands. The bar is about 3 leagues to the eastward of the shore. On the South end of St. Simon's Island is the lighthouse, before described.

The latitude of the bar is about 31° 4' N., and there are 4 and 5 fathoms close to the outside of it. In passing, therefore, it will be prudent not to approach nearer than in 8 or 9 fathoms.

The South end of Simon's Island may be known, not only by the lighthouse, but by four trees, standing thus :—† † † †. On Jekyl Island, to the southward, are some remarkable trees, appearing like umbrellas, and thence called the *umbrella trees*. The beaches, both of St. Simon's and Jekyl Island, are remarkably white.

Directions.—A large black and white buoy is placed off the bar in 5 fathoms water. From it, steer N.W. by W. ¾ W., 3 miles nearly, to a large *black* can buoy, passing a black buoy midway on the course, and keeping the southern end of King's Cotton House, on with the tripod standing on the ruins of the lighthouse.

After passing the second *black* buoy, steer W. by N. ¼ N., 3 miles, to the anchorage, keeping the starboard shore best aboard to avoid a dangerous shoal called "Jekyl Spit," making off the N.E. point of Jekyl Island. A *black* spar buoy is moored in 3 fathoms water, on the outer edge of this shoal, which is bare at very low water. Anchor in from 4 to 7 fathoms water, opposite Mr. T. Butler King's house, on St. Simon's Island.

Fifteen feet at mean low water will be found in the above course over the bar. Mean rise and fall of tide 6¾ ft. From the middle to the inner bar buoy the channel is narrow, with 12 ft. on the South and 9 ft. on the North side. The North bank is bare at very low water, from the inner buoy up.

If bound up to Brunswick, or the Turtle River, you must take a pilot if not acquainted with the navigation.

The tides, on the full and change of the moon, are as follow:—In the sound, 9 o'clock; on the bar, half-past 7; and in the offing, three-quarters after 6 o'clock. The flood, along shore, sets S.S.W., the ebb E.N.E. Ordinary tides rise 6 ft.

ST. ANDREW'S.—The entrance to St. Andrew's is indicated by a *fixed* light, elevated 78 ft., visible 14 miles off, on the South side, and standing on the North end of Little Cumberland Island. The entrance is between Jekyl and Cumberland Islands; and on the bar there are 11 ft. at mean low water, and 14 ft. at high water.

Santilla River empties into St. Andrew's Sound. Crow Harbour lies about 30 miles up Santilla River, and is a great timber depot; about 15 miles above Crow Harbour is the town of Jefferson, where vessels drawing 12 ft. can go.

There are four buoys placed to mark the navigation, besides the buoy at the entrance of the Santilla River. The bar buoy is a second-class can buoy, painted *red*, with No. 2 in white, placed in 19 ft. water at low tide, and must be left on the star-

ST. MARY'S. 139

board hand entering. Little Cumberland light bearing W. by N. ½ N.; South point of Jekyl, N.W. by W.

In running for St. Andrew's Bar, give the land a berth of about 8 miles, until the light bears W. by N. ¼ N., while in 4 fathoms water. When you get the light on this bearing, the course will bring you up to the bar buoy; then haul to the northward until the middle buoy, No. 4, is in range with the light (to avoid the two lumps in a direct line, W. by N. ½ N., between the two buoys), when steer for it, passing it to the southward. From this buoy a N.W. by W. ½ W. course will take you into the channel.

To run in, keep in not less than 6 fathoms water, until the lighthouse bears as above, W. by N. ½ N., then steer for it. When the South point of Jekyl Island bears N.W. ¼ W., steer N.W. by W. ¼ W. until the lighthouse bears W.S.W., then haul in for the anchorage under the N.W. end of Little Cumberland Island, and anchor when convenient.

It is high water, full and change, at the lighthouse, 7^h 55^m. Spring tides rise 7 ft.

ST. MARY'S.—The entrance of St. Mary's Sound and River lies about 8 leagues S.S.W. from Simon's Bar; between there is a depth of 5 and 6 fathoms. This river discharges itself into the Atlantic between Cumberland and Amelia Islands. The town of *Fernandina* is situated a short distance up the Amelia River, on the West side of Amelia Island. It contains several stores and neat dwellings, and is one of the best harbours South of the Chesapeake, having a depth of 11 ft. at mean low water, and 16 ft. 8 in. at high water. The harbour is completely landlocked, and has good holding ground. Vessels can lie in deep water off the Florida railway wharf. The lighthouse and beacon on Amelia Island in line, lead over the bar, on which there is 13 ft. at low water. The channels, however, are liable to such constant changes, that it is advisable not to take a vessel in without a pilot.

Amelia Island Lighthouse, about 2 miles from its North end, and on the South side of entrance to St. Mary's River, is white, 58 ft. high, and exhibits, at 112 feet above the sea, a *fixed* white light, varied by a *flash every minute and a half*, visible 16 miles.

In front of the main lighthouse, in line with the channel, is a skeleton frame tower, painted black, from which is exhibited a *fixed* bright light, at an elevation of 27 ft. above the sea, visible 10 miles.

North Range Lights.—On the North end of Amelia Island are two beacons, half a mile apart, bearing from each other W. ¾ N. and E. ¾ S. The front beacon is painted brown and white, and exhibits a fixed bright light, at 35 ft. above the sea, visible 11 miles. The rear beacon is painted white, and exhibits a fixed bright light, at 53 ft. above the sea, visible 12 miles.

Directions.—Bring the South light beacon in line with the Amelia Island lighthouse at the outer or sea buoy, keep on this line until the North range beacons, which will gradually appear to approach each other, are in line. From this point, follow the line of the North beacons until Amelia Island lighthouse bears S.W. by S., then steer N.W. ¼ W. to No. 6 buoy, when the course should be changed to W. ½ S., which course leads inside Fort Clinch; or when the front North light beacon bears S.W. ¼ W., change course to W. ½ S. Care should be taken to keep the vessel well in hand as the North beacons come together, as the turn is sharp, and there is danger of striking the shoal on the port hand. The North light beacons only mark a turning point, which, at night, sometimes cannot otherwise be found. Vessels cannot run in with them in line.

The bar is very similar to that of Charleston in its general features and depth of water; it is subject to the same vicissitudes from great gales.

Without the bar you may, if requisite, anchor in 7 or 8 fathoms, with the South part of Cumberland Island bearing W. by N. ¼ N. or W. by N., but it is completely exposed to winds from seaward.

NASSAU.—The bar of St. Augustine lies nearly S. by E. about 17 leagues from that of St. Mary. Between lie the rivers of Nassau and St. John. The bar or entrance of Nassau lies nearly 5 leagues to the southward, or S. by E. of St. Mary's, and between there will be found a depth of 5 or 6 fathoms, with sandy ground.

The coast of Amelia Island is a low even coast, but has a range of sand-hills, which serve as a natural dyke against the sea. From each end, the bars of the rivers stretch outward, as described, to a considerable distance.

The *outer buoy* at Nassau inlet is a *red* iron nun in 24 ft. water, with the North point of Talbot Island bearing W. by N. and St. John's light S. by W. The *inner buoy* is similar, but lies in 8 ft. water, with the North end of Talbot Island W. by N., and St. John's light S. ¼ W. The bar is constantly shifting, and should not be entered without a pilot. The buoys are altered as occasion requires, and should always be left on the starboard hand.

St. JOHN'S.—The entrance of St. John's River lies to the southward of that of Nassau. In making this place, when bound southward, *General's Mount* on the South side of the river appears like a high round bluff. The North side of the entrance is formed by Talbot Island, which is 5 miles in length, about the same height as General's Mount, and covered with trees. It is high water here, on the full and change, at half-past 7; the depth on the bar is from 10 to 13 ft. at high, and about 6 ft. at low water. The currents run out until quarter flood, and sometimes half flood. The tides are very much influenced by the winds.

Lighthouse.—Near the mouth of St. John's River and South side of entrance, in lat. 30° 23′ 37″, and long. 81° 25′ 32″, is a lighthouse of reddish grey colour, 65 feet in height, exhibiting a *fixed* light, visible 14 miles off to the northward between N.E. and North. The town of Jacksonville is about 11 miles above the entrance of the river, on the northern side.

There are ten buoys placed to mark the channels in St. John's bar and river; but as the bar, like that of Nassau, is constantly shifting, and ought not to be attempted without a pilot, they need not be described.

Outer buoy is a *red* wooden nun buoy, No. 2, in 29 ft. water; St. John's light bearing W. by S.; Pilot's Station W. ¼ S. *Bar buoy* is a *red* iron conical buoy, No. 4, in 9½ ft. water; lighthouse W. by S. ¼ S.; Pilot's Station W. ¼ S.

Red buoys are to be left on the starboard hand entering, and black buoys on the port hand; striped buoys may be passed on either side.

The entrance of St. John's River forms a long and broad bay, and the effect of the tide is felt up the river full 150 miles from its mouth; the course of the river running nearly parallel with the coast, and affording most excellent navigation; for after passing the bar up to the entrance of Lake George, you will have, in all parts, full 20 ft. water, and this lake to its S.E. extremity has a depth of 10 ft.

In running in to St. John's, bring the lighthouse to bear S.W. ¼ W., and open the top of the chimney on the West end of the dwelling-house, about 3 ft. to the South and East of the light; then run in until within the South Breaker Head; then steer S.S.W. for the General's Mount, within a cable's length of the shore; then haul up to the westward, keeping the shore about the same distance from you, to clear the Middle and North Breakers, which show plainly if there is any wind. When nearly opposite the swash, incline towards the North shore, or Fort George Island, to clear a flat that makes off from the shore a considerable distance.

Vessels having to wait for tide, or becalmed, and inward bound, can anchor in 5 fathoms, good bottom.

Jacksonville is situated on the left bank of St. John's River, about 20 miles from its mouth.

Dames Point Lighthouse, which is about 12 miles below Jacksonville, stands on a shoal about 500 yards S.W. from Dame's Point, in 8 ft. of water, mean tide. There is a channel on either side, one of which passes close under Dame's Point, and the other near the lighthouse on its S.W. side, and they unite a short distance above it. The ironwork of the foundation is painted red, and the superstructure white. The light is *bright* and *fixed*, and can be seen as soon as it is opened by Reddie's Point above, and Mill Cove Point below; elevation, 38 ft. above mean tide.

New Entrance.—The following appeared in the "Mercantile Marine Magazine" for May, 1874:—A new channel has recently been opened through the bar at the mouth of the St. John's River. It is short, straight, and of good width, following the line of beach, and opening well to the South. Vessels drawing 11¼ ft. of water have been taken through the new channel, which is steadily improving, and will eventually be, if not already, the main channel.

St. AUGUSTINE.—Between the river of St. John and St. Augustine, a distance of 25 miles S.S.E. ¼ E., the shore is so bold, as to have 5 and 6 fathoms within half a mile of it. When abreast of Cartel Point, which is the North point of the bay of St. Augustine, you will come in sight of the island of St. Anastasia.

Light.—On the North end of Anastasia Island and South side of entrance to St. Augustine, in lat. 29° 53' N., long. 81° 17' W. is a lighthouse 150 ft. high, painted in black and white spiral bands. This lighthouse was completed in 1874, in a position a quarter of a mile S.W. ¾ S. from the old tower, and a quarter of a mile from the shore. The light exhibited is a *fixed and flashing bright light*, elevated 160 feet, and visible 19 miles off. The flashes occur once in every three minutes. Vessels coming from the northward will run down till the lighthouse bears W. by N., keeping in 3 fathoms water.

The beach between St. John and St. Augustine is even and straight, except about a hill, 4 leagues S.S.E. from St. John's, which is a little higher than the rest of the sandhills. This place, where there are three springs of fine fresh water, was called the Horse-guards.

The bar of St. Augustine is formed by the extremity of a narrow shifting sand, which extends 2 miles E S.E. from Cartel Point, and the point of another sand, which extends half a mile from E. by N. from the N.E. point of St. Anastasia Island. The city of St. Augustine is situated 2 miles back from the Atlantic shore, on the South point of a peninsula, connected with the mainland by a narrow isthmus, protected from the swell of the ocean by Anastasia Island, not sufficiently high to obstruct the sea breezes, or a view of the ocean. The site of the city, though scarcely 12 ft. higher than the level of the ocean, is healthy and pleasant, which makes it a favourite resort of invalids from the North.

The bar at the entrance of the harbour has opened in a new place, rendering the passage more direct and easy than formerly. The depth on the bar at high water is 11 feet 2 inches; at half-tide 9 ft., and at low water 7 ft. In 1869 the buoys were placed as follows:—*Outer buoy*, perpendicular *black* and *white* stripes, nun—lighthouse S.W.; Jack's Mount, S. by W.; and Point North Beach, W.S.W. *North Breaker buoy*, 1 *red* No. 2, nun—Jack's Mount, S. ¼ W.; lighthouse S.W.; Point

ST. AUGUSTINE.

North Beach, S.W. by W. *Spit buoy, red,* No. 4, uuu—lighthouse S.W.; Point North Beach, N.W. Leave the above buoys on the starboard hand entering.

The tide flows, on full and change, at 8 hours 4 minutes, and runs S.E. by S. and N.W. by N.

Vessels bound to this place from the northward should not bring the lighthouse farther to the westward than S.W. by W. If the wind be to the South, bring the lighthouse to bear West; if moderate, come to an anchor, in from 7 to 9 fathoms, muddy ground. All vessels, when off the bar, are required to show, by signal, how much water they draw, by hauling down the flag and hoisting it again so many times as the vessel draws feet of water.

The pilots of St. Augustine board vessels outside whenever the weather admits; if otherwise, they direct them in by a flag, which is waved in the direction the vessel ought to steer. When the flag is erect, the vessel will bear down for the pilot boat.

To anchor in the bay of St. Augustine, bring the signal tower to bear S.W. $\frac{1}{2}$ W. and the fort which stands to the northward of the tower W. $\frac{1}{2}$ N.; the new barracks will then be open of the northernmost part of Anastasia Island; then bring up in 10 fathoms water, good holding ground; the northernmost land in sight will bear N.W. by N., the southernmost land S.S.E., and you will be near the middle of the bay, it being immaterial which way you cast your ship. But should you be too far to the northward or southward, there will be danger of casting the wrong way, and more so on the tide of flood, which sets strongly in the bay. If it should be likely to blow from the eastward, do not attempt to get under weigh whilst the tide of flood runs.

From the 1st of November to the end of February, the hardest gales that blow on this coast prevail, and in general from the N.N.E. to the S.S.E.; the wind any way easterly comes on very suddenly to a gale during the season above mentioned, and these gales give but very little warning.

Vessels bound from Europe to St. Augustine, would shorten their passage considerably by making the lighthouse on the South end of Abaco, or the Hole in the Rock, then running W. by S. to make the Berry Islands, and thence W. by N. or W.N.W., till they get into the Gulf Stream. The only precaution to be observed is, to steer to the westward of North, after you are clear of the Great Bahama Island, because the bank stretches N. by W. nearly, and the currents set partly on the N.W. part of the bank, particularly towards the Memory Rock. Observe also, it is necessary to give the West end of the Great Bahama a good berth, not merely from its shoals, but lest, with the wind hanging south-westward, you should be embayed.

Having gained the Gulf Stream, with the wind blowing strongly from the eastward, by keeping the Bahama shore on board, smooth water will be obtained. If it blows from off the opposite coast, by keeping over towards it, the same convenience will be experienced; not, however, approaching too near. In a gale from the northward, the most prudent way is to retreat before it, in a southerly direction, taking particular care not to approach too near the Florida shore.

ST. AUGUSTINE TO CAPE FLORIDA.

Matanza Inlet.—Nearly 5 leagues S.S.E. from the bar of St. Augustine, and at the South end of the island of St. Anastasia, lies Matanza Inlet, having a bar of only 8 ft. at high water. From St. Augustine to this place there is a channel, for 5 ft. draught, within St. Anastasia Island; this is the usual communication between the two places; so that few vessels enter the inlet of Matanza from sea.

Mosquito Inlet has 5 ft. water on the bar at low water. Rise of tide $3\frac{1}{2}$ ft. The town of *Smyrna* is within the inlet to the southward and Dumbarton to the northward. On the South side of the inlet a lighthouse was erected, but it fell before the light was exhibited.

CAPE CANAVERAL lies S.S.E. $\frac{3}{4}$ E. 31 leagues from Matanza Inlet, and 14 leagues S.E. by S. from Mosquito Inlet. The shore is bold all the way from Matanza Inlet to the Cape, excepting a rocky shoal, which extends $1\frac{1}{4}$ mile from shore, at about 5 miles to the southward of Matanza Inlet.

LIGHTHOUSE.—On the N.E. pitch of Cape Canaveral stand two lighthouses, the old one, now disused, being painted white, and the new one in black and white horizontal bands. The towers are each 55 ft. in height, and the light shown from the new tower is a *revolving bright light* every minute, elevated 139 ft. and visible 18 miles off.

Shoals off the Cape.—From the cape itself a dangerous reef of sand extends to the S.E. some $6\frac{3}{4}$ miles, and breaks at that distance, being a considerable width across. The *Hetzel Shoal* lies N.E. by N., $11\frac{1}{2}$ miles from the lighthouse; the *Ohio Shoal*, N.E. $\frac{1}{4}$ N., $11\frac{1}{4}$ miles; the *Bull Shoal*, N.E. by E. $\frac{1}{4}$ E., $6\frac{1}{4}$ miles. There appears to be a passage between the latter shoal and the cape of 7 fathoms, but no one ought to attempt it until better or more fully explored.

The bank of soundings off Cape Canaveral is very steep; you will have 30 fathoms water at 9 leagues eastward of the cape, and immediately fall off the bank and be in the Gulf Stream, where the temperature of the water is 84° or 85° in August or September. Here there is no bottom with 100 fathoms; at 5 leagues East of the cape are 20 fathoms, broken shells, and at 3 leagues off, 10 fathoms, black sand. To the northward of the cape the bank of soundings sets much broader, so that in 29° an extensive flat of 8 to 12 fathoms runs off the beach, full 10 leagues; beyond which are 40 and 47 fathoms fine black sand, and at 55 miles from the land, in this parallel; this latter depth is near the steep edge of the bank. When approaching Cape Canaveral the lead should be kept going; and when in 18 or 20 fathoms you will be 5 leagues from the cape, when in the parallel of it.

A shoal, awash at low water, is marked on the chart at 7 miles off shore, abreast Cape Malabar, and 26 miles S. by E. $\frac{3}{4}$ E. from Cape Canaveral lighthouse.

Indian River Inlet.—From off Cape Canaveral, with the lighthouse bearing W.S.W. or W. distant about 12 miles, the course and distance to Indian River Inlet is South, 60 or 55 miles. The land to the southward of the cape curves inward, and this part of the coast is flat and not to be trusted to, but is remarkable from the immense number of palm trees. Within the inlets the tides run strong. The River St. Sebastian, and other rivers, empty themselves into the Indian River.

From the northern side of the entrance to Indian River Inlet a reef of rocks runs along shore to the northward, full 7 leagues, extending 2 miles off the land, and a flat of $1\frac{1}{2}$ to $2\frac{1}{2}$ fathoms continues past St. Sebastian's River; but to the northward of this, and in the bight to the southward of Cape Canaveral and its shoals, you will find 7 to 8 fathoms mud, pretty close in. Vessels wishing to lie under the cape in northerly or westerly winds, should bring the lighthouse to bear N.E., and anchor in 15 or 17 ft. water, about one-third of a mile from the beach. To the northward of Indian River Inlet are several hummocks, called the *Tortolas*.

Shoals off Indian River Inlet.—A 4-*fathom patch* lies N.N.E. 16 miles from Indian River Inlet, and S.S.E. ¼ E. 49 miles from Cape Canaveral. A 2-*fathom patch* lies E. by N. 8 miles from Indian River Inlet, and a 2½-*fathom patch* at 5 miles S.S.E. from it. These shoals are surrounded by depths of from 6 to 9 fathoms, by keeping in 20 fathoms you will be eastward of them.

St. Lucie Shoal was first reported in January, 1872, by Capt. Platt, U.S. Navy, when in command of the S.S. *Bibb*, as follows:—" When between Indian River Inlet and St. Lucie Inlet, we suddenly came upon this shoal, and, running over a portion of it, found 17 ft. on it, then suddenly deepened into 10 fathoms. I believe there is much shoaler water upon it, but do not think the shoal extends to the shore. This shoal lies about half-way between Indian River and St. Lucie Inlets, and its outer edge, with 17 ft. water upon it, is nearly 6 miles from the land."

Gilbert Bar, which is the inlet to the River St. Lucia, lies S. by E., distant 16 miles from Indian River Inlet. This bar is in lat. 27° 16', long 80° 20'. Between this and Indian River Inlet the soundings of 6 and 7 fathoms extend 5 miles from the land, and the bank of soundings extends only 20 miles off, and thence into the Gulf Stream.

Jupiter Inlet (closed) lies about 20 miles S.E. by S. of Gilbert Bar, and within the inlet is the river and fort of the same name.

LIGHTHOUSE.—At about 5 miles southward of Jupiter Inlet stands a red brick tower, surmounted by a brown lantern, the height of the building being 94 ft. A *fixed* and *flashing light* is shown, the flashes of 7½ seconds duration occurring every 1½ minute, preceded and followed by partial eclipses of 19 seconds duration. Elevated 146 ft., visible 19 miles off; the partial eclipses, however, are not visible more than 12 miles off.

To the southward of Jupiter Inlet are three hills, and southward of these, about midway between Jupiter and Hilsboro', is *Cooper's Hill*. Abreast of this inlet the bank of soundings extends about 10 miles from the shore.

Grenville Inlet is said to be in lat. 26° 47' N., and will admit small coasters of 5 feet draught. The entrance may be found by a high mound of sand and rocks called Cooper's or Grooper's Hill. At 6 miles southward of the inlet there is a high ridge of rock, out of which a large stream of water rushes into the sea.

Hilsboro' Inlet lies 35 miles to the southward of Jupiter Inlet; the coast runs first S. by E. ¼ E. 16 miles, then South 20 miles. The entrance to this inlet is in lat. 26° 23' 45", long. 80° 5' 30", within which is Hilsboro' River. About 14 miles to the northward of Hilsboro' Inlet the bank of soundings becomes very narrow, and from hence, all the way, southward to the Fowey Rocks, the Gulf Stream runs parallel with the shore, and very near it, in about the meridian of 80°.

At 5 miles northward of New River Inlet is the River Seco or *Dry Inlet*, which has a narrow bar of dry sand at its mouth. The shore forms here a little cove, which affords shelter to small craft.

New River Inlet lies 9 miles S. ¼ E. from Middle River; within this inlet is Fort Lauderdale. A 2½-*fathom patch* lies 3 miles eastward of the inlet.

In case of shipwreck near Cape Florida and the Boca Ratones there is a settlement on the mainland, near the banks of a river, where assistance may be obtained, and by passing through the Boca Ratones, if in boats, the houses will be perceived ahead on the main. If cast away to the northward of Boca Ratones, there are some mangroves thinly scattered, about 2 miles from the Boca, from whence the houses may be seen, and upon making a signal with fire, or otherwise, assistance may be obtained. If to the southward of the New River Inlet, proceed southerly along the beach, where there are posts fixed along the shore, 4 miles from each other, on which are inscriptions in English, French, and Spanish, informing where wells of fresh water have been purposely dug for relief.

CAPE FLORIDA, the S. point of Key Biscayne (or Biscayno), is in lat. 25° 39' 56", long. 8C° 9' 24". This cape is about 5½ miles S. ¼ W. of Boca Ratones, and 4 miles in the same direction from Bear Cut, which is the first opening to the northward. Within Key Biscayne, on the main, stands *Fort Dallas*, and also a settlement. Besides the watering-places on or near Biscayne, the beach will, in almost every part, yield drinkable water in digging, provided the sand does not cover the clay; whenever clay appears, labour is useless.

Fowey Rocks Lighthouse, which superseded that previously existing at Cape Florida, in 1878, is described on page 149.

The shores hereabout are lined with a bank of regular soundings, which run off a considerable distance; and this regularity of soundings extends from Cape Florida to Cape Canaveral. The soundings off Cape Canaveral, with that cape bearing W. by S., are 10, 20, and 30 fathoms, at 10, 20, and 30 miles distance.

From St. Augustine the coast runs about S.E. by S. ¼ S. to Cape Canaveral, from there S. by E. ¼ E. to Jupiter Inlet, and thence S. ¼ E. to Cape Florida.

Bound from St. Augustine, steer S.E. 90 miles, which will bring you to where the light on Cape Canaveral will be S.W., 22 miles. Keep in not less than 13 fathoms, in passing round the shoals of Cape Canaveral. From there the course is S. ⅜ E., 103 miles to Jupiter Inlet.

STEAM VESSELS bound to the southward may steer from Cape Hatteras S. 46° W. (true), 360 miles to long. 80° 20', lat. 31°; from 80° 20' to Cape Canaveral S., 153 miles; from Cape Canaveral to Jupiter Inlet S. 9° E. 90 miles; from Jupiter to New River Inlet S. 5° E., 50 miles; from New River Inlet S. 8° W., 65 miles, past Cape Florida and Carysfort lights, the latter bearing N.W. (true) 8 miles distant; from the last position steer S. 45° W., 34 miles; then S. 67¼° W., 37 miles up to Sombrero, and from Sombrero bearing N.N.E. (true), 9 miles distant, steer S. 30° W., 100 miles to make Havana; be cautious, however, in crossing the Florida Strait, remembering that the stream sets to the eastward at the rate of 1 knot per hour and upwards.

THE FLORIDA REEFS AND KAYS.

The limits of the Gulf Stream to the southward and south-westward consists of the line of submerged reefs and low kays, which were called Los Martires, in the earliest maps after the discovery of America. They have been famous, or rather the dread of them has been great, in all times. The innumerable wrecks and the abundant occupation for the wreckers of the West, and other localities, testify to the reality of this bad reputation. They were carefully surveyed by Mr. Gauld in 1773-5, but their dangerous character was not altered by the possession of his tolerably accurate chart. Since the survey by the U.S. Government the sites of their points of triangulation have been permanently marked by a line of beacons and lighthouses, each distinctively marked as shown presently. This important fence was established on the recommendation of Lieut. James Totten, U.S. Army, in October, 1853. During the progress of the survey the geological and specific characters of the reefs and kays were examined by the well-known naturalist Professor L. Agassiz, and from his report, August, 1851, the following extracts are made :—

The outline of the southern shore of Florida, between Cape Florida and Cape Sable, is well defined, presenting, in almost unbroken continuity, steep bluffs of the same coral limestone which forms the bottom of the everglades, and may be traced, without interruption, along the Miami from the seashore to the everglades.

South of the main land, between it and the range of kays, there are extensive flats, which, even at high water, are but slightly covered, and which the retreat of the tide lays bare, leaving only narrow and shallow channels between the dry flats, with occasional depressions of greater depth. These mud flats extend not only between the main land and the kays as far as Cape Sable, but may be traced to the North along the western shores of the continent, and to the West along the northern shores of the kays, not only as far as Kay West and the Marquesas, but even to the Tortugas.

There is, however, this remark to be made—that to the West the mud flats become covered, by degrees, with deeper and deeper water; or, in other words, that these low grounds, extending between the main land and the main range of kays, dip slightly to the West, being gradually lost in the shoals extending North of the Marquesas and the Tortugas, along the western shore of the peninsula. These flats are interspersed with innumerable low islands, known in the country by the generic appellation of the Mangrove Islands.

The shoals between Cape Sable, Cape Florida, and the main range of kays, are literally studded with these Mangrove Islands. Sometimes they are disturbed without apparent regularity; sometimes, as to the North of Kay Largo, they form a continuous range between the main land and the kays.

The whole tract between Cape Sable and the kays East of Bahia Honda, as far as Cape Florida, or at least as far as Soldier Kay, is so shoal that it will ever remain inaccessible, except to very small vessels.

The kays consist of an extensive range of low islands, rising but a few feet, perhaps from 6 to 8 or 10, or at the utmost to 12 or 13 ft., above the level of the sea. They begin to the North of Cape Florida, where they converge towards the main land, extending in the form of a flat crescent in a south-westerly direction, gradually receding from the main land until, opposite Cape Sable, they have so far retreated as to be separated from it by a shallow sheet of water 40 miles wide. Further to the West they project in a more westerly course, with occasional interruptions, as far as the Tortugas, which form the most western group. They consist either of accumulated dead corals, of coral rocks, or of coral sand, cemented together with more or less compactness. Their form varies, but is usually elongated and narrow, their greatest longitudinal extent following the direction of the main range, except in the group of the Pine Islands, where their course is almost at right angles with the main range.

Most of these islands are small, the largest of them, such as Kay West and Kay Largo, not exceeding 10 or 15 miles in length; others only 2 or 3, and many scarcely a mile. Their width varies from a quarter to a third or half a mile, the largest barely measuring a mile across; but whatever the difference in their size, they all agree in one respect—that their steepest shore is turned towards the Gulf Stream, while their more gradual slope inclines towards the mud flats which they encircle.

The reef proper extends parallel to the main range of kays, for a few miles South or S.E. of it, following the same curve, and never receding many miles from it

The distance between the reef and the main range of kays varies usually from 6 to 2 or 3 miles, the widest separation being South of Kay West and East of the Ragged kays, where the space is about 7 miles. Between this reef, upon which a few small kays rise at distant intervals, and the main range of kays already described, there is a broad, navigable channel, extending the whole length of the reef from the Marquesas to Cape Florida, varying in depth from 3 to 6 and 7 fathoms, and, except off Looe Kay, where the passage is not more than 14 ft. at low water, averaging from 3 to 4 fathoms.

Farther East the average depth is again the same as at Looe Kay; but it becomes gradually more and more shoal towards the East, measuring usually about 2 fathoms, or even less, to the East of Long Kay and Kay Largo, but deepening again somewhat towards Cape Florida, where the reef converges towards the main kays and the main land. Protected by the outer reef, this channel affords a very safe navigation to vessels of medium size, and would allow a secure anchorage almost everywhere throughout the whole length of the reef, were the numerous deep channels which intersect the outer reef well known to navigators, and marked by a regular system of signals. As it is, however, the reef seems to present an unbroken range of most dangerous shoal grounds, upon which thousands of vessels, as well as millions of property have been wrecked.

The reef proper, as we have remarked above, runs almost parallel to the main range of kays from Cape Florida to the western extremity of the Marquesas, where it is lost in the deep. It follows in its whole extent the same curve as the kays, encircling to the seaward the ship channel already mentioned. This is properly the region of living corals. Throughout its whole range it does not reach the surface of the sea, except in a few points where it comes almost within the level of low water mark, giving rise to heavy breakers, such as Carysfort, Alligator Reef, Tennessee Reef, and a few other shoals of less extent, but perhaps not less dangerous.

We see everywhere that the larger boulders and the coarser fragments have been the first to find a resting-place upon the dead reef; the minuter particles and coral sand, which are periodically washed away from its crest during heavy gales, never accumulating upon it till large boulders and more solid materials have collected to such an extent as to form sufficient protection for the more moveable, looser fragments.

A careful survey of the character of the rocks in the kays affords satisfactory evidence that they have been formed at whatever height they may rise, by the same action which is now going on upon the reef—that is, by the accumulation of loose materials above the water-level.

The *broad channel* extending the whole range of the reef, between the main kays and the outer reef, is rather uniform, having the same width throughout, with the exception of those few places where the reef widens, or the mud flats from the kays encroach upon it. Its narrowest passages are between Looe Key and the Pine Islands, between Pickle and French Reefs, and between Kay Rodrigues and Tavernier. It is also somewhat narrowed between Alligator Reef and Indian Kay, and is widest off Kay West. Its depth varies also slightly, being shoaler in its eastern range than to the West. The shallowest part is between Pickle Reef and Kay Rodrigues, and between Looe Kay and Pine Islands.

Between Florida Reefs and the line of kays there are two channels; one known as the Hawk Channel extends all the way from Cape Florida to Kay West. There are buoys on the Triangle Shoal, and on the Hen and Chicken within it.

The other channel is not buoyed out, and is very seldom used, except by wreckers familiar with its bends and intricacies. It runs inside of the outer reef from Cape

Florida to Alligator Bank. Vessels that drift on to the reef and succeed in getting into deeper water inside, may avail themselves of this channel to make their way to the nearest opening between the reefs and through it into the gulf, by means of the chart, and by using the lead and observing the shaded colour of the water.

From Carysfort light the course to run parallel to the reef is S.S.W. (mag.) 22 miles; this will bring you abreast of the Pickles Reef (marked with beacon F), and nearly up with Conch Reef (E); thence steer S.W. by W., 32 miles past Viper Kay, to long. 80° 50'; then W.S.W., 45 miles to beacon A on Kay Sambo (on this course after running 15 miles you will be abreast of Kay Sombrero and lighthouse); from beacon A steer W. by S. for 50 miles, when shape your course to pass between the Tortugas and the reef, or around the Tortugas. Twelve miles on this latter course will be abreast of Sand Kay light at the entrance to Kay West harbour. The passage between the Tortugas and the reef is safe, as there is only the *Rebecca Shoal* of 14 ft. which bears East, 20 miles from Loggerhead Kay, and is marked by a beacon, painted black, and visible 7 miles off in clear weather. Between the shoal and the Tortugas Bank (East Kay), there is a channel, 12 miles in width. During the U.S. Coast Survey a shoal of 13 ft. was discovered $2\frac{1}{2}$ miles to the North of Rebecca Shoal, which there is little doubt is a continuation of that shoal.

LIGHTHOUSES AND BEACONS ON THE FLORIDA REEFS.

During the U.S. Coast Survey of these reefs, signals were placed on the reefs; since when, regular day-marks have been erected to occupy the positions. They are each composed of an iron shaft, 36 ft. in height, erected upon iron screw foundations, distinguished by a vane, upon which one of the letters of the alphabet is painted, and above it a lattice-work, hoop-iron cylinder or barrel.

Three colours (white, black, and red) are used in painting each signal, to render them as striking to the eye as possible, and are so arranged that no two adjacent day-marks have the same colours upon like parts.

The day-marks are placed upon the most projecting and dangerous points of the Florida Reef, and are in general from 4 to 6 miles from the outside (seaward) shores of the Florida Kays, and within half a mile, in every case, of the edge of the Gulf Stream.

The water where these signals stand does not exceed 4 feet at low tide, in any case, and just outside them to the eastward, in the Gulf Stream, it falls into deep water; so that they may be said to be erected on the very edge of the wall of this reef.

You may approach any of these day-marks from seaward within a few hundred yards, but it will always be prudent to give them a good berth, particularly in light winds, or in bad weather. In steering the courses along the edge of the reef, be cautious, in moderate weather, and especially after easterly gales, that the force and direction of the Gulf Stream setting across the reefs, does not imperceptibly set the vessel amidst the dangers. Should you find yourself to the westward of any of these beacons, you may be sure you are between the reef and the kays, and consequently surrounded by shoals and dangerous rocks.

Cape Florida Lighthouse (light discontinued, 1878), erected on the South point of Kay Biscayne, in lat. 25° 39' 56", long. 80° 9' 24', is a *white tower*, 95 ft. in height,

THE FLORIDA REEFS AND KAYS. 149

and rising 100 ft. above the sea. There is a cluster of cocoa-nut trees about the keeper's dwelling.

FOWEY ROCKS BEACON.—Letter P painted red on the vane; hoop-iron lattice-work cylinder, white, shaft and vane black. Bears from Cape Florida lighthouse S. 35° 42' E. (true), 5¼ miles; from Soldier's Kay, S. 89° 58' E. (true), 3½ miles. Lat. 25° 35' 23", long. 80° 5' 51".

FOWEY ROCKS LIGHTHOUSE, completed near the northern extremity of the Florida Reefs in 1878, painted dark brown, and situated 50 yards South of beacon P, in about 5 ft. water, is an iron frame-work, in the form of a truncated pyramid on a pile foundation. The keeper's dwelling, painted white, and about 38 ft. above the sea, is connected with the lantern by a cylindrical staircase, also painted white. Position approximate, lat. 25° 35' 20" N., long. 80° 5' 50" W. The light is a *fixed bright light*, elevated 110 ft. above high water, and visible 16 miles off. On the exhibition of this light, the fixed white light on Cape Florida was discontinued.

TRIUMPH REEF BEACON.—Letter O, painted black, on the vane; cylinder red; shaft and vane, white. Bears from Elliots Kay, No. 1, S. 82° 31' E. (true), 3½ miles; from Soldiers Kay, S. 21° 4' E. (true), 7¼ miles. Lat. 25° 28' 37", long. 80° 6' 50".

LONG REEF BEACON.—Letter N, painted white on vane, cylinder black, shaft and vane red. Bears from Elliots Kay, No. 1, S. 52° 15' E. (true), 3¾ miles; from Soldiers Kay, S. 13° 54' E. (true), 8¼ miles. Lat. 25° 26' 45", long. 60° 7' 21".

AJAX REEF BEACON.—Letter M, painted red, on vane; cylinder white, shaft and vane black. Bears from Elliots Kay, No. 2, S. 79° 36' E. (true), 3¾ miles; from Elliots Kay, No. 1, S. 26° 6' E. (true), 5½ miles. Lat. 25° 24' 9", long. 80° 7' 59".

PACIFIC REEF BEACON.—Letter L, painted black, on vane; cylinder red; shaft and vane white. Bears from Rhodes Kay, N. 76° 30' E. (true), 5¼ miles; from Elliots Kay, No. 1, S. 15° 48' E. (true), 7 1-10th mile. Lat. 25° 22' 13", long. 80° 8' 30".

TURTLE REEF BEACON.—Letter K, painted white, on vane; cylinder black; shaft and vane red. Bears from Rhodes Kay, S. 22° 21' E. (true), 4½ miles; from Cæsar's Creek Bank, S. 6° 28' W. (true), 6 1-10th mile. Lat. 25° 16' 52", long. 80° 12' 34".

Turtle Harbour Beacon, not being one of the series of beacons, is surmounted by a cross. It stands on the West side of Turtle Harbour. Lat. 25° 17' N., long. 80° 14' W.

CARYSFORT REEF LIGHTHOUSE, near the edge of the Gulf Stream, in lat. 25° 13' 15", long. 80° 12' 45", an iron pile lighthouse, tower and keeper's dwelling painted a dark colour, and lantern white, 112 ft. in height, and 106 ft. above the level of the sea, exhibiting a *revolving* light every 30 seconds, visible 18 miles.

The ELBOW BEACON.—Letter J, painted red, on vane; cylinder white; shaft and vane black. Bears from Grecian Shoals beacon, N. 60° 46' E. (true), 2½ miles; from Carysfort Reef lighthouse, S. 29° 30' W. (true), 5½ miles. Lat. 25° 8' 32", long. 80° 15' 40".

GRECIAN SHOALS BEACON.—Letter H, on vane, painted black; cylinder red; shaft and vane white. Bears from Sound Point, S. 45° 58' E. (true), 3⅞ miles; from Basin Bank, S. 21° 25' W. (true), 5½ miles. Lat. 25° 7' 22", long. 80° 17' 57".

FRENCH REEF BEACON.—Letter G, on vane, painted white; cylinder black; shaft and vane red. Bears from Lower Sound Point, S. 32° 34' E. (true), 5 miles; from Point Willie, S. 10° 30' E. (true), 6¼ miles. Lat. 25° 2' 6", long. 80° 21' 5".

The S.W. extremity of *French Reef*, situated about halfway between the French Reef beacon and that on Pickles Reef, is one of the most dangerous points on the Florida range for vessels intending to follow the line of beacons. It projects half a mile to the eastward of a straight line between the two beacons referred to, and has as little as one foot of water upon it.

PICKLE REEF BEACON:—Letter F, on vane, painted red; cylinder white; shaft and vane black. Bears from Point Charles S. 16° 58' E. (true), 5½ miles; from Lower Sound Point, S. 6° 35' W. (true), about 7 miles. Lat. 24° 59' 22", long. 80° 24' 55".

Pickle Reef, as above stated, is marked at its middle by beacon F. In a N.E. and S.W. direction its extent is about a mile and a quarter, with a foot of water at its shoalest part. Between the North end of it and French Kay is an opening, three-quarters of a mile wide, through which 16 ft. may be carried. The southern portion of the reef deepens gradually to 12 ft., that depth being 1¼ mile from the beacon, but here is a narrow cut of deeper water, at less distance in the same direction. Thence on, and to within three-quarters of a mile from beacon E, on Conch Reef, there is an opening of 1¼ mile, which has 3 and 4 fathoms of water.

CONCH REEF BEACON.—Letter E, on vane, painted black; cylinder red; shaft and vane white. Bears from Rodrigues Bank S. 4° 30' W. (mag.); from Kay Tavernier S..43° 30' E. (mag.) Lat. 24° 56' 36", long. 80° 27' 50".

Conch Reef has as little as 18 inches of water on it. It is 1¼ mile long N.E. and S.W., and separated from Little Conch Reef by a narrow cut of 4 and 5 fathoms. The shoalest water on Little Conch is 6 ft., and breaks in moderate breezes.

Davis Reef is about halfway between Little Conch and Crockers or Crocus Reef, with 4 ft. of water, which breaks generally at low tide. This is a small reef, running N.W. and S.E. There are openings of 1½ mile on either side, which give 3 and 4 fathoms water.

Crocus Reef extends about 300 yards N.W. and S.E., and can be approached within 150 yards. On its shoalest part are 2 ft. water. Beacon D, which marked this reef, and beacon C, which was set up on Alligator Kay, were both destroyed in the gale of August, 1861. They have probably been re-established, as they are important.

CROCKER'S REEF BEACON.—Letter D, on vane, painted white; cylinder black; shaft and vane red. Bears from Snake Creek Point S. 39° 15' E. (mag.), distant 4 to 5 miles. Lat. 24° 54' 21", long. 80° 31' 26".

ALLIGATOR REEF LIGHTHOUSE was completed in 1873. It stands near the N.E. point of the reef in 5 ft. water, and within 200 yards of the deep water of the Gulf of Mexico. The structure resembles that on Sombrero Kay, being an iron framework, of the form of a truncated pyramid, with the keeper's dwelling about 37 feet above water. The lower part of the framework, from the water to the dwelling, is painted black; the next part of the structure is white; and the upper part and lantern *black*. The light shown is a scintillating light, *flashing every 5 seconds*, and *every six flash is red*, illuminating the entire horizon; elevated 143 ft. above the sea; visible 18 miles off.

From Alligator Reef light, Indian Kay bears W.N.W., distant 3½ miles; Carysfort Reef lighthouse, which flashes white every 30 seconds, N.E. ¼ N., 31¼ miles; and Sombrero Kay (a fixed white light), S.W. by W. ¼ W., 30 miles. Position, approximate, lat. 24° 51' N,, long. 80° 37½' W.

Vessels in the Gulf Stream, approaching Alligator Reef light from the northward and eastward, should not bring it to bear more to the southward than S.W. by W.; and approaching from southward and westward, it should not bear more eastward than N.E. ¼ E.

To the westward of the Alligator Reef, the reef becomes much narrower.

TENNESSEE REEF BEACON, No. 7, lat. 24° 46' N., long. 80° 46' W.

COFFINS PATCHES BEACON, marked by the letter C, lat. 24° 41' N., long. 81° W., stands near the outer extreme of Coffin Patches, a small dry ledge of rocks, about 10 miles N.E. by E. ¼ E. of Sombrero Kay, and 4 miles S.E. by S. of Crawl Kay.

SOMBRERO LIGHTHOUSE.—The lighthouse on Sombrero Shoal, off Dry Bank, in lat. 24° 37' 36", long. 81° 6' 43", is similar in character to Alligator Reef lighthouse, i.e., an open framework of iron, built an iron piles, 149 ft. in height, and 144 feet above the level of the sea, exhibiting a *fixed* light, visible 19 miles all round the horizon.

LOOE KAY BEACON, No. 6, lies E.N.E., about 14 miles from the eastern Sambo, and about 4 miles from the nearest of the Pine Islands. It is a *white* tower, 30 ft. above the sea, with a staff and *red* ball.

The Florida Reef is here only about three-quarters of a mile broad, and the space between it and Sambo Kays is full of dangers. The kays from abreast this islet as far as Báhia Honda, 12 miles to the eastward, are covered with pine trees, and North of the eastern Sambo they form a remarkable saddle.

AMERICAN SHOALS BEACON.—Letter B, on vane, painted black; cylinder red; shaft and vane white. Bears from Loggerhead Kay S. 22° 17' W. (true), 5¾ miles; from Eastern Sambo beacon, N. 76° 39' E. (true), 8 1-10th miles. Lat. 24° 31' 24", long. 81° 31' 16".

EASTERN SAMBO BEACON.—Letter A, on vane, painted white; cylinder black; shaft and vane red. Bears from Geiger's House S. 3° 29' E. (true), about 4¼ miles; from South Saddle Hills, S. 13° 13' W. (true), distant 5 miles. Lat. 24° 29' 32", long. 81° 39' 55".

BEACON, No. 5, on the shoal on West side of East Channel, is in lat. 24° 28' N., long. 81° 46' W.

EASTERN DRY ROCKS BEACON, No. 4, is in lat. 24° 28' N., long. 81° 51' W.

MIDDLE GROUND BEACON, No. 3, is in lat. 24° 29' N., long. 81° 53' W. It is described on p. 163.

SAND KAY LIGHTHOUSE.—On a small sand and shells island, 7¼ miles from Kay West lighthouse, in lat. 24° 27' 10", long. 81° 52' 43", an iron pile lighthouse, painted a brown colour, and lantern white. It is 121 ft. in height, and at 110 ft. above the level of the sea exhibits a *fixed* light, varied by flashes every 2 minutes, visible 18 miles off. It shows for a space of *one minute* a clear steady light; in every alternate minute there is a *brilliant flash of* 10 *seconds duration, preceded and followed by partial eclipses of* 25 *seconds duration.*

Kay West Lights.—On the inner line of shoals there are the two following lights, which are seen beyond the southern reefs:—

On Kay West Island, to the southward and eastward of the town, in lat. 24° 32' 58", long. 81° 48' 7", a white lighthouse, 60 ft. in height, and 72 ft. above the sea, showing a *fixed* light, visible 13 miles all round the horizon, except between S.S.W. ¼ W. and W. by S. ¼ S. This light serves to guide vessels to Kay West through the different channels across the reef, and also inside of the reef.

N.W. PASSAGE.—An iron screw pile lighthouse, placed on the flats to mark the channel of the bar leading to N.W. channel, in lat. 24° 37' 4", long. 81° 54' 1". The foundation of the structure is of a dark colour, dwelling and lantern white. It is 40 feet above the sea, and exhibits a *fixed* light, visible 12 miles off to the southward between N.W. and N.E.

REBECCA SHOAL BEACON, No. 1, is described on page 158.

DRY TORTUGAS LIGHTHOUSE.—On Loggerhead Kay, the south-western-most kay of the Tortugas Group, in lat. 24° 38' 5", long. 82° 55' 45", is a circular brick tower, lower part white, upper part black, 150 ft. in height, and 152 ft. above the sea, exhibiting a *fixed* light, visible 20 miles off. The keeper's dwelling is two stories high, built of brick, and placed a little South of the tower. Loggerhead Kay is nearly 1 mile in length, N.E. and S.W., and 700 ft. wide, bordered all round with cedar bushes.

GARDEN KAY LIGHTHOUSE.—Dry Tortugas.—At Fort Jefferson or Garden Kay, in lat. 24° 37′ 47″, long. 82° 52′ 53″, a white lighthouse, 65 ft. in height, and 70 feet above the sea, exhibits a *fixed* light, visible 14 miles off.

HARBOURS AND ANCHORAGES IN THE FLORIDA REEFS.

Vessels bound from the North to Legare Anchorage, through what is called the *Hawke Channel*, may run in with the beach, until within 1½ mile of Bear Cut (which is the first opening North of Biscayne, 4 miles from Cape Florida), but be careful not to get into less than 3 fathoms. When fairly abreast of Bear Cut, steer South, 5 miles to where you will have Cape Florida bearing W.N.W.; then S. ½ E., 5½ miles close to the westward of the Fowey Rocks. In this course with the Fowey Beacon P bearing East, and the Soldier Kay W. ¾ S., are 4 fathoms water, and you will have 2 miles of the above course to run, until abreast of the Brewster Reef; from thence S. ¼ W. for 4 miles will lead to Legaré Anchorage, about 4½ fathoms, with the Triumph Reef beacon O bearing S.E. by E. ½ E., distant a little over a mile. In the latter course you will pass a buoy moored on a rocky patch on the port hand, about 1¼ mile from the position of the anchorage we have pointed out.

You may also enter the reef to the southward of Bear Cut, by getting the lighthouse of Cape Florida to bear W. by S., and going in with 4½ to 4 fathoms, and when within 2 miles of the lighthouse, steer S. ½ E. as above, until the Fowey beacon bears East.

No one but those well acquainted can navigate through the inner reef to the shallow bay of Kay Biscayne.

LEGARE ANCHORAGE is within, and to the westward of Triumph Reef, in lat. 25° 29′ 15″, long. 80° 7′ 45″, and N.W. by W. ¼ W., 1 mile from the beacon O on the reef.

Vessels outside the reef from the northward, and bound into the anchorage, when about midway between the beacons P and O, with the beacon P, on Fowey Reef, bearing N. by W. ¼ W., may steer S.W. by W. ¾ W. for the passage between the Star Reefs, and run on that course halfway through it, then haul up to S.W. and steer for the anchorage behind the Star Reefs. The passage is 130 yards wide, with 22 ft. water.

When Beacon O bears S.W. ¾ S., distant 1¾ mile, steer either N.W. ½ N. to the anchorage behind the Star Reefs, through a passage 500 yards wide, with 22 ft. of water, or W. ¼ S. to the anchorage behind the reefs N.W. from Triumph Reef, through a passage 220 yards wide, with 22 ft. of water. In running for this last-named anchorage, the range of the beacons O and N will be passed, and when they are in one, the course for the Legaré Anchorage is S.W. by W., through a passage 800 yards wide, with 20 ft. of water.

With beacon O bearing S.S.W. ½ W., about 2 miles distant, steer S.W. by W. until the beacons O and P are in line, then follow the S.W. by W. course, as before.

When bound into Legaré anchorage from the southward, get the following bearings:—Beacon N, on Long Reef, West, distant 1 mile, and beacon O, on Triumph

Reef, N. by W. ¼ W., distant 2 miles, and a N.W. by N. course will lead to the anchorage through a passage 600 ft. wide, with 22 ft. water.

There is a navigation still further to the westward, on the side of Bache Shoal and Reefs, near to Elliot's Kay, in shallower water, 2½ to 2¼ fathoms, but it is too intricate for directions to avail.

Turtle Harbour.—The next available anchorage to the southward of Legaré is Turtle Harbour, 4 miles to the northward of Carysfort R ef lighthouse.

With Carysfort lighthouse bearing S. ¾ W., distant 4½ miles, and the beacon on Turtle Island S.W., there is white bottom on the reef in 5½ to 5¼ fathoms, steer W.S.W., the soundings being regular; some of the spots, however, give half a fathom less than the clear bottom. Give the beacon on Turtle Reef a berth of half a mile, and when the beacon bears S.E ¼ E., haul up S.W. ¼ S., until the beacon bears E. ½ N., when anchor in 5 fathoms water.

The reef may be crossed at the several undermentioned places, viz.—Tavernier, some 20 miles to the southward of Carysfort lighthouse; at Indian Kay, 16 miles from Tavernier; at Duck Kay, and Knight's Kay; at Bahia Honda, and at Loggerhead Kay. But all these entrances require a local knowledge.

BAHIA HONDA.—From Kay West eastward for 30 miles to Bahia Honda, there are nothing but low mangrove islands forming channels fit only for canoes. The islands eastward of Bahia Honda are somewhat larger, and covered with pine trees, but are low and drowned like the others, and the channels between them are fit only for boats. Of the whole of these islands there is only one, 13 miles from Kay West, of tolerable height; it is rugged, covered with trees, and in whatever direction seen appears in the form of a saddle. Bahia Honda, or Cabbage Tree Kay, is about 2 miles in length, has a sandy beach, and numerous palmetto trees on it, which are the first seen coming from the westward.

Between Bahia Honda and three small kays West of it, is a narrow but snug inlet, with a depth of about 18 ft., and vessels of 7 or 8 ft. draught may pass right through to the N.W. The entrance at the East end of the Pine Islands is about 10 miles West of Sombrero Kay lighthouse. There is good fresh water on Bahia Honda Kay.

The usual method of navigation between the reefs and the kays is to proceed in the day, and anchor at night.

KAY WEST.[*]—This is the first island of consequence to the eastward of the Kay of Boca Grande; the distance between is 6½ leagues. There are some scattered man-

---

[*] WRECKING.—"Irregularities in the rapidity and direction of the current, the causes of which are unknown, the narrowness of the channel, bad weather, bad light, and other causes, have produced annually a large number of shipwrecks on the reefs. Prior to 1821, when Florida belonged to Spain, wrecking vessels from the Bahama Islands constantly cruized along the Florida Reefs, and saved large amounts of shipwrecked property, which they carried to Nassau. In 1821 the country was transferred to the United States by Spain, and soon after that event a small settlement of Americans was made on this island, called by the Spaniards "Cayo Hueso" (Bone Kay), and by the Americans Kay West. In 1822 Congress established a port of entry at this place, and in 1825 prohibited the carrying of wrecked goods found on the coast to any foreign place, and required all such goods to be brought to some port of entry in the United States. This broke up the business of the Bahama wreckers, and Kay West became the central point for the business of wrecking on the coast. The wrecking vessels of Kay West are not allowed to pursue their calling on the Bahama Banks, neither are the Bahama wreckers on the American coasts. A District Admiralty Court of the United States was established at Key West in 1847.

" At the present time seventy-two vessels, with a gross of 2,000 tons, are licensed by the

grove islands between Boca Grande and it, the three southernmost of which have white sandy beaches. Kay West is 6 miles in length, E. by N. and W. by S., and has a sandy beach on its southern coast. The harbour admits mercantile vessels of the largest class, and they are protected from all winds within 200 yards of the N.W. point of the island. Several ponds, for nine months in the year, produce excellent fresh water. The trees are thick upon it, especially towards the West end, where there is anchorage and fresh water.

The town is on the N.W. end of the island, which is also sometimes called Thomson's Island. The census, taken in 1870, gives the population as 5,016; in 1874 it was estimated as 9,000 inhabitants. They may be classed as follows:—Of Bahama birth, four-tenths; Cuban, four-tenths; and American, two-tenths. The principal industry is cigar making.

The harbour of Kay West is considered one of the best within the limits of the United States to the South of the Chesapeake:—1st. For its easy access and egress at all times and with all winds. 2nd. For the excellent anchorage and security it affords both in the inner and outer harbour for ships of the largest class. Leading to the harbour of Kay West are excellent channels, some affording water for the largest class of ships, the others suitable to vessels drawing 10 and 11 ft. water.

"*As a Naval Station*, Kay West (one of the principal naval stations of the United States) is said to possess more advantages for the same than any other port in the union. 1st, For its susceptibility of fortifications. 2nd. For ease and number of approaches with all winds. 3rd. The difficulty of blockade. 4th. The ease in which supplies may be thrown in in despite of the presence of an enemy. 5th. Abundance of wood and water. 6th. The facility of communication with and deriving all the advantages by water, of supplies from the northern and southern sections of the union, provisions from Louisiana, spars and live oak from Florida and Georgia, cordage, iron, canvas, powder and shot, &c., from the North. 7th. It commands the outlet of the trade from Jamaica, the Caribbean Sea, Bay of Honduras, and Gulf of Mexico. 8th. It holds in subjection the trade of Cuba. 9th. It is a check to the naval forces of whatever nation may possess Cuba; it is to Cuba what Gibraltar is to Ceuta; to the Gulf of Mexico what Gibraltar is to the Mediterranean.

"Among the advantages that may be enumerated is an abundance of free stone for building, which, being a concrete of coral and shell, is easily converted into lime. The island is low, the highest part not being more than 15 or 20 ft. above the level of the ocean. The sea abounds in the finest fish in the world.

"A project has long been on foot, and is now receiving the serious attention of capitalists, of connecting the island with the mainland by a railway across the line of reefs. Engineers pronounce it practicable, and should it be carried out, it will vastly increase the importance of the place by making it the chief outlet for American produce to the West India Islands and South America."—*Mr. Vice-Consul Cox*, 1874.

The whole island lies on a bed of limestone about a foot below the surface. Wells are dug into the rock to the level of the sea, which afford fresh water, but rainwater

---

Judge of this Court as wreckers. They have to pay about 2 dollars a year for the licence.

"Between the years 1848 and 1857, an average of fifty vessels a year were wrecked on the Florida Reefs, the average total value being 1,626,000 dollars, and the salvage 115,000 dollars."—*Vice-Consul Cox*, 1874.

KAY WEST.   155

is chiefly used. On no part of the island is their more than a few inches of soil, consequently there are no agricultural products.

The Lighthouse, before mentioned, is erected on the S.W. end of the kay, called *Whitehead Point.* It is elevated 50 ft., and there is another *fixed light* shown from a pile lighthouse, 1½ mile inside the bar of the N.W. Passage. The channel to the harbour is well buoyed, and the buoys generally show the greatest depth of water.

The Main Ship Channel to Kay West is pointed out by the following buoys:—
A *black* can buoy, moored in 18 ft. water, on the West end of a reef 3 miles westward of the Sambo Ledges, with Kay West lighthouse bearing N.N.W., and Sand Kay lighthouse W. by S. ¼ S.

A fairway can buoy, striped *black* and *white* vertically, in 5 fathoms, with Kay West lighthouse N. ¼ W., and Sand Kay lighthouse W. by S. ¾ S.

Two *red* and two *black* nun buoys mark the shoal patches, called the Triangles, about 2 miles northward of the fairway.

A *red* nun buoy, in 18 ft. water, on the S.W. end of the ledge running off a long half mile from Whitehead Point, with the lighthouse bearing N.E. ½ N., 1 1-10th mile.

Near the S.E. extreme of the *Middle Ground* there is a *beacon* shaft (No. 3), octagonal in shape, surmounted by an octagonal box. The shaft, top of the cage, and the box are painted *black*; the sides of the cage are *white*. From the beacon, Kay West lighthouse bears N.E., and Sand Kay lighthouse S. by E.

Directions.—Bring Kay West lighthouse to bear N. ¼ W., and steer for it, until Sand Kay light bears W. by S., then N. ¾ W., passing close eastward of the fairway buoy. When Sand Kay lighthouse bears S.W. by W., it is better to anchor and wait for a pilot if the vessel draws more than 16 ft. water. Drawing less than 16 ft., continue on through the Triangles, leaving the two *black* buoys on the port hand, and the two *red* on the starboard. After passing the northern of these buoys, keep on N. ¾ W. for a quarter of a mile, then steer N.W. by N., passing about a cable westward of Whitehed Spit buoy, when haul up N. by E., and anchor abreast of Fort Taylor, if without a pilot. A vessel will carry 4½ fathoms water on these courses.

At night, if clear, bring the North star over Kay West light, and stand for it; when the light on Sand Kay bears S.W. by W., a vessel of over 16 ft. draught had better anchor and wait for a pilot.

A *dangerous coral head*, with 13 ft. water on it, lies W.S.W. 2½ cables from the fairway buoy. On the East dry rocks, about 2 miles farther westward, is beacon No. 4.

There are no less than six channels into the harbour of Kay West from the southward, but it would be highly imprudent to take them by written directions without the aid of a pilot, or being yourself locally acquainted with the marks, &c. Indeed a pilot is indispensable for a stranger.

East Channel carries 4½ fathoms water, and, in entering, keep the East side of Kay West lighthouse in line with Filor's Observatory, bearing N.W. by N., leaving No. 5 beacon on the port hand. When West Sambo bears E. ⅛ S. steer W. ½ N. until the lighthouse is in line with O'Hara's Observatory N.N.W. ¼ W.; then keep these latter marks on until Sand Kay bears S.W. ¼ W., when steer W. by N. ¾ N. with the East end of A or Snipe Kay, in line with the South end of Mullet Kay. When the lighthouse bears N.E., steer N.N.E., with Tift's and Filor's Observatories in one. When off the fort steer N. ¼ W., and anchor off the lazaretto in 4¾ fathoms water; or steer for the West edge of Fleming Kay, give the wharves, alongside which large vessels load, a berth, and anchor off the town. The least depth of water in this track will be 4½ fathoms. It is advisable to moor, as the holding ground is not good, and the tides are strong.

Rock Kay Channel.—Bring the West end of West Crawfish Kay in line with the middle of Snipe Kay, bearing N. by W. ½ W., and steer for it. When the Middle Ground beacon bears W.N.W., and in line with Man Kay, steer N.N.E. ¾ E. for Tift's Observatory. When the lighthouse bears N.E., bring Tift's and Filor's Observatories in line, and proceed as before.

Sand Kay Channel.—With Sand Kay lighthouse bearing N.E. ¾ E., bring the western end of Snipe Kay to bear N. ½ E., and steer for it; or bring East Crawfish Kay to bear N. by E. ½ E., and steer for it. When Kay West lighthouse bears N.E. ½ E., keep it on that bearing until Tift's and Filor's Observatories are in line, then proceed as before.

West Channel carries 5 fathoms, and to take it is when beacon No. 2 on Western dry rocks and Sand Kay lighthouse are in line bearing E. by N. ¼ N., bring Kay West lighthouse to bear N.E. ½ E., and steer for it until beacon No. 3 on the Middle Ground is in line with Sand Kay lighthouse, bearing S. by E. ¼ E., then steer N.E. by E. ½ E. for 3½ miles towards Rocky Point, until the N.W. angle of Fort Taylor is just on with the Lazaretto, bearing N.E. by N. ½ N.; steer in on this line until abreast Whitehead Spit buoy, when proceed as before.

North-West Channel.—An extensive group of islets and kays lie on a bank about 30 miles in length E.N.E. and W.S.W., eastward of Kay West. These kays and bank are separated from Mangrove shoals on the West, by an opening called North-west Channel, the banks of which are plainly visible, and will serve as a guide; the bar has 12 ft. water on it. *At night*, without a pilot, vessels incur great risk of running on shore, and even with one on board it is not easy to go clear. This channel, although intricate, will be found very convenient for small vessels when bound to, or coming from the N.W., instead of passing round the Tortugas.

Light.—On the flats, 1½ mile inside the bar of the North-west Channel, is an iron screw-pile lighthouse, before described (page 151).

Buoys.—North-West Channel is also pointed out by the four following buoys:—1. A nun buoy, striped *black* and *white*, is moored on the bar in 11 ft. water, with the pile lighthouse, in line with the West end of Mullet Kay, bearing S. by W. ¾ W. 2. A *red* nun buoy, in 15 ft. water, with the pile lighthouse S. by W. ¾ W. distant three-quarters of a mile. 3. A *black* nun buoy, in 24 ft. water, on N.W. tail of Middle Ground, with the East end of Crayfish Kay S. ¾ W., and Flemings Kay E. by S. ½ S. 4. A *black* and *white* striped nun buoy, in 27 ft. water, in mid-channel, with Kay West lighthouse S.E. by E. ½ E., and Flemings Kay E. by N. ½ N.

To pass through the N.W. Channel to the Gulf of Mexico, without stopping at Kay West, when the inner buoy off Whitehead Point bears S.E. ¾ S., and Kay West light is in line with the South end of the fort, steer N.W. ¾ N., passing close eastward of the mid-channel buoy, until Filor's Observatory is seen between the northern and middle churches, bearing S.E. ¾ E., when the N.W. buoy of the Middle Ground will be close-to; then, with the above mark, steer N.W. ¾ W., until the pile lighthouse bears S. by W. ¾ W., and in line with the West end of Mullet Kay; the course will then be N. by E. ¾ E. for the bar buoy, passing it close on either side. A shallow patch, with 9 ft. water on it, lies N.N.E. ¼ E., 8½ miles from the pile lighthouse of North-West Channel.

Entering the N.W. Channel from the northward, bring the bar buoy on with the pile lighthouse, bearing S. by W. ¾ W., and steer on this line, passing close to the buoy on either side. When Filor's Observatory is seen between the northern and middle churches, bearing S.E. ¾ E., steer with this mark on for the N.W. buoy of the Middle Ground; when abreast it the West end of Snipe Kay will be in line with the West end of Woman Kay; then steer S.E. ¾ S. until Tift's and O'Hara's Observatories are in one, when stand for the wharves.

At *night*, when obliged to enter this channel from the Gulf of Mexico, bring the lighthouse to bear S. by W. ¾ W., and steer for it. After passing the bar, anchor anywhere to the northward of the lighthouse in from 16 to 18 ft. In anchoring at Kay West, avoid a 7-fathom rocky hole, bearing N.W. by W. 160 yards from Tift's Observatory; vessels dropping their anchors in it will lose them.

During the recent survey by the officers of the U.S. navy, several dangerous coral heads and shoals were discovered that had not been marked on the former charts; it, therefore, behoves every one to be most careful in navigating among these low kays and dangers.

The Boca Grande.—The passages hitherto noticed through the islands and reefs towards Richmond Bay, are calculated for small vessels which may be desirous of using them in their way to the West Coast of Florida, &c. Of these, the latter by Kay West, or Egmont Channel, is the most frequented; but to the westward are two others, of larger dimensions and deeper water, calculated for ships of all descriptions. The first of these is on the western side of the Mangrove Islands, 13 or 14 miles from the entrance to Egmont Channel; it is called the *Boca Grande*, or the Great Mouth, having the Mangrove Island Bank on its starboard side, and the Marquesas Shoals and Islands on the port. The other, or Tortugas Channel, is between the Marquesas and the Dry Tortugas.

The Boca Grande Kay lies about 13 miles to the westward of Kay West, and is a very much smaller island than Kay West. It lies about N.W. ¼ W., 8 miles from Sand Kay lighthouse, and about S.W. ¾ W., nearly 8 miles from the screw-pile lighthouse in the N.W. channel of Kay West. This island, and the Lavinia Banks to the northward, form the eastern side of the channel of Boca Grande.

The Boca Grande is the large opening to the eastward of Marquesas Kay, and between that island and Boca Grande Kay, and is 4 miles in breadth; the channel runs through to the northward, but it cannot be recommended to strangers, on account of the shoal patches of water in it.

The Marquesas Kays lie about 5⅓ leagues to the westward of Kay West, and about 14 leagues to the eastward of the Tortugas Islands, in lat. 24° 34′ 0″, and long. 82° 7′ 30″. The Marquesas are the westernmost of the range of the Florida Kays, and the easternmost kay is the largest of the group; it is about 3 miles in extent, from East to West, bending to the South and westward, in the form of a horse-shoe. To the westward and north-westward of the Marquesas is a large bank of quicksand, extending full 5 leagues from it, and nearly due South from the western extremity of this bank lies the western end of the general Florida Reef, in lat. 24° 26′, and long. 82° 28′, being the southernmost part of the whole. There is a channel between the reef and the bank above mentioned, and likewise all along between the reef and the kays, which is in many places upwards of 4 miles broad. In that part of the channel to the southward and south-westward of the Marquesas Kays, there are from 5 to 11 fathoms water, on soft mud.

The *West End Bank* of the Florida Reef is about 2¼ miles broad, but the least water on it is 3 fathoms, with irregular soundings from 7 and 8 fathoms; the water over it is all discoloured with white and brown patches of sand and coral rocks, and the bottom is plainly visible. The reef in general is steep, there being from 30 to 20 fathoms, muddy bottom, within 1 or 2 miles of it.

Tides.—The tide ebbs and flows here regularly, and the time of high water on full and change, at and within the northern entrance of the Hawke Channel, opposite Soldier's Kay, is half past 5 o'clock, and spring tides rise only 2 feet 6 inches. To the northward of Kay Biscayne, the stream on soundings is much influenced by the winds, when it blows fresh, but with moderate breezes the ebb tide sets northward, and flood southward, and due attention to this will contribute to shorten a passage over soundings to the reef. The tides flow later, and rise higher, as you go to the westward.

At Kay West Harbour it flows, full and change, at $9^h\ 22^m$, and the rise of the highest tide observed above the plane of reference, 2·7 ft.; fall of the lowest tide below the same, 1·6 ft. Meean rise of spring tides, 1·6 ft.; mean rise of neap tides, 1·0 ft. The flood tide runs about $6^h\ 59^m$; ebb about $5^h\ 25^m$; slack water, $0^h\ 12^m$.

The highest high tide in the 24 hours occurs about $8^h\ 54^m$ after the moon's upper transit (southing), when the moon's declination is South, and about $22^h\ 16^m$ when North. The lowest of the low water occurs about $6^h\ 20^m$ after the highest high water. It is high water at Sand Kay 42^m earlier than at Kay West.

Rebecca Shoal lies about 6 miles westward of the Marquesas Sand spit, and 12¼ miles E. by S. ¼ S. from East kay of the Tortugas. It is a coral bank about half a mile in extent, on which there are only 7 ft. water; on it is placed a *black* iron beacon (No. 1), surmounted by a cylindrical cage, visible about 7 miles. About 1½ mile to the S.E. is *Isaac Shoal*.

The TORTUGAS.—The Tortugas, or Dry Tortugas, consist of ten small islands or kays, upon several flats of sand, coral, and rocky ground. These flats extend about 11 miles in an E.N.E. and W.S.W. direction. The *Middle Kay* appears to lie in lat. 24° 37′, and in long. from Greenwich, 82° 55′ W.

To the West of the Tortugas is the *Tortugas Bank*, extending 9 miles from North to South, by nearly 6 from East to West. It is a large bank of brown coral rocks, intermixed with patches of white sand, and having very irregular soundings of from 5½ to 12 fathoms. Its shoalest part is near the southern extremity. Between this bank and the flats of the Dry Tortugas there is a channel about a league in breadth, and having, in general, from 10 to 12 fathoms, sand, gravel, coral, and shells.

Although, from the clearness of the water on this bank, it appears dangerous, it is not so in reality. Those bound to the eastward, from any port in the Mexican Sea, and meeting with a fierce storm hereabout, which is very common in the summer season, may safely anchor in 4 or 6 fathoms, to the North of the S.W. kay at the distance of one-quarter of a mile from the West side of the long sandy kay called Turtle Kay.

The islets or kays called the Dry Tortugas are all very low, but some of them are covered with mangrove bushes, and may be seen at the distance of 4 leagues. A reef of coral rocks stretches about a quarter of a mile S.W. from this kay, the water on which is discoloured; and, in general, wherever there is danger, it may be easily seen in the day-time from the mast-head.

Several sheltered anchorages will be found within the group; and eastward of Garden Kay, which lies near the middle of the southernmost islets, there is a small inlet of deep water, where a vessel of large draught may careen alongside the kay. The soundings all around are very irregular, and of little assistance when the lights are not visible.

LIGHTHOUSES.—The *fixed light* from a brick tower, 150 ft. high, on *Loggerhead Kay*, has been before noticed, and also that on *Bush* or *Garden Kay*, distinguished by a lighthouse on Port Jefferson, which exhibits a fixed light, 70 ft. above the sea, which may be seen at the distance of 14 miles. It may be approached on the West, South, and round to East, within 4 miles, without danger. On the North it should not be approached nearer than to 9 miles.

THE TORTUGAS.

There is good anchorage in a small but snug harbour near Bush Kay, which is entirely sheltered from the sea by a large reef of rocks, and a flat shoal within them, about half a mile broad; the bottom is soft clay and mud. This harbour is quite smooth, even in a gale of wind; and, in case of necessity, a vessel might be easily hove down there, as there are 3 fathoms close to the bank.

Loggerhead Kay, on which the principal lighthouse is situated, is, according to the United States' authorities, in lat. 24° 38′ 5″, long. 82° 55′ 46″, and is the south-westernmost kay of the group, which in sailing from Pensacola or the Mississippi, is the corner to be turned, and in stretching north-eastward from Cape Antonio is the point to be avoided. A reef of coral rocks stretches about one quarter of a mile S.W. from the kay, the water on which is discoloured; and, in general, whenever there is danger, it may easily be seen in the day-time from the mast-head.

If bound to the eastward, and meeting with a strong easterly gale, which is frequently the case in the summer, you may safely anchor in 5 or 6 fathoms under the lee of the long sandy island, which lies to the northward of the S.W. kay, about one quarter of a mile off shore. There is good anchorage, also, in several other places, particularly in a small snug harbour near Bush Kay, which is entirely sheltered from the sea by a large reef of rocks, and a flat shoal within them, about half a mile broad.

There is a channel 17 miles in width between the eastern kay and the West end of Florida Reef. Thirteen and a quarter miles from the Eastern Kay in an E. 6° S. direction there is the Rebecca Shoal, of 12 ft., marked by its beacon, already noticed, about half a mile in extent. Garden Kay light bears West from the shoal, 17¼ miles distant. With care, and seeing the lights, this channel is preferable to going round the Tortugas. The channel is free of danger, with the exception of the Rebecca and Isaac Shoals, and frequently used by vessels bound to the ports on the West side of the peninsula of Florida. The West end of Marquesas Spit is pointed out by a spar beacon, painted *white*, and 3 ft. above the sea. The beacon is in 15 ft. water, but it is frequently washed away, and it will, therefore, be better to pass westward of the Rebecca Shoal. The soundings will be found irregular, varying from 8 to 16 fathoms.

The bank on the eastern side of the above channel, which stretches to the westward of the Marquesas Kays, is a dangerous and extensive bank of quicksand, on every part of which are no more than 4 to 5 ft. water. It is of a remarkable white colour, especially all along the northern edge, and may easily be avoided in the day-time.

The tide between the Tortugas and Marquesas Kays sets variably through to the northward, and the ebb to the E.S.E.

You may readily know the approach to the Florida Reef in the day-time by the whiteness of the water, in time to avoid all danger; and in the night keep the lead going, so as to be warned of danger at the distance of 2 or 3 miles from the edges of kays or reefs.

In the channel to the northward of Garden Kay there is a shoal spot of 3 fathoms, with 6½ and 7 fathoms on each side of it.

To the southward of the Tortugas, the soundings appear to be very regular, until within 8 leagues of the shore, where, in some places, they become uneven. To the northward of them is fine deep water. In passing by, in the night, it is necessary to sound frequently, and never stand into less than 30 or 35 fathoms.

There is no drinkable water to be obtained on any of the Tortugas, except on the northernmost island, nor is there any wood except a few bushes, which are useful in indicating the Kays at a distance, and, therefore, it would be wrong to cut down. There is a great variety of sea birds, with turtle and excellent fish.

If bound to the eastward, and you meet with a strong easterly gale, which is frequent hereabout in the summer season, you may safely come to anchor, in 5 or 6 fathoms, under the lee of the long sandy island which lies to the northward of the S.W. kay, at about a quarter of a mile from shore.

DIRECTIONS FOR FLORIDA STRAIT.

If from the westward, it is uncertain where the Gulf Stream will be first met. Generally it is found not far to the S.W. of the Tortugas, on the parallel of about 24° N. There are occasions, however, when it is met with much farther to the S.W. and westward, and even to the N.W. of those islands. This probably more frequently happens when light S.E. and southerly winds prevail in the summer season, or in the winter for a short time after heavy north-westers, or at periods when the Mississippi is overcharged; but as yet there is no satisfactory data on which a correct judgment may be formed, of the interruptions which this great stream meets with, in its exit from the Gulf of Mexico through the Florida Strait.

As before stated, vessels having rounded Cape Antonio had better get as quickly as possible on the parallel of lat. 24° N., and work up a short distance on either side of it, until they find the stream. In the winter months, when strong breezes prevail to the northward of East, accompanied by sudden changes to the N.W., they may keep the Florida Kays aboard in the day-time, bearing in mind, however, that they are only visible 8 or 9 miles off, and that the Florida Reefs are steep-to; so that the moment they are sighted, the vessel's head should be placed off shore. It may also be observed, that within this distance from the West end of the reefs to the Carysfort Elbow, there is generally no current, and frequently a strong eddy to the S.W.

After passing Elbow Kay lighthouse on Kay Sal Bank, it will be advisable to keep the Bahama side aboard, and, if possible, without sacrificing too much time, to take a departure from the lighthouse. From abreast Gun Kay light, a track in mid-channel will be better, in order to avoid the dangers on the Little Bahama Bank. Should a vessel be caught with a Norther in this part of the strait, she will be exposed to a heavy short sea, and as the stream runs at this time with perhaps increased force, she had better make short boards under easy but commanding sail, bearing in mind that the wind will shortly veer round to the N.W., making the Florida side a most dangerous lee shore.

In the summer months, when the winds prevail to the southward of East, a vessel may probably get through without having to make a board, making use of the remarkable hills on Cuba to check the reckoning. Extreme care must, however, be taken to give the Colorados a very wide berth. Even in this case it will be as well to sight Elbow Kay light. It need scarcely be said that vessels bound to the N.E., instead of attempting to haul close round Matanilla Reefs, will find it more safe and advantageous to keep in the stream, until they are fully assured of being far to the northward of this dangerous spot.

Vessels proceeding westward from the Great Bahama Bank should endeavour to strike soundings on the N.E. end of Kay Sal Bank. Should the wind be scant from the westward, they may run in on the bank on either side of Dog Rocks, and pass off to the southward of the Elbow; or should the wind be light and tending to calm they may anchor within, to avoid being set to the northward; otherwise it will be better to run down outside, especially in the night, paying great attention to the lead.

Having passed Elbow Kay light, the course should be S.W. ¼ W. until close over to the Cuba shore, to avoid the strength of the current. This course should lead direct towards the peak of Matanzas, and within about 12 miles N.W. of the *fixed* light (varied by a *red* flash every *half* minute), on Kay Piedras, but this will depend upon the set of the current, which is very uncertain, and sometimes strong into the Nicholas Channel.

If bound to the south-western ports of the southern states of America, it will be advisable to run along the Cuba shore as far westward as Mariel, and thence shape a N.W. course, so as to pass at a proper distance westward of the Tortugas. Should the Cuba shore be left in the daytime, an occasional bearing of the high land will enable the mariner to estimate the strength of the stream, and to regulate his course accordingly. He may depend upon finding the current right across, and probably with increased strength as he advances to the northward.

Some navigators recommend vessels to cross over at once from Orange Kay, on the Great Bahama Bank, to the Florida shore, and having struck soundings, to run along the edge of the reef, keeping off the bank during the night. This route might shorten the voyage considerably, but it is attended with great risk and uncertainty. A steamer might accomplish it in safety; but by no means attempt to strike soundings in the night, and be very cautious indeed in doing it in the day, especially if the latitude be at all doubtful.

THE GULF STREAM.

The line of reefs and kays just described form the northern and western limits of the Strait or Gulf of Florida, through which flows the famous *Gulf Stream*, the most strongly marked of all the ocean currents. The causes which give rise to this mighty ocean river, and its ultimate effects, are still involved in much obscurity, although of late years more exact observation has given us a truer insight into its real nature; it has also thrown some obscurity on the entire subject. But as these speculations refer rather to philosophy than to navigation, they cannot be admitted here. Its main features of depth and velocity can only be noticed here, and in this we shall commence at the point where it enters the Gulf of Florida. The observations were made by the officers of the U.S. Coast Survey.

The Gulf Stream at its commencement is confined between the coasts of Florida and those of Cuba and the Bahama Banks, and no other water can reach it during this part of its course.

The first section, that at its westernmost limit, was examined in 1858, between the Dry Tortugas and the entrance to the Havana, a distance of 95 miles, which showed that the water gradually deepened from the North side to the maximum depth of 770 fathoms within 5 miles of the Cuban shore. The next section will be more suitable for demonstration.

THE GULF STREAM.

In 1866 it became necessary to lay an electric cable between the Florida Kays and the Havana; and the United States Coast Survey, under Mr. Hilgard, undertook the examination of the bottom. The line of soundings was carried from Sand Kay to the Moro Castle of Havana in a diagonal line across the main strength of the stream where it first enters the channel which gives its name, a distance of 82¼ miles.

Starting from the northern side the bottom falls away in terraces nowhere abrupt to a depth of 504 fathoms, at the distance of 29¼ miles, and to 687 fathoms at 34 miles, nearly half over. The maximum depth of 845 fathoms is found at 45½ miles from the North side; from this to the Cuban shore the bottom is hilly and precipitous; and at about 20¾ miles from the Moro the summit of a submarine mountain ridge is reached, which rises about 2,400 ft. above the bed of the strait, that is from within 380 to 320 fathoms of the surface; this mountain ridge has been traced for more than 12 miles parallel with the axis of the strait, and falling precipitously toward the South, deep water continuing close up to the South shore.

From the northern side the bottom is rocky, with coral to the depth of 300 fathoms, at depths beyond these it is of that peculiar gray mud, or granular mud, sometimes with red patches, the ordinary type of the organic life of the ocean bed.

The temperature of the waters, varying according to the season from 83° or 84° on the surface, sinks to 60° on the summit of the ridge above mentioned, and is only 45° at the bottom, 13° above the freezing point.

In the northern half of this section, above the terraces South of Florida Reefs, the water lies almost motionless, and it is only over the deep cañons of the southern half of the gulf that the Gulf Stream flows to the eastward. It is thus only 40 miles broad in its greatest strength. Its depth cannot exceed the summit of the submarine ridge, and it was found on hauling in the sounding line that the upper moving stratum is scarcely more than *one-third* of the maximum depth.

The actual sectional area of the Gulf Stream, at its highest temperature and greatest velocity, is not more than from 5 to 8 square miles. Such a well determined fact shows how entirely fallacious were those speculations formed prior to its establishment. It will be no great sacrifice of previously formed opions to curtail the Gulf Stream of those widely extended and majestic features it was formerly endowed with. The data thus acquired as to its initial course is exactly borne out by farther explorations beyond this.

Passing by the next section, between the Sombrero lighthouse and the Salt Kay Bank, about 120 miles farther to the eastward, where it is 45 miles wide, executed in April, 1859, by Commander Craven, U.S.N., which showed that its maximum depth is only 600 fathoms, and the greatest depth still being on its southern side; and also the next, between the Carysfort lighthouse and the Great Bahama Bank (examined by Commander Craven, U.S.N., in May, 1859), 63 miles wide, maximum depth about 500 fathoms; we come to the most important, because it is the crucial test of the magnitude and character of the Gulf Stream.

The narrowest part of the Gulf Stream is also by very much the shallowest part of its course, a fact almost incredible, but that it rests on a solid basis. It was obtained by Commander Craven, in 1855. The distance between Cape Florida and the Bemini Isles is 45 miles, and the maximum depth is only from 300 to 370 fathoms. The temperature of the water at the bed was only 49°, so that here again the warm water does not extend more than one-third or one-half the entire depth, demonstrating the actual cubical amount of warm water passing over this line to be about the same as that shown in the first section, from which this is distant about 250 miles.

Nothing is said here about the cold polar currents in a reverse direction, which have been traced in this its strongest and warmest portion.

THE GULF STREAM.

The stream is here confined between the Little Bahama Bank and the Florida coast, and from this point to its entrance into the Gulf is about 330 miles. Hitherto its course has been one undivided stream, lying over a very cold substratum, probably flowing in a reverse direction, and with cold counter-currents appearing near its margin. To the northward it pursues its course, as is well known, in a direction generally parallel to the inequalities of the United States coast. But it here appears only as one of a series of parallel bands, the warmest of four belts, having one within it, and two or more to the East and S.E. of it, which warm bands are separated by as many belts of cooler water flowing in an opposite direction, and within or inshore of the innermost is the very cold Arctic Current also flowing southwards. The warm belt of the true Gulf stream is so pressed upon the coast, that the exactly defined separation between its dark blue and tepid waters, and the lighter and much colder Arctic stream, has been termed the *Cold Wall*, the division being so nearly perpendicular and well marked to great depths. And this characteristic is preserved as far, and perhaps beyond, the entrance to New York Harbour. The outer edge is very vaguely defined; and, in its northern portion, it imperceptibly blends with the ordinary temperature of the ocean in the latitude. Beyond this it turns more to the eastward, and having arrived on the meridian of the Nantucket Bank, about long. 68° or 69°, its limits become still less defined, and when it reaches the meridian of 50°, or that of the Newfoundland Banks, its southern margin cannot be detected.

The length of its course, after leaving the Gulf of Florida thus far, is about 3,500 miles, and its breadth has increased from about 70 miles off Charleston, 120 miles off Cape Hatteras, at Nantucket to perhaps 300 miles, and the mean velocity of its current is such that it would take from 20 to 25 days in the main strength of the current to reach Nantucket, or 50 days to arrive off the Newfoundland Banks.

In the United States Coast Survey Report for 1869, from January to April the surveyors found the currents along the Florida Reef very changeable. "Some days the current was running at the rate of 2¾ miles per hour, but on other days only six-tenths of a mile the hour. The set of the current was to the northward and eastward, except at one position, 13 miles off Sand Kay lighthouse, where it was running S.S.W. three-tenths of a mile per hour." It is further stated that on carrying soundings on a line between Carysfort light and Orange Kay, one of the Bahamas, the easterly current was observed to have a width of about 30 miles. After passing through this, the vessel suddenly entered water free of current, and in the remaining distance (about 30 miles) to the Bahamas she made her course good. On leaving Orange Kay, April 2nd, to return to Carysfort light, the wind very fresh from the South, no current (as before) was experienced in steaming 20 miles westward, and then the eastward current was met, having a rate of 3 miles per hour.

On our chart of the North Atlantic Ocean, in four sheets, various particulars are given in a graphic form of this important current; and in the North Atlantic Memoir most of the facts relating to it are recorded.

THE BAHAMA BANKS.

The eastern limit of the Gulf Stream is the western edge of the low and singular plateaux, the Bahama Banks. In early times these were most dangerous from the fact that the upper film of the Gulf Stream coming from the westward set across them, and so drifted vessels into destruction. But since the British Government has established some fine and important lighthouses on the more prominent points, much of the danger and most of the uncertainty of the navigation has disappeared.

A more full description of the Bahama Islands and Banks will be found in the book of Sailing Directions which accompanies the chart of the Windward and Gulf Passages, published by the proprietor of this work.

The **LITTLE BAHAMA BANK** is the northernmost of the group, and with the rest was surveyed by Captains Richard Owen and Edward Barnett, R.N., in 1846, &c. The chart will show their general configuration.

On the western edge of the Little Bahama Bank are several kays and dangerous reefs. Off the N.W. point of Great Bahama Island are the Wood and Indian Kays, at a league to the northward of which is *Sandy Kay;* and at 2 leagues to the N. by W. of Sandy Kay is *Memory Rock*, which stands about half a league within the edge of the bank. The rock is only 30 or 40 fathoms in circumference, and 20 feet above water.

From Memory Rock the edge of the bank trends to the N.W., and at 4 miles from the rock is the South end of a reef, which is even with the water's edge, steep-to, and very dangerous. This reef is 2 leagues in length, and is succeeded by several others, to the distance of 3 leagues more to the North. These may be known, in the day, by the white colour of the water. Between these and the Maternillo Reef the ground appears to be clear, with soundings on the bank, in the northern half, 18, 19, and 20 fathoms.

The N.W. extremity of the Maternillo Reef is the western edge of the Little Bahama Bank. From that point the reef extends to the South nearly 30 miles to the Memory Rock, forming altogether a very dangerous coast, steep-to, having sharp coral rocks, and high breakers. The water of the Gulf Stream sets in upon the bank from W.S.W., and when near the reef, sets in towards the centre of the bank.

The **Maternillo or Mantanilla Reefs** extend to the latitude of 27° 25′ N., and the north-western corner of the Little Bahama Bank, which is here deeper than other parts of it, having 40 to 50 fathoms on it, is in long. 79° 8′. The north-westernmost dangerous shoal, the *Maternillo Shoal*, with 12 ft. on it, is in lat. 27° 22′ N., long. 79° 4′. It is of small extent, and lies 4 miles within the edge of soundings. Five miles to the eastward of this, on the same parallel, with 6 and 8 fathoms between, is another 12-feet bank, the *Middle Shoal*, also of small dimensions. The western extremity of the *Maternillo Reefs* is 7½ miles further East, and in longitude 78° 50′. From this the edge of the reef is very shoal and rocky 15 miles, having only 6 to 9 ft. in parts, some of which always break, and the outer edge of the bank, from 1 to 2 miles outside the reef, breaks in moderate weather. Eastward of the Maternillo Reefs the edge of the bank is interspersed with shoal spots as far as the line of kays which forms the northern face of the bank.

When there is a N.E. swell on, upon the edges of the Maternillo Bank, and in 25, 30, and 40 fathoms, the sea jumps up much by the shock of the current, and so forms overfalls or breakers, which seem to indicate a shoal; but there is none; on the contrary, to the southward of these overfalls you may find smooth water, with 16,

15, 8, and 7 fathoms; and may anchor, if you choose, on sand and gravel, with some stones. On this bank the sea is very green, and you cannot see the bottom until in 3 or 2½ fathoms of water.

The **PROVIDENCE NORTH-WEST CHANNEL**, which separates the Great and Little Bahama Banks, is about 9 leagues broad, and leads in a general East and West direction along the southern face of the Great Bahama Island. At its S.W. end it is marked by the important iron *lighthouse* on the Great Isaac Rock.

The **GREAT BAHAMA BANK** is of an irregular figure; its outline is straight, and, like the Little Bahama Bank, it drops at once from the level flat, with 2 to 6 fathoms on it, to the fathomless depths of the ocean. Its south-western face forms, with the North coast of Cuba, the Old Bahama Channel; and, with the Salt Kay Bank, the Santaren Channel.

The **GREAT ISAAC LIGHTHOUSE**, on the N.W. end of the Great Bahama Bank, is an iron tower 145 ft. high, painted with eight broad red bands, with seven white bands between. It stands on the Great Isaac Island, in lat. 26° 2′ N., long. 79° 6′ 30″ W., and shows a brilliant *revolving light* every half minute, at an elevation of 158 ft., seen 16 miles off. A fixed light is seen between the flashes to the distance of 6 miles.

The Great Isaac is a kay of moderate height, about half a league in extent, from East to West. A cluster of little islets and rocks, called the *Hen and Chickens*, lies at the distance of 2 miles to the S.S.W. of its western point. There is also a round rock, called the *Gull*, about 20 yards broad, at the distance of a mile N.E. by N. from the N.E. point; and a reef, called the *Brothers*, at the distance of 4 miles E. by S. from the East point. The ground in other parts is clear, and to the N.W. and S.W. of the isle is good and extensive anchoring ground, with regular soundings, from 15 to 5 fathoms, with soft limestone bottom and broken shells. The larger rocks of the Brothers are two haycock rocks, 1½ mile asunder, lying W.S.W. and E.N.E., the easternmost being about 5 miles from the Great Isaac. The latter, or largest rock, appears to be the *Brigantine* of the Spanish charts, said to be so named because when seen from the E.N.E. it resembles one. On the Great Isaac there are wells of fresh water, and abundance of large shell-fish. The Hen and Chickens are the *Farallons* of the Spaniards, who say that on the West side of them you may anchor in 5½ or 6 fathoms of water, on fine sand. The bank of soundings extends 6 miles to the West of the Great Isaac, with increasing depths from 7 to 16 fathoms; and to the S.W. nearly 6 leagues, with 7, 6, 7, 10 and 17 fathoms.

The **Bemini Isles**, which are the westernmost isles of the Great Bank, are low, with some small trees, or rather bushes on them, particularly on the S.E. part of the South Isle. The ground about these isles is generally shoal and rocky. On each of them is a well of fresh water; and there is good anchorage on the S.W. in 5, 6, 7, and 8 fathoms.

The tide rises and falls between 3 and 4 ft.; flood setting to the N.E., and ebb to the S.W., forming a rippling like the meeting of two currents. The flood here sets at the rate of about 1¼, and the ebb 3 miles an hour.

The inlet or harbour between the Beminis has throughout from 12 and 11 to 10 and 9 ft. at low water.

A shoal, locally known as the *Henry Bank*, is stated to lie about N.N.W. half a mile from the South point of South Bemini Island, and at a distance of half a mile from the shore; this shoal is considered to have a depth of about 3 ft. on it, with 3 fathoms on its inshore side.

From the S.W. point of the southern Bemini a chain of low kays and rocks, called the *Turtle Rocks*, extend about 3 miles to the South. Some of them do not rise to the level of the water. Here the bank is very steep, as, at the distance of a pistol shot, no bottom is to be found; and at the half-length of a ship are 14 and 15 fathoms, on sand. *Barnett's Harbour*, a hole in the bank, of 2¼ fathoms, divides this from the succeeding group of kays, the *Cat Kays*, previously described.

Gun Kay, a narrow ridge of coral, is a mile long N.N.W. and S.S.E., and is the Dog Kay of the Spanish "*Derrotero.*" On its N.E. point is a clump of trees, 20 ft. high. The edge of the bank extends three-quarters of a mile to the westward of the kay. The channel between this kay and the Florida Reefs is 45 miles broad. To the S.E. of Gun Kay is the northern *Cat Kay*, the trees on the south-eastern part of which are 40 ft. high. The edge of the bank does not extend beyond half a mile to the westward of these groups of kays and rocks.

GUN KAY LIGHTHOUSE, at 250 yards from the southern extremity of Gun Kay, was first lighted in May, 1836. It shows a *red revolving light* every 1½ minute, elevated 80 ft. and visible 12 miles off in all directions, except when bearing between S. by W. ¼ W. and S. ¾ E. (by compass), where, at the distance of about 8 miles, it is intercepted by the Bemini Isles. The lighthouse is painted upper part red, lower part white, the lantern also being painted white. Position, lat. 25° 34' 30" N., long. 79° 18' 50" W.

When within the distance of 5 miles vessels should not bring the light to the southward of S.E., as the chain of kays and reefs project in a curve to the westward, and as they lie within a mile of the outer edge of the bank, there might be scarcely time to obtain soundings. The flood tide also sets strongly to the eastward through the intervals of the kays, where is is high water, on full and change, at 7ʰ 30ᵐ, and the tide rises 3 ft.

The Riding Rocks are about 23 miles southward of Gun Kay lighthouse, lying near the western edge of the Great Bahama Bank, and are the southern portion of a range of islets and kays which extend along the N.W. face of the bank, consisting of one rock or kay, about half a mile long, and 12 yards wide in the broadest part, which is divided at nearly one-third from its South point by a bay. This kay is very irregular in its height, and more uneven than Orange Kay. At about 2½ miles to the N.E. of this rock is a small island, about 2½ miles long, and 250 or 300 yards broad in the broadest part; to the northward of the southernmost kay lie three small rocks, about 10 or 12 yards long, each running N.W. by N. These rocks are about 3 or 4 feet high. With the southernmost of the Riding Rocks, bearing N.N.W., distant 1½ mile, are 5 fathoms. With the eastern rock and the northern kay in a line, bearing N. by W. 2½ miles, are 4½ fathoms, fine level sandy bottom; 2¾ fathoms immediately after; and, at 3 miles distant, 3 fathoms. With the northern Riding Rocks bearing West 5 miles, are 3¼ fathoms. The southern kay bearing S.W. by W. 2 miles, are 3½ fathoms. With the main or northern kay W.N.W. 2½ miles, are 3 fathoms. A shoal runs out from this kay in a N.N.E. direction, on which are 6 ft. of water. You have not a passage to the northward of the Riding Rocks for vessels drawing 6 ft. The ebb sets here N.E. 1½ mile per hour.

Between the Riding Rocks and Orange Kay the edge of soundings is very clean, and you may enter without any other precaution than the lead. From the Roquillos the edge trends about S. by E.; it is thence clear, and more or less deep, as shown by the charts, to the parallel of 24° 20'; whence to 24° 7' there are numerous spots, white and black, of shoal ground.

The Orange Kays are a cluster of kays and rocks, about 5 leagues to the southward of the Riding Rocks, and 1 league within the edge of the bank. They extend from lat. 24° 53' to lat. 24° 58', in long. 79° 9'. The main kay is about three-quarters of a mile in length, the broadest part about 120 yards, and the narrowest

8 yards. The highest part is 20 ft. in height. It is a barren rock, the eastern side quite straight, and trends S.S.W. and N.N.E. At S. by W. from the main kay, about three-quarters of a mile, are two rocks, 6 ft. out of water, about 15 ft. in length; and at half a mile S. by W. of these lie two smaller rocks. It is dangerous to attempt passing between either of these rocks and the main kay, as reefs run out, and connect them. These reefs are 30 or 40 yards broad, and directly beyond them are 4 fathoms. At a mile South of these rocks you may sail with safety. Being a mass of solid rock they may be approached, on the West, to their very edge, in 11 ft. of water. To the northward it is not safe to approach within 3 miles, as the water breaks over a ridge which projects to a very considerable extent. There is no sign of verdure on these kays, but around them is plenty of fish.

Many persons have mistaken the Orange Kays for the Riding Rocks, on the North of which a vessel cannot pass; but to the northward of the Orange Kays there is a passage to the bank, which is not, however, recommended to strangers, as there are some black patches of shoal. The western edge of the bank, hereabout, is like an ironbound shore, connected by one grand chain of rocks.

The **SANTAREN CHANNEL**, lies between the Great Bahama Bank and the Kay Sal Bank.

SALT KAY or KAY SAL BANK.—This bank, lying between the Great Bank of Bahama and the Island of Cuba, forms the channels *Santaren* and *Nicholas*. Its greatest extent is from N.W. to S.E. On its S.E. end is the island or cluster of isles called *Anguilla*, which may be seen 4 leagues off. The N.E. part of these is foul, but the western side is clear, with good anchorage. From Aguilla to the N.W. are several groups of kays, which rise almost on the very edge of the bank, and between which, in general, there are clear passages for any vessel, and behind them anchorages. The several groups are denominated *Muertos* (Deadmen's), *Damas* (Ladies'), *Piedras* (Rocky), which are on the N.E. The northern are *Perros*, or Dog's Kays; *Agua*, or Water Kays; and the *Roques*, or Double-headed Shot Kays. The straits between these groups afford free passage; but not so the straits which the kays of each group form among themselves, as they are very narrow. The kays and rocks on the North and N.E. sides of this bank lie in clusters. They are more than fifty in number, but at a distance appear like one island. On the S.W. side of the bank there is only one islet, named *Cayo Sal*, or Salt Kay, and so named from various natural salt ponds on it, which produce very good salt. This kay may be descried at 10 miles off, and water may easily be procured at it, though there is none on Anguilla and the other kays in its vicinity. The bank has three rocky shoals upon it, as shown in the charts; but vessels may navigate upon it without danger, in 7½, 8, and 9 fathoms. Whenever the sky, &c., announce a hard North, it is advisable to enter on the bank, and anchor in the shelter of the kays, or you may lie-to here without any other trouble than that of the lead, until the wind changes, and becomes favourable to your voyage.

The **Salt Kay Bank Lighthouse**, on the N.W. side of the Salt Kay Bank, stands on the highest of the Double-headed Shot Kays, in lat. 23° 56′ 28″, and long. 80° 27′ 38″. The base of the tower is 46 ft. above high water; and the height of the tower is 54 ft. The light is fixed, and may be seen in all directions 15 miles off, except when bearing S.W. by W. ¼ W. (magnetic), where, at the distance of about 9 miles, it will be intercepted by Water Kay.

From the lighthouse the south-westernmost of the Double-headed Shot Kays bears S.S.W. ¼ W. (magnetic), distant 3½ miles.

The Florida Stream is generally found to set strongly to the N.E., within a mile and a half of the rocks; but, through the intervals of the kays, the ebb and flood tides run rapidly off and on the bank, where it is high water, on the full and change, at 9 o'clock, and the tide rises from 2 to 3 ft.

Respecting the tides, they run in various directions on the West part of the bank, being much influenced by the Gulf Stream. There is a regular rise and fall of $2\frac{1}{4}$ to 3 ft. at a spring tides; the flood sets strongly through all the openings, or between the rocks, toward the centre of the bank, and it flows at full and change of the moon at 9 o'clock, nearly. The ebb tide sets the contrary way.

In the Santaren Channel, between the Great Bank of Bahama and the Salt Kay Bank, there is said to be rarely any current, unless after heavy gales, when it runs with great velocity up and down. If it predominates in one direction more than another it is to the N.N.W., and about 1 mile an hour.

THE NORTH COAST OF CUBA.

PORT of SAGUA la GRANDE is considered to extend 13 miles W.N.W. and E.S.E., and 6 miles North and South. Of the several channels leading to the anchorage for loading, the only practicable one for vessels of over 8 ft. draught is the Boca Maravillas. The light at Boca Sagua la Grande is mentioned hereafter.

As the kays which surround the port are low, and the greater portion of them composed of mangroves, the winds cause much sea, notwithstanding the little depth. It is necessary in bad weather, and particularly in the months of September and October, to take every precaution for security.

The mouth of the River Sagua la Grande lies about 4 miles S.S.W. of the entrance to the Boca Marillanes, and is connected with the interior by a railway. The bar is passable for vessels of 6 ft. draught. The town stands about 12 miles in a direct line from the coast, but 21 miles by the windings of the river.

Vessels bound to Sagua la Grande through the Boca de Marillanes should make Cristo Kay, on the East end of which are some huts, with a flagstaff bearing a blue flag with the letter P in white, marking it as the pilot station. When about a mile N.E. of the flagstaff, steer S.S.E. passing westward of the iron buoy on the West edge of the Marillanes Bank. The buoy is in 19 ft. water, and there is as little as 6 ft. water on the bank, the sea generally breaking on it. On nearing the bar a bell buoy, in 17 ft. water, marking the western sandbanks, will be seen, and which should be left to the westward.

When abreast this latter buoy, alter course to S.S.W. $\frac{1}{2}$ W., which, skirting the weather reef, leads in mid-channel between the Mariposa and Cruz Kays; then haul up and pass close westward of the buoy placed near the edge of the spit extending from the former kay; when a S. $\frac{1}{4}$ W. course may be steered, passing the next, a bell buoy, on the port hand. Anchorage may now be taken up in about $2\frac{1}{4}$ fathoms water.

Leaving by this passage, a vessel should take advantage of the land wind, which blows regularly from daylight until 10 a.m., when the sea breeze sets in; the channel is too narrow for working. In case of calm or not sufficient wind, it will be necessary to anchor, the tide not setting fairly through the channels.

Boca Sagua la Grande affords a passage only for vessels of 8 ft. draught, although at the entrance there are between 4 and 5 fathoms water, shoaling within. There is good anchorage in 3 fathoms about half a mile southward of Muertos Point.

LIGHT.—On the N.W. point of Hicacal Kay, East side of the entrance to Boca

Sagua la Grande, a *fixed bright light* is shown from a mast above the keeper's dwelling, 55 ft. above the sea, and visible 8 miles. The keeper's dwelling may be known by its red doors and windows; eastward of it there are a few fishermen's huts.

From Bushy Kay, the western point of entrance to the Boca Sagua la Grande, a chain of rocks, on which the sea breaks, encircles the kay as far as *Verde Kay*, 8½ miles to the W.N.W. Near the edge of the bank, and half a mile northward of Verde Kay, is a reef, having an opening between it and another reef a mile farther westward, affording a passage for small vessels.

At 6 miles N.W. by W. from Verde Kay, is a small flat sandy kay, from which the *Nicolao Reef* sweeps round from N.E. to N.W., distant from 1 to 3 miles, and on which the sea does not always break. About a mile S.W. of it is a shoal which uncovers at low tide, and the sea always breaks over it. This part of the coast bank is extremely dangerous, and not well known. From Médano Islet, Kay Sal bears N. by W., 28 miles.

To the eastward of Bahia de Cadiz Kay, between it and Nicolao Reef, there is a clear space on the bank with from 6 to 2½ fathoms water. Also, immediately eastward of the Médano, there is another clear space with about the same depth of water. A vessel under 10 ft. draught may navigate over this part of the bank, with the lead and lookout for shallow water from aloft.

About 21 miles southward of Médano Islet is the *Morena Mountain*, remarkable, with several pointed peaks; the mountain runs N.W. and S.E. a long distance, and is of moderate height. A short distance westward of the Morena there is another remarkable range of lofty hills, forming three peaks, the centre one being the highest, called the *Bella Paps*, which bears South of Kay Cadiz, and is a good guide for it. Farther westward is the *Limonar Range*, which may also be seen from outside the shoals; and between it and the peaks of *Cumarioca*, still farther westward, is the hill of *Santa Clara*, equally conspicuous.

BAHIA de CADIZ KAY is about 9 miles westward of Médano Islet, and on its N.E. part there are some fishermen's huts and a flagstaff. Under the West side there is good anchorage with the usual winds, but it is exposed to the North. In rounding the West end, vessels drawing not more than 15 ft. may bring the Bella Paps to bear S. ⅛ E. or S. by E., and run in upon that line until the centre of the kay bears about E. by N. ¼ N., then anchor in 4 fathoms water, sandy bottom. Vessels of heavier draught had better anchor in 5 fathoms with the centre of the kay East. In standing in the depths will be 4, 4½, and 5 fathoms, and strangers will probably feel alarmed at the dark appearance of the water, but the bottom is sand covered with weed. There is good fishing and wooding here, but no water.

LIGHT.—Near the N.E. end of Bahia de Cadiz Kay is an iron tower 159 ft. high, painted white, from which is shown, 175 ft. above the sea, a *fixed and flashing bright light*, varied by a flash every minute, and said to be visible 24 miles.*

It is high water, full and change, at Kay Cadiz, at $9^h\ 20^m$, and the rise 3 ft.

Six miles S. ¼ W. of the Médano Islet, is the eastern extreme of *Alcatraces Kays*, which extend W.S.W. nearly 6 miles. Between them and a chain named Falcones, extending S.W. by S. and N.E. by N., is the *Boca Alcatraces*, where vessels of 9 ft. draught will find shelter from all winds.

Cabezas Cay, 7 miles westward of Bahia de Cadiz, has a dangerous ledge running from it to the westward, and as it lies on the edge of the bank, it should be ap-

---

* The Derrotero de las islas Antillas for 1863, states the visibility of this light to be only 17 miles.

proached with great caution. About midway between this kay and Bahia de Cadiz is a shoal, on which the sea does not always break. From the Cabezas Kay the edge of the bank takes a W. ¼ N. direction for 17 miles to the North end of Cruz del Padre Kay, which is the northernmost of the whole range. Thence the bank sweeps round to the S.W., forming a convex to the westward, and terminates off the West part of Yeacos Point.

Five miles W.S.W. of Cabezas Kay is the *Pargo Channel*, and 3 miles farther westward is that of *Barcos*, formed between the reefs; hence several kays continue to the W.N.W. as far as *Galindo*; on the North side of which are two small kays, of which the most distant, about a mile off, is Galindito. From Galindo other kays continue to the N.W. to Cruz del Padre. About a mile N. by E. of Galindito is a shoal near the edge of the bank; and a mile northward of Cruz del Padre Kay a chain of reefs commences and extends 6 miles westward. On these kays, particularly at Cruz del Padre and Galindo, there are wells of *good water*.

Cruz del Padre Kay Light.—On the reef, about three-quarters of a mile N.E. of Cruz del Padre Kay, is a conical white tower, 46 ft. high, from which is shown, 95 feet above the sea, a *fixed* bright light, visible 10 miles. This light is not to be depended on.

Blanco, Mono, Piedras, and Monillo Kays, the westernmost of the kays and islets skirting the North coast of Cuba, lie about a mile from the edge of the bank. About 5 miles S.W. of Cruz del Padre is a group of low kays, extending N.E. and S.W., named Blanco. To the southward of them there is anchorage for vessels of 11 feet draught, with good shelter.

These kays afford convenient anchorage to vessels which cannot advantageously use the harbour of Matanzas. The southernmost and smallest is the Monillo, which lies at the distance of 3 miles from Point Yeacos. From the Monillo to the Cayo de Piedras (Rocky Kay), the distance is only half a mile; and from the latter to Mono Kay it is 2 miles. At a mile and a quarter N.E. by N. from the Mono there is a dangerous reef.

The anchorage in regular soundings of 5 to 7 fathoms, bottom of sand, is to the southward of Mono, and on the East and South of Piedras, where ships may lie defended from any sea coming from the northward. The ground is sandy and clean, with from 5 to 6 fathoms, and vessels here may at all times get under sail. To take the anchorage, so soon as you discover the kays, stand for the middle of either passage, and let go the anchor at pleasure. It is only necessary that, in approaching from the N.E., you must take care to avoid the reef lying to the north-eastward of Mono.

Mono Kay lies about 5 miles W.N.W. from the Blanco group, and from it a shallow ledge runs off to the N.E. a full quarter of a mile; and a mile from the kay in the same direction there is a dangerous rocky shoal, with 1¾ fathom water on it. Piedras Kay, on which is the lighthouse, is composed of rock and sand, partly covered with low bushes, and about 3 cables in extent. It lies 2 miles S.W. of the latter. Close off the N.W. side are three rocks above water, and foul ground extends for about 3 cables nearly round the kay. Midway between these two latter kays is a *coral shoal*, with only 3 fathoms water on it, which should be avoided. This patch lies with the peak of Matanzas between the rocks off Piedras, bearing W.S.W., and Mono Kay N.E. by N.; there is no discoloration of the water, but the sea breaks in heavy weather. There are from 5 to 8 fathoms water on either side of the shoal to within 3 cables of the kays. *Monillo Kay* lies N. ¼ E. 1¾ mile from Yeacos Point, S.W. by W. 1¼ mile from Piedras Kay, and is a small black rock scarcely above the sea; a reef extends around it for about 2 cables.

The channel between Piedras and Monillo is clear. The soundings decrease as it is approached, and in the middle the depth is 6 fathoms. To sail through this channel a vessel should be able to lay up E.S.E. There is also a channel southward of Monillo, but it is not recommended.

Piedras Kay Light.—On Piedras Kay is an iron tower above a house, from which is shown, 74 ft. above the sea, a *fixed and flashing* light, varied by a *red flash* every half minute, and visible 15 miles.

There is good anchorage, as before stated, within the kays, in 6 fathoms water, sandy bottom, with Piedras Kay bearing West, and Mono Kay from N. to N.N.W.; or in 4 fathoms, to the southward of Piedras Kay.

It is high water, full and change, at Piedras Kay, at $8^h\ 0^m$, and the rise is about 2½ feet.

CARDENAS BAY is about 9 miles deep, N.E. and S.W., and from 6 to 10 miles wide. The North side is bounded by a narrow strip of low, sandy, wooded land, which may be said to terminate to the eastward at Mangle Kay; the entrance is so blocked up by small kays and shoals, and the bay itself so shallow, that it is only navigable for vessels of about 11 ft. draught to the anchorages of Cardenas and Siguapa.

The town of Cardenas stands on the swampy shore at the S.W. side of the bay, and is a place of considerable commerce, communicating by rail with Bemba, about 13 miles in the interior. The town of Siguapa is north-westward of Cardenas, and they contain together some 5,000 inhabitants. The best channels are between kays Chalupa and Diana or Anas, and between the latter and Mangle Kay. Pilots are not readily obtained if the breeze is strong. Small steamers and droghers navigate within the kays as far to the eastward as the River Sagua la Grande.

A *fixed bright light* is exhibited from an iron column on the West side of *Diana Kay*, nearly a mile S.E. of Mangle Kay. The light is 43 ft. above the sea, and may be seen 7 miles off.

Vessels bound to the ports on the North side of Cuba, eastward of Cardenas Bay, should approach them from the eastward. The old Bahama Channel is seldom navigated from West to East, except by steamers and coasters.

Yeacos Point is rather low, and lies 1½ mile South of Monillo Kay. At 17 miles W.S.W. of Yeacos Point is *Camacho Point*, which is of sand, with some bushes on it, and 2½ miles farther on the *River Camarioca* empties itself; hence the coast trends about W.S.W. for 4 miles to Maya Point, the East extreme of Matanzas Bay. This part of the coast, which is low, woody, and sandy, may be approached to the distance of a mile.

MATANZAS.—From Point Yeacos the coast trends to the S.W. and W.S.W., 14 miles, to the Point of Maya, which is the eastern point of the great Bay of Matanzas. You may run along this coast at the distance of a league. The *Pan of Matanzas*, 1,277 ft., which distinguishes the bay, appears from this direction like an insulated mountain, having a round surface, and without peaks, watercourses, precipices, or other inequalities, excepting a small fissure near the S.E. part of the summit, which can hardly be noticed at a distance, being of so little depth. The land to the eastward is even, though not very low, but it begins to rise at Matanzas, with a gradual slope; and to the West the coast may be seen at the distance of 3 leagues, but it is alike even or level, without any remarkable height, other than the Pan, which appears over it.

The western coast, at the entrance, is bordered by a reef, which extends off from 1 to 2½ cables. Within the port there are the detached shoals New, Stony, and another. *New Shoal* is 2 cables in length N. and S., and about half a cable in breadth. Its centre lies East 3½ cables from San Severino Castle, and 2 cables from the North shore.

Stony Bank lies to the southward, and separated from New Shoal by a channel 1 cable in breadth, which leads to the anchorage. Its northern edge is marked by a *black* buoy in 12 feet water, E. by S. ¼ S., 5 cables from San Severino Castle. Another bank, about a cable in diameter, with 15 ft. water on it, lies S. ½ E. 3½ cables from the castle, and is also marked by a buoy. Also, 6 cables S. by E. ½ E. of the castle, is another shoal, with 12 ft. water on it, marked by a buoy, and from which shallow water extends to the southern shore. In fine weather these shoals may be seen.

Matanzas Town stands on the western shore, on a tongue of land which separates the rivers Yumuri and San Juan, and communicates by stone bridges with extensive suburbs on the opposite banks. A shallow flat runs off in front of it, which prevents vessels from coming within half a mile of the wharves. The town, with its suburbs, contains a population of about 50,000. There is a steam factory adapted for ordinary repairs. The best water will be found about 3 miles up the River San Juan.

It is high water, full and change, at Port Matanzas at about 8 a.m. and 5 p.m., and the rise 2½ feet. The stream runs in with the sea breeze and out with the land wind.

When bound to Matanzas, the Pan of Matanzas above described, which overlooks it from the West, is an excellent guide; and about 12 miles eastward of the port, and 6 miles inland, there is a small ridge of remarkable irregular hills of considerable elevation, but not nearly so high as the peak, with three distinct summits, called the Camarioca Paps. From the Paps the land westward is level and not very low, without any remarkable object as far as the port, where it begins to rise gently, and can be seen 24 miles off, continuing uniform to the Pan of Matanzas.

Coming from the eastward give Maya Point a berth of 2 miles until the part is well open; then steer to the S.W., hauling up gradually for about a mid-channel course, taking care to avoid the bank of sand and rock which borders the point at the distance of 6 cables. Approaching from the westward, give the western shore a berth of about half a mile. When San Severino Castle, a conspicuous object on the North shore of the port, bears W. by S., steer towards it until the fort of the Vigia, on the shore of the River San Juan, bears S.W. ¼ W., then steer for it, passing northward of the buoy on the Stony Bank, and anchor in 5 or 6 fathoms water, mud, as the shipping will allow, the harbour being generally crowded. No reliance can be placed on the buoys being in position, so that it may be advisable for a stranger to take a pilot.

The port being exposed to the E.N.E., a heavy swell sets in with strong winds. The land wind during northers, from the middle of September to the end of February, is frequently interrupted, and a sailing vessel may probably be detained for a few days, as it is difficult and hazardous to beat out against the stream and sea.

To get out of the harbour it is best to clear yourself by towing, or by the aid of the land breeze, if you have any, at a time when you consider the weather as settled, and there is no appearance of Norths coming on. If agreeable, you may cross over, and come to an anchor on the bank or shoal of Point Maya, which will be a proper situation to make sail from when convenient.

In the S.E. angle of the port, about 2 miles southward of Maya Point, is the mouth of the *River Canimu*, and at the western point of entrance is Fort San Felipe. The river is navigable for 9 miles, and carries from 6 to 15 ft. water; but at the bar there are only from 6 to 9 ft., and it is dangerous during northers. A large num-

HAVANA. 173

ber of small vessels are employed in the river, which convey fruit to Havana and Matanzas.

The coast from the Harbour of Matanzas to the N.W. rounds to *Point Guanos*, which is about 4 miles distant from the mouth of the bay or harbour. A revolving light has been proposed for Point Guanos. From Point Guanos the coast trends nearly true *West* to the Morro of Havana, as already noticed. The coast is mostly clean and bold-to; but a little to the West of *Arco de Canasi* a kind of reef lies out, about 1 cable's length; and, at a mile N.N.E. from the Morro Castle, is the shoal on which the *Mariner* grounded in 1815. A vessel may, however, run along at the distance of a league, or less, if required. There is a rocky shoal, with little water on it, which extends from the coast, between the *Rincon*, or Corner, and the *Point of Tarara* or *Cobre*; but it will be avoided by sailing as above. On this part of the coast are various small harbours, to which droggers resort, such as *Puerto Escondido*, *Arco de Canasi*, and *Santa Cruz*; but they are not fit for vessels drawing above 6 ft. of water. All along the coast are soundings on sand, which extend more or less from shore; but the edge is so steep as to immediately pass from 100 fathoms to 20; but, with the lead going, there is no danger in running along, because the soundings will warn any one of the limits they may stand into without danger; and, in good weather, you may even pass the night, letting go a kedge upon the soundings, a manœuvre which may sometimes be very convenient, either to avoid passing your port, if the breeze blows fresh at night, or not to lose ground if the land breeze is light, or it is calm. The hills or mountains of Jaruco (Iron Hills) which rise nearly in the middle of this coast, serve to recognise it by, and determine your situation.

HAVANA HARBOUR may be distinguished, at a distance, by the Paps of Managua, which lie on the meridian of the entrance; while the land, both to the eastward and westward, is low and equal, with the exception only of the Morro, or little hill surmounted by the fortifications and lighthouse. On advancing, the *Hills of Jaruco*, or *Iron Hills*, which are 6 leagues to the eastward, may be seen. These are of moderate height, and detached. The *Table of Mariel* is about 6 leagues to the westward; and, in advancing, not only these, but the Hill of Cavanas may at times be seen.

The Cabana, or North side of the entrance of Havana Harbour, is a high ridge, as described hereafter, the descent of which is nearly perpendicular; this is crowned with extensive battlements, overlooking the city, and commanding the surrounding country, while fronting the sea the land forms a glacis nearly to the shore. At the extreme point of the entrance the land terminates in a mass of rock, on which stand the Morro Castle, Lighthouse, and Signal Station. This range of fortifications, together with Fort Principe to the West, a row of palm trees and the lesser elevations, encompass the plain on which stands the City of Havana.

Havana is the seat of government of the island of Cuba, and with the suburbs is said to have a population of nearly 250,000, and is the greatest commercial place in the West Indies.

The Entrance to the Harbour lies nearly N.W. by W. and S.E. by E., and the channel for about 4 cables is not more than three-quarters of a cable wide, when it begins to widen, and it then opens out into an irregular-shaped basin, $2\frac{1}{4}$ miles in extent N.E. and S.W., and from half to a mile in breadth. The Morro Point, the North point of the entrance, is steep, and a vessel of the largest draught may pass almost close to it. The soundings extend off in a N.W. by N. direction for about half a mile from the point.

The northern shore of the channel is bordered by the *Cabrestante Bank*, which at the outer part extends off more than half a cable; it is marked by five conical *red* buoys.* The southern shore is also bordered by a sandbank named San Telmo, which about halfway in extends a cable off, with only 15 ft. water on its edge; this side of the channel is also marked by three conical red buoys. Within the harbour, the edges of the shoal that extends off the *Regla Bank* are marked by three red buoys, and the square trunk buoys are moorings; one of the latter may generally be obtained by permission from the Health Officer. Within the harbour the western shore is bold, and vessels lie alongside the wharves of the city. The arsenal is in the S.W. angle of the harbour. From the sewerage, and the tidal stream being weak, the water is very foul.

Vessels generally refit alongside the moles or places for that purpose in the northern part of the port, where there is an *iron floating dock*, 300 ft. in length and 80 in breadth, capable of receiving vessels of heavy tonnage, belonging to the Havana Dock Company. Near the dock are two warping buoys. Dock charges are 80 cents per ton for the first day, 25 for subsequent days, and additional for the cargo.

Light.—A lighthouse, 79 ft. high, stone colour, stands on the Morro Castle, at the N.E. side of the entrance of the harbour, and exhibits a *fixed* and *flashing* bright light, varied by a *flash* every *half minute*. The light is 144 ft. above the sea, and may be seen 21 miles off.

A Pilot will be found off the Morro, by making the usual signal; but, except to a stranger, one is scarcely necessary.

Water.—Vessels of war water conveniently from government tanks, which are allowed to be sent for on making the necessary application. The water is not always good after rain.

It is high water, full and change, in Havana Harbour, at $6^h 14^m$; and the rise is about 3 ft. There is no regular flood and ebb, but with the land wind a slight stream usually runs out.

Approaching Havana from the westward, having rounded Cape San Antonio, with the usual trade wind, and intending to pass to leeward of the Comet and other shoal patches, should not steer higher than N.N.W. ½ W. for 17 miles, when they may haul to the widd. If with daylight the passage eastward of these knolls be taken, the weather reef should be closed, with a good lookout for shoal patches. The current generally sets to the S.W. on the edge of the Colorados Bank; it will therefore be better to stand to the northward, as far at least as the parallel of 24°, before tacking.

It frequently happens that having arrived at a position South of the Tortugas without feeling the influence of the stream (see p. 160), it is perhaps entered soon after the reckoning has been checked in the evening, and in making the land on the following morning the vessel will be found far to windward of the port. The features of the land to the eastward, however, differ so considerably from those to the westward, that there will be no difficulty in making out the position. The land eastward of the Morro is about 200 ft. high and rather flat, but about 18 miles to windward it rises into a remarkable ridge of irregular hills of moderate height, about 3 miles in length East and West, and a short distance from the shore, called the Jaruco Hills; whilst 18 miles westward of the Morro is the Maril table land, and farther on in the same direction the hill of Cabañas, all previously described.

About 13 miles eastward of the Jaruco, and 7 miles South of Guanos Point, is the Peak of Matanzas, before described.

---

* The buoys are not to be depended on.

HAVANA—DIRECTIONS.

Vessels bound to Havana from the North and East will navigate either by way of the Providence N.W. Channel, across or along the western edge of the Great Bahama Bank, round the elbow of the Double-headed Shot Kays, and thence across towards Guanos Point in Cuba, out of the stream; or through the Old Bahama Channel.

Entering Havana, under sail, time will be saved by waiting until the sea breeze has set well in, which commences about 10 a.m., and may be seen from the direction the flags are blowing on the inner heights. In the winter months, from October to June, a vessel will generally fetch up to the anchorage; but in the summer, as the wind prevails to the southward of East, she may have to warp in. In the former case, if coming from the eastward, after passing the Jaruco tower and bank westward of it, run down about half a mile or more off shore, and having brought the lighthouse to bear about S.S.E. (not before, in order to avoid any sweep), haul up under all plain sail, so as to shoot as far in as possible, and with both anchors clear.

Having passed Morro Point at the distance of half a cable, hug the north-eastern shore as near as the wind in general allows, but in a vessel of heavy draught do not go inside the buoys on either side of the channel. The helm must be quickly and well attended, to take advantage of the strong gusts and flaws; and the weather head braces and spanker brails should be in hand, ready to assist it. Having passed the valley between the Morro and Cavaña heights, the wind will become exceedingly variable; but with great attention to the steerage, the vessel will shoot to windward of the black buoy No. 2 on the edge of San Telmo Bank, and through the narrows into the harbour.

When off the East end of the heights the breeze will be more steady, and the sail may then be reduced to enable her to take up a convenient berth among the numerous shipping. Should it be necessary to anchor in the narrows, give a good scope of cable, and shorten sail quickly to avoid dragging, as the wind rushes off the shore with great violence.

If the sea breeze hangs to the southward of East, the vessel will have to be warped in, and most probably to be kedged up the outer part of the channel. In this case, when coming from the eastward and having passed the Morro close aboard, stretch over to the Punta shore, and having tacked under it, shoot in as fast as possible, and anchor under the northern shore, waiting until the breeze slackens in the afternoon to warp up.

A good berth for a ship-of-war is in the N.W. part of the harbour, just past the floating dock; the water here is cleaner. Unless the shipping is crowded, there is no necessity to moor; anchors bury themselves in the mud.

There will be no difficulty whatever in quitting the harbour, as the regular land wind is seldom interrupted except by northers, which sometimes throw a heavy swell into the harbour's mouth. The best time to enter is about mid-day, and for quitting at daylight.

THE COAST OF FLORIDA, ETC., FROM CAPE SABLE TO THE MISSISSIPPI.

The **TORTUGAS BANK**,—The great bank, which extends off the western Coast of Florida, in some parts, 40 leagues from shore, between Cape St. Blas on the North, and the Florida Kays to the South, is generally denominated the *Tortugas Bank of Soundings*. The ground is clean and mostly of sand, there being no known danger. except a doubtful spot of sand, which is in lat. 28° 35', and about 12 minutes to the East of the meridian of Cape St. Blas, and on which it is said there was scarcely 3 ft. of water, though it is so steep that, from 100 fathoms you are aground at once.* The whole of the rest of the bottom of these soundings is very regular, and the depth lessens gradually towards the land; upon it there is good shelter from the North and N.E. sea or swell: and a vessel, commodiously may lie-to upon the bank, observing only that the less depth the less the swell will be; and that even, without much inconvenience, an anchor may be let go in 8 or 10 fathoms.

When entering upon this bank from the southward, without being certain of the latitude, and being near the parallel of the Tortugas (or 24° 30'), the western part of which is very steep, it is most necessary to run with caution, in order to catch the soundings on the edge of the bank, and not to go into less than 40 or 35 fathoms. This is the best precaution for keeping you clear of the Tortugas, around which are 30 fathoms. The same precaution, of not getting into less than 40 or 35 fathoms, ought to be attended to when entering upon the bank from the northward, or on higher parallels, and thence steering to it by its southern edge. This will be sufficient to keep you clear, in any circumstances, from all danger of the Tortugas.

On the edge of the Tortugas soundings the waters run with some strength towards the South; and thus, on entering from the westward, with the intention of ascertaining your position by and on them, and your passage is much retarded by winds from the N.E., E.N.E., or East, you may be sure that you are on the edge of them, if you find, for two succeeding days, differences of latitude of 20 miles or more, to the South of your reckoning. In which case you may consider yourself on the meridian of the edge, reckoning that by this you will not incur an error of more than 10 leagues, and you may prosecute your voyage or route with security.

Proceeding northward from Kay West, the water deepening regularly but rapidly to the eastward, is the bay sometimes called *Gullivan's Bay*, which shoals regularly. Secure anchorage may be found on this coast anywhere between Cape Roman Shoal and Cape Sable, in N.W. to E.S.E. winds, clean bottom, good holding ground. The course from the N.W. bar at Kay West to the point of Cape Roman Shoal is N. ¼ E., distant 72 miles. On this course the water will deepen rapidly to 13 fathoms, after leaving the bar. On approaching Cape Roman Shoal in the night, go no nearer than 7 fathoms, as it suddenly shoals 2 or 3 fathoms on the tail of the bank.

Cape Roman Shoal is not a continuous line, but a succession of lumps and channels, some of which dry at low tide.

CHATHAM BAY, or *Juan Ponce de Leon Bay*, is comprised between Cape Roman, or Punta Larga, and Sable Point (or Punta Tancha), the southernmost point of Florida. The distance between the two points is 19 leagues, the ground generally

---

* A small shoal of *sand*, in such a situation, must, indeed, be considered as a phenomenon.—EDITOR.

clean; but as the depth of water is very small, and the coast lined with shoals, the bay is very little frequented, except by turtles and fishermen.

From Cape Roman to Charlotte Bay the coast trends N.N.W., nearly 11 leagues. The ground all along is very clean, and there are 3 fathoms at 2 miles from the shore.

CHARLOTTE HARBOUR.—About 40 miles to the northward of Cape Roman is the Island of Sanibel, at the N.E. of which is Charlotte or St. Carlos Harbour. To enter by the *Sanibel Pass*, which has 8½ ft. (perhaps 10 ft.) approach from the South, and bring Punta Rasa (which is a point on the mainland) to bear N.W., distant 2¼ miles. Sail inside the point of Sanibel Island to deep anchorage. To enter by Captive Pass (which is 15 miles to the northward of Sanibel Pass, and carries 6 feet) approach from South, distant three-quarters of a mile from land, and cross the bar, sailing due North, then bear N.E. to, and through the Pass, with plenty of water inside the North end of Captive Island.

Boca Grande, 7 miles more to the northward, opens when the North end of Lacosta Island bears East.

Seventeen feet at low water can be carried over the bar of Charlotte Harbour. Inside the bar the channel widens to three-quarters of a mile, with a depth of 3½ to 4 fathoms, the best water being on its northern edge.

Vessels in approaching should not go into less than 5 fathoms, if from the South; and in not less than 6 fathoms if coming from the northward. When off the entrance, with Boca Grande bearing N.E. ½ E., and the North point of La Costa Island E.N.E. vessels can steer N.E. by E. ¼ E. for the entrance, and choose an anchorage in 4 or 5 fathoms inside.

A black and white buoy is placed in 3½ fathoms water in mid-channel, on the edge of the bar.

Gasparilla Pass is 7 miles to the northward of the Boca Grande Pass, and carries only 4½ ft. Bring the tall pine trees on the mainland to bear N.E., in 4½ fathoms, steer towards the North side of the pass, and run into 5 fathoms.

From Gasparilla Pass the coast runs 13 leagues N.N.W. to *Anna Maria Kay*, at the South part of Tampa Bay. In this portion of coast are several kays and inlets or passes to lagoons inside. In running along it will always be proper to give the coast a berth of 2 or 3 leagues; you will then keep in 6 or 10 fathoms, without meeting with any known danger.

From Charlotte Harbour to Tampa Bay the coast continues to the N.W. by W., 22 leagues; there are several kays extending along this coast, a part of which lies out nearly 4 miles from it. The shore is all clean, with the exception of a sand-bar extending out from what is called the *Boca*, or Mouth, of *Sarasota Inlet*, which is an opening formed by two of the longer kays, and which is 7 leagues distant from Tampa Bay. Upon this bar there are 2 fathoms of water; and along the whole coast 4 and 5 fathoms are found at 5 and 6 miles from the shore. There is no danger in running along with the lead kept going.

TAMPA BAY, so called, is an extensive estuary from 6 to 10 miles wide, extending from Egmont Island in a N.N.E. direction about 22 miles, when it forms two arms, the easternmost about 4 miles wide and 6 miles long, North and South; the other 12 miles, from S.E. to N.W., and 6 miles broad. At the head of the former is Fort Brooke and Tampa Village; and at that of the latter, the settlement of *St. Helena*.

The outer part of the estuary is greatly obstructed by a middle ground of hard sand, with depths from 8 to 12 ft.. which stretches two-thirds of the way across from the western shore. Vessels of 18 ft. draught, however, can pass round the

East and North sides, and thence down a lane of deep water on the West side of it, to secure anchorage in 4 or 5 fathoms, within only a short distance of Piney Point.

There is 15 ft. water at about one-fourth of a mile from the Western shore; and at high summer tides perhaps 20 ft. may be carried thus far. Those drawing 10 feet may go up nearly to the head of both arms. A pilot may be had at the lighthouse.

Lighthouse.—On the North point of Egmont Island, in lat. 27° 35½' N., long. 82° 14¾' W., is a white tower, 40 ft. high, which exhibits a fixed bright light of the fourth order, 45 ft. above the sea, visible 12 miles off.

In approaching the *North Channel*, keep in 5 fathoms till Egmont lighthouse bears E. by S., when steer E. ⅛ S., crossing the bar between the red and black buoys, where will be carried not less than 19 ft. at low water. After passing No. 4 buoy, steer N.E. for No. 5 buoy, which having left on the port hand, steer N. by E. ¼ E. for No. 6; leave this on the starboard hand, and steer N.E. by E. ½ E. for No. 7, which must be left to port, at the distance of about a fourth of a mile. Thence the course is North for No. 9, which having left to port, steer for Ballast Point; and giving it a berth of about half a cable's length, steer for the flagstaff at Fort Brooke. The banks on either side of the channel, and at the North end of Egmont Island, are steep-to, and the edges easily seen.

The passage between Egmont and Passage Kays carries 17 ft. at low water, but is so tortuous as to be seldom used. To enter, bring the South point of Egmont Kay to bear N.E., and then steer N.E. ¼ E. for the bar buoy, which having left on either hand, a N.E. by E. ¾ E. course will lead up to No. 4 buoy. Coasters can pass in close round the North end of Palm Kay. There is anchorage to the eastward of Egmont Kay in 4 or 5 fathoms, but the bottom is hard. Wood and water may be easily obtained from the neighbouring shores, and fish got in the greatest abundance with the seine.

It is high water at Egmont Kay at 11ʰ 21ᵐ, and the mean rise and fall is nearly 1¼ ft.

The Coast to the northward is fronted by a range of islands, of a similar character to those to the southward. Of these, St. Joseph's Island is off a N.W. projection of the main coast, which here recedes to the eastward, forming St. Joseph's Bay. The island is about 36 miles northward of Egmont lighthouse.

St. Joseph's Island, which lies at only a short distance to the southward of Anclote Kays, is about 5 miles long N.E. and S.W., and to the southward of it is *Clearwater Island*, about 6 miles in extent North and South. These kays lie not far from the main, and cover *Clearwater Harbour*. On the shore, abreast Clearwater Island, is *Fort Harrison*. The kays which follow lie in a S.E. by E. direction, and are named *Sand, Pine, Arenosa*, and *Cabbage*; the South end of the latter lying 4 miles westward of Piney Point. One of them is higher than the others, and appears like a rounded hill.

From Cabbage Kay, the range takes a more southerly direction across the entrance of Tampa Bay, and the principal islets are named *Mullet, Egmont*, and *Palm*. The opening between the two former is nearly a mile and a half wide E.N.E. and W.S.W., and forms the North pass into Tampa Bay. The two latter are nearly 3 miles apart N.W. by N. and S.E. by S., and form the S.W. pass. At about a mile to the northward of Palm Kay, however, are two small low sand ridges, called *Passage Islands*.

Palm Island nearly connects itself to the South extremity of Tampa Bay; and abreast the North end of the island is *Manatee River*, in the South part of Tampa Bay.

THE CEDAR KAYS.

Anclote or Anchor Kays, the northernmost of the kays just described, are two in number, and occupy a narrow space of about 8 miles in length North and South. The North extreme lies W. by S. ⅜ S., about 7¼ miles from the Anclote River, and the space between them and the main is called *St. Joseph's Bay,* which is about 5 miles broad. Off the South end of the Anclote there is good anchorage in 3 fathoms.

Wekiwahee River.—The entrance of this river is 12½ miles N.N.E. from the North end of Anclote Kays. On this river is the town of *Bayport.* You can carry 9 ft. to the beacon, 4 miles West of the town. Keep off shore 10 miles until you can see the town; when it bears East, run for it until up with the beacon, when anchor.

St. Martin's Reef appears to skirt the whole of the space between the Anclote and Crystal Rivers, at about 5 miles from the land; but its limits are as yet undefined and uncertain. Outside it, in a depth of 9 or 10 ft., the coast is not visible.

Homosassa River disembogues about 16 miles to the northward of the Wekiwahee River a mile or so below the upper end of St. Martin's Reef. There are numerous branches near the mouth, forming a marshy delta; but the navigable entrance is pointed out by two conspicuous large oak trees on a shell bank, at the southern side, and a large rock projecting from the water, a short distance to the northward of them.

The whole of this part is fringed with kays; but it is quite clean and more bold than that to the northward, having 6 fathoms water at the distance of about 9 miles.

Crystal River is about 10 miles farther to the northward, and has two entrances formed by *Shell Island,* which latter is the highest land found along the main shore for some distance, it being 25 ft. above high water mark. The southern channel is the widest and deepest. Off the mouth are several parallel lines of oyster reefs, more or less bare, according to the tides.

Vessels of 10 ft. draught can anchor in safety inside the first of the oyster reefs, the channel being pointed out by a stake, which must be left on the port hand when going in. A number of vessels are employed in getting cedar at this river, which is obtained about 4 miles up, and rafted down to the above anchorage. Those bound higher, or to any of the adjacent rivers, should obtain a pilot at the Cedar Kays; for it is extremely hazardous for a stanger to approach this shore without one, or to attend to any directions he may have received.

We-thlocco-chee River empties itself about 5 miles to the northward of the Crystal River. The banks are marshy at the entrance, and in front of it are many oyster beds, leaving a channel carrying 3 feet of water; inside the bar, however, there is a greater depth. There are two entrances, but only the southern one is available.

Waccasassa Bay.—From Black Point, abreast the Cedar Cays, the coast line runs easterly for about 14 miles, and then turns abruptly southward, forming Waccasassa Bay. When in 2¼ fathoms, with the middle of Snake Kay bearing N.N.W. ¼ W., and its East end just open with the West end of Depot Kay, steer N.E. until Waccasassa Reef bears N.N.E. The course is then N.E. by N. ¼ N. until Waccasassa Reef bears North; this will give good anchorage in 10 ft. at mean low water.

Waccasassa Reef is known by its peculiarly white appearance, and being alone. The channel inside the reefs is not staked out. Vessels bound to Cedar Kays should keep in 3 fathoms water, to avoid the set into Waccasassa and sudden shoalings.

The CEDAR KAYS, which skirt the projection at the entrance of Waccasassa Bay, are a cluster of small, sandy, and mangrove islets, closely grouped together, the three outermost, called North, Seahorse, and Snake, being about a mile apart on a N.W. range. All of them are fringed, more or less, with sand and oyster banks, dry in many places at low water, leaving intricate winding channels into good shelter for small vessels. From Seahorse Kay, the middle and outermost of the above three, a shallow ledge of hard sand runs off S.S.W. ¼ W. about 10¾ miles, where it terminates at a point in 14 ft., with 4¼ fathoms close outside of it. At the extreme edge of the ledge, extending from Seahorse Kay, in 12 ft. water, is a black can buoy, numbered 1, Seahorse Kay lighthouse bearing N.E. by N., and the beacon on S.W. Spit S.W. ¼ W. This beacon is formed by three iron screw piles, from which rises an open framework to 36 ft. above the sea, on the top of which is a tripod surmounted by a ball 8 ft. in diameter, the entire height being 50 ft., and painted black. On the centre of the bar, in 11 ft. water, is a can buoy, striped black and white perpendicularly, the lighthouse bearing N. by E. ¾ E., the N.E. point of Seahorse Kay N.N.E., and the centre of Snake Kay N.E. by E.

Seahorse Kay and Lighthouse.—The islet is about a mile in extent East and West, and 45 ft. high. On a small mound at the East end, in lat. 29° 5¼′ N., long. 83° 4¼′ W., is a dwelling-house, upon which is a white tower, exhibiting a *fixed and flashing bright light*, with a flash every minute at 75 ft. above the sea, and visible at 15 miles off.

All the navigable channels between the kays are staked off, but they require the assistance of a pilot, who will come out on seeing the usual signal. Approaching from the southward, with a view of entering the Seahorse Channel, which is the best, steer up on the meridian of 83° 5′ W., and endeavour to sight the lighthouse on the bearing of N. by E., in 3½ to 4 fathoms, which line leads up along the East side of the Seahorse Ledge, and about 2 miles to the eastward of the extremity. When the lighthouse is situated on the above bearing, from a height of 12 ft., the end of the ledge will bear about West. In the night time it will be better to anchor in the above depths, after making the light, which may be safely done with off-shore winds or moderate weather. Steering N. by E. for the lighthouse, the depths will gradually decrease to the edge of the bar, with Snake Kay bearing N.E. ¼ E.; thence a N.E. ¼ N. course carries up to the bar buoy and through the channel between the stakes in 10 ft. at low water, mean tides. When the depths increase to 2½ or 3 fathoms, keep the West bank close aboard, still guided by the stakes, and anchor just to the northward of the lighthouse in 13 to 15 ft. water, or further in, according to draught. Observe, however, that after strong northerly or easterly winds, the depth of the bar will sometimes be only 7 ft. Within Seahorse Kay the channel becomes extremely tortuous and narrow, but generally 10 ft. can be carried up to the settlement, and alongside the wharves at Depot Kay.

In proceeding to the N.W. Pass, which lies between North Kay and the banks and islets to the northward of it, be cautious of the Seahorse Spit, and do not come into less than 4½ fathoms until to the northward of it, with the lighthouse to the eastward of N.E. by N. Having brought North Kay E. ¼ N. in 3 fathoms water, steer for it, and when the lighthouse bears E.S.E., haul in N.E. for the bar, which line ought to carry 13 ft. water. When the lighthouse bears S.E. ½ E., or the North end of Seahorse Kay is just in with the South end of North Kay, steer E. ¼ N., which leads across the bar between the stakes, and in 10 ft. at low water, mean tides. Within the bar the channel becomes very intricate; and from abreast Middle Kays, where it forms a sharp elbow to Depot Kay, it carries but 8 ft. water. In going into all the channels, the stakes with bushes on them must be kept to starboard. In approaching this Pass from the N.W., a vessel should not come into less than 3 fathoms before North Kay bears E. ½ N.

There is a boat channel to the southward of North Kay, and another called the Swash to the southward of Seahorse Kay.

The water is here so clear that the bottom may be seen in 5 or 6 fathoms.

It is high water at Depot Kay at 1ʰ 15ᵐ; mean rise of spring tides 2¼ ft.; and of neaps, 1¾ ft.

There is good anchorage under the East side of Seahorse Kay, safe in westerly gales.

Suwanee River disembogues about 10 miles from the N.W. point of Waccasassa Bay. The upper part is well settled; and cotton, sugar, and tobacco, are brought down by river steamers, and conveyed to the Cedar Kay Harbour for shipment.

Ocilla River.—The entrance is about 70 miles north-westerly from the Cedar Kays. The entrance to this stream is about 4 cables in width, but it soon grows narrower.

There is anchorage, but not safe, in 3 fathoms, 6 or 7 miles from the entrance, which, however, cannot be discovered at that distance.

ST. MARK'S or Apalache is a port of entry, and is connected with Tallahassee, the capital of Florida, by a railroad, 20 miles long. It lies on the River St. Mark, near the junction of the Wakully River with it, which together form the River Apalaché.

The Lighthouse on Point Casinas, the eastern point of the entrance of the harbour, shows a fixed light at 73 ft. It leads directly towards the entrance when bearing N. ¾ W.

Captain Martin says, "I would advise every one, on coming in for this place, to keep the Florida shore on board, and not upon any account to risk a fall to leeward of the Cape St. George; for should a vessel get in between this and Cape St. Blas, and a gale of wind from the S.W. comes on, she would be placed in imminent danger, between the reefs of the capes. By keeping the bay open, with a beating wind, you may safely stretch into 7 or 8 fathoms; and your lead will warn you of all danger, if kept going, as the soundings are regular, and may be obtained a long way from land.

After making the S.W. cape, give it a berth of at least 4 leagues, in order to avoid the *South Cape Shoals*, so called, and when it bears due West 12 miles from you, you will have the lighthouse about N.N.W., on which course you may safely run into 3 fathoms; but attempt to advance no further, as the Bar is very shoal. With N.W. winds it has not more than 6 ft. upon it; but S.W. winds, having a contrary effect, raise the tides to 12 and 13 ft. The bar has a barrel-buoy at present, lying on the shoalest part about 5 miles South from the anchorage.

Extending East and West there is a dangerous shoal lying off the Okalokana River not inserted in Mr. Gauld's or other charts.

Vessels drawing from 10 to 11 ft. should be prepared with a good stream cable, as it may be of the greatest service on getting over the bar, should your vessel ground, without the assistance of the stream. With perseverance you may get over, when, otherwise you may have your vessel in danger.

The distance that soundings of 5 fathoms may be obtained from the land, on coming in, is about 20 miles from the northern shore. When the wind is N.W. the harbour is not to be attempted on any consideration; with S.W. winds it may be entered safely with a vessel drawing from 9 to 11 ft. The ground may be trusted for holding in a gale of wind from the N.W., which often prevails. If the wind answers, to get once over the bar, you may run the vessel on, and with your stream anchor ahead, about 48 or 50 fathoms, you will be ready for the wind at S.W., which often causes a heavy roll of the sea, when you will be enabled to heave occasionally, as your warp slackens.

Approaching St. Mark's, bring the lighthouse to bear N. ¾ W., and steer for it until up with the buoys; pass between them, steering North. This course carries over the bar, with 9 ft. at mean low water. When in 2 fathoms, steer N.N.W. ¼ W. for buoy No. 4. Anchorage can be found in 2½ to 3 fathoms. S.S.E. of the buoy No. 4, and near buoy No. 6, bottom hard sand, fine broken shells, with slight deposit of mud. The channel is staked out, red on starboard, and black on port hand. Strangers, however, should not attempt the river without a pilot.

It is high water at St. Mark's, full and change, at 1ʰ 38ᵐ. Mean rise of spring tides 2·9 ft.; neaps 1·5 ft.

About S.W. by W., 20 miles from St. Mark's River, is the southern point of James' Island, commonly called the S.W. Cape. Between this cape and the lighthouse is a sort of bay, into which the River Oklokonee empties itself; this river is shoal at its entrance, and the shore from the cape to the light should not be approached nearer than 3 or 4 miles, as it is shoal.

Vessels should not approach the S.W. Cape with it bearing from W. round N., within the distance of 7 or 8 miles, as within that distance there is the Oklokonee Shoal of 3 ft., bearing East from the cape, and the South Shoals South of the cape, with breakers bearing S. ½ E., distant 6½ miles. These will be best understood by the chart, which, although not perfectly surveyed, are there shown with sufficient accuracy to warn the mariner to be on his guard.

ST. GEORGE'S SOUND.—The coast trends W.S.W. from S.W. Cape, 35 miles to Cape St. George, the south-easternmost point of St. George's Island, which is 24 miles long, and, with Dog Island, forms the South side of St. George's Sound. The East end of Dog Island is S.W. ½ W., 7 miles from S.W. Cape, and around it is the *Eastern entrance* to the Sound. Dog Island is about 6 miles in length.

Dog Island Light, on the S.W. end of Dog Island, and eastern side of the Middle Pass, was formerly shown from a lighthouse, built in 1839, and reported destroyed by a hurricane in 1873. The light was a fixed and flashing bright light, a bright flash being shown every minute. The approximate position of the lighthouse is lat. 29° 46′ 48″, long. 81° 38′ 30″ W.

Middle Pass is the channel into the port for large ships, having no bar, and 15 to 16 ft. in it at low water. Ships can get up to about 12 or 13 miles of the town, to load. The gulf inside is perfectly safe, and will hold a large fleet of ships; the ground good and soft; it is an excellent place as a rendezvous for cruizers. The Middle Pass entrance into St. George's Sound is between the East end of St. George's Island and the West end of Dog Island, and is about 3 miles wide; it will be difficult for strangers to find if Dog Island lighthouse is not re-established, as the points of both the islands are low sandy beaches, and there is a sand-beach on the main directly in front of the passage, so that it looks, at 3 or 4 miles distant, like one continued beach.

East Pass.—A new channel, called the East Pass, discovered by Lieutenant Duer, U.S.C.S., leads from sea to St. George's Sound, close in with the N.W. shore of Dog Island, with 20 ft. in the channel-way, by which vessels may be carried from sea to good anchorage in 3½ fathoms, under a reef, and from there around the westernmost point and shoal of Dog Island. On the bar of the East Pass there is, at high water, usually 17 ft. water. It would be unsafe to go beyond the 3¼-fathom anchorage under the reef without a pilot.

To enter, you must bring the S.W. end of Dog Island N., and steer N.N.W. ¼ W.; this will cross the bar. Keep this course until past the point of Dog Island, when haul up S.W. ¾ W. for the anchorage.

Swash Channel.—Stand in as before directed, until Dog Island bears N.E., then

APALACHICOLA.

steer W.N.W. ¼ W., and when the water deepens to 3¼ fathoms haul up for the anchorage.

The outermost buoy of the bar is a perpendicularly striped buoy, bearing S. by W., 2 miles from the lighthouse on Dog Island; the second, *black* buoy on the West bank, lies N.N.W. ⅜ W. seven-eighths of a mile; and the third, a *black* buoy, No. 3, on the Middle Ground, 1¼ mile in the same direction, with the lighthouse bearing E. ¼ N., distant 2¼ miles. Another *black* buoy, No. 5, lies W.S.W. ¼ S., 2¼ miles from the lighthouse, called Sand Island buoy, and a *black* buoy, No. 7, on the reef off the West end of St. George's Island, with the point bearing S.E. ¾ E., distant three-quarters of a mile. High water, full and change, at 1^h 31^m; rise of spring tides, 1·8 inches; neaps 0·8 inches.

The *Western Pass* into St. George's Sound is between the S.W. point of St. George's Island, and Vincent's Isle to the North of it.

The Lighthouse on the western point of St. George's Island shows this entrance, and exhibits a *fixed* light at 77 ft., in lat. 29° 35' 15", long. 84° 58' 29"; but is of little use as a day mark, as it does not appear until open to the westward of Cape St. George. The bar of this pass is about 60 ft. broad, and of hard sand. Vessels bound for it ought not to draw more than 12 ft. of water: for, when over the bar, if a vessel loads in the gulf, very little more will be found. A vessel of 12 ft. may lie aground on the soft bottom. There are vast numbers of oyster beds all along shore.

To the South of the point on which the lighthouse stands, there is a reef of shoal water extending to the distance of 7 miles from the land, with the Inner and Outer Channel and Fifteen-feet Swash across the shoal. At 1¼ mile from the lighthouse there are only 9 ft. water, and at 1¼ mile further, 7 ft. At 3¼ miles from the lighthouse, 12 ft., and 1¼ mile further, 10 ft.; this latter bearing about South 4¾ miles from the lighthouse. Beyond this is a 4¾-fathom shoal, with the southern channel across the reef.

Three miles to the eastward of the lighthouse, on St. George's Island, is New Inlet, having 3½ fathoms; and 2 miles N.W. from the same is Sand Island Pass, but neither of these are much use to navigation.

APALACHICOLA is situated on a bluff at the mouth of the Apalachicola River, on the West side. The river forms a broad estuary, called Apalachicola Bay, which connects with St. George's Sound. It is navigable for small vessels to the junction of the Chattahoochee and Flint Rivers. The Chattahoochee, the largest branch, is navigable for boats nearly 400 miles from the Gulf of Mexico. The town of Apalachicola is a port of entry, and is also a considerable cotton mart. It occupies a square mile, and is regularly laid out.

West Pass.—This pass is about 3¾ miles to the north-westward of the lighthouse, in lat. 29° 37', and is the principal entrance to Apalachicola; on each side of the entrance, banks project to the W.S.W., to the distance of 2½ miles. These are called the East and West Banks, both of which show breakers, and the West Bank has two sandy islets upon it, called Flag and Sand Island. On the bar is a fairway buoy, moored 2¼ miles S.W. of the entrance, and on the South point of St. Vincent Island is a beacon. This beacon is painted white, and can readily be seen at the distance necessary to get bearings. It is in the form of a pyramid, and neither of the pilot's ranges (which are of entirely different shape, and stand considerably to the westward) must be mistaken for it. The South point of the island of St. George is thickly wooded, and can be distinguished when in 10 fathoms, bearing N.E.

To cross the bar of the West Pass, you must bring the lighthouse of St. George to

CAPE ST. BLAS AND LIGHTHOUSE.

bear E. ¼ N., and the beacon on the point of St. Vincent Island N.E. by N., and steer N. by E. ¼ E.; this course will cross the bar in 13 ft. at mean low water. Keep this course until the lighthouse bears E. by S., when steer N.E. ¾ E. until the beacon bears W.N.W. and the lighthouse S.E. ¼ S., then steer E.S.E. 3¼ miles. When the channel stake bears N. ½ W., haul up N.E. ¼ N., which course you must keep until the town of Apalachicola bears N.N.W. ¼ W., and anchor in 11 ft., at mean low water.

Should you have a foul wind, and be obliged to turn to windward, keep the island of St. George on board; when fairly to the westward of the South point, the water is good near the beach, and the soundings are regular.

Bound to the *eastward*.—From the bar of the West Pass, steer S.E. by compass until the lighthouse on Cape St. George bears N. by W.; then haul up East, and when in 5 fathoms the channel has been cleared.

Bound to the *westward*.—When about 4 miles from the land, and in 5 fathoms, get the lighthouse to bear N.N.W., and steer East until it bears N. by W., when steer N.W. into 4½ fathoms. Continue on this course if bound to Apalachicola. When crossing the shoal keep the lead going, as the set of the currents is always uncertain. This channel was discovered in 1858 by Lieut. Duer, U.S.C.S.

Tides.—The rise and fall of tides at the western entrance to St. George's Sound is usually small. The time and height of high and low water are irregular and much influenced by the direction and force of the wind. The mean low water depth over the bar is 13 ft. The average rise and fall, 1·1 ft. There is generally but one high and low water in 24 hours, the rise and fall being greatest when the moon's declination is greatest. The high water remains at the same height, with small fluctuations, from 6 to 9 hours. When the moon's declination is very small, or northing, there are from 3 to 4 days, two small irregular tides in 24 hours.

Capt. Jos. Cornforth, of the brig *Harbinger*, of Newcastle, favoured us with the following directions:—

"From Cape St. Antonio or the Dry Tortugas, steer for the middle of St. George's Island. The soundings will be regular as you approach the land, which is extremely low all about, and they will shoalen gradually. The above course will take you to the eastward of St. George's Reef, extending 8 miles from the South point of St. George's Island. The soundings near the western edge of this reef are very irregular, and not to be depended upon. By running along the island you will meet the reef, and by keeping your lead going it will carry you outside; for should you fall to the westward and make Cape St. Blas, or to the westward of it and a S.W. wind come on, and blow hard, you are then between the two reefs, and the current setting along St. Blas Reef and winding into Apalachicola Bay, you will find some difficulty in keeping to windward; but, by being to the eastward of St. George's, you will have the current setting to the southward and westward toward the gulf, and farther to the eastward the stronger you will feel it going to windward.

CAPE ST. BLAS is a low point which trends to the South by East about 2 miles. From the woody part of the point a sandbank extends to S.S.E. to the distance of more than 3 miles; there are, also, from the S.S.E. to the S.S.W. of the point various shoal spots, or small sand-banks, which have not above 3½ fathoms over them; the southernmost of the whole of them lies 4 leagues from the point. Between these spots there are channels with 7, 8, and 9 fathoms of water.

The LIGHTHOUSE stands near the South point of Cape St. Blas. It shows, at 96 ft., a bright fixed light, varied every 1½ minute, or 90 seconds, by a bright flash. The light is visible 16 miles off, and is in lat. 29° 39′ 46″, long. 85° 21′ 38″ W.

ST. JOSEPH'S BAY.—The tongue of land, which forms the western boundary of the Bay of St. Joseph, is 17 miles long, and is so narrow, that, in some places, its breadth is not more than 2 cables' lengths. There are various breaks in it, by which during storms and the rains, the waters of the sea join those of the bay; and there is some wood on it. This piece of coast presents good anchorage, sheltered from the East winds, in 6 and 7 fathoms of water, which you will gain at a mile and a half from the shore.

To enter by the *Bar of St. Joseph*, it is necessary to coast the tongue of land in 4 or 5 fathoms, until you pass a small tongue of sand, which lies a little way without the mouth; thence you must steer N.E. and E.N.E for the interior, coasting always along the tongue, near which is the deepest water. There is always a swell on the bar. This bay is entirely unsheltered, especially in the winter, when the winds prevail from the S.W. and N.W. quarters, and raise much sea, in addition to the usual swell on the bar.

A *new passage* into St. Joseph's was laid out. The entrance is $2\frac{1}{4}$ miles W.N.W. from the lighthouse. Bring two pine trees, on the eastern side of the bay, painted white, in range (they then will bear N.E. by N.) and run for them; keep this course on, until you get the eastern shore aboard, when you may shape your course for the town, keeping the eastern shore aboard until you get to the southward of the lighthouse.

St. Joseph's Bay is 20 miles long, and 7 or 8 wide. The water becomes more shoal 4 miles from the S.E. end of the bay. There is a picturesque island 2 miles from the S.E. end, covered with live oak, cedar, and palms. The N.E. shore is intersected by ponds and lagoons.

From Cape St. Blas to the Bar of St. Andrew's the coast trends N.N.W. for 28 miles. From the Island of St. Andrew a sand-bank, with only 4 ft. water on it, extends on the direction of S.S.E. 10 miles. This shoal, which may easily be discovered from the water turning white on it, extends about a league and a half from the inner coast.

St. Andrew's Bay and Sound are easy of access, and good anchorage within, sheltered from all winds. One mile from the sea beach an arm extends 20 miles parallel with the coast. Ten miles from the sea another arm extends East for 30 miles, from 1 to 10 miles wide. The main body of the bay extends 12 miles North, with an average breadth of from 2 to 5 miles. The bay has some fertile settlements on its borders.

St. Andrew's Bay is covered by Crooked and St. Andrew's Islands, which form three entrances to the sound, leading to the bay. The eastern entrance is through the opening between Crooked Island and St. Andrew's Island; the depth is 18 ft. on the bar, and the channel, which is one-sixth of a mile wide, is close to Crooked Island. The distance between the islands is above two-thirds of a mile. The middle or main entrance is near the western end of St. Andrew's Island; the depth 21 ft., and the channel 200 yards wide. The western entrance is 2 miles N.W. of the latter; the depth on the bar 10 ft. This bay is very large, but as yet there can be no motive for vessels to go into it, except for temporary shelter. If such should be the case, the bay is said to be shoal, but from the main to the eastern entrance you have 3 fathoms in the sound, and good shelter under St. Andrew's Island.

From the Bay of St. Andrew to Santa Rosa Bay the coast trends N.W. by W. and W.N.W. for 48 miles; the trees are very thick on the coast between and close to the shore; there are also various hillocks of red and white sand.

STA. ROSA BAY.—The Island of *Santa Rosa* extends from Pensacola along the coast above 40 miles; but its greatest breadth does not exceed half a mile; there are many hillocks of white sand upon it, and some scattered trees. The eastern extremity of the island, which is the West point of the entrance of the bay of Santa Rosa, is a very low sandy point. The eastern point of the entrance of this bay may be known by some barrancas, or broken cliffs, of a bright red colour, which are upon it. The channel or mouth of the bay is very narrow, and has a bar, on which the depth is only from 6 to 7 ft. The entrance over the bar must be made with the prow to the N. by W., keeping in the middle of the channel until you pass the extreme East point of Santa Rosa Island, when, altering course to N.W., you may anchor as soon as you are sheltered. This bay is of extraordinary extent, being about 24 miles in length, to the eastward, and from 4 to 6 miles broad. The greatest depth in it is 3 fathoms, which is found only when you are to the West of the ravines, or red bluff, at the entrance; that is to say, at the distance of about 2 miles within the bar. The rest of the bay is full of shoals and old trees or stumps, so as merely to be passable for boats.

PENSACOLA BAY is a good harbour, but it has, at its entrance, a bar of only 22½ ft. of water.* The East point of the entrance is the West point of the long island of Santa Rosa, which is so low that the sea washes over it. To the N.W. of this point of the island, which is named *Point Siguenza*, there are some red gaps or gullies (*barrancas*) on the coast, which are in the highest land of it. At these gullies is a fort, and it is where the pilots reside. Between these and Siguenza Point is the entrance of the gulf, extending nearly East and West, and which would be very difficult to recognise from sea, were it not for the barrancas, which are unequivocal marks for knowing it by.

The principal channel entering Pensacola is from the S.S.E., leaving the Caucus Shoal projecting from the western point of entrance to the westward; and the East bank, stretching from Sta. Rosa Island to the eastward; it then sweeps round a Middle Ground which projects about half a mile from Point Siguenza, and turns to the eastward towards the bay.

Several buoys mark the entrance and the outermost channel. A perpendicularly *striped* buoy lies about 2½ miles from the entrance, nearly in range with the principal lights; the next is a *red* buoy, No. 2, nearly a mile in the same direction, marking the S.W. end of the East bank; West of this buoy half a mile is a *black* buoy, No. 1, and N.W. at a little farther distance from the same is a *black* buoy, No. 3; these two latter buoys mark the S.E. end of the Caucus bank. Nearly half a mile farther to the N.W. is a *red* buoy, No. 4. This buoy apparently marks the deep water of the channel, and the main channel course is to the westward thereof.

There are six lights exhibited to render the navigation of Pensacola Bay, or rather the entrance thereto, less intricate. These we shall next enumerate :—

Lights.—Near Barrancas, on the North side of entrance to the bay, in lat. 30° 20' 49" N., and long. 87° 18' 32" W., stands a lighthouse, 160 ft. in height, the upper two-thirds of which are painted black, and the lower third white. From this tower is shown, at 210 ft. above the sea, a *revolving bright* light every minute, visible 21 miles off.

---

* Extract from a letter written in the year 1873, respecting a ship which loaded timber at this port:—"I am glad to be able to write you of our being safe at sea, although we stirred up the mud coming over the bar, ship drawing 19 feet 7 inches aft. Some ships have lain a week and ten days after being laden, waiting water to take them out. One large ship belonging to Greenock, drawing 22 ft., had been lying fourteen days, and remained waiting."

In connection with the above light there is a beacon painted white, exhibiting a *fixed* light, visible 4 miles. This beacon is 470 ft. from the main light on a S.S.E. ¼ E. bearing; the two lights forming a range to cross the bar N.N.W. ¼ W.

Beacons.—On the West side of entrance, a little to the S.W. of Fort McRae, are the two Caucus beacons, painted white, bearing W.N.W. and E S.E., distant 619 feet from each other; these beacons in range W.N.W. will clear the Caucus Shoal.

Nearly half a mile to the eastward of the principal light are the *Barrancas Beacons*. These beacons are also coloured white, and bear N. ¼ E. and S. ¼ W. of each other, distant 506 ft.; they form a range to the westward of the Caucus Shoal.

Directions.—Vessels making the land should keep off 4 or 5 miles until they make the lighthouse, which cannot be seen until nearly opposite, as the trees on Rosa Island on the East, and on the mainland to the West, obscure it from the river. As will be noticed from the description of the lights, there are three ranges established for the Main Channel.

No. 1.—The *Bar Range*, marked by the front beacon and the Main Light. The course on this range is N.N.W. ¼ W., leaving the two first mentioned buoys close on your starboard side, and the first black buoy, No. 1, on your port side, at nearly half a mile distant.

No. 2.—The *Caucus Range*, marked by two beacons to the southward and westward of Fort McRae. The course on this range is W.N.W.

No. 3.—The *Barrancas Range*, marked by the two beacons to the eastward of the Main Light. The course on this range is N. ¼ E.

To enter.—When in 10 fathoms water bring the Pensacola light to bear N.N.W. ¼ W., and stand in for it. This will make the bar range. Cross the bar on this range, leaving the outer channel buoy and the buoy No. 2 close on starboard hand. When up with the mid-channel buoy, and on the Caucus range, run on this range, until up with the Barrancas range. Then stand in on the Barrancas range. When the Barrancas range crosses the Bar range, haul up E. ½ N. for the anchorage off the Navy Yard. The course from here to the city is N.N.E. ½ E.

Swash Channel.—Vessels drawing less than 14 ft. can make a direct course from the crossing of the bar, and the Caucus ranges by standing in for the front beacon of the Barrancas range on a N. by W. ¼ W. course, giving the N.W. point of Santa Rosa a berth of 120 yards.

Tides.—The ebb tide sets S.W. and the flood N.E., which should be carefully observed by all vessels going in, lest an ebb tide should drift them on the Caucus Shoal, or a flood upon the Middle Ground, as it sets directly over that shoal. The tides are irregular and affected by the winds, running with great velocity in the mouth of the port. The rise and fall of the tides at Pensacola is usually small. The time and height of high and low water are irregular, and much influenced by the direction and force of the wind.

The average rise and fall for two months hourly observations at Fort Pickens, in September and October, 1852, was 1 foot. The average rise and fall at the time of the moon's greatest declination was 1·5 ft.; at the time of least declination 0·4 foot. The rise of the highest tide observed above mean low water 2·2 ft.; the fall of the lowest tide 0·9 ft.

There is generally but one low and one high water in 24 hours, the rise and fall being greatest when the moon's declination is greatest, and the interval from high to low water being less by some hours than from low to high water.

MOBILE BAY.

About the time of the moon's declination being zero, the rise and fall is least, and there are sometimes two small tides in 24 hours.

Time of High Water.—At the time of the moon's greatest northern declination it is high water at Fort Pickens about 12¼ hours after the moon's meridian passage, or southing. This rule will be good for three or four days before and after the day of greatest declination, giving, however, the time too early before, and too late after that day by from 10 to 15 minutes a day.

The bay of Pensacola is an extensive inlet, entirely landlocked. Several rivers fall into it, of which the largest, called the *Escambia*, is navigable for small craft, but to the distance of a few miles only.

The town or city of Pensacola is situate on a plain, and defended by a fort on a sandhill, close under which all vessels must pass to the town. It lies along the beach of the bay, is of an obling form, and contains some spacious and elegant buildings. The streets are wide, crossing each other at right angles.

The United States Navy Yard is 8 miles from the city, and 5 from the entrance of the harbour, and covers nearly 80 acres of ground, enclosed by a high brick wall. From Pensacola to the lake and river *Perdido* is 4 leagues eastward. The entrance of the lake is narrow, with a bar of 4 or 5 ft.; but afterwards, widening considerably, it extends first to the N.E. and then towards the N.W. From this to a small lake, which is 4 leagues from Mobile Point, the coast presents a great number of hillocks along the shore. This lake is navigable for boats, and surrounded with high and thick wood. From Mobile Point, in the space of 3 leagues to the eastward, the coast is sufficiently remarkable, from the spaces it alternately presents, with and without wood.

MOBILE BAY is an estuary, about 30 miles in extent North and South. Just within the entrance, on the East side, a bight is formed in that direction, called Bon Secours Bay, which is about 10 miles deep, and the same dimensions in width; but to the northward of Bon Secours Bay the estuary is from 10 to 7 miles in breadth.

The River Mobile flows into the N.W. corner of the bay, and is navigable for large-sized steamers about 53 miles. At the entrance on the West bank is the town of Mobile, whence the principal articles exported, in 1877, were cotton to the value of £2,538,347, lumber, resin, staves, and shingles. Here is a capacious floating dry dock. A *fixed bright* light is exhibited on the iron screw-pile lighthouse erected on the ruins of Gladden Battery, which stands in 7 ft. water, three fifths of a mile East of Choctaw Point, mouth of Mobile River. The piles are painted *red*, and the dwelling and tower *straw* colour. The light, elevated 47 ft., is visible 12 miles off.

On the eastern shore, about 20 miles from the entrance of the bay, is the town of *Alabama*, and a little to the northward of it, on the western shore, is the entrance to the Dog River.

The entrance to the bay between Mobile Point on the East and Dauphine Island on the West is 2¾ miles wide; bu it is obstructed outside this by the Pelican and Sand Islands, stretching off 3 miles to th southward of Dauphine Island; and at 2 miles farther out, by a narrow bar, which carris 22¼ ft. at high water, and 20½ ft. at low water spring tides; and 22 ft. at high water, and 21 ft. at low water mean tides. Mobile has a bold entrance, and it should not be attempted without a pilot on any account. Even when there is not a fresh breeze the currents set strongly in various directions.

Dauphine Island is about 6 miles in length, and 2 in width, where broadest. The western part of it is a narrow tongue of land, with some withered trees; the rest of it is thickly covered with pines, which, at the East part, almost come down to the beach.

Dauphine Island forms the West part of the entrance of the Bay of Mobile; and on the North another island, named *Gillori*, succeeds it; from this to the continent there is a chain of shoals, through the straits, among which boats only can pass. Within a mile to the South of Dauphine Island is *Pelican Island*, which is arid and small; about 3 miles from Pelican, to the East of it, is *Mobile Point*, with its lighthouse.

Pelican Island is very narrow, and extends about 1½ mile S.S.E. To the south-eastward of Pelican Island, at the distance of 1¼ mile, is the western point of the Western Sand Island. This is the western point of the two Sand Islands, which extend to the S.E. nearly 2 miles, being separated by a little gut at 1½ mile from the western end. On the Eastern Sand Island is the light, to be noticed presently.

Little Pelican Island, upon Little Pelican Bank, divides the entrance between Pelican and the Sand Islands into two channels, termed respectively the Little Pelican Channel, next to the Sand Islands; and the Middle Pelican Channel next to the southern point of Pelican Island; while the narrow passage between Pelican Island and the shore of Dauphine Island is the Pelican Channel. N. by E., 2¾ miles from Sand Island, is Mobile Point, having on it Fort Morgan lighthouse, and a thicket of low trees.

Sand Island Lighthouse is a brick tower 125 feet high, painted black, and situated near the middle of Sand Island, which is situated well inside the entrance of Mobile Bay. The light shown is a *fixed* bright light, elevated 132 ft., and visible 17 miles off.

Mobile Point Lighthouse, on the East side of entrance to Mobile Bay, is a black iron tower, supported on an open framework on the S.W. bastion of Fort Morgan. The keeper's dwelling, painted white, is 50 yards south-westward of the lighthouse. A *fixed red light* is shown, elevated 50 ft. above the sea, and visible 13 miles off. Vessels drawing 18 feet of water may approach the lighthouse on the West side, within 300 yards. A *shoal* extends southward from the lighthouse 4 miles. Over this shoal, running E. and W., and lying three-fourths of a mile from the light, is the *Swash Channel*, with 6 ft. water.

Bell Boat.—At the bar is a bell boat, moored in about 8 fathoms, 2 miles distant from Sand Island lighthouse. Buoys and beacons are also placed to mark the Main Ship Channel and shoals.

Directions.—Vessels of heavy draught caught off this part of the coast in bad weather, with the wind from the southward, should endeavour to keep a wide offing, for there is no safe anchorage off the Mobile Bar, and no shelter nearer than Nassau or Naso Sound, 45 miles distant.

The land in the neighbourhood presents nothing remarkable to strangers, and the entrance is only discovered by the lighthouses and two high umbrella trees near Fort Morgan Point, and coming from the southward by the woods of Dauphine Island, which are first seen, and make as a wooded bluff. In the night a vessel should not come into less than 10 fathoms water until the Sand Island light is sighted. S.E. and South of the lighthouse at the distance of 12 miles, the depth is 15 fathoms.

MOBILE BAY.

Being off the bar, in 9 fathoms of water, sticky bottom, bring Sand Island lighthouse to bear N.N.W. ½ W., the lighthouse will then be open to the westward of the scattered trees on the East end of Dauphine Island; keep on this course until over the bar and in 4½ fathoms, then steer N. by W. ¼ W., until Sand Island bears W., passing halfway between Sand Island and Revenue Point Shoal, which is bare at high water. Then the course is N. ¼ E., passing Mobile Point, one-third of a mile distant, until Mobile Point lighthouse bears S.E. ⅜ S. The course from here is N.W. ½ N., passing midway between West Bank Buoy, No. 7, and Middle Ground buoy, No. 8, when the course is N. by W. ¾ W., 2 to 4 miles, to anchorage in Lower Fleet, where there is about 3¼ fathoms.

Those of 12 ft. draught, from abreast Sand Island may steer at once North, which will lead across the Middle Ground in 15 ft. water, and to an anchorage in the Upper Fleet in 12¼ ft. about midway between Dog River and the town of Alabama.

"From the report of the United States engineer officer superintending the improvements in Mobile Bay, it appears that during the past year the channel through *Dog River Bar*, about 9 miles below Mobile, has been completed to a width of fully 200 ft., with a depth of 13 ft., at mean low tide, throughout its entire length. It was intended to widen Choctaw Pass, at the mouth of Mobile Harbour, from 200 to 300 ft. during the past year, but on account of the freshets the work has been much delayed. The work on the pass is progressing and nearly completed, and when finished a clear channel of 13 ft. at mean low tide will be available from the lower bay to the city. In consequence of the above improvements, many British and foreign vessels have lately come up to the city and been freighted with cotton, lumber, and other articles, thereby saving the lighterage expenses as in former years."— *Mr. Consul Cridland*, 1876.

Mobile Bay Breakwater was commenced in September, 1876, and when completed will form a safe and secure place for loading vessels in the lower part of Mobile Bay, free from interruption by any weather that may occur. The breakwater is constructing in Navy Cove, and in January, 1878, was of sufficient length to afford protection to a number of vessels from North, N.E., and N.W. winds, and timber ships will find that it will give them ample security from the loss of timber by the said winds. The company have erected a building on the western end of the structure, with a mast 30 ft. high, to suspend a *light* from at night, and during the season of the arrivals and departures of vessels it will be kept constantly lit to designate the locality of the breakwater.

A bank with 6 fathoms lies E. by S., 5½ miles from Sand Island lighthouse, and E.N.E. ¼ E. 5 miles from the bar, hard bottom, light sand and black specks. Between this and the shore there are 8¼ fathoms water, sticky bottom.

A bank with 5¾ fathoms, hard sand, lies S.W., 3 miles from Sand Island lighthouse, and W. ¾ S., 3 miles from the bar.

Sand and Pelican Islands are increasing in length, and Pelican Channel is getting narrower every year. No dependence can be placed upon the soundings between Pelican and Sand Islands, as they so constantly change.

Pelican Bay is available only for vessels drawing less than 12 ft. water. The entrance from outside should not be attempted by strangers.

Grant's Pass is artificial, with a depth through in May, 1849, of 6½ feet at mean low water. The channel is staked on both sides at intervals of 150 to 200 yards; those on the North side being marked by bushes on their tops; those on the South side being bare.

TIDES.—The rise and fall of the tide at the entrance to Mobile Bay is usually small. The time and height of high and low water ar irregular, and much influenced by the direction and force of the wind.

MISSISSIPPI SOUND.—From Mobile Bay to the entrance of St. Louis Bay is 60 miles, the bearing being about W. ¾ S.; the chain of iislands which lies parallel to the mainland forms Mississippi Sound, fit for small coasting vessels, but only those that are well acquainted. The inland navigation commences between Dauphine Island and the main; here the bottom is principally composed of oyster beds, between which there are three shallow passages. *Huitres*, the northernmost, carries 3 ft. at high water. *Guillori*, or *Grant's*, the middle one, has only 2 ft. at ordinary tides; and the *Heron*, or southernmost of the three, has nearly 5 ft.

Dauphine Island, the easternmost of the group of islands forming the South part of Mississippi Sound, is about 9½ miles East and West, and at its East end about a mile in breadth, is thickly wooded; but its middle and western portions are very narrow and low. In 1852 a hurricane made a shallow opening through the centre of the island. The West end of the island appears to be increasing in extent.

Petit Bois Island, the East end of which lies W. by S. ¼ S., 1¼ mile from the West end of Dauphine Island, is 10 miles long, about E. by N. and W. by S., and three-quarters of a mile across in its broadest part, which is near the West end. At the southern side of the West extremity are two clumps of wood, 2 miles apart, with a group of large sandhills between them, distinguishing this from Horn Island (to the westward), which is entirely wooded. The hurricane of 1852, mentioned above, tore away about 2 miles of the East Spit of Petit Bois Island, leaving an opening between it and Dauphine Island 2¼ miles wide, and a channel through it from the Sound into the Gulf, carrying from 12 to 18 feet water. In 1855, however, this channel was only 30 yards in width, with 5 ft. water, and changed with every gale that occurred South of East or West.

Horn Island is about 3 miles to the westward of Petit Bois Island, forming between Horn Island Pass. The island is about 11¼ miles long East and West, and very narrow; it is wooded nearly its entire length, and on the East extreme is a square black beacon, and a mile to the westward of it is a signal post. The opening between it and Sand Island is 6 miles wide East and West.

A *lighthouse* is erected at the East end of Horn Island, West side of Horn Island Pass. It shows a *fixed light*, varied by a *red flash* every minute, elevated 42 ft., and 12 miles off. The lighthouse is situated about 500 yards within the extreme end of the island, and is a square wooden building, painted white, erected on screw piles, painted black. In thick weather a *fog-bell* is sounded once every 15 seconds.

Horn Island Pass.—A shallow sandbank stretches across, between Petit Bois and Horn Islands, with but 6 ft. water from Petit Bois to about midway, leaving close to Horn Island a narrow intricate cut into the Sound, with 17 ft. water.

Vessels approaching this pass from the eastward should keep in not less than 6 fathoms, until the beacon on the East end of Horn Island is in line with Round Island lighthouse N.W. ½ W.* This mark leads close to the westward of the outer

---

* Round Island is a small island situate about the middle of the Mississippi Sound; the lighthouse showing a *fixed* light.

shoal off Petit Bois, which has 5 ft., and lies with the sand-hills bearing E. by N. ¼ N. Being to the westward of this, bring the woods on the East point of Pescagoula River to bear N.N.W. ¼ W., a little open to the eastward of Horn Island beacon, and steer on this course until the large sand-hills on Petit Bois are nearly shut in with the woods on that island, E. ¾ N., which will be close outside the bar, in 4 fathoms. Then steer N. by W. ¼ W. until Horn Island beacon is in line with Round Island lighthouse N.W. ¼ W.; then N.W. ¾ N. until the northern side of the woods on Horn Island is open to the northward of the beacon, when alter course to W. by N., and anchor in 3½ fathoms, sticky bottom, from half to three-quarters of a mile to the westward of the point, with signal-staff S. by W. ¼ W.

Vessels drawing but 12 ft. may run in with the beacon in line with the woods on the West side of Pascagoula River, N.W. by N. After passing the bar, open out the woods gradually to the East, and round the point of Horn Island, as above directed. The course and distance from Mobile Outer Bar to the above pass are W. ¼ S. 24 miles.

Ship Island lies 6½ miles to the westward of Horn Island, and is 7 miles long E.N.E. and W.S.W. About 2 miles from the East end, where the island is about a mile broad, there is a grove of pine trees, and the western part is low and barren. A dangerous hard bank stretches off the N.E. end, having only 12 ft. water, at the extremity of a spit, with the above point W. ¾ N., distant 3 miles, and Ship Island light, E.S.E., 2½ miles. To the eastward of this the depths increase to 3 fathoms at about half a mile, leaving a channel close to Ship Island, carrying 20½ ft. at high water, and 18¾ ft. at low water springs, and 20¼ ft. at high water, and 19 ft. at low water mean tides. Near the beach, West of the pine grove, is a well of good water.

Light.—On the West end of Ship Island, in lat. 30° 12′ 54″, long. 88° 56′ 58″ is a white lighthouse, 48 ft. in height, and at 51 ft. above the sea exhibiting a *fixed red light*, visible 13 miles off. This light bears N.W. by N., 10½ miles from Chandeleur lighthouse.

Biloxi Bay.—Upon the main land, opposite Ship Island, is the *Bay of Biloxi*, of very little depth; and, about 9 miles to the East of it, the River Pascagoula discharges its waters. From this the coast trends nearly East, 21 miles, and then abruptly turns to the North, and forms the western side of the great bay of Mobile. The last portion of coast is shut in by the *Massacre* and *Dauphine Islands*, which lie to the East of Horn Island, with several smaller ones. The space of sea shut in between these islands and the coast is about 7 miles in width, but very shallow, and navigable for small vessels only. The shore is full of lagoons, with clayey bottoms; but, at 2 or 3 miles in from the shore, the land is covered with oaks and pines, and the third part is sandy.

N. by W. 13 miles from the northern extremity of the Chandeleurs is *Ship Island*; to the West of this, and at the distance of 5 miles, is *Cat Island*, and to the S.S.W. of that, a group of kays, named *San Miguel's*, or *St. Michael's*, extend from the southern shore. Between these and Cat Island is the pass into *Lake Borgne*, or *Blind Lake*, and *Lake Pontchartrain*, in which there is very little depth. From Lake Borgne, eastward, the main land trends to the E.N.E., and extends thus to the northward of Cat and Ship Islands, which lie about 6 miles from it.

Cat Island and Lighthouse is about 5 miles to the westward of Ship Island, and is 5 miles long East and West, but very narrow; the East end of the island is formed by a similar narrow strip of land, 4½ miles in extent North and South. A *fixed* and *flashing* light, the flashes occurring once in every 1½ minute, elevated 45 ft.

and visible 11 miles off, is shown from a pile lighthouse on the western end of Cat Island. The lighthouse is painted red, and the dwelling white.

On Merrill Shell Bank, W. ½ S. 4¼ miles from Cat Island light, is a lighthouse, on a screw pile foundation, which exhibits, at the height of 45 ft. above the sea, a *fixed bright light*, visible 11 miles off. A *Fog-horn* and *bell* is used in foggy weather.

Between Cat Island and Ship Island there is a great shoal, with little water on it, which, running out from the East end of the first, leaves a channel of only a mile in width between them. To the northward of the westernmost part of Ship Island, and at the distance of a mile and a half there is anchorage in from 4 to 5 fathoms; but, as the channel has a bar, with only 12 ft. on it, large vessels cannot reach it. *Ship Island* is narrow at its extremities; and its middle, which is broader, is covered with grass, and has some pine trees on it, but the rest of it is entirely barren. There is a well of very good water on its North shore, and near the middle of it.

From Ship Island, at 5 miles to the eastward, is the West end of *Horn Island*, and between them there is a little islet named *Peros*, or *Dog's Isle*. From Ship Island extends a shoal, which not only surrounds Dog's Isle, but advances so much to the East, that it leaves a channel of only one-third of a mile wide between it and Horn Island; and although in this channel there is a depth of 5 fathoms, yet on a bar at its entrance are only 15 ft. water.

Chandeleur Islands.—South, about 10 miles from Ship Island, is the northern part of the Chandeleur Islands, a string of islands which stretch to the southward, in the direction of the entrances to the Mississippi River.

The whole of these islands are low, with myrtle bushes scattered about them, and are very dangerous, inasmuch as they cannot be seen at any distance, and the wintry S.E. winds blow directly upon them; nevertheless, there is good shelter to be found within them, particularly at their northern part, in the Road of Naso.

Light.—On the northern extremity of Chandeleur Island, in lat. 30° 3′ 8″, long. 88° 52′ 36″, is a white lighthouse, 50 ft. in height, and the same above the level of the sea, exhibiting a *fixed* light, visible 13 miles off. This light is a good guide into Cat and Ship Island anchorages. There is safe anchorage inside the point on which the lighthouse is erected, in 4 fathoms water, the light bearing N.E., about 2 miles distant.

In entering the above anchorage you will double the northern part of the Chandeleurs in 5 or 6 fathoms water, at a distance of about a mile from the land, then turn in round from the West to the southward, keeping in 6, 5, or 4 fathoms, to the anchorage; should you prefer deeper water, do not run so far South, but come to an anchor when the North point bears E.N.E., in 5 or 6 fathoms. You may obtain fresh water on any of the islands, by digging wells, but there is no wood, except the myrtles, which produce green wax. (See page 197.)

RIVER MISSISSIPPI.—This noble river, in its higher latitudes, receives the waters of the Ohio and Illinois, and their numerous branches from the East, with those of the greater river *Missouri*, and other rivers, from the West. These mighty streams, united, are borne down with increasing majesty, through vast forests, and prairies, or meadows, and are at length discharged into the Mexican Sea, from the several channels or passes here noticed. From the mouth of the South Pass of the Mississippi, the distance to the *City of New Orleans* is about 90 nautic miles, and here the river is about as wide as the Mersey at Liverpool. There is no tide, but when the snow and ice of the N.W. melt, the water rises some 3 ft. above the level of the adjacent streets, and is kept from overflow by artificial banks called *levees*. On the river face of these levees are built the wharves at which ships discharge and load, and on the land side is the road along which all sorts of merchandize, whether exports or imports, have to pass. From the first to the last wharf at which sea-going ships find a berth on the New Orleans side is a distance of 7 miles. On the opposite side (Algiers) are the floating docks, and a few wharves where railway iron is discharged, and cotton-seed oil and cake loaded. The business on this bank is insignificant. The leveer are, or were, in 1878, in a very bad state of repair, making loading and discharging very troublesome.

The Mouths of the Mississippi are formed by mud-banks, continually increasing, which owe their origin to the great number of trees that incessantly float down the river, and ground at its entrance into the sea. These banks are not discernible from the mast-head at above 4 leagues distance, in clear weather, and are about 10 or 12 ft. above the water, covered with reeds and rushes.

Deer Island Lighthouse is situated at the head of the Passes, or at the point of land where the S.W. Pass and South Pass divide. It is a white building, in lat. 29° 8' 37" N., long. 89° 15' 6" W., and from it is shown a *fixed red light*. A *Fog-bell* is sounded at this lighthouse, two blows and one blow at alternate intervals of 10 and 20 seconds.

The Passes or principal entrances to the Mississippi are five in number, and the delta through which they run has been compared in form to that of the human hand, Pass a l'Outre representing the thumb, S.W. Pass the little finger, and N.E. Pass, S.E. Pass, and South Pass the intervening fingers. The principal of these entrances is now the South Pass, engineering operations (presently described) having cleared a good channel over its bar. Previously, the Pass a l'Outre and S.W. Pass were those chiefly used, their entrances being deepened by dredging. Naturally, these latter passages would have a depth of but about 14 ft. at their mouths, and the South Pass but 7 ft.; this is owing to the deposit of mud which takes place immediately the stream of the river loses its velocity by getting beyond the limits of the embankments formed by nature. The improvement of the South Pass of the Mississippi has been effected in the same manner as that of the Danube entrance in the Black Sea. Artificial embankments are formed, in order to continue the channel as far out as the deep water of the Gulf of Mexico, a deep channel by this means being scoured across the bar. We shall first describe the Pass a l'Outre, and then the others in succession to the westward.

Pass a l'Outre or Otter Pass, the north-easternmost of the whole, flows in an E.N.E. direction from the main river, also by two narrow outlets, one about 2 miles to the northward of the other. The southernmost lies N. by W. about 2¾ miles from the N.E. Pass; and at spring tides carries 13¼ ft. at high water, and 11¾ ft. at low water; and at mean tides 13 ft. at high water, and 12 ft. at low water. The North channel carries at high water springs 10½ ft., and at low water 9¼ ft.; and at mean tides 10¼ ft. at high water, and 9½ ft. at low water. The South channel is said to be deepening; and it has the advantage of the wind blowing more generally right up it, into the main stream of the Mississippi.

Light.—On the middle ground, at the North side of the entrance, is a black iron tower, 69 ft. high, which shows a *fixed and flashing bright light*. The flashes occur once every 45 seconds, elevated 77 ft. above the sea, visible 14 miles off.

A Steam Fog-whistle is sounded in thick weather for 15 seconds, at intervals of 45 seconds.

On the South side of the South bar is a stake beacon, and on the North side is a keg buoy; there is also a fairway buoy off this entrance, chequered red and white, in 7 fathoms water, about half a mile to the eastward of the bar, and E. ¾ S. from the lighthouse. About 3 cables to the northward of the keg buoy is the East signal post; and on the Middle Ground, about midway between the two channels, is the

North stake. At the West end of the Middle Ground, on the North side of the South channel, about 1½ mile within the bar, is another stake beacon.

North-East Pass, or *Old Ship Channel*, taking an easterly direction, discharges itself 3 miles southward from the Pass a l'Outre by two small mouths a little more than half a mile apart North and South. The South channel carries at high water springs 10¼ ft., and at low water 8¾ ft.; and at mean tides 10 ft. at high water, and 9 ft. at low water. The North channel carries at high water springs 10½ ft., and 9¼ feet at low water; and at mean tides 10½ ft. at high water, and 9½ ft. at low water.

On the mud-bank which separates the above mouths are two stake beacons, the southernmost having a barrel on the summit; and on the South side of the South channel is another stake beacon. On the North bank of the fork, W. ¼ N. from the South bar, and W. ¼ S. about 2¼ miles from the North bar, is a conspicuous *white* tower, formerly a lighthouse, the summit of which is 70 ft. above the sea.

South-East or Balise Pass, or *Main Ship Channel* is situated S.S.W. 5 miles from that of the N.E. Pass, and N.E. by N. 6¼ miles from the South Pass; and the bight between forms Garden Island Bay.

N.W. by W. 4½ miles from the bar, on the South bank of the main fork, is a large blockhouse, with a lofty signal post, called the Balise or Beacon, which from the N.E. is visible about 9 miles, in 15 or 18 fathoms water, and serves as a guide to the pass and anchorage. Vessels of 14½ ft., in being dragged through the soft mud, often lie aground on the bar for several days. The channel at high water springs carries 11¼ ft., and at low water 9¾ ft.; and at mean tides 11 ft. at high, and 10 ft. at low water.

SOUTH PASS lies S.W. by S. 6¼ miles from S.E. Pass, and E.N.E. about 15 miles from the S.W. Pass; and the dangerous bight between is called East Bay. On the bar at spring tides, previous to the improvements, there was a depth of 7¾ ft. at low water; and at mean tides 9 ft. at high water, and 8 ft. at low water.

Light.—On the West bank, near the South point of Gordon Island, N.W. ¼ W., 2 miles from the South bar, is a slate-coloured wood tower on the keeper's dwelling, 54 ft. high, from which is exhibited at 60 ft. above the sea a *revolving bright light*, every 1½ minute, visible 13 miles off. *Red lights* are shown on the jetties.

A *Whistle-buoy* is placed off South Pass. It is painted *black* and *white* in vertical stripes, giving frequent blasts of a 10-inch whistle, and is moored in 10 fathoms water, with the entrance between the jetties bearing N.W. by N., about 1 mile, and South Pass lighthouse N.W. Position, lat. 28° 58′ 45″ N., long. 89° 8′ 0″ W.

The Jetties, or artificial banks of the pass, constructed by Mr. James B. Eads, commence at what was the land's end, and extend seaward over the bar, and out into deep water. They are placed about 950 feet apart, and are parallel with each other. The East jetty is about 2¼ miles in length, and the West jetty about 1½ mile. The jetties are built of willows and stone. The results of this work, commenced in June, 1875, have been—1st, a most remarkable deposit of sand and clay over the whole space outside of the jetties, amounting to several hundred acres, now dry at average tide. 2nd, a deepening of the bar throughout its whole extent, so that where there was formerly but 7½ to 16 ft. of water, there is now from 23½ to 95 ft., and also the formation of a wide, straight channel, which can be navigated without the least difficulty. 3rd, a deepening of the old bar and gulf bottom seaward of the ends of the jetties. This action is due to the strong current discharged through the ends of the jetties and the cross current of sea water, also increased by the jetties, so that although upwards of 5½ millions of cubic yards of material have been excavated in the channel between the jetties, and thrown out to sea, yet there is deeper water immediately in front of and adjacent to the ends of the jetties than previously existed. The progressive development of the channel has of course been subject to fluctuations, depending upon the condition and progress of all the works, and upon the varying conditions of the river; but taking the whole history of the channel into consideration, the progress towards a depth of 30 ft., and width sufficient for all the wants of commerce has been steady and sure.

The result officially reported by the engineers, in 1877, is a channel, nowhere less than 200 ft. wide and 22 ft. deep, from the South Pass between the jetties to the deep water of the Gulf of Mexico, the width between the 22-feet curves varying from 200 ft. to more than 500 ft. A practicable channel of 22 ft. 4 in. exists through the whole extent of this portion of the pass. At the head of the pass a channel 264 ft. wide and 22 ft. deep exists, and a practicable channel of 23 ft. deep is also found.

South-West Pass carries generally 14½ ft. at high water, and 12¾ ft. at low water springs; and 14 ft. at high water, and 13 ft. at low water mean tides. This pass runs nearly straight about N.N.E., and the banks are so bold that in many parts there are 7 fathoms water almost alongside them.

It is to be observed, however, that no sure directions can be given. Mud knolls are continually formed and washed away by the action of the winds and currents, and the buoys and stakes are moved accordingly. During the year 1876, 128 vessels struck on the bar, and remained there on an average twenty hours each. The longest detention of a steamer (the *State of Alabama*, drawing 20 ft. 4 in.), was 360 hours, that of a sailing ship (the *Success*, drawing 18 ft.), was 117 hours.

The highest tides occur at the moon's greatest declination.

Light.—On the low marshy land, forming the western side of S.W. Pass, and near the entrance of the pass, stands a white lighthouse, of iron, 68 ft. high, in lat. 28° 58′ 53″ N., long. 89° 22′ 20″ W. From it is shown a *fixed bright light*, elevated 128 ft. above the sea, and visible 17 miles off.

A *Steam Fog-whistle* is established 20 yards S.E. of the tower. The whistle will be sounded in thick weather, with blasts of 5 seconds, at alternate intervals of 5 and of 45 seconds.

In approaching the bar, vessels should not pass inside of 10 fathoms without a pilot. When the outer bar buoy (black can) bears about N. by E., steer for it. There is good anchorage near this buoy in 8 to 10 fathoms. Three red buoys mark the channel over the bar.

PILOTS.—Vessels are seldom detained from want of pilots or tow boats, as they cruize at sea from 10 to 15 miles off the passes in fair weather, and lie in readiness just within the bars in foul weather. Steam Tugs sometimes run out as far as 40 miles or more from the mouths of the river. The pilot boats are from 50 to 80 tons, and carry a number on their jib on the starboard side and on the port side of the mainsail, besides wearing a blue flag. The steam tugs are similar to those of the Havana, but have much more power.

Directions for Approaching the Mississippi.—The currents between the delta of the Mississippi and the Tortugas and West end of Cuba are so uncertain—fogs and haze so prevail, especially in the summer and fall of the year—the mud banks of the forks are so low, the tops of the rushes which cover them being only from 10 to 12 ft. above the sea—and the winds so generally blowing from the eastward—that vessels approaching from the S.E. should strike soundings well to windward.

The line of 100 fathoms lies only 14 miles S.E. of the South Pass, whence it runs E.N.E. for about 50 miles to lat. 29° 10′ N. (the parallel of l'Outre Pass) on the meridian of 88° W. The depths within this decrease rapidly to the passes, the 50-fathom line being but 7 miles off.

In the night, if the weather is clear, the lights will guard from all dangers off the mouths of the Mississippi; but, if hazy, vessels should not run down for any of the passes into less than 50 fathoms; if less is obtained, she should immediately haul seaward.

In the day time, the first objects seen will probably be the light towers or Balise Flag, visible at 9 or 10 miles off, or the masts of any shipping that may be aground or waiting at anchor off the bars. When the river is low, the dirty white muddy waters will be met with about 10 miles, and when high about 15 miles off. In some places dark patches will appear in the river water, and strong ripplings which have an alarming appearance; but there is no danger, except a few shifting mud-banks which lie close to the delta.

In approaching from the southward or south-westward very great attention must be paid in checking the latitude, for the bank is so steep that the first cast may be 35 fathoms at only 3 or 4 miles from the South Pass; and it is equally abrupt, if not more so, off the S.W. Pass. Beating up from the westward, the pilotage may be made by the lead, for on a line between the Ship Island shoal, and the S.W. extremity of the delta, there is no greater depth than 20 fathoms.

In running from abreast the l'Outre to the S.E. Pass in the day time the depth may be 10 fathoms, but in the night time it should not be less than 15 fathoms. Being off the former in 15 fathoms, a S.S.E. course will lead round the N.E. Pass in 10 fathoms; and from thence a S.S.W. course $4\frac{1}{2}$ miles will carry to an anchorage in 8 to 11 fathoms off the S.E. Pass, with the Balise Tower bearing W. by N. $\frac{1}{2}$ N.

The streams issuing from the forks take generally an easterly direction, but at the edge of the white water there is often a strong south-westerly set, which is apt to drive a vessel to leeward of the passes, and cause her some delay in getting back again. To the westward of the delta the current is variable; the lead should therefore be closely attended. The thermometer will also be found a useful guide.

Anchorage.—In the event of being driven to the northward of the eastern mouths by a strong S.E. gale, which sometimes happens, shelter will be found, in a case of necessity, round the northern extremity of Chandeleur Islands, about 55 miles to the northward of l'Outre Pass. Care should be taken to skirt the Chandeleur Islands in not less than 8 fathoms until near the North end. The bottom will be light blue mud mixed with white shells, and further in the shells will be broken. The North end of the Chandeleur Islands may be rounded at 1 mile distant, and a sheltered position found at 2 miles to the S.W. of the light in 4 or 5 fathoms. Observe, however, that when the wind lulls, and comes from the N.W., the water will fall 4 to 6 feet. In thick weather there is no other guide on the first approach but the lead; but if the land is visible, the spit which runs off from the East side of Chandeleur, and breaks with East and S.E. winds, may be rounded by the eye. (See page 193.)

APPENDIX.

CAUTIONARY WEATHER SIGNALS.

The chief of the United States' Signal Service calls attention to the following:—

"The cautionary signal of the Signal Service, United States' army—a red flag with black square in the centre by day, and a red light by night, displayed at the office of the observer and other prominent places, signifies:—

"1. That from the information had at the Central Office in Washington, a probability of stormy or dangerous weather has been deduced for the port or place at which the cautionary signal is displayed, or in that vicinity.

"2. That the danger appears to be so great as to demand precaution on the part of navigators and others interested—such as an examination of vessels and other structures to be endangered by a storm—the inspection of crews, rigging, &c., and general preparation for rough weather.

"3. It calls for frequent examination of local barometer and other instruments by ship captains or others interested, and the study of local signs of the weather, as clouds, &c., &c. By this means those who are expert may often be confirmed as to the need of the precaution to which the cautionary signal calls attention, or may determine that the danger is over, estimated or past."

Orders to display cautionary signals will be issued from the office in Washington whenever they are considered necessary. These orders will be sent, at such hours as the necessity of the case may demand, to the observers at the chief seaports on the coast of the United States.

INDEX.

Abaco, 142
Abbot's Rock, 11
Absecum, Inlet and Light, 87
Adam's Fall, 63
Agua Kays, 167
Ajax Reef Beacon, 149
Alabama, 188
Alatamaha Sound, 137
Albemarle Sound, 114, 116
Alcatraces Kays, 169
Aldridge's Ledge, 18
Allerton Point, 17
Alligator Reef, 147, 150
Altamaha River, 136
Amelia Island, 139, 140
American Shoals Bcn., 151
Ammen's Rock, 5
Anas Kay, 171
Anastasia Id. & Lt.-ho., 141
Anchoring Island, 86
Annapolis, Point, River, and Roads, 108
Ann, Cape 6
Anne, Cape, and Harbour, 5, 7
Antonio, Cape, 160
Apalache and River, 181-2
Apalachicola, 183
Apple Island, 16
Aqua-vitæ Rocks, 12
Archer's Rock, 9
Arco de Canasi, 173
Ashepu River, 128
Asia Bank, 33
Assateague Inlet, Island, and Light, 95
Astoria Ferry, 70
Augusta, 129
Avery's Rock, 7

Babson's Ledge, 8
Bache Shoal & Reefs, 153
Back River Light, 99
Bahama Banks, 160-1, 164, 168
Bahia de Cadiz Lt., 169
—— Honda, 146, 151, 153
Baker's Island, 6
—— —— Lights and Breakers, 9, 10

Bald Head, 119
Baltimore and River, 108, 110
Bar Neck Wharf, 44
Barnegat Inlet, Light, and Sound, 81, 83—85
Barnett's Harbour, 166
Barnstaple, 21
Barrancas Light, 186
Barrel Rock, 15
Barslow Rock, 46
Bartlett's Reef and Light, 59, 61
Basin Bank, 149
Bass River and Light, 36, 39
Bass Rip Shoal, 31-2
Battery Island, 120
Baum's Windmill, 113
Bayport, 179
Bayside Beacon, 77
Beach Channel, 125
Bear Cut, 145, 152
Beaufort Harbour and Directions, 117-18
Beavertail Light, 46
Bedford Reef, 53
Bella Paps, 169
Bell Boat, 94
Bemba, 171
Bemini Isles, 165
Ben's Point, 53
Berry Islands, 142
Beaufort River, 130
Beverley, Harbour and Bar, 8, 10
Billingsgate Island, Light, and Shoal, 21-2
Billingsport, 94
Biloxi Bay, 192
Bird Island Light, 17, 43, 45-6
Biscayne Kay, 145, 152
Bishop and Clerks & Light, 37
Bishop's Rock, 47
Black Bay Rock, 61
Blackbeard Island, 136
—— Buoy Reef, 61
—— Fish Bank, 95
—— Flat, 33

Blackland, 24
Black Ledge, Channel, and Point, 54, 59—61
—— Rock, Channel, and Harbour, 10, 12, 18, 60, 64-5
Blackstone's Island, 106
Blackwell's Island, 70-1
Blake's Channel, 93
Blanco Kay, 170
Block Island & Soundings, 79—81
—— Island, Channel, and Lights, 48-9
—— Island Sound, 56
Bloodsworth Island, 107
Blue Hills, 18
Blunt's Channel, 90
Bobell Rock, 46
Boca Ratones, 144
Body Island and Light, 113
Bolle's Hill, 56, 60
Bombay Hook and Light, 92
—— —— Roads and Point, 93
Bone Kay, 153
Borgne Lake, 192
Boston to New York, 1
—— Harbour, Bay, and Lights, 5, 13, 14, 19
Botany Bay Island, 128
Bottle Channel, 122
Bowditch's Ledge, 9
Brandywine Shoal & Light, 90, 92
Branford Reef, 63
Brant Point and Light, 20, 33
Bread and Cheese, 70
Breakwater Light, 91
Brenton's Reef and Light, 46-7
Brewerton Channel and Lights, 110
Brewster Islands and Bar, 15
Brewster Island, Little, 14
Bridgeport and Lights, 64
Brigantine Shoals & Beach, 87

U. S.—Part II.

2 D

INDEX.

Brimbles Rock, 10, 12
Broad Sound Channel, 18
Broken Rips and Shoal, 27, 38
Brother, North, 69
Brothers Reef, 165
Brown Shoal, 90
Brown's Island, Bank, and Reef, 20, 63
Brunswick Port, 137
Budd's Reef, 66
Bug Light, 38
Bulk Head, 93
Bull River, 127
—— Shoal, 143
Bull's Bay and Island, 124
Bunker Hill Monument, 16
Bush Kay and Lt., 158-9
Bushy Kay, 169
Butler's Flats, 45
—— Hole, 27, 33, 38
Buzzard's Bay, 28, 40, 43

Cabezas Kay, 169
Cabrestante Bank, 173
Calf Island, 18
Calibogue Sound, 131
Camacho Point, 171
Camarioca Peaks and River, 169, 171
Canaveral Cape, 143, 145
Caninna River, 172
Cape Island, 91
Cape Roman Shoal, 176
Cap, The, 97
Captain's Hill, 20
—————— Islands & Light, 66
Captive Pass, 177
Cardenas Bay, 171
Carolina Shoals, 119
——, Remarks on the Winds, &c., on the Coast of South, 126
Carysfort Lt.-ho., 148-9
Cashe's Ledge, 4
Casinas Point Lt.-ho., 181
Castle Hill Point, 46
—— Island Rock, 18
—— Pinckney Light, 125
Cat Island, 9
Cat Island Lighthouse, 192
—— Kays, 166
Caucus Shoal, 187
Cayo Sal, 167
Cedar Island and Point, 19, 52, 107
Cedar Kays, 179-80
Centre Island and Point, 68
Centreport Inlet, 67
Centurion Buoys, 18
Cerberus Shoal, 51
Chandeleur Ids., 193, 197
Channel Islands, 22
Chapel Hill, 77

Chappaquiddick Id., 28, 29
Charles, Cape, and Light, 94, 96, 97, 99
Charles's Neck, 46
Charles River, 19
Charleston, 85
Charleston Lights, Buoys, and Channels, 125
Charlotte Harbour, 177
Chatham Bay, 176
Chatham, Beach and Harbour, 19, 25-6
Chattahoochee River, 183
Chehaw River, 128
Cherrystone Inlet & Light, 104
Chesapeake, 83, 98
————, Directions for entering the, 102
———— Entrance Lts. and Signals, 99, 100
Chester Island, 93
—— River, 109
Chilmark, 29
Chincoteague Inlet and Shoals, 83, 95, 97
Chop and Light, East and West, 35
Choptank River, 108
Christiana River, 93
Clark's Point, Bank, & Lt., 4, 43
Clay Ponds Lights, 22
Clearwater Harb. & Id., 178
Clement's Island, 106
Cliff Beacons Light, 33
Clump Islet, 59
Coasters Channel and Harbour, 47, 90
Cockenoe's Island, 66
Cockspur Island Lt., 133
Cod, Cape, Harbour, Peninsula, and Light, 2, 19, 22-3
Coffins Patches Bcn., 150
Cohansey and Light, 88, 92
Cohassets Light, 17
Cohasset Rocks, 15
Cold Spring Harbour and Inlet, 68, 87
Cold Wall—Gulf Str., 163
Coles Care Shoal, 129
Colorados & Bank, 160, 174
Columbus, Fort, 78
Combahee Banks Bcn., 128
Comet Shoal, 174
Comfort Point, 77, 84
Compass, Variation of, 1
Conanicut Island, 46, 48
Conch Reef Bcn., 148, 150
Concord Point and Light, 112
Connecticut River, 61
Conover Beacon, 77
Coosaw and River, 127-8

Cormorant Rock, 43, 45-6
Cornfield Point and Reef, 62
Corson's Inlet, 87
Cove Point, 107
Cow Harbour, 67
Cows Rocks, 65
Cowyard, 21
Craighill Channel and Lts., 111
Crams Bank, 70
Crane Neck Point, 67
Crane Reef, 62
Craney Island and Light, 102
Craven's Shoal, 80
Crawfish Kays, 156
Cristo Kay, 168
Crockers Reef Bcn., 150
Crocus Reef and Bcn., 150
Croket's Bay, 107
Crook, 48
Cross Ledge and Light, 91, 92
—— Rip Light, 33
Crow Harbour, 138
Crow Shoal, 52, 90
Cruz del Padre Kay & Lt., 170
—— Kay, 168
Crystal River, 179
Culloden Point, 51
Cumberland Sound, 138
Currents between Capes Fear and Hatteras, 121
Currituck Inlet and Strait, 113
Cuttahunk and Lt., 28, 40

Damas Kays, 167
Dames Point Lt.-ho., 141
Darien Inlet, 136
Daufuskie Id. and Lts., 131
Dauphine River, 188-9, 191
Davis Reef, 150
Davis's Bank, 32
—— Ledge, 17
—— South Shoal, 30
Deadmen's Kays, 167
Deer Island Lt.-ho., 194
Deer Island and Point, 16, 17
Delaware Bay and River, 88—93
Derby Wharf, 11
Devil Island Bank, 112
Devil's Back, 15
—— Bridge Shoal, 40
Diamond Shoal, 114
Diana Kay and Light, 171
Dobell Rock, 43
Doboy Inlet, 136, 137
Dog Bar and Ledge, 7, 8
Dog Island and Lt., 182
—— Kays, 161, 167

INDEX.

Dog River, 188, 190
Dog's Isle, 193
Drum Point, 107
Dry Inlet, 144
Dry Romer, 78
—— Tortugas and Lt.-ho., 151, 158—160
Duck Kay, 153
Dumbarton, 143
Dumpling Rocks and Light, 43, 45
Dutch Island and Light, 48
Duxbury Pier Light, 20
Dyer's Reef, 47

Eagle Island, 10, 12
East Bank Shoal, 122
—— Church, 7
Eastern Bay, 109
—— Point and Light, 7
Eastham, 25
East Harbour River, 25
—— Greenwich, 48
—— Point Channel, 57
—— River, 50, 69, 76
Eaton's Neck and Light, 67-8
Edgar Town, 28-9, 35
Edisto Inlets, 127
Eel Grass Ground, 57
—— River, 20
Egg Harbours, 85, 87
—— Island Flats, 45
—— —— Light, 92
—— Rock and Light, 14, 18, 20
Egmont Channel, 157
—— Island and Lt.-ho., 177-8
Elbow Ben., Florida Reefs, 149
—— Kay Light, 161
Eldridge Shoal, 39
Eleven-feet Bank, 45, 60
Elisha's Point, 21
Elizabeth Islands and Light, 28, 40, 41
—— Roads, 102
Elliots Kay, 149, 153
Ellis's Spindle, 57
Elm-tree and Light, 77, 80
Escondido, Puerto, 173
Execution Rocks, 66
—————— and Light, 69

Fairfield Bar, 64, 66
Fair Haven, 45, 64
Fairweather Island & Light, 65
Falcones Kays, 169
Falkner's Island and Light, 62
Falmouth, 28, 42
False Approach, 100

False Channel, 100
—— Hook Channel and Shoals, 78, 80
—— Spit, 17
Farallones Rocks, 165
Faun Beacons, 18
Fear, Cape, and River, 113, 119, 120
Federal Point & Light, 119
Fenwick Hall, 62
—————— Island, Shoal, and Light, 94, 97
Fernandina, 139
Field Rocks, 8
Fig Island Beacon Lt., 133
Filor's Observatory, 155
Fingers Bank, 120
Fippenies Bank, The, 5
Fire Island and Lights, 74, 75, 79, 82
Fish Island, 66
Fisher's Island and Sound, 51, 54, 56-7
Fisher's Rock, 73
Fisherman Island, 100
Fishing Rip, 33
Five-fathom Bank and Lt., 83, 88
Five-mile Beach, 87
—————— Point and Light, 63
Flag Island, 183
Flat Neck Point, 66
Fleming Kay, 155
Flint River, 183
Flogger Shoal, 91
Flood Rock, 70, 72
Florida Cape and Lt.-ho., 144, 145, 148
—— Reefs & Kays, 145—150
—— Strait, 160-1
Flushing Bay, 69
Flynn's Knoll, 78
Fog Point Light, 107
Folger Shoal, 92
Folly Island, 127
Fort Flat and Point, 8, 45, 59
—— Pond and Bay, 51
—— Sumter Light, 125
Fourteen-feet Bank, 33, 93
—————— Channel, 80
Fowey Rocks Beacon and Lighthouse, 144, 149, 152
Fox Island, 48
Frank's Ledge, 59, 60
French Reef and Beacon, 147, 149
Fresh Brook Hollow, 25
Friar's Head, 67
Frying Pan Shoals & Light, 119
—————— and Ripple, 70, 71

Gale's Ledge, 11
Galindito Kay, 170
Galindo, 170
Gallatin Rocks, 37
Gallop Island, 17, 18
Gallows Hill, 71
Gammon, Point, and Light, 28, 36
Gangway Rock, 37, 57, 58, 69
Garden Kay Light-ho., 152, 158-9
Gardiner's Island & Light, 50, 52
Gaskin Bank, 129, 133
Gay Head and Light, 28-9, 39, 40
Gazelle Rock, 37
Gedney's Channel & Lights, 77, 79
General's Mount, 140
George Lake, 140
George's Bank and Shoals, 2
—————— Island, 16
Georgetown Harbour and Light, 121-2
Georgia, 131
Gibb's Point, 71
Gilbert Bar, 144
Gilgo Inlet, 75
Gloucester Harbour and Light, 7
Gloucester Point, 94
Goat Island, 47
Gooseberry Ledge, 9, 10
—————— Neck, 43
Goose Island, 63
Goshen Point and Reef, 60, 61
Governor's Island, 78
Graves Rocks, 15
Gray's Rock, 10
Great Bahama Bank, 161, 165
Great Egg Harbour, 83
—— George's Bank, 2
—— Ledge, 44
—— Mill Rock, 70-1
—— Point Light, 29, 33
—— Rip Shoal, 32
—— Rock, 37
—— Swamp, 87
Grecian Shoals Beacon, 149
Greenberry Point and Lt., 108
Green Island, 15, 135
Greenport & Light, 52-3
Green Run, 95
Grenville Inlet, 144
Gridiron Rock, 71
Griswold Fort Monument, 61
Groton, 59, 60
Grove Point, 112
Guanos Point, 173

INDEX

Guillori Passage, 191
Gulf Stream, 80, 142, 144, 148, 161—163
—— Weed, 83
Gull Banks, 95, 97
—— Island Light, 54
Gullivan Bay, 176
Gull Reef, 53
—— Rock, 165
—— Rocks, 47
Gun Kay and Lt.-ho., 160, 166
Gunpowder River, 112
Gurnet Point & Lights, 20

Hacket's Point, 109
Halbert Point, 7
Hale, Fort, 63
Half-tide Rock, 15, 37
Half-way Rock, 8, 10, 12
Hallet's Cove and Point, 70, 71
Hampton Roads, 101
Handkerchief Shoal and Light, 27
Hangsman Rocks, 16
Harding Ledge, 15, 17
Hardy's Rocks, 9, 10
Hart Island, 109, 112
Haste Shoal, 10
Hatchett's Reef & Point, 61
Hatfield's Store, 86
Hatteras, Cape, &c., 83, 113—116
Hatter's Dock, 70
Havana Harbour, 173—175
Havre de Grace, 111
Hawes Shoal, 35
Hawke Channel, 152
Hawkins Point and Light, 110
Hay Beach Point, 53
Head Fort, 13
Hedge Fence Shoal, 39
Hell Gate, 70
Hempstead, Bay and Harbour, 68
Hempstead Hill, 76, 84
Hen & Chickens Rks., 147, 165
Hen and Chickens Reef and Light, 43, 62, 90, 96
Henlopen, Cape, & Lights, 88-9, 97
Henrietta Rock, 45
Henry Bank, 165
Henry Capo to Charleston, 113
Henry, Cape, Light, 97, 99
Hereford Inlet and Light, 87
Herring Cove, 19, 24
Herod's Point, 67
Heron Passage, 191

Hetzel Shoal, 143
Hicacal Kay and Lt., 168-9
Highland Lts., New York, 76
Highlands Light, Cape Cod, 22
High Pine Ledge, 20
Hilsboro' Inlet and River, 144
Hilton Head, 129
Hog Island Inlet, 75
—— —— and Light, 96, 97
—— Point. 68, 107
Hog's Back, 60, 70
Hogshead, Point, 63
Hogstack Island, 92
Hole-in-the-Rock, 142
Holmes Hole and Light, 28, 29, 35
Homosassa River, 179
Hook Channel, 78, 80
Hooper's Island and Light, 107
Horn Id. Lt.-ho., 191
Horn Point, 109
Horn's Hook, 71
Horse-shoe Channel, 120
—— —— Reef, 57
—— —— Shoal, 39, 101
Horton's Point & Light, 66
Hospital Point, 11
—— —— Shoal, 16
House Island, 10
Howell Point, 112
Howland's Rock, 20
Hudson River, 76
Huitres Passage, 191
Hummocks, 24, 57
Hunting Creek, 105
Hunting Id. and Lt., 128
Huntington Bay and Harbour, 67
Hunt's Harbour, 74
Hursell Rock, 45
Hyannis and Harbour, 23, 36
Hypocrite Channel, 15, 18

Indian Riv. Inlet, 94, 97, 143
Inez Rock, 45
Inner Middle Ground, 100
In-shore Channel, 60
Iron Hills, 173
Isaac Island, 100
Isaac Shoal, 159
Isle of Wight Shoal, 94

Jacksonville, 140, 141
James Island and Point, 108
James Island, 182

James River, 102
James's Head and Lights, 26
Jaruco Mountains, 173
Jefferson, Port, 67
Jekyl Id. and Sound, 137-8
Jersey, 77, 79
Joe Flogger Shoal, 92
Joiner's Bank, 129
Jones's Falls, 110
Juan Ponce de Leon Bay, 176
Judith Point and Light, 48
Jupiter Inlet & Lt.-ho., 144

Kay Sal Bank, 167
—— West & Lights, 146, 148, 151, 153—157
Kedge's Strait, 107
Keeper's Shoal, 129
Kelly's Rock, 16
Kent Island Spit, 108-9
Kill Van Kull, 78
Kimberley's Reef, 63
Knight's Kay, 153

La Costa Island, 177
Ladies Kays, 167
Lafayette, Fort, 77
Lambert's Point and Light, 102
Largo Kay, 146
Latimer's Reef and Spindle, 57
Lavinia Banks, 157
Lawrence Reef and Point, 69
Lazaretto Point and Light, 110
Leading Point and Light, 110
Ledge Shoal, 39
Legare Anchorage, 152
Lewistown Roads, 89
L'Homme de Dieu Shoal, 39
Lighthouse Island, 17
Lime Rocks and Light, 47
Limonar Mountains, 169
Little Bahama Bk., 160, 164
—— Cumberland Island & Light, 138
Little River Inlet, 121
Lloyd's Neck and Point, 67
Lobster Rocks, 10
Lockwood's Folly, 121
Locust Point, 112
Loggerhead Inlet, 113
Loggerhead Kay and Light-ho., 148, 151, 153, 158-9
Londoner Ledge, 6
Long Bay, 121

INDEX. 203

Long Beach, 53, 86
—— Branch Beach, 83
—— Island and Light, 15, 16, 18
—— Island and Sound, 50—75
—— Island Lights, 133
—— Ledge, 19
—— Neck, 44
—— Point and Light, 22, 48
—— Reef Beacon, 149, 152
—— Sand Shoal and Light, 62
—— Wharf and Light, 63
Looe Kay & Ben., 147, 151
Look-out, Cape, &c., 117
——— Point and Light, 105-6
Loose Shoal, 39
Lord's Channel, 57-8
Los Martires Reefs, 145
Lovel's Island, 16, 18
Lovely Rocks, 48
Love Point and Light, 109
Low Point, 36
Lucas Shoal, 41
Luddington Rocks, 63
Lumbert's Cove, 42
Lumpfish Rock, 22
Lynde Point and Light, 61, 62
Lynhaven Roads, 101
Lynn Harbour, 14, 18

Machipongo Island, &c., 96, 97
Maffits Ledge, 15
Mahon River Light, 92
Malabar, Cape, and Light, 26
Malabar Cape & Shoal, 143
Manatee River, 178
Manchester Harbour, 8, 10
Mangle Kay, 171
Mangrove Islands, 146, 157
———— Shoals, 156
Manhatten, 71, 76
Manomet Point, 21
Marblehead Harbour, 8, 12
———— Rock, 10
———— Neck, 9
Marcus Hook, 93
Mariel, 161
————, Table of, 173
Marillanes, Boca, 168
Mariner Shoal, 173
Mariposa Kay, 168
Marquesas Kays, 147, 157
Marshall's Shoal, 120
Marshfield, 20
Marsh Islands, 119
Martha's Vineyard, 28-9, 40
Martinicock Point, 68

Martin Ledge, 10, 15
Martin's Industry Shoal, 129, 130, 133
Mary Ann Rocks, 21
Maryland, 94
Mason's Island, 58
Massachusetts Bay, 5, 6
Matanilla Reefs, 160
Matanza Inlet, 143
Matanzas, 161, 171—172
Maternillo Reefs, 164
Matomkin Harbour, 97
Mattapoiset Harbour and Ledge, 45
Maurice River, 92
Maya Point, 171, 172
May, Cape, and Light, 75, 87—89, 90
Mayo's Beach and Light, 22
Mc Blair's Shoals 32, 34
Mc Cries Shoal, 88
Medway River, 131
Melton's Ledge, 60
Memory Rock, 142, 164
Menemsha Bight, 40
Mercer's Rock, 60
Merrill Shell Bank Lt., 193
Metompkin Harbour, 96
Middle Ground and Light, 41, 64, 93, 97, 100
Middle Ground Ben., 151, 156
Middle Kay, Tortugas, 158
———— Rock, 22
Mifflin, Port, 94
Miik Island, 7
Mill Cove Point, 141
Miller's Island, 111
Mill Rocks, 71
Millstone Point, 61
Minots Ledge & Light, 14
Misery Island and Ledge, 9, 10
Mishaun Point, 43, 45
Mispillion River and Light, 94
Mississippi River, 193—197
————— Sound, 191
Mistic River and Light, 55, 57
Mitchell Bluff, 112
————, Mount, 76
Mobile Bay, 188—191
Mob Jack Bay, 104
Monillo Kay, 170
Monomoy Island and Light, 26, 36
Montauk Point and Light, 49, 50, 74, 80-1
Monumet, 20
———— River, 44
Morena Mountain, 169
Morgan's Point Light, 57, 59

Morris Island and Light, 125
Morro Castle and Lt., 173
Mosquito Cove, 68
Mosquito Inlet, 143
Mount Misery Shoal and Point, 67
Mud Holes, The, 81
Muertos Point, 167, 168
Mullet Island, 155, 178
Mummy Shoal, 90
Muskeget Island and Channel, 28, 34
Mussel Point, 7
Mutton Shoal, 35

Nag's Head, 113
Nahant Bay and Peninsula, 13, 14
Namset, 22
Nantasket Roads, 18
Nantucket and Shoals, 28, 29, 79
———— and Harbour, 33-4
———— Sound, 28, 39
Napatree Point, 57-8
Narragunset Bay, 48
Narrows, The, 76
———— Light, 15
Nashawina Island, 40, 42
Nashon Island and Light, 28
Nash Rock, 16
Nassau River, 140
Naumkeag, 11
Nauset Beach and Lights, 22, 25
Naushon Island, 40
Nautilus Shoal, 100
Navesink, 83
———— Islands & Light, 75-6, 85
Nayat Point, 48
Neapeague Bay & Harbour, 51-2
Neck Point, 13
Necunkey Cliff and Point, 42
Ned's Point and Light, 45
Negro Point, 69, 70
Newark Bay, 77
New Bedford, 43-4
—— Castle, 93
—— Comfort Bay, 104
—— Dorp, 77
—— Haven and Light, 63
—— Inlet, 75, 113, 119
—— Jersey, 82-3, 92
—— London & Light, 51-2, 55, 59
New Orleans, 193
—— Point Comfort Light, 104
Newport, 72

INDEX.

Newport Harbour, 46, 48
New River Inlet, 144
New Shoal, 30, 32, 171
New South Shoal & Light, 30
Newton's Point, 106
Newton Rock, 46
New York, 76—84
Niantic Bay, 61
Nicholas Channel, 161, 167
Nicolao Reef, 169
Nissequaque River, 67
Nix's Mate, 16, 18
Nobsque or Nobska Point & Light, 28, 39, 42
Noman's Island, 49
—— Land, 40
Norman's Woe, 7
North Hill, 55
—— Inlet, 121
—— Point and Light, 112
Northport and Bay, 67
North River, 76
Norwalk Islands, 65
Nye's Ledge, 43, 45

Oak Island Lights, 120
—— Neck Point, 68
Ocean House, 60
Ocilla River, 181
Ocracoke Inlet and Light, 116
Ogeechee River, 135
O'Hara's Observatory, 155
Ohio Shoal, 143
Oil Spot, 78, 80
Okalokana River, 181
Old Bartlemy, 45
—— Bug Shoal and Light, 33-4
—— Cock Rock, 43
—— Eph Shoal, 89
—— Field Point & Light, 67
—— Hen Rock, 69
—— Inlet, 86
—— Point Comfort Light, 99
—— Man, The, 31
—— —— Rocks, 40
Oliver Reef Light, 116
Old Silas Rock, 54
—— Sow Rock, 67
—— Stage Harbour, 36
—— Topsail Inlet, 118
Orange Kays, 161, 166-7
Oregon Inlet, 113
Orleans, 26
Ossabaw Sound, 135
Otter Island, 128
Outer Shoals, 114
Overfalls, The, 90
Oyster Bay and Harbour, 68, 75

Oyster Beds Beacon Lt., 133
—— Pond Point, 52-3
—— River Point, 63

Pacific Reef Beacon, 149
Packet Rock, 45
Palmer's Island and Light, 44-5
Pamplico Sound, 113, 116
Paramore Bank, 96
Pargo Channel, 170
Parker's Neck, 44
Pasqui Island, 40, 42
Passage Islands, 178
Patapsco River and Lights, 110
Patuxent River, 106-7
Peach's Point, 9
Peaked Hill, 25
Pea Patch and Light, 93
Pelican Island, 188
—— Shoals, 136
Penfield's Reef and Light, 65
Penikese or Penequese Id., 40, 43
Pensacola, 186—188
Peros Isle, 193
Perros Kays, 167
Perth Amboy, 78
Petit Bois Island, 191
Phelps Bank, 33
Philadelphia, 93-4
Phillip's Point, 13
Pickering, Fort, and Light, 11
Pickle Reef & Beacon, 147, 148, 150
Piedras Kay & Light, 161, 167, 170-1
Pig Rocks, 13
Pilots, Mississippi, 196
——, Carolina, &c., 127
Pine Island, 59
—— Island Channel, 53
Pine Islands, 146, 147, 149
—— Kay, 178
Piney Point and Light, 106
Pinnacle Rock, 8
Pleasant Bay, 26
Plum Island, Gut, & Light, 52—54, 62
—— Tree Point, 99
Plymouth, 20
Pochick Rip, 31
Pocomoke Sound, 106
Pocosin Flats, 101
Poge, Cape, 28, 35
Point North Beach, 141
Point Rip Shoal, 29
Pole's Hill, 51
Pollock Rip Light, 27, 29, 36
Pond Bay, 51

Pondquogue Point & Light, 74
Pool Island and Light, 111
Pope's Head Rock, 9, 12
Poplar Point, 48
—— Island, 108
Porpoise Bank, 96
Port Royal, 129, 130
Potanumagunt Beach, 25
Pot Eddies and Cove, 70
Potomic River, 104—106
Powder Island, 59, 60
—— Hole, 26, 36
President Road, 15, 17, 18
Price's Creek, 120
Prince's Bay and Light, 78
Prospect, Mount, 51
—— Point, 69
Providence Channel, 165
Providence River & Point, 47-8
Provincetown, 19, 22-3
Prudence Island, 47
Pulpit Rock, 69
Pumpkin Hill Channel, 125, 126
Pune Island, 40

Quarantine Rocks, 16
Quick's Hole, 42, 44
Quinipeag Rock, 61
Quixe's Ledge, 63

Raccoon Kay & Light, 123
Race, The, 19, 54
—— Point, 5, 19, 22-3
—— Rock and Channel, 55, 59, 73
Racoon Island, 135
Ragged Kays, 147
Ragged Point, 106
Rainsford Island, 16
Ram Head, 16, 18
Ram-horn Rock, 10
Ram Islands, 13
Rappahannock River, 104-5
Rapid Rock, 60
Raritan River, 78
Rattlesnake Shoals & Light, 124
Rebecca Shoal and Beacon, 148, 158, 159
Reddie's Point, 141
Reedy Island and Light, 93
Regla Bank, 174
Rehoboth Bay, 97
Rhode Island, 46, 49
Rhodes Kay, 149
Richmond Bay, 157
Ricorda Channel, 90-1
Rikor's Island, 69
Rip, The, 119
Roanoke Point, 67
—— Sound, 113
Roaring Bull Rocks, 13, 15

INDEX.

Robins Reef & Light, 77-8, 80
Rochester Harbour, 46
Rockaway Inlet, 75
Rock Kay Channel, 156
Rock Point, 46
Rockport, 6
Rocky Kays, 167
Rocky Point, 66
Rodrigues Kay, 147, 150
Roman Cape, 170
Roman Cape, &c., 123
Romer Bank & Beacon, 78
Roques Kays, 167
Rose and Crown Shoal, 32
—— Island and Light, 47
Roslyn, 68
Round Hill Point & Channel, 43-4
—— Rock, 7
—— Shoal, 86-7, 90
Rously's Point, 107
Ryulander's Reef, 71

Sable Cape, 146, 176
Sachuset Point, 46
Saddle Rock, 47
Sag Harbour, 52
St. Andrew's Bay, 185
— —— Sound, 138-9
— Augustine, 141-2
— —— —— Bar, 140-2
— Blas Cape, 176
— Catherine's Island and Sound, 135-6
— George's Island Lt., 183
— George's Island, 106
— —— —— Sound, 182
— Helena, 177
— —— Sound, 127-9
— John's River & Lightho., 140-1
— Joseph's Bay, 184-5
— Joseph's Island & Bay, 178-9
— Lucia River, 144
— Lucie Shoal, 144
— Mark's, 181-2
— Martin's Reef, 179
— Mary's River, 106
— Mary's Sound & Riv.,139
— Michael's Island, 192
— Philip's Island, 129
— Sebastian River, 143
— Simon's Sound, 137-8
— Vincent Island, 183
Sagua La Grande, and Lt., 168-9
Salem Harbour and Lights, 8, 10, 11
Salthouse Beach, 20
Salt Kay Bank & Lightho., 160, 167
Salvages, The, 6
Sambo Kay, 146, 151

Sammy's Rock, 13
San Antonio, Cape, 174
—— Felipe Fort, 172
—— Juan River, 172
—— Severino Castle, 172
—— Telmo Bank, 174
Sand Island & Lightho., 189
—— Kay, 178
—— —— & Lightho., 148, 151, 155
Sand Rocks, 22
—— Spit, 45
Sand's Point and Light, 69
Sandwich Harbour, 46
Sandy Bay, 7
—— Hook and Bay, 78—83
—— —— and Lights, 76
Sandy Kay, 164
—— Neck and Light, 21
—— Point and Light, 28-9, 108-9
Sanibel Island, 177
Saukaty Head Light, 29, 30, 32, 38
Santa Clara Hill, 169
—— Cruz, 173
Santee River, 123
Sarah's Reef, 60
Sassafras River, 112
Satan Rock, 10, 12
Saughkonnet Point & River, 46
Saulis Rock, 10
Savannah and River, 131-4
Saybrooke and Light, 61-2
Scaly Rock, 71
Schuylkill River, 94
Scituate and Harbour, 16, 19
Scraggy Neck Shoal, 43
Seaflower Reef, 57, 59
Seahorse Kay and Lightho., 179, 180
Seal Rock, 57
Searl's Rock, 9
Senator Shoal, 37
Setauket and Bay, 67
Seven-foot Knoll, 110
Severn River, 108
Sewall, Fort, 10
Shag Rocks, 15
Shagwong Reef and Point, 50
Shank-painter Bar, 23
Shark Shoal, 96
Sharp's Island and Light, 108
Shears Shoal, The, 90
Sheffield Island and Light, 66
Shelter Island, 52
Shinnicock Bay and Light, 74
Ship Channel, 11

Ship Island Lightho., 192
Ship John Shoal Light, 92
—— Shoal, 96
Shovelfull Shoal and Light, 27, 36
Shrewsbury Inlet, 83
Siasconset, 31
Siguapa, 171
Sill's Rock, 67
Sinepuxent Shoals, 95
Sinking Ledge, 45
Sippican Harbour, 46
Slate Ledge, 18
Slue Channel, The, 118
Smith's House, 60
—— Island Light and Shoal, 96-7
—— Point and Light, 105-6
Smithtown Bay, 67
Smyrna, 143
Snow Rock, 45
Sod Channel, 86
Soldier Kay, 146, 149
Sombrero Kay & Lightho., 148, 151
South Breaker, 124
S.E. Pass, 122
South River, 108
S.W. Ledge, 60, 63
Sow and Pigs Rocks, 40
Spectacle Island, 17
Spesutic Island, 111
Spindle Rock, 8
Squid's Ledge, 49, 56
Squan Beach, 83
Squash Meadow, 39
Star Reefs, 152
Staten Island, 76, 84
Stellwagen's Rock, Shoal, & Bank, 5, 6, 21
Stepping Stones Reef, 69, 74
Stewarts Bend, 26
Stingray Point and Light, 105
Stone Horse Shoal, 27
Stoney Brook Harbour, 67
Stonington and Light, 53, 57-8
Stouts Creek, 25
Straitsmouth Island, 6
Stratford Point and Light, 63-4, 66
Strong Island, 25
Success Rock, 69
Succonesset Light, 39
Sullivan Island & Lights, 125
Sunbury Port, 135
Superb's Reef, 52
Susquehanna River, 112
Suwanee River, 181
Swamp Inlets, 84
Swan Point, 109

www.ingramcontent.com/pod-product-compliance
Lightning Source LLC
Chambersburg PA
CBHW031817220426
43662CB00007B/682